ADVANCES IN SOCIAL WORK
PRACTICE WITH THE MILITARY

ADVANCES IN SOCIAL WORK PRACTICE WITH THE MILITARY

Edited by

Joan Beder

Routledge
Taylor & Francis Group

NEW YORK AND HOVE

First published 2012
by Routledge
711 Third Avenue, New York, NY 10017

Simultaneously published in the UK
by Routledge
27 Church Road, Hove, East Sussex BN3 2FA

Visit the Taylor & Francis Web site at
http://www.taylorandfrancis.com

and the Routledge Web site at
http://www.routledgementalhealth.com

Routledge is an imprint of the Taylor & Francis Group, an informa business

© 2012 by Taylor & Francis *Group, LLC*

Library of Congress Cataloging in Publication Data
Advances with social work practice in the military/[compiled by] Joan Beder.
  p. cm.
  Includes bibliographical references and index.
  1. Soldiers—Mental health—United States. 2. Soldiers—Mental health services—
  United States. 3. Veterans—Mental health—United States. 4. Veterans—Mental
  health services—United States. I. Beder, Joan, 1944–
  U22.3.A36 2012
  362.2´042508835500973—dc23   2011044371

ISBN: 978-0-415-89133-2 (hbk)
ISBN: 978-0-415-89134-9 (pbk)
ISBN: 978-0-203-82574-7 (ebk)

Typeset in Bembo
by RefineCatch Limited, Bungay, Suffolk, UK

Printed and bound in the United States of America on acid-free paper.

Printed and bound in the United States of America
by Edwards Brothers, Inc.

This volume is dedicated to the individuals who have served our country in war and to the many devoted and hard-working professionals who give of themselves on a daily basis to care for them. With deep appreciation to all who have participated in writing for this volume; I also wish to thank family, friends and especially Matthew who keeps me focused on the future.

And a special dedication to a dear colleague, Lt. Col. David Cabrera, MSW, PhD., co-author of Chapter 3 on Combat Medics, who was killed in combat on October 29, 2011. Dr. Cabrera was practicing what this book promotes: caring for others as a social worker. Dr. Cabrera was on his way to help soldiers in Afghanistan when a suicide car-bomber struck his transport. His voice will be missed.

For now, however ...

> *... let us strive to finish the work we are in, to bind up the Nation's wounds, to care for him (and her) who shall have borne the battle and for his (her) widow and his (her) orphan ...*
> *Abraham Lincoln, Second Inaugural Address, March 4, 1865*

CONTENTS

FIGURES AND TABLES

Figures

Tables

PREFACE

How This Book Came To Be

In 2007, I watched the HBO documentary *Alive Day*, produced by James Gandolfini. In the film, Mr. Gandolfini interviewed ten soldiers and Marines who had been seriously wounded during their military service in Iraq. The interviews were powerful and wrenching; they were augmented by harrowing insurgent footage using embedded cameras and soldier home videos. In each interview, the service member was encouraged to tell the story of their Alive Day—the day they realized that they were alive and had narrowly escaped death due to their injury—and what they anticipated for their future. As noted by Mr. Gandolfini in the beginning of the film, each soldier would forever remember two dates: their birthday and their Alive Day. Most of those interviewed were very seriously challenged by their life-altering injuries while displaying grit and courage about their future.

I was deeply impacted by the film and, as a social work educator, I realized that I wanted to know as much as possible about the travails of service members and those who helped them. As such, my research and writing interests since 2007 have all focused around issues related to the experience of those in the military and those who serve them. I traveled extensively over the years since 2007, visiting military bases across the United States and Veterans Administration and Department of Defense hospitals and interviewing numerous service members and service providers. I spoke with dozens of compassionate professionals who are dedicated to caring for the military population and their needs. However, the more I learned about the military experience and the care offered our service members by the government systems, the more I began to realize that there was a need for civilian social workers and other civilians in the helping professions to become aware of the issues faced by those returning from war. This is based on the likelihood that we will be called upon to care for them within our agencies and private practice areas. This realization suggested that educating civilian practitioners about the unique and pressing needs of the returning military was essential.

In 2010, I approached the editor of *Social Work in Health Care*, Dr. Gary Rosenberg, and suggested that he consider dedicating an issue of the journal to the needs of the military, with primary concern for those returning from Iraq and Afghanistan. Specialists in areas of care related to the military would write the articles; I would serve as the editor, making contact with the authors and keeping the work focused and timely. He readily agreed and the January 2011 issue became the first of two issues, and the second issue was published in August, 2011, with this special focus. In the initial meeting with Dr. Rosenberg, he suggested that I consider editing a book on the same topic; thus this volume.

Structure of the Book

A specialist(s) who works in a particular area devoted to the care of the service member and his/her family has written each chapter in this book. All authors had the same set of instructions: write about your specific area of expertise, include case material (assessment and intervention approaches) and write to educate a civilian audience, i.e., a practitioner who does not have employ and the experience of working at a VA or DoD hospital. I was amazed at the enthusiasm expressed by each author(s) and their willingness to take on this assignment. In recognition of the unending intensity of their work and time constraints, I was gratified at the welcome response to participate in this endeavor.

The book is divided into five parts. In Part I—The World of the Military—Hall's chapter and that of Coll, Weiss and Yarvis, introduces the reader to the culture of the military and how that affects the service member and his/her family and the subsequent development of mental health services. This understanding, so beautifully described in these two chapters, sets the stage for a preliminary orientation to the military environment, an understanding essential for the clinician to grasp the nuances of the experience of the service member.

Part II—Special Populations—looks at six different groups with specific needs based directly on their military service. Yarvis and I describe the needs of those with post-traumatic stress disorder (PTSD), and offer diagnostic indicators and treatment approaches. Closely aligned to PTSD, and considered the signature injury of the war, are the needs of those with traumatic brain injury (TBI) expertly described by Parkinson, French, and Massetti. Bell and Reardon's contribution focuses on the needs and treatment approaches of those who have survived sexual harassment and assault during their military service, noting that both women and men struggle with this experience. Wounding, always a by-product of war, is the focus of my chapter with Helen Jones. We note that the experience of being wounded often impacts the whole family; we specifically include details on intervention we believe to be helpful in their care. Often overlooked in the many systems of care are the needs of the combat medic described by Cabrera, Figley, and Yarvis. The medics serve the needs of the wounded and often have to absorb the anguish and offer support to others while needing support for themselves. They are overlooked and often suffer in silence. The authors describe this situation and offer suggestions for addressing the needs of the combat medic. The final article in this part describes the physiology of the war zone experience. Bruner and Woll discuss the physical changes that one experiences in battle and the impact of this on the service member's physical and emotional outlook and behavior both during and after the war exposure.

Clinical Challenges are presented in Part III of the book. My chapter begins this section and describes the challenges faced by the reintegrating service members as they attempt to find their place with, and rejoin, their family and their pre-war life. Family issues are additionally described by Chapin who uses a model of care described by McCubbin to work with families when there has been wounding and/or a death. An on-going risk for service members is suicide, and in the chapter by Jackson and Branson this risk is discussed with a specific focus on assessment and intervention strategies. Harrington LaMorie tackles an especially complex area of care: the needs of those bereft by the wartime experience. She describes the rituals that the military follow when there is a death and offers the clinician treatment approaches that are helpful with this population. Everson and Perry's chapter is about the experience of wives (and significant others) both pre- and during deployment, noting areas that are critical for the practitioner to understand in order to effectively intervene with a couple. The final chapter, by Roy and Skidmore, describes the assessment and treatment of those with substance abuse disorders, so common in those back from service. They too describe assessment and intervention strategies that they have found helpful.

Animal assisted interventions and the services offered by the Veterans Administration are the two chapters in Part IV of the book entitled Services. I worked with Sullivan-Sakaeda and Martin to write the chapter on animal assisted interventions that focused on companion dogs, horses, and trout fishing, animals used to help service members, especially those with physical and emotional problems associated with their war experience. Amdur and her colleagues, in the final chapter in this part, describe the numerous services offered to Veterans through the VA integrated system of care.

Part V—Unique Concerns for Practitioners—looks at ethical concerns faced by practitioners working with the military. Beckerman describes several situations faced by clinicians that are not always black and white, and suggests an approach to resolving these ethical challenges. Finally, Figley and I worked on our chapter which centers on the needs of practitioners, noting that there is a cost to caring and that we must all be aware of our needs in order to provide the highest level of care to the service member and their family.

Final Thoughts

My hope is that this volume will serve as the basis of understanding for civilian practitioners as they address the needs of returning service members. It is anticipated that more and more schools of social work will be offering courses designed to educate students to the needs of the military, and that this volume will be a starting point to understanding this complex cohort.

It has been an honor and privilege to work with the authors who contributed to this work. Each is an expert in their field and gave of their time and expertise to contribute to this effort. I am grateful to each of you.

ABOUT THE EDITOR

Joan Beder, DSW is Professor at Yeshiva University's Wurzweiler School of Social Work. She has been teaching social work students for over 20 years in both clinical and practice course areas. Her research interests have focused on medical social work as well as areas of grief and bereavement. Dr. Beder is the author of *Voices of Bereavement: A casebook for grief counselors* (2004), and *Medical Social Work: The interface of medicine and caring* (2006); and is co-editor of *Community Health Care in Cuba* (2010). For the past five years, her research has been on issues related to the military, with particular concern on how it impacts social work practice. She has written extensively on this and other subjects and has presented at numerous conferences both nationally and internationally.

ABOUT THE CONTRIBUTORS

Deborah Amdur, LCSW, is the Chief Consultant in the Care Management and Social Work Service at the Department of Veterans Affairs Central Office in Washington, DC. Ms. Amdur leads the VACO office that provides policy guidance and program oversight to the VA field offices, and champions the development and implementation of VA key programs to serve the returning wounded, ill and injured from the wars of Iraq and Afghanistan. She and her office work in collaboration with the Department of Defense, the Department of Health and Human Services, TRICARE and myriad other federal, state, public, and private enterprises to optimize and ensure Veteran centric care to Service members, Veterans and their families.

Alfonso Batres, MSW, PhD, is the Chief Officer of the Readjustment Counseling Service in Iraq. He received his MSW (Masters of Social Work) while working at Ireland Army Hospital, Ft. Knox, Kentucky, from the University of Louisville Kent School of Social Work and his PhD from University of Colorado, Boulder. He has served Veterans and their families for most of his 30 years of government service.

Nancy Beckerman, LCSW, DSW, Professor and Director of Faculty Development at the Wurzweiler School of Social Work, Yeshiva University in New York. She has published widely in the areas of HIV/AIDS, the psychosocial impact of illness in health care, social work values and ethics, the diagnosis and treatment of PTSD, family and couple therapy. She is a clinical consultant to numerous hospitals and community-based health care agencies, and is a psychotherapist.

Janet Belisle, MHA, RHIA, FACHE, is a Health System Specialist in Care Management and Social Work Service at the Department of Veterans Affairs Central Office in Washington, DC. Ms. Belisle develops policy and coordinates national care management issues for the OEF/OIF/OND Care Management and VA Liaison Programs. She has a Masters Degree in Healthcare Administration, a Bachelor of Science Degree in Health Information Management, and is a Fellow in the American College of Healthcare Executives.

Margaret Bell, PhD, earned her doctorate in counseling psychology from Boston College, a program that has a particular emphasis on community-based collaboration and the promotion of social justice. Her research and policy work has largely been driven by a desire to use knowledge about the aftereffects of trauma and the context of women's lives to inform the development of effective, victim-sensitive intervention programs and policies. Currently employed by the Department of Veterans Affairs, she has worked with a number of interdisciplinary, policy-oriented teams designed to help systems, community agencies, and victims work collaboratively to respond to and prevent violence against women.

Yvette Branson, ME, PhD, has been with the VA since 2006, first as a post-doctoral student in behavioral health research and now as the coordinator in Mental Health services of the suicide prevention program. As Suicide Prevention Coordinator, she has trained over 1,000 staff members in the Gatekeeper training known as Operation SAVE, a training that uses the public health model to prevent suicide. Dr. Branson works with Veterans in crisis, in affiliation with the Veterans Crisis Line, and offers training throughout the NY Metropolitan area in crisis management. In addition, she has a personal interest in the issue of stigma and barriers within our community to seeking help in mental health services. She earned her PhD in Clinical Health Psychology in 2006 from Yeshiva University. Dr. Branson was formerly an orchestral musician and teacher, holding a Masters in education as well as in music performance. She has a private practice on the Upper West Side of Manhattan.

John H. Brown, Jr., MHA, MPA, has served as Director of the Department of Veterans Affairs (VA) OEF/OIF/OND Outreach Office since October 1, 2007. He is responsible for improving access to VA health care by optimizing linkages to VA services for OEF/OIF/OND Active Duty Warriors in Transition, the National Guard and Reserve Forces through specialized programs and initiatives. Prior to Mr. Brown's assignments at Walter Reed, during his 26 years on active duty, he served in many other health and medical related administrative and command positions, retiring as a full colonel in 2002.

Victoria Bruner, RN, LCSW, BCETS, specializes in treating traumatic stress. On 9/11 she was one of the first responders onsite at the Pentagon. Now she is

Senior Clinician with the Department of Defense Deployment Health Clinical Center, Walter Reed Army Medical Center, where she treats complex combat trauma and has led research efforts on women in the military and innovations in trauma treatment. Her positions there have included Trauma Therapist, Director of Clinical Education, Acting Clinical Director and Deputy Director of Program Replication. She was a private practitioner for 30 years, an international consultant, and author on the impact of exposure to traumatic stress and violence.

David Cabrera, PhD, LCSW, BCD, was a board certified Social Worker and Child and Family Fellow, and his specialties included trauma, PTSD, and child/family therapy.

> Sadly, David died in October 2011 while deployed. At the time of his death, he was a Major in the U.S. Army and was serving as an assistant professor for Family Medicine and Director of Social Work at the Uniformed Services University in Bethesda, Maryland. He was also involved in research, teaching, and direct practice with a Joint Force population (Army, Air Force, and Navy). David's previous assignments had included being Deputy Director of the Soldier and Family Support program which is responsible for behavioral health care across Europe, Military Corrections, Combat Support Hospital, and two deployments to Bosnia and Iraq to name but a few.

Mark Chapin, PhD, retired from the Army in July 2007 after serving 28 years as a Social Work Officer. He has worked with hundreds of soldiers returning from battle who had experienced posttraumatic stress, including combat Veterans not only from Iraq and Afghanistan, but also Vietnam, Panama, Grenada, Somalia, Rwanda, survivors of bombing of the Marine Corps Barracks in Beirut, survivors of terrorist attacks in Germany in the 1980s, and the Ramstein Air Show disaster in 1988. He has numerous publications and presentations on the topics of violence exposure, traumatic stress, and alcoholism. On September 12, 2001, Dr. Chapin was deployed to the Pentagon as part of Walter Reed Army Medical Center's Special Medical Augmentation Response Team (Stress Management) after the terrorist attack. After retiring from the Army, Dr. Chapin worked as a clinical social worker at Walter Reed Army Medical Center, where the majority of his practice was serving families of injured soldiers. In 2009 he accepted a position with the Veterans Health Administration to start up the Annapolis Vet Center, a VA counseling center for combat Veterans and serve as the Team Leader.

Jose Coll, PhD, is an Associate Professor of Social Work and Director of the Office for Veteran Student Services at Saint Leo University. Prior to his current appointment, Dr. Coll was Clinical Associate Professor and Director of the San Diego Academic Center and Military Social Work program at the University of Southern California. As a Marine Corps veteran who served with 1st Force

Reconnaissance Company, Dr. Coll is acutely aware of the needs, and the struggles, faced by our military personnel and their families. As director of the Military Social Work and Veteran Services specialization program, he advocates and develops a curriculum that emphasizes the challenges faced by our military and their families. His research interests include development and cognitive complexities, underage college substance abuse, and counseling practices with Veterans. Dr. Coll received his PhD in Counseling Education and Supervision from the University of South Florida, and was the recipient of the University of South Florida Latino Doctoral Fellowship, and the American Association of Hispanics in Higher Education Graduate Fellowship.

Micaela Cornis-Pop, PhD, is a speech pathologist with broad experience in academic teaching, clinical care, administration and program development in polytrauma and brain injury rehabilitation. In her position in VA Central Office, Rehabilitation Services, she has participated in the development of the VA Polytrauma/TBI System of Care. She is a frequent presenter and author on topics related to brain injury rehabilitation and cognitive-communication disorders.

R. Blaine Everson, PhD, is a marriage and family therapist in private practice with The Samaritan Counseling Center in Athens, Georgia. He was awarded a PhD in Family and Child Science from The Florida State University, and is a clinical member of The American Association for Marriage and Family Therapy. His practice includes extensive work with military families and readjustment issues associated with military service, along with a special interest in the recovery from emotional trauma at the familial level. He is a part-time member of the teaching faculty in The Department of Child and Family Development at The University of Georgia. He has published several book chapters and journal articles. He recently co-authored and edited *Families Under Fire: Systemic therapy with military families* with Charles R. Figley, which was published in 2010 by Routledge.

Charles R. Figley, PhD, MS, is the Paul Henry Kurzweg Distinguished Chair and Professor in Disaster Mental Health. Both his PhD and MS are from Penn State University and he has held professorships at Purdue University (Princeton), Cornell Medical School, and Florida State before joining the Tulane University in his current position. Among his more than 200 scholarly publications are *Stress Disorder among Vietnam Veterans* (1978), *Combat Stress Injuries* (in 2007 with W. Nash), and *Families under Fire* (in 2010 with B. Everson). He is founding President of ISTSS, founding editor of the *Journal of Family Psychotherapy*, the *Journal of Traumatic Stress* (1987-92), and the journal *Traumatology* (1995-2011).

Louis M. French, PsyD, is the Chief of the Traumatic Brain Injury Service at the Walter Reed National Military Medical Center at Bethesda. He also serves as Site Director of the Defense and Veterans Brain Injury Center, Walter Reed.

Dr. French is an Assistant Professor of Neurology at the Uniformed Services University of the Health Sciences in Bethesda, Maryland. He received his doctorate in clinical psychology from the George Washington University and completed fellowships at the National Institute of Mental Health, and the Defense and Veterans Brain Injury Center at Walter Reed Army Medical Center.

Lynn Hall, EdD, is Dean of the College of Social Sciences at the University of Phoenix and oversees numerous counselor education, human service, and psychology programs around the country. In addition to working for almost 15 years as a mental health counselor, she spent almost 10 years as a school counselor with the Department of Defense schools in Germany, where she worked with military dependents and their families. She is the author of the book, *Counseling Military Families: What mental health professionals need to know*, published in 2008 by Routledge, as well as numerous other articles and chapters in edited books dealing with the same subject. She is the mom of an Air Force Non-Commissioned Officer.

Greg Harms, MS, is a Readjustment Counseling Service Program Analyst. Greg served in the U.S. Army from 1985-8 with tours in Germany and at Ft. Campbell with the 101st Airborne Division. He has been with the Readjustment Counseling Service since 1988, first doing work-study at the Eugene Vet Center (1988-91) while earning his undergraduate degree from the University of Oregon. Greg worked in the RCS Regional Office in northern California from 1991-2001 and has been in Central Office since 2001.

Stephen C. Hunt, MD, MPH, is a VA primary care physician and national director of the Post-Deployment Integrated Care Initiative. He has been providing care for returning combat Veterans in an integrated, multi-disciplinary post-combat care clinic at the VA Puget Sound since shortly after the end of the first Gulf War.

Christie Jackson, PhD, is a licensed clinical psychologist and Clinical Assistant Professor of Psychiatry at the NYU School of Medicine. She obtained her PhD in clinical psychology from the University of North Dakota, and completed a postdoctoral fellowship in trauma and dissociative disorders at McLean Hospital. Prior to her current position as Suicide Prevention Coordinator at the Manhattan Veterans Administration Medical Center, she worked at the NYU Institute for Trauma and Resilience. Dr. Jackson also maintains a private psychotherapy practice with specializations in complex trauma, personality disorders, and various forms of CBT, including Skills Training in Affective and Interpersonal Regulation (STAIR) and Dialectical Behavior Therapy (DBT).

Helen Jones, MSW, BA, is a Clinical Social Worker who received her MSW degree from the University of Texas at Arlington, and her BA degree from the University of Texas at Dallas. As a Licensed Clinical Social Worker, she has worked with psychiatric in-patient programs, general medical hospitals, and physical rehabilitation facilities providing clinical social work and hospital social work services. Helen has had a private clinical practice for 20 years. She has worked as a clinician with the military as a community provider and as civilian staff as well as serving as an intern with the Veteran's Administration. Ms. Jones presently works for a government employee assistance program, and she continues to see clients privately.

Peggy Kennedy, MSN, RN, is the National OEF/OIF/OND Care Management Program Manager at the Veteran's Administration Headquarters in Washington, DC. In this position she overseas policy and coordinates national care management issues with VA's national leadership, VISN and facility level care management team program managers, case managers, and Transition Patient Advocates (TPAs). She represents the Care Management and Social Work Service Office on national issues as part of the Primary Care Services VACO Program Office and liaises with other program offices including VBA, the VA/DoD Outreach Office and other specialty areas such as mental health and polytrauma.

Jill Harrington LaMorie, MSW, DSW, is currently a field scientist at Uniformed University of the Health Sciences, Center for the Study of Traumatic Stress, Child and Family Program. She is the former Director of Professional Education at the Tragedy Assistance Program for Survivors. Dr. Harrington LaMorie received her undergraduate degree in Psychology from The Catholic University of America, her MSW from Adelphi University, and her DSW from the University of Pennsylvania School of Social Policy and Practice. She has extensive experience working with individuals and families affected by crisis, trauma, grief, loss, life transitions and illness. Dr. LaMorie worked on the Project Liberty Team in the aftermath of the 2001 World Trade Center attack, has been an oncology social worker, and has worked with military surviving families. She is the proud mother of two children, Madeline and Alexander.

Heather Mahoney-Gleason, LCSW, is the National Caregiver Support Program Manager within Care Management and Social Work Service, at the Department of Veterans Affairs Central Office in Washington, DC. Ms. Gleason is responsible for policy, program development, and implementing a nationwide approach to supporting Veteran caregivers.

Tamar P. Martin, PhD, is a licensed counseling psychologist with a subspecialty in clinical neuropsychology. She is also certified as a rehabilitation counselor. Her background includes several years experience working in the field of education and rehabilitation medicine. In addition to teaching, she has a private practice in Greenwich Village, NY. Dr. Martin was the project psychologist for the Traumatic Brain Injury—Technical Assistance Project at Mount Sinai

Medical Center, Department of Rehabilitation Medicine from 1995-2001. For the past few years, she has been a research psychologist with the Research Foundation, Hunter College, NY. Currently, she is coordinator for the Research and Rehabilitation Training Center sponsored by the National Institute on Disability Research, focusing on several topics including women with disabilities, pediatric brain injury and educational adaptations and behavioral strategies in the classroom.

Marianne Mathewson-Chapman, PhD, ARNP, Major General (ret), Army National Guard, and Nurse Outreach Consultant to Guard/Reserve and Families at the Department of Veterans Affairs, Washington, DC.

Silvia Massetti, MSW, is a Social Worker in the Traumatic Brain Injury Service at Walter Reed Army Medical Center. Ms. Massetti received her MSW from The Catholic University of America. Upon graduating she worked at the Pentagon in a program to provide support and assistance to employees of the Pentagon after the September 11 attacks. She has been working at Walter Reed Army Medical Center since 2005 in the Traumatic Brain Injury Service as a social work case manager. She provides case management for individuals with traumatic brain injury. She also serves as the TBI Service intake coordinator.

Glenn W. Parkinson, MSW, MA, is a Licensed Independent Clinical Social Worker practicing psychotherapy at the Defense and Veterans Brain Injury Center at Walter Reed Army Medical Center. She received her MSW at Fordham University and a Master of Psychology at New York University. She also completed post-graduate training at the International Trauma Studies Program at New York University.

Jennifer Perez, LICSW, serves at the National VA Liaison Program Manager in the Veterans Health Administration and as such is responsible for the programmatic oversight of VA Liaisons stationed at 18 Military Treatment Facilities throughout the country. Ms. Perez has a Masters Degree in Social Work from Virginia Commonwealth University and is a Licensed Independent Clinical Social Worker in Washington, DC.

C. Wayne Perry, DMin, PhD, has been a practicing psychotherapist since 1971, with backgrounds in both pastoral psychotherapy and marriage and family therapy. He is currently a licensed marriage and family therapist and supervisor of therapy, a Clinical Member and Approved Supervisor in the American Association for Marriage and Family Therapy, and a Fellow in the American Association of Pastoral Counselors. Wayne has published two books, *Basic Counseling Techniques* and *Learning to Talk Sheep: Understanding those you lead*, as well as numerous articles in professional journals. In addition to his clinical work, Wayne is the Clinical Programs Director at Amridge University.

Annemarie Reardon, PhD, received her PhD in Clinical Psychology from Illinois Institute of Technology, Chicago in 2006, and completed a postdoctoral fellowship in VA Boston Healthcare System's Clinical Research Fellowship Program of the Boston Consortium in Clinical Psychology. At the VA's National Center for PTSD, in her capacity as a Research Lab Manager for the Structure of PTSD Comorbidity (SPC) and the NIMH-funded Genetics of Negative Conflict Behavior (GNCB) studies, she has served as Primary Diagnostician administering in excess of 300 structured clinical interviews for the assessment of PTSD and other Axis I and II disorders. Clinically, she specializes in working with Veterans with PTSD.

Monica Roy, PhD, received her PhD in Clinical Psychology from Nova Southeastern University. She completed her clinical training in the VA Boston Healthcare System in the Substance Abuse Treatment Program. She is currently the Director of the residential and outpatient substance abuse treatment programs at the VA Boston Healthcare System. In that role, she focuses on promoting and implementing state of the art assessment treatment for Veterans with substance use disorders, working with psychology trainees, and collaborating in research related to the assessment and treatment of substance use disorders.

Carol Sheets, LICSW, serves as National Director of Social Work within Care Management and Social Work Service, Office of Patient Care Services, Veterans Health Administration (VHA) in VA Central Office. There she develops policy on the provision of Social Work services in VHA facilities and offers guidance and consultation on the professional practice of social work to VA Central Office and the field.

W. Christopher Skidmore, PhD, received his PhD in Clinical Psychology from Northwestern University. He completed his clinical training in the VA Boston Healthcare System and the National Center for Posttraumatic Stress Disorder (PTSD). He currently works as a psychologist treating substance use disorders (SUD) and PTSD in Boston. In that role, he focuses his efforts on promoting the wellbeing of Veterans and service members, working with multiple interdisciplinary teams on the assessment and treatment of SUD and PTSD, and treatments for SUD and PTSD. He also has an interest in diversity issues and decreasing the stigma around mental health treatment.

Laurie Sullivan-Sakaeda, MS, PhD, is a licensed clinical psychologist in the state of Utah. She grew up in Wisconsin and has been working with trauma survivors, mostly children and women survivors of sexual abuse, for over 20 years. She received her MS in psychology from California State College in Bakersfield, and her PhD from the combined scientific-profession psychology program at Utah State University in Logan, Utah. Dr. Sullivan-Sakaeda did not grow up with horses but had a fling with ownership while in Montana. Following marriage and two children, horses were left behind. Years later when one daughter needed occupational therapy, a horseback riding program was developed. There are now eight horses living in pastures behind the family home. Dr. Sullivan-Sakaeda has provided mental health services through community practice. She owns and operates A Helping Hoof, PLLC, and works part time for the State of Utah Department of Disability Services.

Terry Washam, LISW, FACHE, has held a variety of mental health positions during his 30 year career with the Department of Veterans Affairs. His current assignment is Senior Military Outreach Liaison with the VHA OEF/OIF/OND Outreach Office. Terry is a Vietnam Veteran and currently serves as a Social Work Officer in the U.S. Army Reserve holding the rank of Colonel.

Eugenie Weiss, PsyD, LCSW, is a licensed clinical social worker and a licensed psychologist. She received her doctorate from Alliant International University in Clinical Psychology, and her Masters from the University of Southern California in Social Work. She is currently Clinical Assistant Professor at the University of Southern California, School of Social Work, military social work sub-concentration. Dr. Weiss has maintained a private practice since 1995, working with individuals, couples, families and children/adolescents, with a special emphasis on military personnel and their families. She is bilingual-bicultural in Spanish. Her areas of expertise include the treatment of trauma, substance abuse, and mood disorders. Dr. Weiss is co-author of *A Civilian Counselor's Primer for Counseling Veterans* (2nd Ed., 2011).

Pamela Woll, MA, CADP, is a Chicago-based author and consultant in writing and instructional development. Pam has been writing books and manuals in addiction, mental health, and other human service fields since 1989, on topics including stigma reduction, strength-based treatment, resilience, trauma, depression, cultural competence, addicted families, violence, and disaster human services. Since 2007, her primary focus areas have included resilience, neurobiology, trauma, and the needs of service members and Veterans. She is the author of the *Finding Balance* series of materials, for and about service members, Veterans, and military families, available for free download from https://sites.google.com/site/humanprioritiesorg/.

LTC Jeffrey S. Yarvis, MSW, MEd, PhD, currently serves as the Deputy Commander and Department Chair of Psychiatry at Fort Belvoir, Virginia, and as an Assistant Professor of Family Medicine and Psychiatry at the Uniformed Services University of the Health Sciences (USUHS) in Bethesda, MD. He also is an adjunct professor of social work at Virginia Commonwealth University, the University of Houston and the University of Windsor. He was recently honored as the 2008 U.S. Army and Uniformed Services Social Worker of the Year. He has presented on, treated, and researched the mental health concerns of military beneficiaries worldwide for 24 years. A published scholar in the field of traumatic injuries, he has received numerous military decorations, including the Bronze Star Medal and Combat Action Badge for leadership under fire in Iraq. LTC Yarvis received his PhD in social work from the University of Georgia, his MSW from Boston College, his MEd from Cambridge College, and his BA from Indiana University. LTC Yarvis and his wife Laura have two children, Jacob and Olivia, who all serve together.

ACKNOWLEDGMENTS

The editor would like to thank those concerned for the following chapters, and especially the Taylor & Francis Group which published each of the journals involved:

Chapter 1 Adapted with permission from Hall (2011). The importance of understanding military culture. *Social Work in Health Care*, 50(1), 4–15.

Chapter 2 Adapted with permission from Coll, Weiss, & Yarvis (2011). No one leaves unchanged: Insights for civilian mental health care professionals into the military experience and culture. *Social Work in Health Care*, 50(7), 487–500.

Chapter 3 Adapted with permission from Yarvis (2011). A civilian social worker's guide to the treatment of war-induced PTSD. *Social Work in Health Care*, 50(1), 51–72.

Chapter 4 Adapted with permission from French, Parkinson, & Massetti (2011). Care coordination in military traumatic brain injury. *Social Work in Health Care*, 50(7), 501–514.

Chapter 5 Adapted with permission from Bell and Reardon (2010). Experiences of sexual harassment and sexual assault in the military among OEF/OIF Veterans: Implications for health care providers. *Social Work in Health Care*, 50(1), 34–50.

Chapter 8 Adapted with permission from Bruner & Woll (2011). The battle within: Understanding the physiology of war-zone stress exposure. *Social Work in Health Care*, 50(1), 19–33.

Chapter 10 Adapted with permission from Chapin (2011). Family resilience and the fortunes of war. *Social Work in Health Care*, 50(7), 527–542.

Chapter 12 Adapted with permission from LaMorie (2011). Operation Iraqi Freedom/Operation Enduring Freedom: Exploring wartime death and bereavement. *Social Work in Health Care*, 50(7), 543–563.

Chapter 14 Adapted with permission from Skidmore and Roy (2011). Practical considerations for addressing substance use disorders in Veterans and service members. *Social Work in Health Care*, 50(1), 85–107.

Chapter 16 Adapted with permission from Amdur, Batres, Belisle, Brown Jr., Cornis-Pop, Mathewson-Chapman, et al. (2011).VA integrated post-combat care: A systemic approach to caring for returning combat Veterans. *Social Work in Health Care*, 50(7), 564–575.

PART I
The World of the Military

1

THE IMPORTANCE OF UNDERSTANDING MILITARY CULTURE

Lynn K. Hall

All of us in the helping professions have a passion for helping others find solutions to the issues that are causing them concern, as well as helping to make their lives more productive. In order for that to happen when working with military personnel and their families, we first must pay attention to the culture of the military. Social workers can make a significant contribution to military service members and their families, but first it is essential that the worldview, the mindset, and the historical perspective of life in the military are understood. Social workers, just like other helping professionals, already pay attention to the cultural diversity of the people they are working with. The unique culture of the military is, indeed, a diverse group of people in American society that must be understood as uniquely different from the civilian world. "All experiences originate from a particular cultural context; the [social worker] must be attentive to this context and the role that cultural identity plays in a client's life" (Dass-Brailsford, 2007, p. 78). As Reger, Etherage, Reger and Gahm (2008, p. 22) state, "to the extent that a culture includes a language, a code of manners, norms of behavior, belief systems, dress, and rituals, it is clear that the Army represents a unique cultural group". While the article written by these authors focuses on the Army, each of the military services have components that are unique to that service, as well as common across the military.

David Fenell (2008, p. 8) points out that while there is "cultural, religious and ethnic diversity within the military, the military is a culture in its own right". It is, therefore, the responsibility of ethical practitioners to be well versed in the three multicultural competencies (Sue, Arredondo & McDavis, 1992) which include:

1   becoming aware of our own behavior, values, biases, preconceived notions, and personal limitations;

2   understanding the worldview of our culturally different clients without negative judgment;
3   actively developing and practicing appropriate, relevant and sensitive strategies in working with our culturally diverse clients.

(Hall, 2008)

While this chapter will not attempt to cover all three multicultural competencies, it is essential to consider the second competency of understanding the unique worldview and culture of the military in order for social workers to work to the best of their ability with this culturally diverse population. Some of the challenges in working with military members and families include an understanding of the acronyms, the rank and grade system, the beliefs and assumptions—both spoken and unspoken—held by most who chose this lifestyle, the fears, goals, and complications of living with long and frequent absences of one parent (or two in some cases) as well as the required frequent moves, and the more subtle lifestyle changes that military families must endure and, in most cases, survive with amazing resilience and success. It is also important sometimes to be aware of what is not being said, and understand the restricted nature of the military with its many boundaries, rules, regulations, and habits. It may also be necessary to acknowledge that some members of the military may actually feel "trapped", particularly those who are from multi-generational military career families (Hall, 2008).

Reasons They Join

One place to begin is to consider why people join the military. Wertsch (1991) identified four key reasons why young people in our society make that life-changing decision. These are: (a) family tradition (b) benefits (c) identification with the warrior mentality, and (d) an escape. While it would be impossible to identify every reason why young people join the military, some aspects of these four seem consistently to be present in making the decision.

Family Tradition

When asked why a young woman chose to join and then make the military a career (Hall, 2008), she said she came from a military family so she understood the culture and explained that she was rather anxious about the possibility of living in the civilian world. Having spent most of her life living on military installations and going to schools either near or on the installation, she realized as an adult that she knew nothing about living outside of the military. As she experienced the civilian world through friends and college, she found it was an uncomfortable, insecure world, with too many choices and too much freedom. Young people who grew up in the military often share that they later joined the military because it was more comfortable than civilian life. An Air Force Veteran stated: "I think it is important to note that many families have numerous members who have served our country proudly and have provided them the emotional support to complete their tasks" (Wakefield, 2007, p. 23).

Benefits

Henderson (2006) suggests that financial concerns almost always contribute to a decision to join the military. She points out that those who join for the amount of money they will receive from the military "tend to come from places that lack other economic opportunities" (p. 22). The military is often also seen as an option for young people who don't have clear future plans and see the military both as a transition and a place of service, until they decide what they want to do with their lives. These young people may not yet see themselves as college material, but they are aware that working for minimum wage is not what they want out of life. In addition, the Post 9/11 GI Bill has greatly expanded tuition and housing benefits for those who have served overseas. There are minimal requirements for period served and the opportunities are great and well financed (Henderson, 2006).

In addition to the benefits of a steady income and a transition period, the military has been called the "great equalizer" for many in our society. In the wake of the current economic recession/depression, with double-digit unemployment in many parts of the country, joining the military presents itself as a viable option for job and job training. A high percentage of lower income youth have correctly seen the military as a road to upward mobility, education, respect, and prestige that they perceive would be impossible if they remained in the civilian world (Hall, 2008). The military has indeed set a standard for the integration of ethnic groups and gender, as it remains a relatively safe world for the families of lower income service members and their families (Schouten, 2004). Wertsch shared that many of the African-American military brats she interviewed experienced racism for the first time as adults in civilian communities and often "grew up acutely conscious of the contrast between their safe, secure life in the military and the tenuous existence of their civilian relatives in small rural towns or big city ghettos" (1991, p. 338).

Identity of the Warrior

On a more psychological level, many who join the military feel a need to "merge their identity with that of the warrior" (Schouten, 2004, p. 17). The structure, the expectations, the rules, even the penalties and overriding identity as a "warrior" are reassuring while, at the same time, providing service members with security, identity and a sense of purpose. Those whose personality and needs fit with the military culture often find themselves making the military a career. A San Diego therapist (Hall, 2008) noted that the profile of the service member who made the military a career during the time of the draft is often similar to those who now volunteer, as the military offers a re-enforcement of a belief system and a personal identity.

Previous work on the topic of war (Nash, 2007, p. 17) has explored the "psychology of war as a test of manhood and a rite of initiation among males in many cultures", so it is not uncommon for young men to merge their identity with that of a warrior by being a part of something meaningful. Gegax and Thomas (2005) suggest that while military sons tend to talk about duty when asked why they followed their fathers to war, their more personal motivations may have more to do with passing the test of manhood. Throughout the history of warfare, combat is often seen as a test, and certainly in some cultures *the* test, of manhood. "There is no better way to win a father's respect than to defy death just the way he did. Indeed, the effort to surpass one's father's or brother's bravery has gotten more than a few men killed" (p. 26).

An Escape

The military also satisfies a need for some young people to escape from painful life experiences, "a need for dependence … [drawing them] to the predictable, sheltered life … that they did not have growing up" (Wertsch, 1991, p. 17). Ridenour (1984) believes that military service becomes the extended family that was not experienced growing up. Sometimes, young married couples come into the military "as an escape from their respective families [only to] unconsciously run toward becoming part of a third extended family system" (p. 4). However, as Wertsch (1991) points out, "joining the military in order to put one's self in the care of a good surrogate parent is hardly the sort of thing one is likely to advertise; in fact, it is a secret so deep-seated that those who act upon it … guard the secret carefully" (p. 17). This attempt to flee from childhood or family problems at home, however, often does not solve most problems; sometimes the violence, gang mentality, or addiction issues are simply brought with them into the military (Hall, 2008).

Characteristics of Our Military Culture

Most of the unique facets of military life that were described almost three decades ago remain true for military families today, including:

- frequent separations and reunions;
- regular household relocations;
- living life under the umbrella of the "mission must come first" dictum;
- the need for families to adapt to rigidity, regimentation and conformity;
- early retirement from a career in comparison to civilian counterparts;
- rumors of loss during a mission;
- detachment from the mainstream of nonmilitary life;

- the security of a system that exists to meet the families' needs;
- work that usually involves travel and adventure;
- the social effects of rank on the family;
- the lack of control over pay, promotion, and other benefits.

(Ridenour, 1984)

While "it is evident ... that large segments of our society deal with one or more of these aforementioned concerns and stresses ... there may be no other major group that confronts so many or all of them" (1984, p. 3) at any given time.

Mary Wertsch (1991) defined this military society as a "Fortress" to differentiate it from the democratic society of most U.S. citizens. "The great paradox of the military is that its members, the self-appointed front-line guardians of our cherished American democratic values, do not live in democracy themselves" (p. 15). A number of characteristics of the Fortress that Wertsch discovered in her many interviews with adults who had grown up as military dependent children, are shared here. Having spent almost a decade working as a school counselor with military dependent children and youth, the author can attest to the validity of these characteristics.

Authoritarian Structure

The first characteristic is that the military world is maintained by a rigid authoritarian structure. The family must learn how to adapt its natural growth and development to the rigidity, regimentation and conformity that is required within the military system, as these characteristics often extend from the world of the service member into the structure of the home. It is important to point out, however, that while 80 percent of the military brats Wertsch interviewed described their families as authoritarian, "there are warriors who thrive in the authoritarian work environment without becoming authoritarian at home" (Wertsch, 1991, p. 25), so it is important to understand that authoritarianism is not the only model of military family life. However, in those families where authoritarian parenting is present, some of the following characteristics often exist:

(a) There are clear rules, often with narrow boundaries, for behavior and speech.
(b) There is little tolerance for questioning of authority or disagreements.
(c) There are often frequent inappropriate violations of privacy.
(d) Often children are discouraged from engaging in activities or behavior that hint at individuation.

(Hall, 2008)

The authoritarian structure can be a factor in the reintegration experience of returning service members, as many homes are not necessarily arranged with the degree of structure imposed by the military. The service member, used to the structure and boundaries of the military, may seek to impose structure and an authoritarian work environment upon returning home.

For many, this authoritarian parenting structure works, at least when children are young or if children attend schools on military installations. However, when families live "on the economy" (in a civilian community), the children, particularly once they reach adolescence, often rebel against this authoritarian parenting style because they associate with kids from very different family structures (Hall, 2008). Within the military community this can be both comforting and suffocating at the same time. It becomes a culture that is very inward focused, with a consistent hierarchical structure. The children sometimes blame the military for all their problems, as they see no escape and realize that even their extended family cannot step in to help. "They have a sense of betrayal by the military because they do not have the right to make the choices they see other young people making, but they realize their parents are not in a position to make many personal choices either" (2008, p. 47).

Isolation and Alienation

The necessity for extreme mobility results in military families becoming characterized by isolation and alienation from both the civilian world and the military family's extended family. The wife of an active duty service member reported that she had made 11 moves in the last nine years. One can only speculate on the degree of disruption for her and her three children. The language, often spoken in acronyms and other idiosyncratic terms, magnifies another aspect of this isolation. Someone "who does not understand … a word or phrase is faced with a dilemma. She must balance the risk of missing important clinical information with the cost of asking for clarification" (Reger, Etherage, Reger, & Gahm, 2008, p. 25). This vocabulary is a significant part of the military culture and if the words and phrases are not understood could have significant implications for assessment, intervention, and care.

One of the implications of the issues of mobility and language is that the military family may not be available for long-term care; "therefore, pragmatic reasons often force therapists to conceptualize treatment in brief terms" (Reger et al., 2008, p. 28). In addition, work with families could be interrupted for numerous military enforced reasons—including frequent moves—suggesting that social workers need to pay attention to issues of continuity of care.

Another obvious example of isolation is that the average tour of duty is three years, but, in many cases, moves are much more frequent; for some as often as every year. There are many students in the Department of Defense middle and high schools in Germany who had never visited their extended families' homes in the U.S. or lived anywhere near their "home of record." The irony is that every time the family moves, it is called a PCS, or Permanent Change of Station; permanent, that is, until the next move (Hall, 2008).

This isolation is often experienced as if life is temporary, with children and families not able or willing to make commitments to friends or communities, and always wondering about the next place, the next community, the next school. For those families who spend time living abroad, the isolation can seem overwhelming as most housing areas in foreign countries are walled off from the outside culture. The world of the military can become "an oddly isolated life, one in which it is possible to delude oneself that one is still on American soil" (Wertsch, 1991, p. 330). While there are those families who value the experience of living in a foreign country by learning the language and taking part in the culture, there are also those who are more anxious about this experience and may spend their entire tour of duty within the walls of the military installation.

Even when military dependent children attend public schools in the United States, they almost always "know" they are different from the other students. Wertsch states that it is "next to impossible to grow up in the warrior society without absorbing the notion that civilians are very different and sometimes incomprehensible" (Wertsch, 1991, p. 315). Gegax and Thomas (2005) share that this isolation of the military from the rest of society can be readily understood because the United States is, in fact, divided between the vast majority who do not have military service experience and the tiny minority who do.

Class System

Nowhere in America is the dichotomy so omnipresent as on a military base; nowhere do the classes live and work in such close proximity; nowhere is every social interaction so freighted with class significance ...The thousands of people on a military base live together, have the same employer, dedicate their lives to the same purpose—yet they cannot, must not, socialize outside their class.

(Wertsch, 1991, p. 285)

The military has two distinct subcultures, the world of the officer and that of the enlisted; each with very different lifestyles. The non-commissioned officers (non-coms or NCOs), who are usually the top five grades within the enlisted ranks, seem sometimes caught in the middle.

So, while members of the military and their families usually experience a sense of isolation from their civilian counterparts, this rank structure creates a distance within the military itself. The families are impacted, as well, as the spouses of officers and their children are also expected to maintain their distance from the enlisted spouses and children. The military has its reasons to make these distinctions and more than likely it could not exist without them, but it seems that "the only equality among officers and enlisted is in dying on the battlefield" (Wertsch, 1991, p. 288).

The United States has made great strides in the past five decades to affirm the importance of and equalize the differences in available services between rank and grade. But it is a universal assumption of all military systems that it is essential for the functioning of the organization to maintain a rigid hierarchical system, based on dominance and subordination. The importance for social workers is that it is also an essential ingredient in a clinical setting. In doing an assessment and initial intake, rank can give us important information: such as stressors, military history of the client/family, length of service, and possibly certain duties and experiences that will impact assessment, intervention, and care. Another consideration is that professional care givers, i.e., social workers, counselors, etc., will more than likely be viewed by those in the military as "civilian/officer-equivalent/authority" figures. Practitioners may need to be aware that enlisted service members may respond differently than officers, based on this common belief, possibly leading to initial difficulties in establishing the all-important practitioner/client alliance (Reger et al., 2008)

While the children of the enlisted and officers go to the same school, they almost always are uncomfortable associating outside of school with children of the other rank. Housing is separated, with single military in one area, enlisted family housing in another, and officers' quarters in another; each with clear distinctions in appearance, quality and size (Hall, 2008). In speaking with numerous adult military brats, virtually all will share that, as kids, they could, almost instantaneously, recognize an officer's kid or an enlisted kid. It is not a distinction to be taken lightly.

Parent Absence

This is a society with a great deal of parent absence and, with the changes in the military of the past two decades, sometimes both parents are absent at the same time. "Parent absence during important events can be crushing for young people; but for these families, nothing new. A parent is often absent for the prom, the big football game, the drama production, or graduation" (Hall, 2008, p. 51). But, more importantly, parents are absent for the routines of daily life: the first step, the first day of school, losing the first tooth, the first date, starting middle school or a special birthday. These are the times that cement relationships and often are missed by at least one parent. For single military parents, it can be even more difficult as they may not even live with their children on a regular basis. In the current conflicts in Afghanistan/Iraq, the use of Internet technology through email, SKYPE and other communication tools, has enabled a certain level of connection and contact. However, on both sides (from home and battlefield), many report that they severely edit communication so as to not alarm or upset the recipient.

In understanding the military family system, it is also important that while the absence of parents is stressful, "sometimes this constant coming and going results in either the military parents protecting themselves from the pain of separation or the family forming a kind of cohesive unit that keeps the military parent out" (Hall, 2008, p. 52). The military parent may distance from the family, either physically by working long hours or spending time away from home, or emotionally through alcohol or other ways of soothing the self. Families, on the other hand, may become so comfortable in their roles without the military parents that when the service members return, they simply put up with the intrusion, knowing that it won't be long before it ends. If the military parent expects or demands major changes upon returning home, the adjustments are often resented by the non-military parent or children. We must "be aware of the dynamics of military life that can introduce dissension into the relationship. Readjusting to family life, only to be pulled away yet again … places enormous stress on all those involved" (Dahn, 2008, p. 56). The issues of reintegration are complex. Interventions that normalize some of the struggles with families are often considered the most helpful as the family is reassured that what they are going through is "normal" and "expected" under the situation of military service.

Importance of Mission

The conditions and demands of "a total commitment to the military—typically a commitment to one's unit, the unit's mission and its members" (Martin & McClure, 2000, p. 15) is the very essence of military unit cohesion. This felt sense of mission is, indeed, the purpose of the military; for each service member, the commitment is not just about having a better education or training for a job but is, in fact, a sense of mission to make the world a better and safer place (Hall, 2008). Houppert (2005) explains that basic training is not designed to bring an adolescent into independence but rather to shift the recruit from dependence on his family to dependence on the team; "the soldier must learn that he can trust no one but his buddies" (p. 84). As "incongruous as it may seem for the millions whose closest brush with battle is on [TV], Soldiers and Marines on the front line are proud to be there and willing to serve again. The overall effect is to heighten the sense that the military is becoming a proud cult that fewer and fewer outsiders want to join" (Gegax & Thomas, 2005, p. 26). Those working with the military need to "recognize several common values shared by military personnel, including: (a) always maintaining physical fitness; (b) training hard before deployment to reduce casualties; (c) never abandoning fellow warriors in combat; (d) making sure the mission and the unit always come before the individual; and (e) never showing weakness to fellow warriors or to the enemy" (Fenell, 2008, p. 9). While the last two items point directly to this issue of the importance of the mission, the first two also indirectly relate to the imperative of readiness.

This dedication to the country and fellow soldiers (Fenell & Weinhold, 2003) can create difficult times for the family. Service members often see themselves as part of what might be described as a second family. Conflict at home emerges when this second "military family" is perceived to be more important than the family. While it has been shown that military service members who have solid families perform better on the job, it is always a difficult balancing act to be a part of two families who are so integral to the success of the mission (Fenell & Weinhold, 2003). A therapist interviewed had been a career military officer's spouse and was also the mother of a career officer (Hall, 2008). She experienced this demand of the military for loyalty, dedication, dependency and a sense of mission as virtually a form of brainwashing. As a clinical issue, social workers need to be attuned to the potential for this divided loyalty and help clarify loyalty issues.

One of the major determining factors in most military families is that all-powerful presence, which was often unacknowledged by the family, called the Military Mission; it is this presence that goes with them everywhere, and without which their lives would have no meaning (Wertsch, 1991). "From the viewpoint of the military's extended family style and demands, the mission takes precedence and, therefore, often the service member's relationship with his peers is found to take precedence over [the relationship] between himself and his spouse, children, or parents" (Ridenour, 1994, p. 7).

Preparation for Disaster

> Civilians often seem to blithely overlook a central truth military people can never afford to forget: that at any moment they may be called upon to give their lives—or lose a loved one—to serve the ends of government. Even if it never comes to that, [they] sacrifice a great deal in the course of doing a job that most civilians on some level understand is necessary to the country as a whole.
>
> (Wertsch, 1991, p. 316)

Unlike most civilian occupations, with certainly a few exceptions such as the police and firefighters, the military is a world set apart from the civilian world because of its constant preparation for disaster. This constant preparation for disaster also places a great deal of pressure and stress on the military family. "Military readiness is like a three-legged stool. The first leg is training, the second equipment. The third leg is the family. If any of these three legs snaps, the stool tips over and America is unprepared to defend herself" (Henderson, 2006, p. 5). While the military cannot exist without this constant preparation, it means the family is also living under the constant threat of disaster, i.e., the potential for death or injury to the military parent.

Psychological Results of Living in the Fortress

The above general characteristics of the military culture often lead to the three psychological traits that Mary Wertsch (1991) identified when interviewing a large number of adult military brats. These traits include:

1   Secrecy, the importance of keeping what goes on at work separate from home, as well as making sure that what goes on at home stays home. The dictate is also a present in many military job categories often producing a level of psychological shutting off even between spouses, as well as between parents and children.

2   Stoicism, or the importance of keeping up the appearance of stability and the ability to handle whatever stress the family encounters. Having to live under this constant preparation for change, whether it be disaster, just another deployment, or a PCS, means that if these fears and other feelings were expressed, families would have to acknowledge constant emotional turmoil. As the National Military Family Association (NMFA) stated recently, "complete elimination of stress, especially for a military family member, is an impossible task" (NMFA, nd-a, ¶ 1) and while military families are resilient and able to successfully manage multiple stressors, "sometimes it can take additional help to relieve the underlying feeling that life is coming at you too fast and becoming too complicated" (¶ 3). Often this help is unavailable to families unless they take the risk to ask for it.

3   Denial, or the need to keep all the feelings, fears, and even other "normal" developmental stresses of the family under wraps. While in a relatively few number of families this includes domestic violence, child abuse or other "reportable" offenses, what it does mean for most families is that the expression of feelings is not encouraged, fears are not shared, and the need to ask for help or request assistance goes unnoticed. The National Military Family Association states that "teens especially carry a burden of care that they are reluctant to share with the non-deployed parent … as they are often encumbered by the feeling of trying to keep the family going, along with anger over changes in their schedules, increased responsibility, and fear for their deployed parent" (¶ 2).

Secrecy, stoicism and denial are, in fact, crucial for success of the warrior, success of the mission, and ultimately success of the military (Hall, 2008). At the same time, these traits often determine whether military members, and sometimes their families, seek treatment. "To the extent that seeking psychological treatment is defined as 'weakness,' soldiers may be slow to pursue services" (Reger et al., 2008, p. 27). Often this reluctance delays treatment, resulting in many being pushed beyond tolerable stress levels. Addressing these beliefs during intake may lower the chance of military members minimizing symptoms, and thereby benefiting from a professional's ability to normalize their beliefs about fears, stigma and future treatment.

These three traits of secrecy, stoicism and denial also suggest that many military families may, on a regular basis, be experiencing Type II Trauma (National Institute for Trauma and Loss in Children, n.d.) or the type of trauma that results from constant fear, the constant planning for disaster and the constant readiness for change. These restrictions from grieving may mean that military families are not allowed the growth that can come from the expression and "work" done in grieving the experience of loss. "When the culture encourages secrecy, stoicism and denial and discourages or even punishes the expression of fears and grief, families and service members are often faced with the same kind of consequences we see in clients who suffer from constant levels of Type II trauma" (Hall, 2008, p. 58).

Honor and Sacrifice and the Male Military Psyche

These dynamics of secrecy, stoicism and denial also can help us understand the important concepts of honor and sacrifice in the military. It is difficult to understand the importance of the concepts of military honor and sacrifice without relating it to the male psyche and the traditional stereotypes of the military as a male domain. While we know that more and more women are entering the military, the culture of the military has historically been a very "male" culture. From the perspective of a therapist in San Diego who has worked with military service members for three decades (Butler, 2006), this issue could easily be overlooked, or at least not understood, particularly by professional females working with male service members. Because the military is still predominately male, and most social workers are predominately female, Dr. Butler's insights are invaluable.

It is also these concepts of honor and sacrifice that help us to understand the inherent stigma that is so predominant in the military. "Military personnel are expected to 'soldier up' and get through the rough times on their own" (Dahn, 2008, p. 56) because they have been warned that seeking professional help "could be detrimental to career advancement or seen as a sign of weakness by their chain of command" (p. 56).

To work with men in the military, it is important to give due attention to the concept of "honor" that is so central to the psychology of the military, and so central to male psychology. There is a marked difference between men and women in studying the culture of honor. The reality is that the military probably couldn't do its job without the strongly held beliefs of service members regarding the importance of honor (Gilligan, 1996).

Through leadership, training and unit cohesion, stress reactions are managed and honor is maintained; "searching for ways to become more comfortable or safe in war can be not only a distraction from the real business at hand, but also a serious hazard to success and even survival" (Nash, 2007, p. 15).

Relationships at Home

One of the obstacles that the concept of honor presents in therapy is the possibility that military men, because of their military commitments, believe they should be "given a pass when it comes to relationship issues with family and children" (Hall, 2008, p. 63), leading to a form of neglect at home. In a metaphorical way, the career military male marries his military service and the male–female marriage becomes an extramarital affair (Keith & Whitaker, 1984).

A female therapist, who was also a wife of a former military officer, talked about family get-togethers when the officer husbands returned from deployment. She shared that, invariably, the military members wanted to spend the time together instead of with the families. While these were difficult times for her and the children, she began to understand that the time her husband spent with the other officers was the only time he believed that those around him would understand the memories that were constant in his mind. She also realized this was the only way the military husbands could cope with the tremendous shame for what they believed they had done, and for what they had witnessed (Hall, 2008). One way of reframing this for families, especially spouses, is to point out, as Lyons (2007) suggests, that a reluctance to divulge horrible details may very likely be due to the importance of the home relationships, rather than an indication of the contrary.

Implications for Practice

Social Workers practice in a variety of settings from private practice to medical clinics, schools, Veteran's hospitals, community agencies and many, many more. As noted in the introduction, having an understanding of the culture of our military clients, families, and children is the best place to begin. Not unlike other culturally diverse groups, the military has standards, a jargon of its own, and beliefs that must be incorporated into the practice of those in the helping professions. Some of the characteristics of this culture, such as frequent moves, deployment and training schedules of the service member, and the psychological issues of secrecy, stoicism and denial add a layer of difficulty and possibly confusion for professionals who may see the world from a place of openness, fairness, and egalitarianism. Virtually all reported best practices when working with the military suggest that coming from a strength-based approach, usually incorporating a more cognitive modality, is more effective than a longer-term approach with a strong focus on feelings and emotions. Service members and their families need to get things done and move on, which is how the expertise of social workers can be so valuable. While longer term distress, such as PTSD, have to be a part of the assessment, treatment and referral, building on the family and the service members' strengths by helping them to resolve issues through CBT, Solution-Focused or Rational Emotive Behavior Therapy modalities often are the most effective approaches. However, from whatever approach and in whatever setting, social workers will encounter military families; therefore, having an understanding of their culture and what has shown to be most helpful is essential.

Summary

Acknowledging and understanding the many unique characteristics of the military is essential before attempting to intervene and work with this diverse culture. Unless we understand how these characteristics impact the military family and lead to the need for stoicism, secrecy and denial, we cannot work effectively with the military service members or with their families In addition, unless we understand their language, their structure, why they join, their commitment to the mission, and the role of honor and sacrifice in military service, we will not be able to adequately intervene and offer care to these families. This care must come from within the military framework and be consistent with the worldview of their culture.

References

Butler, H. (2006). Love, honor and obey: Musings on working with military men and their families (Personal communication).

Dahn,V.L. (2008). Silent service in the soldier's shadow. *Counseling Today*, 51(4), 55–57.

Dass-Brailsford, P. (2007). *A Practical Approach to Trauma: Empowering interventions.* Thousand Oaks, CA: Sage Publications.

Fenell, D. (2008). A distinct culture: Applying multicultural counseling competencies to work with military personnel. *Counseling Today*, 50(12), 8–9 & 35.

Fenell, D.L. & Weinhold, B.K. (2003). *Counseling Families: An introduction to marriage and family therapy* (3rd Ed.). Denver, CO: Love Publishing Company.

Gegax,T.T. & Thomas, E. (2005).The family business. *Newsweek,* 145(25), 24–31.

Gilligan, J. (1996). *Violence: Reflections on a national epidemic.* New York: Random House.

Hall, L.K. (2008) *Counseling Military Families: What mental health professionals need to know.* New York: Routledge:Taylor and Francis.

Henderson, K. (2006). *While They're at War:The true story of American families on the homefront.* New York: Houghton-Mifflin.

Houppert, K. (2005). *Home Fires Burning: Married to the military—for better or worse.* New York: Ballantine Books.

Keith, D.V. & Whitaker, C.A. (1984). C'est la Guerre: Military families and family therapy. In F.W. Kaslow & R.I. Ridenour (Eds.), *The Military Family: Dynamics and treatment* (pp. 147–166). New York: Guilford Press.

Lyons, A.J. (2007). The returning warrior: Advances for families and friends. In C.R. Figley & W.P. Nash (Eds.), *Combat Stress Injury: Theory, research and management* (pp. 311–324). New York: Routledge.

Martin, J.A. & McClure, P. (2000). Today's active duty military family: The evolving challenges of military family life. In J.A. Martin, L.N. Rosen, & L.R. Sparacino (Eds.), *The Military Family: A practice guide for human service providers* (pp. 3–24). Westport, CT: Praeger Publishers.

Nash, W.P. (2007). The stressors of war. In C.R. Figley & W.P. Nash (Eds.), *Combat Stress Injury: Theory, research and management* (pp. 11–32). New York: Routledge: Taylor and Francis.

National Institute for Trauma and Loss in Children (n.d.) *Grief and Trauma.* Retrieved May 13, 2007 from: www.tlcinst.org/griefandtrauma.html

National Military Family Association (nd-a). *Caring for Kids*. Retrieved February 2, 2010, from: www.militaryfamily.org/get-info/mental-health-care/caring-for-kids

National Military Family Association (nd-b). What's normal. Retrieved February 2, 2010, from: www.militaryfamily.org/get-info/mental-health-care/whats-normal

Reger, M.A., Etherage, J.R., Reger, G.M., & Gahm, G.A. (2008) Civilian psychologists in an Army culture: The ethical challenge of cultural competence. *Military Psychology*. 20, 21–35.

Ridenour, R.I. (1984). The military, service families, and the therapist. In F.W. Kaslow & R.I. Ridenour (Eds.), *The Military Family: Dynamics and treatment* (pp. 1–17). New York: Guilford Press.

Schouten, F. (2004). No soldier's child left behind: Defense Department school system gets results. *USA Today*, p. D7.

Sue, D.W., Arredondo, P., & McDavis, R.J. (1992). Multicultural counseling competencies and standards: A call to the profession. *Journal of Counseling and Development*, 70, 477–486.

Wakefield, M. (2007). Guarding the military home front. *Counseling Today*, 49(8), 5 & 23.

Wertsch, M.E. (1991). *Military Brats: Legacies of childhood inside the fortress*. New York: Harmony Books; currently published by Brightwell Publishing, St. Louis, MO, at www.brightwellpublishing.net

2

NO ONE LEAVES UNCHANGED— INSIGHTS FOR CIVILIAN MENTAL HEALTH CARE

Professionals into the Military Experience and Culture

Jose E. Coll, Eugenia L. Weiss, and Jeffrey S. Yarvis

This chapter aims to elucidate an understanding of military culture and experience, so as to better frame the services offered by civilian clinicians. Service members indoctrinated into such an influential culture can experience adjustment problems upon reentry into the larger society, and thus social workers must be ready to address the reintegration process with Veteran clients. Furthermore, the chapter highlights a few of the major mental health concerns that are prevalent in combat Veterans, especially for those returning from Operation Iraqi Freedom (OIF), Operation New Dawn (OND), and Operation Enduring Freedom (OEF); and presents a brief overview of treatment modalities implemented both within and outside of the military. Practical therapeutic suggestions for clinicians with little or no knowledge of the military are discussed. The objective is to educate and prepare civilian social work practitioners to administer culturally sensitive prevention and intervention services to meet the unique needs of this population.

Military personnel form a fairly distinct subset of American society, governed by a separate set of laws, norms, traditions, and values (Exum & Coll, 2008). Upon leaving military service, many service members encounter the same type of culture shock that immigrants experience when first arriving in the United States; there is the disorientation, change of status, and a search for identity and meaning. It is highly likely that some military personnel will return to civilian life with adjustment issues beyond culture shock. Some will return with a loss of trust in the U.S. government, while others will return with a wavering faith in God. Many will return with physical disabilities resulting from combat injuries, while others will return with less apparent but equally disturbing emotional and psychological disabilities.

Data from the Medical Department of the Army (2008) indicate that the current suicide rate among active duty service members is the highest it has been in the 26 years of the Department's record keeping. Fifteen to 30 percent of all returning Veterans will meet the *Diagnostic and Statistical Manual of Mental Disorders* (APA [American Psychiatric Association], 2000) criteria for serious mental health disorders involving post-traumatic stress disorder (PTSD), mood disturbances, anxieties and co-morbid substance abuse (United States Army Medical Department, 2008). Perhaps the most salient disorder associated with combat Veterans is PTSD, which involves the impairment of functioning after having experienced or witnessing actual or threatened death or serious injury to self or others (APA, 2000). This disorder is particularly devastating because Veterans will often self-medicate with drugs and alcohol to alleviate the symptoms of PTSD. Research suggests that approximately 64–84 percent of Veterans with PTSD will also suffer from a life course of alcohol abuse (Brady & Sinha, 2005). Moreover, Veterans suffering from PTSD experience significantly higher rates of marital and familial problems (i.e., often resulting in domestic violence and child abuse) than those without PTSD. The rates of interpersonal violence in both active duty and Veteran populations are estimated to be three times greater than those of civilian populations (Houppert, 2005). This statistic is disconcerting considering the fact that a significant number of returnees will "fly below the radar," that is, Veteran's PTSD and associated problems will go undetected until they instigate disruptions in their families, in their places of employment or in their communities. Therefore, it is critical for social work practitioners to be well informed of the military experience in order to administer culturally sensitive interventions to effectively meet the needs of military personnel that will ultimately impact their families and communities.

Additionally, due to the nature of the conflicts in OEF/OIF/OND, service members are suffering from the effects of severe blast injuries from Intermittent Explosive Devices (IED), and acquiring traumatic brain injury (TBI); considered the "signature wound" of these wars (Okie, 2006). The biopsychosocial effects of TBI along with the occurrence of PTSD are just beginning to be understood and the efficacy of treatment approaches over the long-term has yet to be demonstrated.

Military Culture and Values

Military culture is comprised of the values, traditions, norms, and perceptions that govern how members of the armed forces think, communicate, and interact with one another and with civilians. Though each branch of the military has a unique set of core values, there are unifying qualities across the various divisions of the military, such as honor, courage, loyalty, integrity, and commitment (Exum & Coll,

2008; Exum, Coll & Weiss, 2011). Military values serve as the standards of conduct for military personnel and these rules regulate their lives on a daily basis. The military believes that the ubiquitous application of their standards of conduct is necessary because members of the armed forces must be ready at all times to be deployed into combat.

The often-overlooked virtues that shape the military professional include peacefulness, restraint, and obedience (DeGeorge, 1987; Exum & Coll, 2008). The military upholds the value of peacefulness by preserving harmony, which sometimes ironically involves waging war. From a civilian perspective, this may seem contradictory, yet from the military perspective, there is a clear difference in the motivation behind force. The virtue of peacefulness coincides with the virtue of restraint, which is often exercised when service personnel direct attacks at opposing armed forces while avoiding civilians or noncombatants. This restraint can be difficult to sustain, especially when civilians from foreign countries instigate conflict by attacking American troops. In the current wars, the enemy is often indistinguishable. One such vivid example of this involves the Taliban's use of women and children as suicide bombers. Restraint is also observed in the rationale that drives a war. The "Just War Doctrine" states that war should be waged as a last resort when all other peaceful alternatives have been exhausted (DeGeorge, 1987). The doctrine indicates that there must be a "just cause" that necessitates recourse to war, and that the expected costs of the war in terms of human life and destruction of property should be a "proportionate price for the good to be achieved by defending the just cause" (O'Brian, 1984, p. 59). The doctrine maintains that the use of force must be limited to attaining the just cause and should not be motivated by hatred or by the desire for revenge.

Obedience, on the other hand, is more complex than the simple act of compliance (DeGeorge, 1987). DeGeorge states that obedience is only a virtue when the orders are legitimate and morally sound. The commander's moral obligation is to accomplish legitimate military objectives while minimizing the deaths of those under his command and of civilian populations on either side of the conflict (Viotti, 1987). Hence, a service member is not obligated to follow an order that he deems to be either immoral or illegitimate. Having said this, it becomes unlikely that a subordinate will challenge the direct order of a superior. In a recent U.S. Navy and Marine Corps Conference on Combat Stress, there was much discussion among mental health professionals over the notion of "moral injury" as a form of combat stress. Moral injury is defined as "the stress arising from witnessing, perpetrating or failing to stop actions that violate a person's deeply held belief systems; in combat this could be the killing of a woman or child, the inability to save a fellow Marine or the failure of leadership to live up to a moral code" (McCloskey, 2011). Interestingly, there was dissension between the commanding officers and the mental health professionals who attended this conference, where the officers posited that the Marine Corps "trains Marines to have the skill and the will to kill", and that this is based on "an ethical standard"

(McCloskey, 2011). Additionally, service members who question the integrity of the military system may often prove to be liabilities during missions.

By surveying military virtues and ethics, it becomes imperative for a clinician to separate the service member from the underlying political agenda involving war. Though soldiers, airmen, sailors and marines may function as the precipitating agents of violence and conflict abroad, they do so in compliance with direct orders issued by the U.S. government. It is important for social work professionals to recognize the service member's values to fight for peace, exercise restraint and obey the chain of command. In any case, engaging former military personnel or active duty service members in political discussions in the therapeutic setting, is not advisable. Additionally, the clinician should self-monitor instances of countertransference that may spark controversy and negatively impact the therapeutic relationship. In an effort to remain strengths-based, the social worker could acknowledge the virtues of the military, and commend clients on their willingness to serve (keeping in mind that the U.S. armed forces consists of an all-volunteer force) at a personal sacrifice and for a purpose larger than the self (Cook, 2004). Davenport (1987) states that military personnel often form their own separate specialized society that is psychologically distant from that of the civilian world. This phenomenon is due to the establishment of unit cohesion, which involves the formation of trusting bonds between members of the same team that ensures survival in battle. Thus, civilian clinicians need to be versed in military culture in order to be able to penetrate effectively the military mindset and establish a rapport with Veteran clients.

Mental Health Concerns

As previously mentioned, military personnel with combat exposure are at a high risk for developing PTSD, major depression, substance abuse, and anxiety disorders; as well as suffering from impairments in such areas as social, occupational, and physical functioning (Hoge, Auchterlonie, & Milliken, 2006). The generation of military personnel returning from Iraq and Afghanistan are perhaps even more at risk than prior generations of Veterans since they have served substantially longer tours of duty throughout the course of multiple combat deployments. Experiencing combat-related stressors can produce a considerable amount of distress within a service member, which ultimately yields acute biopsychosocial stress reactions such as psychomotor deficiencies, withdrawal, anxiety, extreme paranoia, and interpersonal problems (Litz & Orsillo, 2003).

The set of stressors associated with the war zone experience are unlike that of any other occupation in civilian society. Although police officers may experience similar violent situations to military service members, the significant difference is that police officers operate in a domestic context and have continuous access to sources of emotional support. Whereas military personnel experience the added stress of being in a foreign land, spending endless hours in a miserable work environment punctuated by moments of transcendental terror and unimaginable,

TABLE 2.1 Potential stressors

Type of stressor	Examples of stressor	Bio-psycho-social effects of stressors
Environmental	Extreme weather conditions Loud noises from explosions Toxic agents	Poor unit cohesion Grief and depression Resentment Aggression
Physiological and physical	Sleep deprivation Dehydration Bodily injury Brain injury (from IED)	Abusive behaviors towards prisoners Malingering (feigning illness to avoid responsibility) Restlessness Nausea and vomiting
Cognitive	Sensory overload	Stuttering Confusion
Emotional	Fear Insecurity	Suspiciousness and distrust Self-isolating tendencies Physical injury Medical conditions

Note: Adapted from Exum & Coll (2008).

horrific destruction of human life and property. Thus, no one leaves combat without incurring profound physical, psychological, existential, and emotional changes. This is not to imply that all of those who experience combat will necessarily suffer from PTSD; in fact the majority of service members do not, and may in fact experience intrapersonal and interpersonal growth as a result of this life changing experience—often referred to in the literature as posttraumatic growth (Calhoun & Tedeschi, 1999). Table 2.1 offers examples of the various types of potential stressors that service members may endure, including those related to the environment, physiological/physical, cognitive and emotional; and the possible negative effects resulting from the exposure to such stressors. This list is not meant to be a complete description of problems and symptoms associated with the current wars; for a comprehensive review please refer to Hoge et al. (2006) or Seal, Bertenthal, Nuber, et al. (2007).

Combat zone experiences may produce more chronic maladaptive symptoms, as is the case with PTSD. An individual who experiences PTSD suffers from an increased risk of dysfunctional interpersonal relationships, vocational difficulties, and educational problems. It is therefore important to devote significant time to assessing the presence and the severity of PTSD in Veteran clients.

Posttraumatic Stress Disorder

The DSM-IV-TR (APA, 2000) classifies the symptoms of PTSD under three headings, as shown in Table 2.2.

TABLE 2.2 PTSD symptom classifications

PTSD symptom classification	Description
Intrusion	The event is persistently re-experienced in one or more of five possible ways (e.g., recollections, flashbacks, dreams)
Avoidance	Stimuli associated with the traumatic event are avoided and accompanied by numbing of general responsiveness
Disordered arousal	Persistent symptoms of increased arousal as indicated by at least two of five symptoms (e.g., sleep disturbance, irritability, hypervigilance, exaggerated startle response)

Source: APA (2000).

Under the current diagnostic system, it is important to note that even if a service member exhibits all the symptoms of PTSD, an individual cannot be diagnosed unless he or she meets the criterion for exposure. The Veteran must have been exposed to an event that involved actual or threatened death or serious injury to self or others, where the person's response involved intense fear, helplessness, or horror (APA, 2000). If all criteria have been fulfilled and symptoms have persisted for more than one month, a diagnosis of PTSD is made. If the symptoms have persisted for less than one month, the diagnosis of Acute Stress Disorder (ASD) should be considered instead (APA, 2000).

Individuals who suffer from PTSD are apprehensive in moments of re-exposure to previously disturbing or unsettling experiences. As a consequence, there is an interruption of thoughts, actions, or feelings (Friedman, 2004). Intrusive recollections can persist for more than 50 years (waxing and waning), and symptoms may become worse over time. Those suffering from PTSD also develop avoidant behaviors or emotional numbing in order to ward off the intolerable emotions and memories associated with the traumatic events. Clients with PTSD may suffer from autonomic hyper-arousal, meaning that they are always on guard and fearful of re-encountering the terrifying circumstances that haunt them. Isolation is common for those suffering from PTSD because these individuals find it difficult to trust other people and environments, and their need for safety and protection outweighs all considerations for intimacy, socialization, or pleasurable pursuits. In order to reduce the likelihood of mental health or interpersonal problems resulting from combat reactions in service members of active duty status, the U.S. military has developed resilience-building programs to promote individual and family wellness.

Resilience-Building Programs Within the Military

The U.S. Army has recently developed a program for promoting the psychosocial wellbeing of its service members and their family members, titled the

Comprehensive Soldier Fitness (CSF) Program. This program entails resiliency skills training for military personnel and their families in preparation for deployment. The concept behind CSF training is to prepare the service member and their spouse through strengths-based and cognitive skill building and communication types of exercises. Training objectives include identifying strengths that the individual and the family bring to the deployment experience and assist in the anticipation of possible deployment and post deployment reactions. The U.S. Navy and Marine Corps have their own version of a resilience building program, titled Families Overcoming and Coping Under Stress (FOCUS, 2011). A family-centered resiliency-training program serves families with children that wish to strengthen their relationships, highlighting family strengths, adaptive coping responses, and the use of available resources.

Combat Stress Control Teams

Another military-based approach to treating the psychological effects of warzone experiences is summarized by the principles of Proximity, Immediacy, Expectancy, and Simplicity (PIES) (Litz & Orsillo, 2003). This concept was originally designed in World War I as an early intervention program to normalize combat experiences and recycle soldiers back into combat as expeditiously as possible. Since then, the military has established Combat Stress Control (CSC) teams that incorporate the "PIES" system to provide front-line behavioral health care for military personnel. The CSC teams have proven to be very effective in Operations Desert Shield, Desert Storm and in Somalia, and thus, both the Army and Navy currently deploy CSC teams to OEF/OIF/OND.

The CSC team usually consists of a behavioral specialist, a social work officer, a psychiatric nurse officer, a psychiatrist, and an occupational therapy officer. Together, the team works to promote a mentally stable and mission-oriented combat force through several interventions. These include the following: consultations with command, preventative resiliency skills training, brief individual therapy, anger management skills, stress management, substance abuse counseling, and PTSD symptom related group therapies. On occasion, CSC teams may deem it necessary to place a distressed service member on "restoration hold" for up to three days, under which the service member is not allowed to return to the combat zone and is provided with food and rest while being monitored by CSC staff. The goal of the CSC team is to return the service member back to duty. Return-to-duty rates from 2004 indicate that 98 percent of soldiers treated by the CSC unit returned to assume their combat zone duties (Litz & Orsillo, 2003). Even with these clinical services available in the warzone, many military personnel will still return to the U.S. with serious psychological disorders as a consequence of combat experiences. Once home, if the service member is of active duty status (whether they are Active Duty, Reserve or in the National Guard) they can access services on military installations or through local Vet Centers. If they are separated or retired from the military and are eligible, they can access services through the Veterans Affairs (VA) hospitals and clinics. However, for a variety of reasons, many Veterans are accessing mental health care at community mental health agencies or through private practitioners. One of the reasons for the Active Duty to seek services outside of the military has to do with the fear of negative work repercussions or stigma (Hoge et al., 2006). For those that are separated from the military and have a *less than honorable discharge* and consequently are not entitled for services through the VA, or those individuals that have served under private contractor firms and do not have medical benefits, these individuals will often end up in the civilian mental health sector. There are also those disabled Veterans who are disappointed with service delivery through the VA and elect to seek mental health services in the community. As the reader can ascertain from this description of possibilities in Veteran care, it becomes imperative for the civilian social worker to understand the complex system that surrounds Veteran care that is essentially based on a continuum of care that hinges upon where the service member falls in relation to military service.

Military Identity Transitions and Continuum of Care

According to Daley (2011), there exists a continuum of care for a Veteran that depends on where the individual is in the military life cycle (and corresponding identity), and that each phase of care entails a different culture driven perspective and mission. For instance, for those individuals who are "active duty" status, their culture and perspective becomes centered on the military needs of "mission readiness." Whereas for those that have been injured as result of military service (i.e., "wounded warriors") their culture and mission is to rehabilitate and either return to duty or separate from the military. In fact, the military offers a Wounded Warrior Program which entails long-term rehabilitative care along with the provision of needed supports for the warrior and the caregivers with the purpose of returning the warriors to duty. If the military deems it unfeasible for the soldier to return to duty (as in many cases of PTSD and TBI), the soldier is then medically separated from service and is routed to the VA for continued care. Some amputees fitted with prosthetic limbs can continue in active duty status in a specialized unit through the wounded warrior battalion. Finally, the last phase of military identity transition and continuum of care entails Veterans retiring or separating from military service and accessing Veteran services and benefits (e.g., disability pay, GI Bill, medical care through the VA, and pension) and reintegrating into civilian culture. The transition involves a new identity formation, new career plans and perhaps the pursuit of higher education. Each phase in this model includes a set of unique challenges and demands where the mediating factors towards adaptation in all of these transitional scenarios have to do with the support systems available to the service member. The support systems include the service member's internal resilience as well as family and community supports. Here, community support relates to both the military's formal and informal networks and the support derived from the civilian sector and society. The notion of support as a central principle is derived from Huebner and colleagues' (2009) model of "community capacity." An additional component that needs to be considered as part of the model is the influence of race or ethnicity as an overlapping element in each of the military life cycle phases. Ethnic and minority cultural variables play a role in help-seeking behaviors (Sue & Sue, 1999); may also play a part in bolstering resilience through differing worldview orientations (Weiss, Coll, & Metal, in press) and response to trauma (Weiss, Coll, Mayeda, et al., in review). Please refer to Figure 2.1.

Mental Health Treatment Outside of the Military

Civilian social workers and mental health professionals need to be prepared to handle the psychological aftermath of the Veteran experience. In addition to acute stress reactions to combat, returning soldiers may also present with general adjustment issues while reintegrating back into the civilian world. Treatment for any of these clients, whether they present with acute symptoms or not, should be specifically catered to their needs and based on where they lie on the continuum of care and should involve a holistic approach to recovery. Table 2.3 provides a brief overview of some treatment modalities that have proven to be effective for working with Veterans.

Treatment interventions for working with Veterans include psychoeducation, coping skills training, cognitive restructuring, exposure therapy, substance abuse

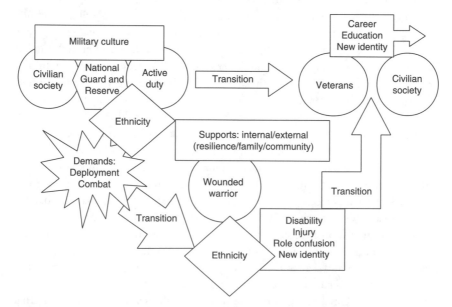

FIGURE 2.1 Military identity transitions and continuum of care

TABLE 2.3 Treatment modalities

Treatment modality	Symptoms addressed	Therapeutic goals	Clinical notes
Education	Adjustment/ reintegration problems	• To reduce shame • To normalize experiences including loss and emotional cycles of deployment	Emphasis should be placed on teaching clients about the recovery process and how to recognize symptoms
Coping skills training	Emotional instability	• To manage anger and anxiety • To foster interpersonal communication • To promote emotional grounding • To teach skills that support recovery • To instruct in non violent problem solving skills	Treatment entails an instruction/education component followed by role-played rehearsals, feedback and coaching, real-world practice and self-monitoring notes
Cognitive restructuring and logo therapy	• Self-defeating thoughts • PTSD	To develop alternative interpretations of thoughts, feelings and behaviors; recreate meaning	Emphasis should be placed on increasing an awareness of the relationship between thoughts, emotions and behaviors
Exposure therapy	PTSD	To help clients confront traumas by exposing them to traumatic memories or fear provoking situations	• Clients repeatedly verbalize incidents that trouble them until fear and anxieties diminish • May involve revisiting sites of trauma or simulation of traumatic experience • Helpful when used in conjunction with other treatment modalities
Family Counseling	• Readjustment problems • Domestic violence • Spousal/ partner distress • Child abuse/ neglect	• To resolve family conflicts • To build long-term healthy support systems for client	• Family education • Couples counseling • Parenting workshops

(Continued)

TABLE 2.3 *(Continued)*

Treatment modality	Symptoms addressed	Therapeutic goals	Clinical notes
Pharmacology	• Readjustment • PTSD	To reduce symptoms of stress disorders through the use of psychotropic drugs	• Must be prescribed by physician/psychiatrist • Often used in conjunction with other treatments • Know the names of drugs and possible effects

counseling, family counseling, and pharmacological treatment as needed (Exum & Coll, 2008; Exum et al., 2011). The psychoeducational component often involves the clinician explaining the homecoming process and what to expect during the various stages of deployment (pre-deployment, deployment and post-deployment) in terms of emotional functioning in the self and in the family (Pincus, House, Christenson, & Adler, n.d.). Clinicians can also provide psychoeducation about common symptoms associated with PTSD reactions. Coping skills training often involves anger management techniques, and relaxation exercises—including anxiety management and interpersonal communication skill building (Ruzek, Curran, Friedman, et al., 2003). Motivational Interviewing can be utilized to address co-morbid substance use and health care issues (Rollnick, Miller, & Butler, 2008). Cognitive Restructuring (or Cognitive Processing Therapy) is an evidence based treatment approach for PTSD and for general adjustment problems that is designed to help Veterans challenge negative and distorted thinking patterns in order to come up with more positive interpretations of their beliefs (Foa, Keane, & Friedman, 2000). Logotherapy (derived from Frankl, 1959) is a meaning making based intervention for altered worldviews and survivor guilt, resulting from combat experience can also be utilized as an adjunctive approach to combat PTSD (Southwick, Gilmartin, McDonough, & Morrissey, 2006). Acceptance and Commitment Therapy (Hayes, Strosahl, & Wilson, 1999) is an approach to problems that is based on a cognitive model that utilizes mindfulness techniques, gaining acceptance of the human condition and values-based living. Other evidence-based treatments that are geared to address PTSD specifically include cognitive-behavioral and exposure based therapies, such as Prolonged Exposure Therapy (Foa, Hembree, & Rothbaum, 2007); Eye Movement Desensitization and Reprocessing (Shapiro, 2001), which incorporates bilateral neurobiological stimulation with a guiding Adaptive Information Processing model; and Virtual Reality Exposure Therapy that is based on combat trauma therapy within a human–computer interaction paradigm (Rothbaum, Difede, & Rizzo, 2008). The Seeking Safety model as proposed by Najavits (2007) addresses PTSD and substance abuse co-morbidity has also been a successful model in the treatment of Veterans. The literature on PTSD and related therapies is too extensive for review in this chapter. Please refer to the above named authors and to the subsequent chapters in this book for a more comprehensive understanding.

Practical Advice for Engaging Veterans

A clinician's approach to counseling a Veteran client will vary depending on how far removed the Veteran is from military service. No blanket assumptions should be made about the Veteran's experience. However, in most situations, it can be helpful to initiate the conversation with preliminary questions about the client's military service. Questions might include:

- In which branch of the armed forces did you serve?
- Where were you stationed?
- What was your military occupational specialty (MOS)?
- Do you have any family or friends who are still deployed?
- Were you engaged in combat?

Some Veterans may be apprehensive and skeptical when talking to civilians about military experiences. Therefore, it is crucial to cultivate a safe, neutral and yet encouraging therapeutic environment in which the client may feel comfortable enough to share when he or she is ready. Until then, the clinician should watch for turning points in dialogue and shifts in affect, as well as triggers that might invoke repressed feelings and memories; it is critical for the clinician to be emotionally present and attentive. The client's thoughts may be desultory and disorganized and, as with any client, the clinician must be flexible and adaptable.

Regardless of where the Veteran is in terms of the continuum of care, clinicians need to anticipate issues of grief and loss in all the phases of adaptation: through the transitions from active duty status to Veteran status to civilian status. Combat related losses in terms of the Veteran's loss of functioning, disability and the death of fellow comrades, as well the shattered assumptive worldviews in the Veteran returning from combat, would all need to be explored. The role of the clinician during this transitional process is to listen and validate the client's feelings and to encourage their internal and external resources. It would also be appropriate to normalize grief by providing education into the stages of grief (Kubler-Ross, 1969). The clinician is encouraged to ask questions about what the losses mean to the client, and to offer validating statements such as "I'm sorry this happened to you," or "I'm sorry that you are struggling with this." It is not appropriate to offer presumptuous or negating statements such as "I understand how you feel," or "You'll get over it." As a clinician, it is imperative to appreciate the uniquely subjective nature of the transitional process and how grief is expressed differently for everyone and that the duration of grief associated with the transitions will vary interpersonally.

Often, for clinicians, there may be an emotional distancing that takes place when interacting with the bereaved (Knake, 1995) which can prompt the mourner to stop sharing. As a therapist, it is important to monitor any countertransference that may be hindering the client's willingness to share. The clinician may offer empathic support to the client as he or she accepts the variety of loss experiences that may be associated with the loss of physical or mental functioning, the bereavement resulting from the loss of peers, or the loss that accompanies the shift in identity and roles. The goal for the therapist is to help the client work through the grief in order to adjust his or her life and perceptions to accommodate the loss or multiple losses (Knake, 1995) and adapt to a "new normal." A clinician should not expect the client to "get over" a loss; rather, the clinician should remain available as the client learns how to accommodate the loss. Additionally, when deciding which of the best practice approaches to take with which particular client situation, we concur with Sprenkle, Davis, and Lebow's (2009) position that clients will utilize whatever is offered in therapy in their own idiosyncratic ways to achieve their goals; and that the foundational factors for treatment effectiveness involve the strength of the therapeutic alliance, the building of client motivation, and therapist competence.

Discussion

This chapter is based on the perspective that the training, socialization and indoctrination provided by the U.S. armed forces creates a belief system, values and a lifestyle among service members that is distinct from civilian mainstream culture. Although service members discharged from military service are no longer active duty soldiers, they may carry their military identities into the civilian world. Some service members retain values, attitudes, and behaviors that are distinctly military and significantly set apart from civilian ways. Additionally, most Veterans seem to be able to readjust to the civilian lifestyle. This group of Veterans is apparently able to negotiate the values, traditions and behaviors of military culture with those of civilian culture. Many other Veterans, however, are not able to make the transition back to civilian society due to cultural dissonance, mental health problems, and/or physical disabilities. Though some mental health services are available in the military, Veterans may require additional counseling and therapy upon re-entry into civilian life. Counselors must demonstrate a cultural competency of this military subculture when treating Veteran clients, and must also become informed of the various treatment modalities that have been effective at alleviating adjustment and PTSD related issues. By acquiring a more informed understanding of the military experience, clinicians can better position their therapeutic interventions to accommodate the host of biopsychosocial needs of service members that will depend on where they are in their military identity transition, on the continuum of care and in the utilization of resources.

References

APA (American Psychiatric Association) (2000). *Diagnostic and Statistical Manual of Mental Disorders—Text Revision* (4th Ed.). Washington, DC: Joan Beder.

Brady, K.T. & Sinha, R. (2005). Co-occuring mental and substance use disorders: The neurobiological effects of chronic stress. *American Journal of Psychiatry*, 162(8), 1483–1493.

Calhoun, L.G. & Tedeschi, R.G. (1999). *Facilitating Posttraumatic Growth: A clinician's guide.* Mahwah, NJ: Erlbaum.

Cook, J.M., Riggs, D.S., Thompson, R., & Coyne, J.C. (2004). Posttraumatic stress disorder and current relationship functioning among World War 2 ex-prisoners of war. *Journal of Family Psychology*, 18, 36–45.

Daley, J. (2011). *Continuum of Care.* Presented at the Families Impacted by Military Service: Understanding and Intervening—Continuing Education Course. Center for Innovation and Research on Veterans and Military Families, University of Southern California, School of Social Work.

Davenport, M. (1987). Professionals or hired guns? Loyalties are the difference. In M.M. Watkin, K. Wenker and J. Kempf (Eds.), *Military Ethics: Reflections on principles—the profession of arms, military leadership, ethical practices, war and morality, educating the citizen soldier* (pp. 5–12). Washington, DC: National Defense University Press.

DeGeorge, P.T. (1987). A code of ethics for officers. In M.M..Watkin, K. Wenker, & J. Kempf (Eds.), *Military Ehics: Reflections on principles—the profession of arms, military leadership, ethical practices, war and morality, educating the citizen soldier* (pp. 13–29). Washington, DC: National Defense University Press.

Exum, H. & Coll, J.E. (2008). *A Civilian Counselor's Primer for Counseling Veterans.* Deerpark, NY: Linus Publications, Inc.

Exum, H., Coll, J.E., & Weiss, E.L. (2011). *A Civilian Counselor's Primer for Counseling Veterans* (2nd Ed.). Deerpark, NY: Linus Publications, Inc.

Foa, E.B., Hembree, E., & Rothbaum, B.O. (2007). *Prolonged Exposure Therapy for PTSD: Emotional processing of traumatic experiences, Therapist Guide.* New York: Oxford University Press.

Foa, E.B., Keane, T.M., & Friedman, M.J. (2000). *Effective Treatment for PTSD: Practice guidelines from the International Society for Traumatic Stress Studies.* New York: Guilford Press.

FOCUS (Families Overcoming and Coping Under Stress) (2011). *Learning 5 Key Skills.* Retrieved from: http://www.focusproject.org/how-it-works

Frankl, V. (1959). *Man's Search for Meaning.* New York: Simon & Schuster.

Friedman, M.J. (2004). PTSD diagnosis and treatment for mental health clinicians. In M.J. Scott & S. Palmer (Eds.), *Trauma and Post-traumatic Stress Disorder* (pp. 1–14). Thousand Oaks, CA: Sage Publications.

Hayes, S.C., Strosahl, K.D., & Wilson, K.G. (1999). *Acceptance and Commitment Therapy: An experiential approach to behavior change.* New York: Guilford Press.

Hoge, W.C., Auchterlonice, C.J., & Milliken, S.C. (2006). Mental health problems, use of mental health services, and attrition from military service after returning from deployment to Iraq or Afghanistan. *The Journal of the American Medical Association*, 29, 1023–1032.

Houppert, K. (2005). *Base Crimes: The military has a domestic violence problem.* Foundation for National Progress. Retrieved from: http://www.motherjones.com/news/featurex/2005/07/base_crimes.html

Huebner, A.J., Mancini, J.A., Bowen, G.L. & Orthner, D.K. (2009). Shadowed by war: Building community capacity to support military families. *Family Relations*, 58, 216–228.

Knake, B. (1995) .What to say/not say to the grieving. *The Forum*, March/April, 13–14.

Kübler-Ross, E. (1969). *On Death and Dying.* New York: Scribner.

Litz, B. & Orsillo, S.M. (2003). The returning Veteran of the Iraq War: Background issues and assessment guidelines. *The Iraq War Clinician Guide* (pp. 1–13). Palo Alto, CA: Department of Veterans Affairs, The National Center for Post-Traumatic Stress Disorder.

McCloskey, M. (April 28, 2011). Combat stress as "moral injury" offends Marines. *Stars and Stripes.* Retrieved from: www.stripes.com

Najavits, L.M. (2007). Seeking safety: An evidence-based model for substance abuse and trauma/PTSD. In K.A. Witkiewitz & G.A. Marlatt (Eds.), *Therapist's Guide to Evidence Based Relapse Prevention: Practical resources for the mental health professional* (pp. 141–167). San Diego, CA: Elsevier Press.

O'Brian, C. (1984). Special ops in the 1980s: American moral, legal, political and cultural constraints. In F.R. Bennett, B.H. Tovar, & R.H. Shultz (Eds.), *Special Operations in U.S. Strategy* (pp. 54–84). New York: National Defense University Press.

Okie, S. (2006). Reconstructing lives—a tale of two soldiers. *New England Journal of Medicine*, 355, 2609–2615.

Pincus, S., House, R., Christensen, J., & Adler, L.E. (n.d.) *The Emotional Cycles of Deployment: A military family perspective.* Retrieved from: *http://hooah4health.com/deployment/familymatters/emotionalcycle.htm.*

Rollnick, S., Miller, W.R., & Butler, C.C. (2008). *Motivational Interviewing in Health Care: Helping patients change behavior.* New York: Guilford Press.

Rothbaum, B.O., Difede, J., & Rizzo, A. (2008). *Treatment Manual Virtual Reality Exposure Therapy: Posttraumatic stress disorder in Iraq combat Veterans.* Decatur, GA: Virtually Better, Inc.

Ruzek, J., Curran, E., Friedman, M.J, Gusman, F.D., Southwick, S.M., Swales, P., Walser, R.D., Watson, P.J., & Whealin, J. (2003). *Treatment of the Returning Iraq War Veteran. The Iraq War Clinician Guide* (pp. 14–26). Palo Alto, CA: Department of Veterans Affairs, The National Center for Post-Traumatic Stress Disorder.

Seal, K.H., Bertenthal, D., Nuber, C.R., Sen, S., & Marmar, C. (2007). Bringing the war back home: Mental health disorders among 103,788 U.S. Veterans returning from Iraq and Afghanistan seen at Department of Veterans Affairs Facilities. *Archives of Internal Medicine*, 167, 476–482.

Shapiro, F. (2001). *Eye Movement, Desensitization and Reprocessing: Basic principles, protocols and procedures* (2nd Ed.). New York: Guilford Press.

Southwick, S.M., Gilmartin, R., McDonough, P., & Morrissey, P. (2006). Logotherapy as an adjunctive treatment for chronic combat-related PTSD: A meaning-based intervention. *American Journal of Psychotherapy*, 60(2), 161–174.

Sprenkle, D.H., Davis, S.D., & Lebow, J.L. (2009). *Common Factors in Couple and Family Therapy: The overlooked foundation for effective practice.* New York: Guilford Press.

Sue, D.W. & Sue, D. (1999). *Counseling the Culturally Different* (3rd Ed.). New York: John Wiley & Sons.

U.S. Army (2011). *Comprehensive Soldier Fitness Program.* Retrieved from http://csf.army.mil/.

United States Army Medical Department, Mental Health Advisory Team (MHATV) (2008, March). *Army Report on Mental Health of Soldiers in Afghanistan and Iraq.* Retrieved from

U.S. Army Medical Department Website: www.armymedicine.army.mil/news/releases/20080306mhatv.cfm

Viotti, P.P. (1987). Morality in targeting objects of military value: A response. In M.M. Watkin, K. Wenker, & J. Kempf (Eds.), *Military Ethics: Reflections on principles—the profession of arms, military leadership, ethical practices, war and morality, educating the citizen soldier* (pp. 171–5). Washington, DC: National Defense University Press.

Weiss, E.L., Coll, J.E., & Metal, M. (in press). The influence of military culture and Veteran worldviews on mental health treatment: Implications for Veteran help-seeking and wellness. *International Journal on Health, Wellness & Society.*

Weiss, E.L., Coll, J.E., Mayeda, S., Mascarenas, J., & Krill, K. (in review). An ecosystemic and worldviews perspective of PTSD and substance use in Veterans: Seeking safety and beyond. *Journal of Social Work Practice in the Addictions.* Wounded Warrior Project. Retrieved from: http://www.woundedwarriorproject.org/#ixzz1LPuPBoYQ.

PART II
Special Populations

3

CIVILIAN SOCIAL WORKER'S GUIDE TO THE TREATMENT OF WAR-INDUCED POST-TRAUMATIC STRESS DISORDER

Jeffrey S. Yarvis and Joan Beder

Introduction

Post-traumatic stress disorder (PTSD), as defined in DSM IV-TR, is the most common psychiatric problem associated with the stress experienced by soldiers in combat. Diagnosis of PTSD requires exposure to a traumatic event that involves experiencing, witnessing, or being confronted by death or serious injury to self or others; a response of intense fear, helplessness, or horror; and the development of a set of symptoms that persists for at least a month and cause significant impairment of functioning (APA [American Psychiatric Association], 2000). Studies have demonstrated four basic PTSD symptoms: re-experiencing (e.g., nightmares, flashbacks), avoidance (e.g., efforts to avoid thinking about the trauma), numbing of general responsiveness (e.g., restricted range of affect), and hyperarousal (e.g., exaggerated startle response) (Forbes, Creamer, Bisson, Cohen, et al, 2010; McWilliams, Cox, & Asmundson, 2005). Most individuals who develop chronic PTSD experience immediate distress that then persists over time (Buckley, Blanchard, & Hickling, 1996). However, a small but significant number of individuals report increases in PTSD symptoms over time defined as delayed onset PTSD (Palm, Strong & MacPherson, 2009; Tanielian & Jaycox, 2008).

Current data suggest that approximately 5-20 percent of armed forces personnel deployed for combat, peacekeeping, or humanitarian disaster relief will develop PTSD following their tour of duty (Bramsen, Dirkzwager, & van der Ploeg, 2000; Dohrenwend, Turner, Turse, et al., 2006; Litz, Orsillo, Friedman, et al., 1997; Mehlum & Weisaeth, 2002; Tanielian & Jaycox, 2008; Ward, 2002). Current estimates for those serving in Iraq/Afghanistan run as high as 15 percent and while exposure to specific combat traumas are the single best predictor for the development of PTSD, service members who have experienced more lengthy and more frequent deployments are at the greatest risk (Tanielian & Jaycox, 2008).

In considering the problem of PTSD, it should be acknowledged that problematic reactions to trauma are not limited to full-blown PTSD disorder. A considerable percentage (i.e., 10%–25%) of those not meeting diagnostic criteria for PTSD experience significant symptoms that may require treatment. Even for those who have partial PTSD, there are differing levels of impairment of social, occupational, and family functioning (Gellis, Mavandadi, & Oslin, 2010; Stein, Walker, Hazen, & Forder, 1997; Weiss, Marmar, Schlenger, et al., 1992; Zlotnick, Franklin, & Zimmerman, 2002), often similar to those reported in individuals with full-blown PTSD. Those diagnosed with PTSD—full or partial—almost always experience concurrent additional mental health disorders, such as substance use disorders, other anxiety disorders, and major depressive disorder (Breslau, Davis, Peterson, & Schultz, 2000; Kessler, Sonnega, Bromet, et al., 1995; Kulka, Schlenger, Fairbank, et al.,1990; McDevitt-Murphy, Williams, Bracken, et al., 2010; Schnurr, Lunney, Bovin & Marx, 2009).

Risk factors for development of PTSD include characteristics of the traumatic event itself, pre-trauma factors, and post-trauma factors. Event characteristics that increase the risk for chronic PTSD include the type of trauma, a greater amount of exposure, injury, involvement in atrocities, and perceived life threat (Wolfe, Erickson, Sharkansky, et al., 1999; Schnurr et al., 2009). The degree of exposure to potentially traumatic combat events during deployment is strongly associated with development of PTSD (Hoge, Castro, Messer, et al., 2004) as is military sexual trauma (Himmelfarb, Yaeger, & Mintz, 2006; Yaeger, Himmelfarb, Cammack, & Mintz, 2006). In a sample of women Veterans seeking treatment for stress disorders, sexual stress was found to be almost four times as influential in the development of PTSD as duty-related stress (Fontana & Rosenheck, 1998; Luxton, Skopp, & Maguen, 2010). In Veterans, predisposing factors have included non-Caucasian ethnicity, lower intelligence or education, younger age at exposure, lower socioeconomic status, family problems in childhood, pre-trauma psychopathology, and childhood behavior problems (Engdahl, Dikel, Eberly, & Blank, 1997; D.W. King, King, Foy & Gudanowske, 1996; Kulka et al., 1990; McNally & Shin, 1995).

Post-event factors that predict chronic PTSD in Veterans include low levels of social support, negative homecoming experiences, poor coping, and adverse life events post-trauma (Boscarino, 1995; Brewin, Andrews, & Valentine, 2000; L.A. King, King, Fairbank, et al., 1998). While many risk factors exert a similar effect in military and civilian populations, trauma severity and post-trauma social support may be more important in *military* than in civilian samples.

This chapter will explore the etiology of PTSD, present several approaches to care for those with war related PTSD, and provide direction for clinicians on assessment and evaluation. Throughout the chapter, the case of JG will be used to illustrate critical concepts.

JG—28 years old, Caucasian, male. *He spent 11 months in Iraq and returned with PTSD. Although not technically discharged from the military, he was sent home for further evaluation. His family—wife and two children aged 7 and 9—have been very concerned about his behavior which includes major outbursts of anger, sleeplessness, and inability to work. JG had been employed as a postal clerk before going to Iraq. He presented at an out-patient counseling center for help with his "problem." While not eager to enter counseling, he knew he had a problem and his family had been urging him to get help soon after he returned to the states from Iraq.*

Psychological Theories of PTSD and Treatment

Conceptions of the etiology of PTSD, both psychosocial and biological, have implications for the understanding of treatment. Many such theories have focused on the intense fear often experienced during traumatic experiences and the impact of fear on conditioned emotional reactions and storing of traumatic memories.

While most theories of PTSD emphasize the relationship of fear to the development of PTSD, combat and other deployment-related traumas often activate other intense emotions—including sadness, anger, and guilt—that can be connected with the development of PTSD and other post-trauma problems. In Operation Iraqi Freedom, for example, substantial percentages of Army and Marine Corps personnel reported experiencing potentially traumatic experiences that included not only events likely to be associated with fear (e.g., "being attacked or ambushed"), but also those related to loss (e.g., "knowing someone seriously injured or killed"), moral conflict (e.g., "being responsible for the death of a noncombatant"), horror (e.g., "handling or uncovering human remains"), or helplessness (e.g., "seeing ill or injured women or children whom you were unable to help") (Hoge et al., 2004). These types of experiences are associated with a range of intense emotions that can continue to trouble trauma survivors and are stored as deeply troubling memories.

Generally, cognitive-behavioral psychological theories of PTSD and its treatment instruct that the trauma memory needs to be actively confronted, elaborated, and integrated into the context of an individual's preceding and subsequent experience; that problematic appraisals that maintain a sense of threat and other negative emotions need to be modified; and that dysfunctional coping strategies that prevent emotional processing of the trauma and thus recovery need to be reduced.

JG reported that soon after his arrival in Iraq, he had been instructed to patrol a certain area, not move from that area, and to keep guard. He spent the night sitting on what he thought was a mound of dirt only to find that in the morning light, he realized that he had been sitting on a grave that had been newly dug that afternoon. He was "freaked" from that moment on and hardly slept for the first several weeks in Iraq. Subsequent events were also problematic, i.e., seeing a friend who was seriously wounded and had to leave Iraq, "having to kill on a regular basis" and not being able to connect to home due to constant phone problems. All in all, JG wanted to leave the battlefield almost from the time he arrived. Depression, fear, and anxiety were his "constant companions."

The Process of Treatment of Deployment-Related PTSD

Treatment of PTSD must depend upon a careful assessment of the individual. The assessment includes the formulation of a treatment plan that is based on judgments about the factors that may have caused problems for that particular person, identifying those factors that maintain them, identification of the co-occurring problems of the person, and the priorities for intervention.

Assessment

Assessment of military-related PTSD requires a multi-method approach in which various measures are used to assess the different domains of functioning, both to improve diagnostic confidence and to identify targets for intervention (e.g., Keane, Street, & Stafford, 2004). Veterans of the wars in Afghanistan and Iraq initially present in myriad ways. Some may be very frail, labile, emotional, and compelled to share their experiences. The more usual presentation is likely to be defended, formal, respectful, laconic, and cautious (as if they were talking to an officer). Generally, it is safe to assume that it will be difficult for Veterans to share their thoughts and feelings about what happened during the war and the toll those experiences have taken on their mental health. It is important not to press any survivor of trauma too soon or too intensely, and to respect the person's need not to feel vulnerable and exposed. Clinical contacts should proceed in a logical sequence from triage (e.g., suicidality/homicidality, acute medical problems, and severe family problems that may require immediate attention), screening, formal assessment, to case formulation/treatment planning, with an emphasis on prioritizing goals for intervention.

It is important for the provider to gather information about the individual's experiences during deployment. Ask specifically: about the traumatic event(s); symptoms as a result of the traumatic event(s); and what kinds of stressors they experienced before, during and after combat/traumatic exposures. Were there real or perceived threats? What was the nature of the weapons—if in active combat—used against them? How were their living conditions? What were work conditions like inside and outside their operating base, and could they communicate with the home front? Was the home front doing OK, or was it a distraction? How has the family handled military-induced family separations? Were they exposed to harassment or other job-related non-combat stressors? Were there control issues; for example, ask did they feel they could effect what was going on around them? Asking these questions will help determine whether or not the Veteran is on a trajectory toward PTSD. Throughout the assessment session(s), note and look for signs of depression, suicidal or homicidal thoughts, memory loss, anxiety, sleep impairment, substance use as well, as the clinical criteria used in the DSMIV.

Quick Screening for PTSD

For civilian social workers and other mental health providers, there are a number of screening tools that are useful in diagnosing and assessing PTSD. A useful scale is the Post-traumatic Stress Disorder Checklist–Military Version (PCL–M). This scale is an adult self-report and is available through the National Center for PTSD and is used with a military population: http://www.ncptsd.org/publications/assessment/adult_self_report.html. The PCL-M is a 17-item self-report checklist of PTSD symptoms based closely on the DSM-IV criteria. It can be used to assess symptom severity or to determine a PTSD diagnosis. The military version of the PCL (PCL-M) assesses PTSD symptoms in relation to military experiences (Weathers, Litz, Herman, et al., 1993). The standard procedure for determining PTSD is to compute the questionnaire's subscales. The three subscales of the PCL-M are re-experiencing, avoidance/numbing, and hyperarousal.

Two other commonly used screening instruments are the Traumatic Life Events Questionnaire (TLEQ) and PTSD Screening and Diagnostic Scale (PSDS) (Western Psychological Services, 2010 http://portal.wpspublish.com/). The TLEQ is a brief self-report inventory that asks about current and prior exposure to 21 kinds of potentially traumatic events (from natural disasters to sexual abuse). All events are described in behavioral terms, avoiding emotionally charged words such as "rape" or "abuse." Clients use a seven-point response format to indicate frequency of occurrence. Completed in just 10 to 15 minutes, the TLEQ is written at a 9th-grade reading level.

The PSDS, available from Western Psychological Services, is a 38-item self-report inventory that assesses the six DSM-IV criteria for making a diagnosis of PTSD. Respondents are asked to indicate the degree to which they experienced each of 17 symptoms that correspond to the 17 key features of PTSD. They are also asked whether they have experienced any symptom for longer than 30 days and, if so, for how long. Other items inquire about specific areas of functioning (such as social life) and trauma-related anger, guilt, and grief. All items are written at an 8th-grade reading level. Used together, the TLEQ and PSDS constitute a quick trauma history/PTSD screen that is extremely useful in settings where clinicians have no prior knowledge of a patient's background or experiences.

In addition, there are a number of shorter self-report questionnaires such as the Deployment Risk and Resilience Inventory (L.A. King et al., 2006) and the PTSD Checklist developed by the National Center for PTSD. This PTSD Checklist is designed for both civilians and military personnel/Veterans. Another scale, the Primary Care PTSD Screen (PC-PTSD) designed by Prins, Ouimette, Kimerling, Caeron, Hugelshofer and Shaw-Hegrew (2004) poses four questions regarding symptoms over the past month: the presence of nightmares, avoidance behaviors, watchfulness, and detached feelings. If the respondent answers yes to three of the four questions, they should be considered positive for PTSD. Use of these scales can make the assessment process more complete and efficient for the provider. However, they cannot be relied upon fully as they are self-reports; the scales can supplement a fuller diagnostic workup.

> *JG screened positive for PTSD not only through the use of the PC-PTSD but from general discussion of his war experiences and the problems he was experiencing on a daily basis. He was unable to sleep, had terrible nightmares when he was able to sleep and was generally hypervigilant and "edgy" all of the time. Classically, loud noises alerted him and caused him to assume "combat mode". He described himself as "angry all the time at almost nothing" and was unable to spend any time with his children. Work was out of the question in his current state.*

In-depth assessment—initially and on-going

In addition to the various scales, there are many potentially important variables to assess as part of the on-going treatment program. Education for the soldier and his/her family on each of these domains is considered important and helpful. The National Center for PTSD recommends evaluation and education on the following domains: (http://www.ptsd.va.gov/professional/pages/vets-iraq-war-guidelines.asp):

- Work functioning
- Interpersonal functioning
- Recreation and self-care
- Physical functioning
- Psychological symptoms
- Past distress and coping
- Previous traumatic events
- Deployment-related experiences.

Content versus process

Often, when working with Veterans who have been exposed to potentially traumatic experiences, there is pressure to begin with an assessment and education on traumatic exposure, and to encourage the Veteran to talk immediately about his or her experiences. However, it is often recommended that it is most useful to begin the assessment process by focusing on current psychosocial functioning and the immediate needs of the Veteran, and to assess trauma exposure, as necessary, later in the assessment process. It is advised to follow the patient's lead in approaching a discussion of trauma exposure. Clinicians should verbally and non-verbally convey to their patients a sense of safety, security and openness to hearing about painful experiences, and create a holding environment as many Veterans begin to view the therapist's office as hallowed ground. However, it is also equally important that clinicians do not urge their patients to talk about traumatic experiences before they are ready to do so.

Specific Areas of Functioning—Work

Many who return from warzones way have difficulty making the segue to a non-military or pre-military life. This includes work. For those with PTSD, it may be very difficult and sometimes impossible to pick up the pieces and return to productive work as issues of concentration, hypervigilance, anxiety and sleep-lessness intrude. Veterans in this situation might have to be encouraged to try to put returning to work at a lower priority until they are better able to deal with day-to-day stressors. Some may benefit from employment related assessment and rehabilitation services including an exploration of career interests and aptitudes, counseling in resume building and job interviewing.

> JG was unable to consider working, as his inability to concentrate with frequent bouts of crippling anxiety and anger issues precluded that option. He was placed on disability for an extended time.

Interpersonal Functioning

Another important area of assessment involves interpersonal functioning. Veterans of war hold a number of interpersonal roles including son/daughter, husband/wife/life-companion, parent, and friend—and all of these roles may be affected by the psychological consequences of their military service. A number of factors can affect interpersonal functioning, including the quality of the relationship pre-deployment, the level of contact between the Veteran and his or her social connections during deployment, and the expectations and reality of the homecoming experience. Perceived versus received social support can play an important role in recovery and re-adjustment.

> One of the strengths for JG was the level of social support that was forthcoming from his wife and his parents. Even though there were numerous tough times, his wife was steadfast and his parents and brother were also supportive and caring.

As with all areas of post-deployment adjustment, Veterans may experience changes in their interpersonal functioning over time (Fontana & Rosenheck, 2010; Yarvis & Schiess, 2008). It is not uncommon for families to first experience a "honeymoon" phase of reconnection marked by euphoria, excitement, and relief. However, a period of discomfort, role confusion, and renegotiating of relationships and roles can accompany this phase, and the risk for suicide and domestic violence can occur as well, confounding the notion of a so-called honeymoon phase. Therefore, repeated assessment of interpersonal functioning and on-going educations is needed between or after deployments so that anticipated relational difficulties that threaten the well-being of the Veteran are detected and addressed. There should be education about transitioning caregivers, role changes, and phase of life changes as part of educating Veterans on interpersonal issues that may arise.

Recreation, Self-care, and Spiritual Well-being

Participation in recreational activities and engaging in good self-care are foundational aspects of positive psychological functioning. However, they are often overlooked in the assessment and education process. Some Veterans who appear to be functioning well in other domains may be attending less to these areas of their lives, particularly if they are attempting to mask, deny or control any painful thoughts, feelings or images they may be struggling with. Thus, a brief assessment of engagement in and enjoyment of recreational and self-care activities may provide some important information about how well the Veteran is coping post-deployment. Spiritual functioning and behavior can also be addressed here because loss and grief, war and horror can challenge a Veteran's spiritual beliefs.

Current Physical Functioning

Early assessment of the physical wellbeing of Veterans is critical. Sleep, appetite, energy level, and concentration can be impaired in the post-deployment phase as a result of exposure to potentially traumatizing experiences, the development of any of a number of physical disease processes, and/or simply the normal operational fatigue associated with military duty. Clinicians are again charged with the complex task of balancing the normalization of transient symptoms with the careful assessment of symptoms that could indicate more significant psychological or physical impairment. It is important to ensure that a Veteran complaining of these and other somatic/psychological symptoms is referred for a complete physical examination to investigate any potential underlying physical pathology, and to provide adequate interdisciplinary treatment planning.

Current Psychological Symptoms

Once the clinician gains an overall sense of the Veteran's level of psychosocial functioning, a broader education about psychological symptoms, and responses to those symptoms that may be impairing forward motion can be useful. Clinicians must use their judgment in responding to transient normal responses to potentially traumatizing events versus symptoms that may reflect the development and/or exacerbation of a psychological disorder. Sometimes assessing both psychological responses and responses to those responses can help determine whether or not some form of treatment is indicated. For instance, Veterans may appropriately respond to the presence of painful thoughts and feelings by crying, talking with others about their experiences, and engaging in other potentially valued activities such as spending time with friends and family. However, others may attempts to suppress, diminish or avoid their internal experiences of pain by using alcohol and/or drugs, disordered eating, self-injurious behaviors (such as cutting), dissociation, and behavioral avoidance of external reminders or triggers of trauma-related stimuli.

Past Distress and Trauma-Spectrum Disorders

In determining the extent of education needed for a particular presenting problem, an assessment of the history of the problem and the Veteran's previous responses to similar stressful experiences is useful. A general sense of pre-deployment work and interpersonal functioning, along with any significant psychological history, can place current distress in context. Orienting the Veteran toward previous successful coping can combat and challenge cognitive distortions or misperceptions about their ability to re-adjust to "normal" life. To get back to this "new normal", coping skills training can prove helpful.

Given that a full-range of psychological responses may be seen, and given that co-morbid disorders may be present, one challenge to the clinician during the assessment process is to prioritize treatment goals. The National Center for PTSD recommends the following:

- First, attend to symptoms that may require emergency intervention such as significant suicidal or homicidal ideation, hopelessness, self-injurious behavior and/or acute psychotic symptoms or situations putting others at risk.
- Second, it is useful to address symptoms that the Veteran perceives to be the most interfering.
- Third, the best way to develop a treatment plan with a Veteran with diverse complaints is to develop a case formulation to functionally explain the potential relationship between the symptoms in order to develop a comprehensive treatment plan.

> In a more in-depth discussion of JG's situation, it had to be acknowledged that he was struggling in most areas of his life—he was unable to work, his interpersonal relationships were troubled, and he was physically challenged with lack of sleep and anxiety. One of his strengths was that he and his wife had had a strong marital bond before he was deployed and his wife was very present and supportive as were his parents who lived nearby. While minimally motivated, the challenge for JG was to successfully engage him in treatment.

Stigma

Once diagnosed, and in order for treatment of PTSD to commence, individuals with PTSD must present for care. However, many are reluctant to seek mental health treatment, and those experiencing higher levels of symptoms may be less likely to seek help and report more barriers to help-seeking (Sayer, Friedmann-Sanchez, Spoont, et al., 2009). Consistent with military culture, barriers to help-seeking include concern about being seen as weak, feelings of embarrassment, and concern about reactions from leadership. For some, another barrier to seeking treatment for PTSD within a Veterans Healthcare Administration (VHA) or Department of Defense (DoD) setting is fear that documentation of PTSD-related problems in the medical record might have an adverse effect on advancement in a military career or later employment in some occupations (e.g., police).

Addressing the Issue of Stigma

Stigma is a problem. While it is a societal issue, it is much more pronounced in the military. There is a perception among the troops that seeking mental health care means you may be weak or a coward. A recent Defense Department study looking at combat troops returning from Iraq found that soldiers and Marines who needed counseling the most were least likely to seek it. As many as 16 percent of the troops questioned admitted to symptoms of severe depression, Post Combat Stress Disorder and other problems. Of those, six out of 10 questioned felt their leaders would treat them differently and that fellow troops would lose confidence in them. As many as 65 percent said they would "be seen as weak" (Hoge, Terhakopian, Castro, et al., 2007). Col. Charles Hoge, lead author of the study, said, "Our most important finding was this concern about stigma and barriers to care, that is, the number of soldiers who have mental health who don't seek care."

According to Hoge and colleagues (2007), the key to reducing that stigma is to present mental health care as a routine aspect of health care, similar to getting a check up or an X-ray. Soldiers need to understand that stress reactions—difficulty sleeping, reliving incidents in your mind, and emotional detachment—are common and expected after combat. The treating social worker or mental health professional needs to normalize as many of these symptoms as possible. The soldier should be told that wherever they go, they should remember that what they're feeling "is normal and it's nothing to be ashamed of."

Even in the combat zone, officials have made a conscious effort not to call troops seeking mental health care "patients." It cuts to the very heart of the stigma issue. Treating soldiers like other kinds of casualties could help reduce the sense that problems coping with the horrors of combat are no different than bleeding from a gunshot wound.

Confidentiality is one of the biggest barriers to reducing stigma. Firm laws are in place protecting patient privacy and the soldier still has HIPPA rights. There are, however, a few circumstances in which mental health providers are required to inform authorities of safety risks. These include suspected harm to self or others that the soldier reveals. It is indeed the case that there are limits to confidentiality, and it is those that create the perception that confidentiality is not kept. However, violating confidentiality is the rare exception rather than the norm. In order to protect the privacy of soldiers, most providers will also remind them of these limits if it appears that they might report something that will require a disclosure to authorities.

JG was not seen at a military-based facility. He explained that he was afraid that someone "might see me going into the VA and report me" and then "I would really be in trouble." He was reassured about confidentiality and told that only under circumstances of harm would confidentiality be broken. Nevertheless, he was guarded, edgy and tense throughout most of the first few sessions. While reassurances were given as to the "normalcy" of most of his reactions, there was on-going concern related to his potential to blow-up and do harm to himself or his family. This was discussed and he said that he was self aware enough to get out of the house when he felt very angry. He was less concerned about appearing weak than about "being seen not only going in for counseling" but being seen as a "baby, someone who couldn't take it."

Fortunately several family members had had positive experiences with counseling and they were urging him to seek help. He felt certain that he had PTSD and, while resistant, finally did seek care.

Approaches to Treatment

Coping Skills Training

Skills training methods are commonly used to help those suffering with PTSD to increase their ability to reduce anxiety, communicate with loved ones, manage anger, and respond assertively (not aggressively) to conflict situations. Through a cycle of instruction, demonstration, rehearsal/practice, feedback/coaching, and more practice, survivors learn skills in treatment sessions and practice them in the natural environment. In some cases they keep written records of their attempts to apply the skills, which help them learn and provide both practitioner and survivor with real-world experiences to review. Clinical experience indicates that survivors are typically attracted to the idea of learning skills ("tools") for coping. The methods of skills training help to actively involve the survivor in treatment, provide him or her with a greater sense of control (and responsibility for active participation in treatment), and strengthen the transfer of what is learned in treatment to the natural environment of the client.

Deliberate, Planned Confrontation of Trauma Memories and Reminders

The core element of PTSD treatment is active discussion and exploration of traumatic experiences and their implications. The treatments that focus explicitly on traumatic memories and meanings—PE (Prolonged Exposure therapy), CPT (Cognitive Processing Therapy), and EMDR (Eye Movement and Desensitization and Reprocessing) have received the most empirical support to date.

Methods of direct therapeutic exposure involve confrontation of memories and reminders. Prolonged Exposure therapy involves a repeated retelling of the trauma story. According to Foa and Jaycox (1999), PE therapy assists the individual in incorporating new information into the memory, by reducing cognitive avoidance of trauma-related feelings, demonstrating that remembering the experience is not dangerous, and that anxiety will diminish over time. The main components of PE, imaginal exposure and *in vivo* exposure, entail the revisiting of trauma memories and triggers with the goal of overcoming the instinctual response of fear. During treatment, subjects are asked to revisit the trauma experience(s) with their eyes closed while emotionally engaging in the memory. The subject is then asked to retell their experience repeatedly over numerous sessions. Theoretically, each telling "deposits" some of the toxic aspects of the memory. This enables the processing of the trauma experience and allows the subject to approach activities, people and environments (Cukor, Olden, Lee & Difede, 2010) that have been avoided to allow comfort in what was once a hostile environment.

Successful implementation of PE can also result in modification of distressing trauma-related cognitions by disconfirming beliefs ("anxiety stays forever" or "I will go crazy"), and by helping the survivor differentiate the trauma from similar but safe events (disconfirming "the world is extremely dangerous"). PTSD symptoms themselves may begin to be associated with mastery rather than incompetence (disconfirming "I am incompetent"). Negative thoughts can be challenged through direct review of the belief and consideration of alternatives, and through encouraging real-world experiences that can help to disconfirm them. For example, having a successful experience in disclosing personal information to another person can help challenge the belief that "other people cannot be trusted."

Exposure to trauma memories is an element of a number of treatments other than PE that are supported in the research literature. For example, individuals being treated with Cognitive Processing Therapy (Robjant & Fazel, 2010) are asked to write out the details of their traumatic experience and to read their account on a regular basis. EMDR is an eight-stage information processing treatment that includes an exposure component, in that it involves bringing to mind an image of a traumatic event while visually tracking a therapist's finger as it moves back and forth in front of the subject's visual field (or tracking a light moving back and forth, or listening to tones alternating from one ear to the other). The treatment is said to work by enhancing processing of the trauma memory with new connections that have more positive associations with the memory. The trauma memory is no longer able to stimulate an emotional or physiological response (Cukor et al., 2010). EMDR is a specialized approach that requires specific training by the therapist.

Challenging of Negative Trauma-related Thoughts

Cognitive therapy is a systematic approach that includes education about the role of beliefs in causing distress; identification of distressing beliefs held by the individual; discussion and a review of evidence for and against the beliefs; generation of alternative beliefs; and rehearsal of new, more adaptive beliefs. In the briefest terms, cognitive therapy avers that thinking shapes behavior. Thoughts that create significant distress (e.g., trauma–related guilt, exaggerated thoughts about danger) are replaced with more realistic and self-supportive thoughts. For example, if an individual has the thought "I will never be safe again, the world is a very dangerous place," then cognitive therapy might focus on helping the individual to consider evidence for and against the belief and move toward a more realistic appraisal (e.g., "I am safe in most situations and the chances of harm coming to me are quite small in the civilian world").

Technology-based Treatments

Internet-based treatments are becoming useful as a delivery method for PTSD; these techniques address some logistical impediments to treatment including geography and fiscal constraints and may be useful for those concerned about stigma related to treatment. One model—DE-STRESS—is an eight-week cognitive behavioral internet-delivered program that entails the therapist using some PE techniques with writing and reaction sessions using some of the principles of PE treatment (Cukor et al., 2010).

Family/Couples Treatments

Since PTSD frequently impacts marital and family relationships, therapists might consider working with couples and family members to address issues of stress that may exist within the family system. In addition, spouses and partners of the PTSD sufferer can benefit from education toward symptoms and symptom relief/management. Several couples-based treatments have been developed including cognitive behavioral conjoint therapy (CBCT). This focus of the work is improvement in behavioral and communication techniques as well as addressing maladaptive thoughts about the trauma and its impact on significant relationships (Cukor et al., 2010).

Pharmacotherapy

Medication is an important treatment option that should be considered for almost all with significant symptoms of PTSD. The use of a medication for treating PTSD may be directed at PTSD symptoms generally, specific PTSD symptoms, common co-occurring symptoms, or at co-morbid conditions (e.g., depression).

Medications, particularly antidepressants, may reduce the global severity of PTSD symptoms and serve as useful tools in the treatment of PTSD. Antianxiety medications are also viewed as helpful. In addition, psychotropic medications may be used to treat associated features and/or co-morbid conditions.

Associated Problems in PTSD Treatment

As noted above, approximately 80 percent of those diagnosed with PTSD experience concurrent additional mental health disorders (Kessler et al., 1995). In addition, they experience a range of problems in living that are often addressed in treatment. PTSD symptoms are associated with reduced quality of life before treatment and, encouragingly, evidence suggests that change in PTSD is significantly associated with change in quality of life (Schnurr, Hayes, Lunney, et al., 2006).

> *JG engaged in his treatment that initially lasted for 6 months. During that time, several of the preliminary sessions were used to reassure him of the "normalcy" of most of his symptoms. A behavior contact was initiated and he agreed to absent himself from his home when he felt his anger rising and feelings that he might hurt his wife or their children. Once during the early months, JG called feeling very "out of control" and an emergency session was initiated. From that point on, he began to realize both the severity of his condition and the need for him to work on his PTSD. Prolonged exposure therapy was initiated and JG was able to recall many of the most traumatic events during his 11-month tour. A psychiatric evaluation was ordered and he was given medication to address both his anxiety and sleeplessness. Both conditions improved. On several occasions, his wife who was instrumental in furthering JG's management of his PTSD joined in the twice-weekly sessions. The strength of the marriage was tested and weathered the storm. The memories that JG recalled were often about those who were wounded in battle and his fear for his own safety. JG is currently being seen once a week and while tremendous strides have been made in terms of his understanding and management of his PTSD, not all areas of his functioning are improved. He still is not able to consider working and soon that will be problematic as the family resources are dwindling. He still has occasional flashbacks but is able to move past them adequately. It was suggested and he agreed to continue treatment for at least 6 more months. That time will be used to address his stress level to enable him to return to some form of work, to continue to manage his anger and resume what for JG will be his "new normal."*

Conclusion

Management of deployment-related PTSD has been changing rapidly. Screening for PTSD is widespread, returning personnel are informed about the disorder, and the Veterans Healthcare Administration and Department of Defense have collaborated to establish practice guidelines for responding to the specific needs of those with PTSD. As treatment systems evolve, it is critical that more and better quality evaluation of treatment effectiveness be undertaken. The reality is that the VA and DoD are overwhelmed with the struggles of the returning service members. More and more the civilian mental health sector will be called upon to offer services to those who return from Iraq/Afghanistan.

The necessity for civilian social workers to be attuned to the nuances of PTSD is imperative. As more and more returning service members are seeking care in the private sector, social workers and other non-government mental health care providers will be working with those with PTSD and those close to them. Management poses many challenges and understanding both the challenges and approaches to care will benefit service members to better return to civilian life.

References

APA (American Psychiatric Association) (2000). *Diagnostic and Statistical Manual of Mental Disorders—Text Revision* (4th Ed.). Washington, DC: Joan Beder.

Boscarino, J.A. (1995). Post-traumatic stress and associated disorders among Vietnam Veterans: The significance of combat exposure and social support. *Journal of Traumatic Stress*, 8, 317–336.

Bramsen, I., Dirkzwager, A.J.E., & van der Ploeg, H.M. (2000). Pre-deployment personality traits and exposure to trauma as predictors of posttraumatic stress symptoms: A prospective study of former peacekeepers. *American Journal of Psychiatry*, 157, 1115–1119.

Breslau, N., Davis, G.C., Peterson, E.L., and Schultz, L.R. (2000). A second look at co-morbidity in victims of trauma: The posttraumatic stress disorder–major depression connection. *Biological Psychiatry*, 48, 902–909.

Brewin, C.R., Andrews, B., & Valentine, J.D. (2000). Meta-analysis of risk factors for posttraumatic stress disorder in trauma-exposed adults. *Journal of Consulting and Clinical Psychology*, 68, 748–766.

Buckley, T.C., Blanchard, E.B., & Hickling, E.J. (1996). A prospective examination of delayed onset PTSD secondary to motor vehicle accidents. *Journal of Abnormal Psychology*, 105, 617–625.

Cukor, J., Olden, M., Lee, F., & Difede, J. (2010). Evidence-based treatments for PTSD, new directions and special challenges. *Annals of the NY Academy of Sciences*, 1208, 82–89.

Engdahl, B., Dikel, T., Eberly, R., & Blank, A. (1997). Posttraumatic stress disorder in a community group of former prisoners of war: A normative response to severe trauma. *American Journal of Psychiatry*, 154, 1576–1581.

Foa, E.B. & Jaycox, L.H. (1999). Cognitive-behavioral theory and treatment of post-traumatic stress disorder. In D. Spiegel (Ed.), *Efficacy and Cost-effectiveness of Psychotherapy* (pp. 23–61). Washington, DC: American Psychiatric Press.

Fontana, A. & Rosenheck, R. (1998). Duty-related and sexual stress in the etiology of PTSD among women Veterans who seek treatment. *Psychiatric Services*, 49, 658–662.

Fontana, A. & Rosenheck, R. (2010). War zone Veterans returning to treatment: Effects of social functioning and psychopathology. *Journal of Nervous and Mental Disorders*, 198(10), 699–707.

Forbes, D., Creamer, M., Bisson, J., Cohen, J., Crow, B., Foa, E., Friedman, M., Keane, T., Kudler, H., and Ursano, R. (2010). A guide to guidelines for treatment of PTSD and related conditions. *Journal of Traumatic Stress*, 23(5), 537–552.

Gellis, L. Mavandadi, S., & Oslin, D. (2010). Functional quality of life in full versus partial PTSD among Veterans returning from Iraq and Afghanistan. *Journal of Clinical Psychology*, 12(3), 1–6.

Himmelfarb, N., Yaeger, D., & Mintz, J. (2006). Posttraumatic stress disorder in female Veterans with military and civilian sexual trauma. *Journal of Traumatic Stress*, 19, 837–846.

Hoge, C.W., Castro, C.A., Messer, S.C., McGurk, D., Cotting, D.I., & Koffman, R.L. (2004). Combat duty in Iraq and Afghanistan, mental health problems, and barriers to care. *New England Journal of Medicine*, 351, 13–22.

Hoge, C.W., Terhakopian, A., Castro, C.A., Messer, S.C., & Engel, C.C. (2007). Association of posttraumatic stress disorder with somatic symptoms, health care visits, and absenteeism among Iraq War Veterans. *American Journal of Psychiatry*, 164, 150–153.

Keane, T.M., Street, A.E., & Stafford, J. (2004). The assessment of military-related PTSD. In J.P. Wilson & T.M. Keane (Eds.), *Assessing Psychological Trauma and PTSD* (2nd Ed., pp. 262–285). New York: Guilford Press.

Kessler, R.C., Sonnega, A., Bromet, E., Hughes, M., & Nelson, C.B. (1995). Posttraumatic stress disorder in the National Comorbidity Survey. *Archives of General Psychiatry*, 52, 1048–1060.

King, D.W., King, L., Foy, D., & Gudanowske, D. (1996). Prewar factors in combat-related posttraumatic stress disorder: Structural equation modeling with a national sample of female and male Vietnam veterans. *Journal of Consulting and Clinical Psychology*, 64(3), 520–531.

King, L.A., King, D.W., Fairbank, J.A., Keane, T.M., & Adams, G.A. (1998). Resilience/recovery factors in posttraumatic stress disorder among female and male Vietnam Veterans: Hardiness, postwar social support, and additional stressful life events. *Journal of Personality and Social Psychology*, 74, 420–434.

King, L.A., King, D.W., Vogt, D.S., Knight, J., & Samper, R.E. (2006). Deployment risk and resilience inventory: A collection of measures for studying deployment-related experiences of military personnel and Veterans. *Military Psychology*, 18, 89–120.

Kulka, R.A., Schlenger, W.E., Fairbank, J.A., Hough, R.L., Jordan, B.K., Marmar, C.R., & Weiss, D.S. (1990). *Trauma and the Vietnam War Generation: Report of the findings from the National Vietnam Veterans Readjustment Study*. New York: Brunner/Mazel.

Litz, B., Orsillo, S., Friedman, M., Ehlich, P., & Batres, A. (1997). Posttraumatic stress disorder associated with peacekeeping duty in Somalia for U.S. military personnel. *American Journal of Psychiatry*, 154, 178–184.

Luxton, D., Skopp, N., & Maguen, S. (2010). Gender differences in depression and PTSD symptoms following combat exposure. *Depression and Anxiety*, 27(11), 1027–1033.

McDevitt-Murphy, M., Williams, J., Bracken, K., Fields, J., Monahan, C., & Murphy, J. (2010). PTSD symptoms, hazardous drinking, and health functioning among U.S.

OEF and OIF Veterans presenting to primary care. *Journal of Traumatic Stress*, 23(1), 108–111.

McNally, R. and Shin, L. (1995). Association of intelligence with severity of posttraumatic stress disorder symptoms in Vietnam combat Veterans. *American Journal of Psychiatry*, 152: 936–938.

McWilliams, L.A., Cox, B.J., & Asmundson, G.J.G. (2005). Symptom structure of posttraumatic stress disorder in a nationally representative sample. *Journal of Anxiety Disorders*, 19, 626–641.

Mehlum, L. & Weisaeth, L. (2002). Predictors of posttraumatic stress reactions in Norwegian U.N. Peacekeepers 7 years after service. *Journal of Traumatic Stress*, 15(1), 17–26.

Palm, K., Strong, D., & MacPherson, L. (2009). Evaluating symptom expression as a function of posttraumatic stress disorder severity. *Journal of Anxiety Disorder*, 23(1), 27–37.

Prins, A., Ouimette, P., Kimerling, R., Camerond, R.P., Hugelshofer, D.S., Shaw-Hegwer, J., Thrailkill, A., Gusman, F.D., & Sheikh, J.I. (2004). Primary care PTSD screen: Development and primary care characteristics. *International Journal of Psychiatry in Clinical Practice*, 1(6), 9–14.

Robjant, K. & Fazel. M. (2010). The emerging evidence for Narrative Exposure Therapy: A review. *Clinical Psychology Review*, 30, 1030–1039.

Sayer, N., Friedemann-Sanchez, G., Spoont, M., Murdoch, M., Parker, L., Chiros, C., & Rosenheck, R. (2009). A qualitative study of determinants of PTSD treatment initiation in Veterans. *Psychiatry*, 72(3), 238–254.

Schnurr, P.P., Hayes, A.F., Lunney, C.A., McFall, M., & Uddo, M. (2006). Longitudinal analysis of the relationship between symptoms and quality of life in veterans treated for posttraumatic stress disorder. *Journal of Consulting and Clinical Psychology*, 74(4), 707–713.

Schnurr, P.P., Lunney, C.A., Bovin, M., & Marx, B. (2009). Postraumatic stress disorder and quality of life. Extension of findings to Veterans of the wars in Iraq and Afghanistan. *Clinical Psychology Review*, 29(8), 727–735.

Stein, M.B., Walker, J.R., Hazen, A.L., & Forder, D.R. (1997). Full and partial posttraumatic stress disorder: Findings from a community survey. *American Journal of Psychiatry*, 154(8), 1114–1119.

Tanielian, T. & Jaycox, L.H. (2008). *Invisible Wounds of War: Psychological and cognitive injuries, their consequences, and services to assist recovery*. Santa Monica, CA: RAND MG-720-CCF.

Ward, J. (2002). Stress hits 1 in 5 Afghan war vets, ombudsman says: Stigma "is still very much alive." Marin warns of possible law suits. *Toronto Star* (p. A06).

Weathers, F.W., Litz, B., Herman, D.S., Huska, J.A., & Keane, T.M. (1993). *The PTSD checklist: Reliability, validity, and diagnostic utility*. Paper presented at the Annual Meeting of the International Society for Traumatic Stress Studies, San Antonio, Texas.

Weiss, D.S., Marmar, C.R., Schlenger, W.E., Fairbank, J.A., Jordan, B.K., Hough, R.L., & R.A. Kulka (1992). The prevalence of lifetime and partial post-traumatic stress disorder in Vietnam theater Veterans. *Journal of Traumatic Stress*, 5(3), 365–376.

Wolfe, J., Erickson, D., Sharkansky, E., King, D., & King, L. (1999). Course and predictors of posttraumatic stress disorder among Gulf War Veterans: A prospective analysis. *Journal of Consulting and Clinical Psychology*, 67, 520–528.

Yaeger, D., Himmelfarb, N., Cammack, A., & Mintz, J. (2006). DSM-IV diagnosed posttraumatic stress disorder in women Veterans with and without military sexual trauma. *Journal of General Internal Medicine*, March Supplement, 21, S65–S69.

Yarvis, J. and Schiess, L. (2008) Sub-threshold PTSD as a predictor of depression, alcohol use, and health problems in Veterans. *Journal of Workplace Behavioral Health*, 23(4), 395–424.

Zlotnick, C., Franklin, C.L., & Zimmerman, M. (2002). Does "sub-threshold" posttraumatic stress disorder have any clinical relevance? *Comprehensive Psychiatry*, 43(6), 413–419.

4

CARE COORDINATION IN MILITARY TRAUMATIC BRAIN INJURY

Glenn W. Parkinson, Louis M. French, and Silvia Massetti

Introduction

Traumatic brain injury—an injury to the brain that may or may not create lasting impairment for the survivor—has been recognized as a major public health problem by the Centers for Disease Control (Langlois, Rutland-Brown, & Thomas, 2006). Ongoing conflicts in Iraq and Afghanistan have highlighted the problem for the military (Warden, 2006). Along with post-traumatic stress disorder, traumatic brain injury (TBI) has become known as one of the "signature wounds" of the current conflicts—Operation Enduring Freedom and Operation Iraqi Freedom (Altmire, 2007). Modern warfare in Iraq and Afghanistan includes the widespread use of Improvised Explosive Devices (IED). Detonation of IEDs exposes service members to multiple risks for traumatic brain injury including injury from projectile material, or shrapnel, as well as from the primary blast wave itself. It is estimated that at least 30 percent of troops engaged in active combat in Afghanistan/Iraq for four months or more had suffered a mild TBI as a result of IED blast waves (Hoge, McGurk, Thomas, et al., 2008). While the majority of traumatic brain injuries that occur are classified as mild and have excellent prognosis overall (Iverson, 2005), both for civilians and the military, persistent problems do occur in some individuals.

For those injured under combat conditions, even mild TBI can have a complicated recovery course when it occurs in the context of multi-system trauma (French & Parkinson, 2008). Those with more severe TBI typically need ongoing treatment and support to achieve maximal recovery. This usually includes inpatient and residential treatment. For those individuals with persistent problems following a TBI of any severity, the assessment and treatment process works best when all relevant symptoms are addressed, and care is organized and coordinated.

There is no discipline that can lay claim to "owning" the care of one with TBI. In many cases, multiple providers will be seeing the patient to address a range of issues including cognitive complaints, pain (including headache), dizziness, emotional concerns, and sleep disturbances. In the military care setting, the care plan is sometimes driven by the type of injury (Belanger, Scott, Scholten, et al., 2005) as much as the specific diagnosis. As blast is the most common method of injury in the current military operational setting (Bell, Vo, Neal, et al., 2009), the evaluative process needs to start by investigating the full range of potential sequelae to blast exposure. This often-complicated care model requires significant co-ordination, and the role of the TBI-specific case manager is key in helping to organize the care needed and to assist the patient and family in navigating the care system.

This chapter is intended to help educate civilian social workers and other mental health providers on the issues faced by those with mild traumatic brain injury and its impact on both the service member and their family. As service members and newly separated Veterans increasingly access care in civilian care systems. The case of Sergeant First Class L (SFC L) and a few intermittent vignettes will serve to illustrate some of the issues faced by a service member with mild TBI.

Definition of TBI

The United States Department of Defense and the United States Department of Veterans Affairs define TBI as:

> a traumatically induced structural injury and/or physiological disruption of brain function as a result of an external force that is indicated by new onset or worsening of at least one of the following clinical signs, immediately following the event:

1 any period of loss of or a decreased level of consciousness;
2 any loss of memory for events immediately before or after the injury;
3 any alteration in mental state at the time of the injury (e.g., confusion, disorientation, slowed thinking);
4 neurological deficits (e.g., weakness, balance disturbance, praxis, paresis/plegia, change in vision, other sensory alterations, aphasia) that may or may not be transient;
5 intracranial abnormalities (e.g., contusions, diffuse axonal injury, hemorrhages, aneurysms).

Penetrating TBI is defined as something, often a bullet or fragment, penetrating the dura that surrounds the brain. Other traumatic brain injuries are defined as "closed" and then further defined according to injury characteristics. Although penetrating brain injuries have historically been of significant concern in warfare (and remain so), much attention is now being placed on closed TBI and brain injuries at the milder end of the spectrum, especially mild TBI (or concussion) caused by IEDs. Closed TBI severity is classified by characteristics of the injury itself, and not by the severity of the symptoms that result, although, in general, more severe TBI results in more lasting and severe symptoms. Severity is based on the duration of the loss of consciousness (brief, or even absent in mild TBI) and posttraumatic amnesia (the period after the injury during which the individual cannot reliably encode new memories).

In 2009, penetrating brain injury accounted for just 1.4 percent of the total reported brain injuries, and severe closed brain injury accounted for less than 1 percent of the total. Of the almost 28,000 traumatic brain injuries reported in 2009, about 78 percent (21,859) were classified as mild (available at http://www. dvbic.org/TBI-Numbers.aspx). Overall, some studies have shown that during deployment as many as 20%–30% or more may have suffered a concussion or mild TBI (Terrio, Brenner, Ivins, et al., 2009), although other studies have shown rates to be lower. It will primarily be service members or Veterans with mild TBI who will be accessing care through civilian social workers and mental health providers. However, caregivers and family members of those with moderate or severe injuries will likely present for services and support for themselves.

Sergeant First Class L—Mild Traumatic Brain Injury

Sergeant First Class L was a 37-year-old married male, U.S. Army E-7, who was injured when an Improvised Explosive Device (IED) detonated under the right front tire of his HMVEE. SFC L, who had 11 years time-in-service, was the restrained right front passenger wearing full body armor and was the truck commander (TC) of the vehicle when it was hit. He reported having an immediate loss of consciousness which lasted for less than a minute, with clear memories leading up to the blast and some hazy memories after regaining consciousness. The length of SFC L's posttraumatic amnesia was estimated to be a few seconds and he was determined to have sustained a mild traumatic brain injury. SFC L sustained a traumatic amputation of his right leg just below the knee. He also sustained a fractured right hand and significant soft tissue damage to his face due to shrapnel. He underwent several surgeries to address his amputation, which finally resulted in a right knee disarticulation. He declined plastic surgery to correct scarring on the right side of his face.

System of Care and Evaluation

At Walter Reed Army Medical Center (WRAMC), TBI evaluations are conducted by a multidisciplinary team of providers. Following medical air evacuation from theater, inpatient and outpatient arrivals are routinely screened for TBI. In some cases, while a diagnosis of TBI has already been established, the patient has failed to recover as expected and is therefore referred to WRAMC for other evaluative and treatment resources. Evaluations for inpatients and outpatients are conducted in similar ways. The system of care for evaluation at Walter Reed will be delineated below as an exemplar, though these processes (or parts of them) can be replicated in the civilian sector.

The WRAMC TBI service begins screening patients before they arrive at WRAMC. A TBI clinician performs a thorough review of air evacuation manifests and in-theater medical databases that provide description of injuries, initial surgical procedures and radiological evaluations. Common TBI causes of injury include being in or near a blast/explosion, a motor vehicle accident, a fall, or injury to the head, face or neck, and, therefore, incoming patients with these mechanisms of injury are flagged for further screening.

After the medical record and history are reviewed, a member of the TBI team conducts a thorough clinical interview when the patient is able to participate. Collateral information is also obtained by interview with family members, or other service members that may have witnessed the incident. This interview allows the clinician to ask probative questions to help the patient describe what occurred. Through the interview process the length of loss of consciousness (LOC) and/or posttraumatic amnesia (PTA) can be more accurately established to help determine the severity level of the TBI. This is accomplished by asking detailed questions about how events transpired and what memories of the injury event patients have retained. These interviews can be conducted in free-form, or in a structured way (Corrigan & Bogner, 2007).

The first step in an interview is to obtain general information about a patient's history of concussion. Initial questions involve asking if a patient has ever sustained an injury to their head or neck in a motor vehicle accident, in a fall, by being hit by something or someone (including being in a fight), or if they have ever been nearby when an explosion occurred. If the patient answers yes to any of the questions, then they are asked if they know or have been told if they sustained a loss of consciousness. Patients may state, "I was unconscious for a few seconds, I remember the explosion but then I was slumped inside the vehicle," or "I remember the blast and then I remember being dragged out of the vehicle." When asked if they remember details such as how they fell in the vehicle from standing in the turret or who pulled them out of the vehicle, they may or may not recall the answers. Patients often assume that they were unconscious in these moments, however reviewing records or consulting collateral sources sometimes reveals that they were awake and responding to others around them but have no independent recall for this period. This helps differentiate posttraumatic amnesia from loss of consciousness.

Next, questions should be asked targeting the reported gap in memory. This line of questioning might include, "What is the first thing you remember after the blast/crash/shot?," or "Can you tell me in detail what you remember that happened next?" (Ruff et al., 2009). A typical response may be, "I remember coming to on the ground and the medics were already working on me." Another response may be, "I remember feeling dazed, kind of out of it, then I remember returning fire because we were in a firefight and I was the gunner." In the first example it is likely that the patient sustained other injuries and there may be medical documentation to supplement the patient's recollection in determining LOC. Patients that sustain other injuries are usually transported to hospitals or aid stations for treatment and their TBI may be diagnosed relatively quickly after the injury event. The second example is typical of patients who may not have been evaluated after the event, therefore the interviewer has to rely solely on current reporting for a diagnosis. Patients who do not seek immediate medical attention may have a gap in months if not a year or more between the exposure and their TBI diagnostic interview. The amount of time that has passed since the injury event impacts the narrative that is built around the patient's recall.

A critical factor that needs to be considered is the patient's emotional state at the time of the event. Traumatic events can cause acute distress, fear and anxiety in patients that may induce an amnestic period that is not caused by an organic disruption of brain functioning. Patients who experience psychogenic amnesia instead of true posttraumatic amnesia often may report, "I don't remember, I don't know what happened. I felt like things were moving in slow motion. I remember the explosion, the white flash of the blast, the dust. I remember falling to the ground but I can't remember if I hit my head. Then I remember my ears ringing and my squad leader calling my name but everything was fuzzy and it felt like things were moving slowly." This is a typical example of psychogenic amnesia as a stress reaction to an acute event. The patient initially states that they don't remember what happened but with further questioning they are able to report events in detailed continuous memory.

Once PTA and/or LOC are/is established the interview focuses on assessing reported symptomatology. The interviewer asks questions related to physical, psychological and cognitive symptoms. These would be open-ended questions such as:

- How did you feel after the blast?
- What, if any, changes have you noticed in yourself since then?
- What feedback have family members or people from your unit given you about changes they have noticed at home or at work?
- When did you start experiencing the headaches/dizziness/irritability?

The onset of symptoms is important to determine because it gives clues as to whether they are likely related to the TBI or to other factors. Patients may state, "I got headaches right away then they got better over the next few days, but now I have been getting headaches again recently." In this example, it is probable that the patient recovered from the initial concussion and might lead the clinician to inquire about any new onset of stressors in their life to see if there is a correlation to the new onset of headaches. Alternately, when asked to pinpoint onset of sleep disturbance, a service member might say, "Well, my sleep got bad right when I deployed, but after the blast it got worse—much worse." This illustrates a clear worsening of symptoms post-exposure and would likely be the resultant from some aspect of the event.

Assessing cognitive changes is important during this step in the interview process. Patients often simply refer to "memory problems" and say that they forget things easily. However, upon further questioning they may also report difficulty with concentration, problem solving, or executive functioning, although they are not able to define them as such. Examples of how a patient might report these deficits include: "I cannot multi-task any more." "I can't stand going grocery shopping; I get overwhelmed and leave with a cart full of groceries except the one thing I came in for." "When I try to read a book, I read the same paragraph over and over again."

Addressing the patient's symptomatology and offering education about TBI recovery is the next step in the interview process. Educating patients regarding cognitive symptoms associated with TBI is very important. Working with a patient who may have sustained a mild TBI but did not start noticing symptoms until years later leads to a further discussion about how lack of sleep, depression or medical conditions can also cause cognitive changes. Given the amount of attention TBI has received in the media, some patients misattribute a symptom to a prior TBI. Education is particularly important if a civilian social worker has the opportunity to work with service members who have recent injuries. Providing basic information on the course of recovery from mild TBI can help set up the expectation of a full recovery. These simple interventions can greatly reduce the anxiety and uncertainty that may otherwise slow down the recovery process.

Standardized questionnaires are administered to all patients with TBI at WRAMC. Using questionnaires allows for further evaluation of symptoms and monitoring progress in treatment. For a newly formed civilian program, the choice of questionnaires used would be informed by both the expertise of the clinicians administering and interpreting them as well as the scope of support services available in the larger community. Of note, given the emotional context in which the injuries had occurred, stress symptoms are common and expected. In some cases, normalization, monitoring and general support are all that is required (Wain, Bradley, Nam, et al., 2005). Regardless of the etiology, symptoms are monitored and treated, consistent with standardized DoD/VA practice guidelines (The Management of Concussion/mTBI Working Group, 2009).

During his inpatient stay, SFC L denied any cognitive difficulties and did not evidence cognitive deficits during interviews. He was initially administered a Repeatable Battery for the Assessment of Neuropsychological Status (RBANS) (Randolph, Tierney, & Chase, 1998) about one month after his injury. Results showed intact functioning in all domains with his lowest score being low average on a verbal fluency measure. Since he was still on narcotics for pain management at that time, it was recommended that he be retested in 3-6 months.

Five months later, SFC L underwent comprehensive neuropsychological testing. He reported that his awareness of cognitive deficits had increased over time which, for him, constituted a significant drop from pre-morbid functioning. He also reported acute irritability, poor sleep and some re-experiencing symptoms including intrusive thoughts. His testing generally was not indicative of impairment. There were areas of improvement and a few areas of decline, most particularly on a measure of attention. SFC L was offered comprehensive education about mild TBI including the normal trajectory of recovery following mTBI. It was pointed out that whereas his focus had been on physical issues early on in his recovery, his subsequent focus on cognitive issues might create the impression that things had worsened. Additionally, his discharge from the hospital to an outpatient setting had presented more demands from, greater variability in, and less structure to his environment, again creating the possible impression that things had worsened. Myriad factors, which can affect attention including poor sleep, anxiety and pain, were all discussed with the patient and his wife.

Following comprehensive evaluation at WRAMC, outpatient treatment for service members occurs in a multidisciplinary outpatient TBI clinic to ensure delivery of comprehensive care. The TBI clinic is composed of providers from: Physical Medicine and Rehabilitation, Neurology, Psychiatry/Behavioral Health, Neuropsychology, Audiology, Optometry, Ophthalmology, Physical Therapy, Speech Language Pathology, Occupational Therapy, Rehabilitation Psychology, and Case Management. Each TBI-positive patient undergoes comprehensive evaluations by these services individually to determine the scope of their ongoing rehabilitative needs.

Patients return to TBI clinic for continuous monitoring of progress jointly by the rehabilitation services and physicians. During the clinic, patients' dispositions, plans of care and medical needs are established, reevaluated and updated as their individual needs change over time. If a patient endorses mood symptoms, then behavioral health is consulted. Patients who endorse headaches are referred to neurologists. Speech language pathologists and occupational therapists often treat cognitive symptoms. Vestibular changes may be assessed by audiologists and otolaryngologists (ENT) and treated by specially trained physical therapists. Additionally, specialized clinics have been established to treat common symptoms such as dizziness, memory/attention problems, or headaches. Unfortunately, in the civilian sector it is often only patients in rehabilitation programs who have the services of a comprehensive rehabilitation team; patients often have to go to many different providers in different locations and these providers often do not communicate with each other.

Within the military system of care, patients with a moderate or severe TBI who exhibit impaired cognitive functioning and/or physical limitations are usually transferred to one of the Veterans Affairs Polytrauma Centers identified in order to provide acute inpatient TBI rehabilitation. Treatment course and length of stay at the polytrauma center is contingent upon the patient's progress in the program.

As the majority of injured service members and their families live outside of the Washington, DC area, their prolonged stays in the hospital can place significant strains on the individual and family. Normal community social supports may not be close by. Parents or spouses may have to leave work to be near the injured service member, thereby placing financial burdens on the family. Children are also affected. Assessment and interventions must be extended to the children and family unit (Cozza, Guimond, McKibbeb, et al., 2010). Programs have been developed to get service members closer to their homes and support as soon as possible (Dominguez, 2008). Patients may be referred to either VA or civilian providers in their home community, and continue to receive case management services from a remotely located military case manager. This way, they can return home and receive their medical care within their own community and support systems, which will usually enhance their recovery and community reintegration. The specific role of the civilian case manager in this context is coordination and support.

SFC L's wife and two children were still living in Texas and had, as yet, been unable to move to WRAMC to be with him because of his kids' school schedules. SFC L had a solid and open relationship with his wife of nine years who was an important source of support for him. He was also very close with his children who were a motivating force for his rehabilitation. His stated goals were to be able to play catch and football with his son and to dance with his daughter at her wedding.

SFC L was referred for behavioral health treatment for his reported difficulty with irritability and persistent subclinical posttraumatic stress symptoms. He had been seen by the Speech Language Pathology service for some initial difficulty with verbal fluency but had been discharged following satisfactory resolution of his symptoms. He was also followed by Physical Therapy and Orthotics for physical rehabilitation and prosthetic care. SFC L's case manager was instrumental in advocating for his transfer to the Warrior Transition Unit at Brooke Army Medical Center (BAMC) in San Antonio so that he could be closer to home and would have the advantage of enhanced social and familial support while he underwent the Medical Retirement process.

TBI Case Management

The role of case management for TBI patients is important to help facilitate care both in the military and the civilian sector where many TBI patients may end up receiving services. The TBI case manager's role is to implement, monitor, review and revise the plan of care to ensure that patients' ongoing needs are met. One of the key functions of the TBI case manager in any setting, civilian or VA/DoD, is to gather relevant information from a range of sources, including the individual and/or their family and different rehabilitation/medical disciplines. They develop an overarching view and understanding of the individual's injury and their course of treatment. This involves playing an active role in any clinical setting where a patient is discussed with a multi-disciplinary team. The TBI case manager reviews all medical records, contacts patients and reviews past recommendations to communicate to physicians who evaluate the patient.

For social workers working with TBI patients in a civilian setting, the roles would be similar and this ability to maintain broad oversight over the patient's comprehensive care would be essential. As stated previously, there is no single discipline which "owns" the care of the traumatically brain-injured patient. As a result, TBI patients in an outpatient civilian setting may have what feels like fractured care. They may see a neurologist for headaches, a mental health provider for mood dysregulation and a physical therapist for vestibular dysfunction.

In the civilian sector, these providers may not be co-located, may not be in a system of care that is collaborative, and may even not be aware that other specialists are seeing the patient. Due to TBI patients' frequent difficulty communicating, the broad spectrum of patients' deficits may not be conveyed to individual providers. Patient care can easily be "stove-piped" such that symptoms end up being treated in a vacuum by individual providers who may not have an understanding of how they fit into an overall constellation of post-concussive symptoms. A civilian social work case manager can make a significant impact by linking these formerly unconnected providers so that they can consult each other as an ad hoc inter-disciplinary team. These sorts of informal networks that are created by social workers and case managers in civilian community-based settings are invaluable in terms of integrating patient care more seamlessly.

Another function of the case manager is to help facilitate the development of the treatment plan for the TBI patient. At WRAMC, this involves coordinating appointments and communicating with the military case managers assigned to oversee the patient's overall care. For this task, TBI case managers need to be aware of both military and civilian resources available for TBI patients. A third function of the TBI case manager is to educate patients and their family members on the TBI recovery process, the military system of care, and to make sure their needs, both clinical and psychosocial, are met as fully as possible. The TBI case manager needs to evaluate resources of care, family supports, and military regulations when helping to develop the treatment plan. Case managers can be available to make sure patients are heard and understood, to help understand medical terminology, and to facilitate communication between patients and providers.

A unique service provided by the Defense and Veterans Brain Injury Service (DVBIC) is the Care Coordination system. This consists of monitoring patients' progress at routine time intervals to ensure that their clinical needs continue to be met. At WRAMC a social worker has been assigned to contact patients who are identified as TBI positive via telephonic interview. It has been shown that telephonic follow-up and monitoring over time can enhance post-deployment adjustment (Martin, French, & Janos, 2010). The Care Coordinator's role is to review medical records and to contact patients to conduct an intake assessment. The subsequent telephone contacts consist of ongoing assessment of symptoms, ensuring that patients are connected with services, providing education, and contacting other case managers involved in patient care to make sure any concerns are properly communicated. This model of care can and should be replicated by the civilian social worker in a non-military setting. The DVBIC Care Coordinator may also assign the civilian social worker as a "point person" to oversee and supplement the care of the patient. This is particularly helpful for service members as they transition to life as a civilian.

One of the main functions of the Care Coordinator is to link patients back into services when they become disengaged from systems of care or otherwise become isolated. They are tasked with being knowledgeable about all available resources for patients. This ranges from formal treatment settings, to local municipal resources, to community-based support groups, and to any more informal networks of support. On behalf of retired or medically discharged patients, they might work closely with civilian social workers to ensure that patients are as integrated into their home communities as possible. Similarly, it would be the task of a civilian social worker who is setting up their own system to monitor TBI patients in their community to develop these same sorts of formal and informal networks. The most fundamental task of a case manager working with TBI patients is to ensure that they remain linked with services. For a population that may have difficulty remembering appointments, managing social interactions, or simply feeling that they belong in the civilian world to begin with, the risk of isolation is great. Social workers can play a critical role in maintaining connection with this highly vulnerable population that is at considerable risk of falling through the cracks.

TBI Education

Education is a critical aspect of recovery from a TBI. When seen on an outpatient basis, it is the role of the clinician who evaluates them to provide education about the expected recovery process. Education should be conducted in several ways including oral communication, printed materials, group classes, and providing web-based resources (see Table 4.1). This is especially true for a population that may have difficulty with receptive language, productive language, attention or concentration. Every format offered increases the chance of making the information more accessible to the service member and their family members. It is also important in that a social worker may not know how much ongoing contact they will have with the patient so frontloading educational materials is best in case they only get one chance to offer it.

As they transition to outpatient status, all TBI patients at WRAMC are required to attend educational classes. Patients and their families learn about the TBI

TABLE 4.1 Ways in which education should be communicated

Brainline: www.brainline.org
  Interactive site with broad resources and links to services.
Defense and Veterans Brain Injury Center: www.DVBIC.org
  Resources for military personnel, families, and providers about TBI.
Deployment Health Clinical Center: http://www.pdhealth.mil/TBI.asp
  Resources for military clinical guidelines and policies.
Brain Injury Association of America: www.biausa.org
  Resources for advocacy, support, education, and research for individuals with TBI,
  their families and professionals. Links to individual State offices available.
CDC-National Center for Injury Prevention and Control: www.cdc.gov/ncipc/
  tbi/TBI.htm
  Educational information about TBI, Concussion in sports, clinical diagnosis and
  management, and statistics. Free downloadable education materials, and request forms
  for shipment of materials.
Defense Health Board—The Center of Excellence for Medical Multimedia:
  www.traumaticbraininjuryatoz.org
  Informative and sensitive exploration of Traumatic Brain Injury (TBI) including
  information for patients, family members, and caregivers.
**National Institute of Neurological Disorders and Stroke (NINDS) Traumatic
  Brain Injury Information Page**: www.ninds.nih.gov/disorders/tbi/tbi.htm
  Organizations that provide assistance for TBI patients and their families.

---

diagnostic criteria, symptoms of TBI along with some techniques to address some of those symptoms, and how caregivers can provide support to the patient with a TBI. Themes discussed in the classes include: behavioral and emotional effects of TBI; family and caregiver issues; physical effects of TBI; and sleep issues. In the class, participants are exposed to TBI diagnostic criteria, mechanisms of injury, symptomatology, the recovery process, factors that affect recovery, compensatory strategies and the overlap of PTSD and TBI. The interaction between physical symptoms, cognitive issues, headaches, and the environment are also explored at length. The education classes are easily replicable by civilian providers and can be conducted by clinicians with a variety of training backgrounds.

Transition to the Community

A critical task for any service member during long-term recovery is a successful transition back into the community. Community reintegration is a multilayered process which encompasses an individual's resumption of former roles. This may require adapting the service member, the system or even the physical environment to allow the individual to participate as fully as possible in those roles. In general, this will include successfully reentering family, social and often civilian residential and workplace settings. This may be fraught with feelings of doubt, anxiety and anger for some individuals who are either not able to, or not confident about their ability to, resume certain roles from their lives prior to injury. It is often the case that expectations are adapted in the process. It falls to the civilian social worker to help facilitate this adjustment that can be taxing to both the service member and his/her family.

For those with TBIs on the milder end of the spectrum, reintegration is often centered around issues related to the deployment process. Adjustment to life after serving in theater can be difficult for some. It can be particularly challenging when someone is injured in theater and is medically evacuated out. Abrupt removal from the theater of operations precludes a person's ability to anticipate and emotionally and psychologically prepare for transition back to peacetime environs. Service members may struggle with feelings of guilt or shame if they feel as though they have let down their unit or their buddies by not being there to support them. This may also be complicated if there were other service members who were injured or died in the same event. These are important areas of discussion between the service member and counselor.

Part of the process of early reintegration is redefining community to reflect those around them instead of the intense, intimate connections that are often formed within a unit during deployment. Formation of those connections is an adaptive means of securing protection and support in an austere environment. The loss of those relationships can sometimes inspire feelings of grief and vulnerability, and it is a testament to the intensity of the bonds formed during deployment that such loyalty and commitment persist even in the aftermath of sometimes catastrophic injury. It is often helpful to attempt to connect the injured service member with other Veterans in his/her community. In many parts of the country, Vet Centers exist in communities where service members can go to be with other Veterans. While part of the VA system, the Vet Centers have more of a drop-in atmosphere where informal discussions and groups occur.

For patients who are able to return to active duty, community reintegration entails successfully transitioning from a hospital-based therapeutic environment back to a more traditional military unit, often called a line unit. Transition may include negotiating expectations from command and fellow service members regarding duty hours, adherence to military standards of physical fitness, and an ability to resume prior responsibilities at the same pace and frequency as before.

Transition from the relatively stable setting at WRAMC may also reveal to service members the extent of their deficits. Living within the context of a contained, safe environment wherein a patient's medical care, nutritional needs and basic supports are provided may mask some of the more challenging aspects of recovery. When a patient returns to their home community and is responsible for keeping track of their own appointments, driving to new locations and managing the basic structure of their environment, challenges may emerge. The lack of structure may also make time management more difficult. This is another capacity in which civilian social workers can make a significant contribution.

Helping patients to develop compensatory strategies that work for them in their own unique environment has the potential to make a meaningful impact on a patient's functionality.

Simple problem solving and strategizing how to structure personal space, appointments, and to introduce effective reminders into the patient's routine can effectively enable them to act more independently. This sort of collaboration can be very helpful for a patient who may be too irritable or overwhelmed or distracted to focus on developing ways to structure their lives more effectively. Sometimes simple life skills training can make a radical difference in someone's life and routine. One such intervention might be suggesting that a Veteran who is going back to school schedule their classes in the morning. That way they might have assistance from a working or otherwise committed spouse or parent to get them out of bed and out the door on time. This also could allow them to take advantage of increased energy and focus which may tend to wane as they day goes on. For someone who has difficulty with executive functioning, such simple tips to help organize or structure their day can make a big impact.

While awaiting transfer, SFC L was seen by a Rehabilitation Psychologist who helped him explore goals for his future. He expressed interest in pursuing a college degree in the field of mechanical engineering, because he had served as a combat engineer and had found the work stimulating and satisfying. Given evidence of his high pre-morbid level of intelligence, his overall performance on testing measures, and his motivation, he was encouraged to pursue these goals. He was offered suggestions regarding possible academic accommodations, and upon his formal transfer to BAMC, SFC L was linked with the regional Care Coordinator for that area. While the expectation was that he would continue to do very well, the Care Coordinator served as a safety net to help assess and address any unforeseen challenges that might arise upon his departure from the security and familiarity of WRAMC or when he began a more rigorous academic program. SFC L was reminded of the change he had noticed when he transitioned from the structure of being an inpatient to the novel challenges faced as an outpatient. The expectation of transitional challenges was conveyed and normalized, as was the expectation of his successful adaptation.

Connections were made with the local VA and a civilian social worker in the family's community. The civilian social worker was initially able to help SFC L link to some educational resources for tutoring and time management as he started his coursework. These skills turned out to be rusty—more so because of how long it had been since he was a student than because of any residual deficit. Yet the social worker's involvement and willingness to step in and help him served to develop a rapport between them. SFC L had intended to be career military and was not initially open to receiving any kind of services outside of the military until he was formally discharged. Making this connection early on diminished some of the anxiety he felt about "waking up one day and being a civilian all of a sudden." The social worker ended up playing a significant role in working with the family to help the adjustment to home, the departure from active duty, and community-based adaptations based on his amputations.

Community reintegration entails the re-absorption of an individual back into their family. The experience at WRAMC repeatedly demonstrates how critical the involvement and support of family members is to the effective recovery of a loved one following TBI. It can be tremendously healing for an individual to leave a clinical rehabilitative setting and return to home and thereby regain the sense of autonomy that is elusive in a hospital setting. This same process, however, also is rife with challenges and potential obstacles for the family. One of the most common and universal advisements for patients returning to their families is to "Go Slow." This applies to the resumption of most of the roles associated with family membership. A partner/spouse who has been gone for a while due to deployment or rehabilitation may feel both familiar and foreign at the same time. It can take a while to regain a sense of ease with someone who has been absent even if they have been married or partnered for many years. Deployment and the experience of injury can change the most basic dynamics within a couple.

This is also true of sexual intimacy. For patients who struggle with depression or body image issues related to physical injury, lack of interest in sex may be a factor. For some with more severe TBI, structural damage to the brain may increase sexual impulsivity, lessen inhibition, or modify levels of desire (Weinstein & Kahn, 1961). Endocrine dysfunction after TBI can affect sexual desire also (Hohl, Mazzuco, Coral, et al., 2009). Interventions to address these challenges would include a full medical evaluation to determine the organic and hormonal basis of these changes; this may include referral to an endocrinologist. Couples therapy or various kinds of individual therapy for the patient can also help ameliorate some of the effects of depression or impulse control problems. It is important that social workers ask about issues related to intimacy and sexual functioning. Patients often will not bring them up out of embarrassment or discomfort. Simply asking about these issues normalizes them and creates an opportunity to support what can otherwise be a hidden source of pain and shame.

For people who sustain moderate and severe TBIs, this process of family reintegration can be largely characterized by the redefinition of roles. If someone is unable to perform certain roles or is unable to participate in family life in the way that they used to, the meaning of their relationships may alter significantly (Olkin, 1999). This is most characteristically true in the context of a marriage if a person who was formerly a partner providing emotional support, social interaction and income, is rendered incapable of performing activities of daily living. A spouse may take on some basic caretaking functions that render the relationship more similar to that of parent/child than a spousal one. Many times, in such families, children also end up taking on some caretaking roles. Often an adult child who has recently become independent and autonomous sustains a TBI and is rendered reliant once again upon parental support and care.

Neurobehavioral sequelae of TBI often present the most painful challenges for families in terms of reintegrating an injured family member. Families in which loved ones evidence personality changes, impulsivity or disinhibition after injury may struggle with reintegrating someone who does not, in very fundamental ways, feel like the loved one who was injured (Olkin, 1999). Other permanent changes may include chronic health problems associated with either the TBI or the other injuries sustained. This may include pain, mood disorders, long-term health problems associated with amputation, or limited mobility. Family members may be concurrently grieving for the loss of the person or personality of the person who was injured, even if they survived the injury event. This can be a complex and confusing tangle of experiences and emotions, and is further complicated by the strain that is placed upon a family when their loved one is living at WRAMC or another rehabilitation facility that is far from their home. Many families make profound sacrifices in terms of professional pursuits, financial commitments, changing children's school arrangements, and mobilizing the involvement of extended family members in order to attend to and support the service member who was injured.

Conclusion

Despite the range of severity of traumatic brain injuries, the majority of those who have sustained a TBI have a mild injury. While immediate sequelae may include alterations in multiple domains of functioning (including mood changes, sleep dysfunction, cognitive deficits and physical symptoms), the vast majority of symptoms will fully resolve and patients will be able to function well within the family, community and greater society. For those more seriously injured, service members and their families will be adapting to a life with permanent deficits and ongoing challenges. Because much of the care of the traumatically brain injured is administered outside of large military medical centers such as WRAMC, civilian social workers and other mental health providers will play an important role in their care.

Authors' Note

The views expressed in this article are those of the authors and do not reflect the official policy of the Department of Army, Department of Defense, or U.S. Government.

References

Altmire, J. (2007). *Testimony of Jason Altmire*. Hearing before the Subcommittee on Health of the House Committee on Veterans Affairs, Washington, DC.

Belanger, H.G., Scott, S.G., Scholten, J., Curtiss, G., & Vanderploeg, R.D. (2005). Utility of mechanism-of-injury-based assessment and treatment: Blast Injury Program case illustration. *Journal of Rehabiliation Research & Development*, 42(4), 403–412.

Bell, R.S., Vo, A.H., Neal, C.J., Tigno, J., Roberts, R., Mossop, C., Dunne, J.R., & Armonda, R.A. (2009). Military traumatic brain and spinal column injury: A 5-year study of the impact blast and other military grade weaponry on the central nervous system. *Journal of Trauma*, 66(4 Suppl), S104–S111.

Corrigan, J.D. & Bogner, J. (2007). Initial reliability and validity of the Ohio State University TBI Identification Method. *Journal of Head Trauma Rehabilitation*, 22(6), 318–329.

Cozza, S.J., Guimond, J.M., McKibben, J.B., Chun, R.S., Arata-Maiers, T.L., Schneider, B., et al. (2010). Combat-injured service members and their families: The relationship of child distress and spouse-perceived family distress and disruption. *Journal of Trauma Stress*, 23(1), 112–115.

Dominguez, M.A. (2008). The comprehensive care plan: Building the strength to do well tomorrow. *U.S. Army Medical Department Journal*, Jan.–March, 8–16.

French, L.M. & Parkinson, G.W. (2008). Assessing and treating Veterans with traumatic brain injury. *Journal of Clinical Psychology*, 64(8), 1004–1013.

Hoge, C.W., McGurk, D., Thomas, J.L., Cox, A.L., Engel, C.C., & Castro, C.A. (2008). Mild traumatic brain injury in U.S. Soldiers returning from Iraq. *New England Journal of Medicine*, 358(5), 453–463.

Hohl, A., Mazzuco, T.L., Coral, M.H., Schwarzbold, M., & Walz, R. (2009). Hypogonadism after traumatic brain injury. *Arquivos Brasileiros de Endocrinologia & Metabologia*, 53(8), 908–914.

Iverson, G.L. (2005). Outcome from mild traumatic brain injury. *Current Opinion in Psychiatry*, 18(3), 301–317.

Langlois, J.A., Rutland-Brown, W., & Thomas, K.E. (2006). *Traumatic Brain Injury in the United States: Emergency Department visits, hospitalizations, and deaths*. Atlanta, GA: Centers for Disease Control and Prevention, National Center for Injury Prevention and Control.

Martin, E.M., French, L.M., & Janos, A. (2010). Home/community monitoring using telephonic follow-up. *NeuroRehabilitation*, 26, 279–283.

Olkin, R. (1999). *What Psychotherapists Should Know About Disability*. New York: The Guilford Press.

Randolph, C., Tierney, M.C., & Chase, T.N. (1998). The Repeatable Battery for the Assessment of Neuropsychological Status (RBANS): Preliminary clinical validity. *Journal of Clinical Experimental Neuropsychology*, 20(3), 310–319.

Ruff, R., Iverson, G., Barth, J., Bush, S., Broshek, D., & the NAN Policy and Planning Committee (2009). Recommendations for diagnosing a mild traumatic brain injury: A national Academy of Neuropsychology education paper. *Archives of Clinical Neuropsychology*, 24, 3–10.

Terrio, H., Brenner, L.A., Ivins, B.J., Cho, J.M., Helmick, K., Schwab, K., et al. (2009). Traumatic brain injury screening: Preliminary findings in a U.S. Army Brigade Combat Team. *Journal of Head Trauma Rehabilitation*, 24(1), 14–23.

The Management of Concussion/mTBI Working Group (2009). VA/DoD clinical practice guideline for management of concussion/mild traumatic brain injury (mTBI). Retrieved April 18, 2010, from: http://www.healthquality.va.gov/mtbi/concussion_mtbi_full_1_0.pdf

Wain, H., Bradley, J., Nam, T., Waldrep, D., & Cozza, S. (2005). Psychiatric interventions with returning soldiers at Walter Reed. *Psychiatric Quarterly*, 76(4), 351–360.

Warden, D. (2006). Military TBI during the Iraq and Afghanistan wars. *Journal of Head Trauma Rehabilitation*, 21(5), 398–402.

Weinstein, E.A. & Kahn, R.L. (1961). Patterns of sexual behavior following brain injury. *Psychiatry*, 24, 69–78.

5

WORKING WITH SURVIVORS OF SEXUAL HARASSMENT AND SEXUAL ASSAULT IN THE MILITARY

Margret E. Bell and Annemarie Reardon

Introduction

When clinicians evaluate their competency to provide care to Veterans who served in Operation Enduring Freedom or Operation Iraqi Freedom (OEF/OIF) or other eras, they typically think about their skills and knowledge in working with combat trauma. However, few consider their ability to address issues related to sexual harassment and sexual assault in the military. This is problematic given the frequent occurrence and well-documented deleterious impact of these experiences on both women and men (Kessler, Sonnega, Bromet, et al., 1995; Kilpatrick, Acierno, Resnick, et al., 1997; Kimerling, Gima, Smith, et al., 2007; Ullman & Brecklin, 2003; Vogt, Pless, King, & King, 2005). While the Department of Veterans Affairs (VA) provides an array of free, specialized outpatient, inpatient, and residential services for survivors of sexual trauma in the military, some Veterans choose not to seek care from the VA, despite the particular expertise that might be available. For this reason, it is important for all healthcare providers working with Veterans to have a basic working knowledge of sexual trauma in the military.

This chapter is designed to assist with this, by giving clinicians an overview of issues that may arise when providing clinical care to survivors of sexual harassment and sexual assault in the military. We recognize that readers may be working with survivors in a variety of different roles and, as such, focus on general themes and issues that may come up in working with survivors, as opposed to specifics about provision of psychotherapy or other forms of treatment.

That said, it is important to note that psychotherapy, case management, and other care focused on mental health and psychosocial issues with sexual trauma survivors is similar in many ways to work with other trauma survivors. As such, we strongly encourage readers with less experience working with trauma survivors in general to acquire additional expertise in this area. Providers who have experience working with civilian sexual trauma survivors will find that the skills and conceptual models for working with these survivors generally accord to working with survivors of sexual trauma in the military. However, there are key ways in which the experience and impact of sexual trauma in the military can differ from sexual trauma in civilian settings. Understanding how the military context and, in the case of OEF/OIF Veterans, deployment to a warzone, can affect the dynamics of sexual harassment and assault will help providers to better appreciate the precise stressors faced by survivors at the time of the experiences, in the immediate aftermath and, currently, as they progress in their recovery.

In the sections that follow, we first briefly review key terms and provide information on prevalence. We then discuss the impact that sexual trauma in the military can have on survivors, with a particular emphasis on the ways in which various aspects of the military context may shape survivors' reactions and subsequent difficulties. Finally, we focus on application of this material, with case vignettes illustrating general principles that may assist providers in working with survivors. Throughout, our goal is to share information that may be useful in helping providers understand why survivors behave and react in the ways that they sometimes do. Our hope is that, armed with this understanding, providers can more effectively tailor their work, whatever their role, to the particular needs of each Veteran under their care.

Background

Definitions

Although "trauma" has a specific DSM-IV (APA [American Psychiatric Association], 1994) definition, the term "sexual trauma" is at times used more loosely as a general term encompassing sexual harassment, sexual assault, and other coercive sexually-based experiences.

Similarly, although the terms "sexual harassment" and "sexual assault" have precise behaviorally-based legal definitions, in clinical settings these terms are typically used more expansively in order to particularly emphasize the survivor's subjective experience. This is appropriate given that a healthcare provider's primary interest is in the health impact of these experiences. "Sexual harassment" can be considered an overarching term of sorts in that it refers to a continuum of unwanted sexual experiences occurring in the workplace. Experiences fall into the category of sexual harassment when they create an intimidating, hostile or offensive working environment, or when employment or employment decisions are contingent on cooperation with them (EEOC, 1990). Behaviorally, this may include unwanted sexual advances, offensive comments about a person's body or sexual activities, or the display of pornographic or other sexually demeaning objects in the workplace.

One particularly severe form of sexual harassment is workplace sexual assault, or unwanted physical sexual contact involving some form of coercion. This coercion can take many forms including threats of punishment (for example, lowered performance evaluation with implications for promotion), or promises of rewards (for example, better job assignments); and as such, may not always involve physical force. It also includes situations where the victim cannot or does not consent to sexual activity (for example, due to intoxication or cognitive impairment). The nature of the physical contact involved in sexual assault may range from touching or fondling to vaginal, anal, or oral penetration (rape).

As a workplace, the military is an all-encompassing one, particularly during deployments such as those in service of OEF/OIF. Men and women work *and* live in the same environment with the same people for many months, often making it difficult to escape harassing behavior even when officially off duty. Compounding the problem, the strict hierarchy and chain of command can create ample opportunities for coercion. Many sexually harassing behaviors in the military look very similar to those occurring in a civilian context; however, in the military the consequences may be even more profound: not only may performance evaluations or promotions be at stake, but there may also be the possibility of receiving less hazardous duty assignments or ensuring that someone "has your back" during combat encounters.

One final term to be familiar with is "military sexual trauma," or MST, which is used by the Department of Veterans Affairs. While the official definition of MST is delineated in federal law, generally speaking this term refers to sexual assault and repeated, threatening experiences of sexual harassment during military service.

Prevalence

Unfortunately, data from several large-scale studies suggest that sexual harassment and assault are frequent events during military service, at least in peacetime. For example, a nationally representative sample of female and male reservists who were discharged prior to OEF/OIF (Street, Stafford, Mahan, & Hendricks, 2008) found that 60 percent of women and 27.2 percent of men had experienced repeated or severe sexual harassment at some point during their military service. In the sample as a whole, 13.1 percent of women and 1.6 percent of men reported being sexually assaulted at least once during their service. Little data exists on sexual harassment and assault among deployed military personnel, particularly among personnel deployed in support of OEF/OIF or other conflicts (Lipari, Cook, Rock, & Matos, 2008). Given key differences between these environments and those of non-deployed personnel, caution should be used in attempting to generalize from the peacetime rates just reviewed to deployed contexts. (For a more detailed discussion of these issues, please see Street, Kimerling, Bell, & Pavao, in press.)

Regardless, although a range of studies have documented that rates of sexual trauma in the military are higher among women, the disproportionate ratio of men to women in the military means that there are considerable numbers of both men and women who report having had these experiences (Kimerling, Gima, Smith, et al., 2007). It is thus important to remember that while many practitioners think of sexual trauma survivors as being female, clinicians working with military personnel will almost certainly encounter male survivors as well.

Impact

As with other forms of trauma, most survivors of sexual harassment or sexual assault in the military will experience mental health and other difficulties in the immediate aftermath of their experiences. Although many individuals will recover on their own within a few months without needing clinical intervention, others may continue to struggle even years afterwards. The particular toxicity of sexual trauma is well-documented among both treatment-seeking and non treatment-seeking samples (Kessler et al., 1995; Kilpatrick et al., 1997; Kimerling et al., 2007; Suris & Lind, 2008; Ullman & Brecklin, 2003; Vogt et al., 2005) with sexual assault being, for example, more likely to lead to symptoms of posttraumatic stress disorder (PTSD) than most other types of trauma, including combat (Kang, Dalager, Mahan, & Ishii, 2005; Kessler et al., 1995). Readers with less background in this area are urged to consult Street, Kimerling, Bell, & Pavao (in press) and Street, Bell, & Ready (in press) for more information about the health and psychosocial consequences of sexual trauma. However, in brief, along with PTSD, sexual trauma survivors often experience problems including depression, substance abuse, dissociative disorders, eating disorders, personality disorders and physical health problems (Frayne, Skinner, Sullivan, et al., 1999; Hall, 2007; Kimerling et al., 2007; van Berlo & Ensink, 2000; Vogt et al., 2005). They may also experience disruptions in important relationships, have difficulties trusting themselves or others, have difficulty identifying and setting appropriate interpersonal boundaries, and express concerns about sexual functioning and sexuality (Hall, 2007; van Berlo & Ensink, 2000).

It is important to remember, though, that different sexual trauma survivors may have very different reactions to their experiences. Gender, race/ethnicity, religion, sexual orientation, socioeconomic status, and lifetime trauma history are some factors that may have a powerful impact on a survivor's presentation. For example, although the reactions men and women have to sexual trauma are similar in some ways, gender norms for help-seeking and expression of distress can often lead men and women to present differently and to struggle with somewhat different issues. For example, few men believe they are vulnerable to sexual assault, making it that much more confusing for them to experience sexual trauma. This may lead them to question their masculinity or sexual orientation. For women, sexual trauma may strengthen preexisting concerns about safety, especially in environments dominated by men. Women Veterans in particular may also struggle to reconcile victimization with the toughness they had to exhibit as women in the military.

In general, however, there is empirical evidence to suggest that sexual trauma in military settings may be even more strongly associated with negative mental health consequences than sexual trauma in other contexts (Himmelfarb, Yaeger, & Mintz, 2006). In our clinical experience, there are also ways in which some of the aftereffects common among sexual trauma survivors in general may be heightened, take on different meaning, or manifest themselves somewhat differently among Veterans who are survivors of sexual trauma in the military. For example, given the emphasis on toughness and self-sufficiency in military training, it can be very hard for many Veteran survivors to acknowledge that their experiences of sexual trauma in the military had a powerful impact upon them. This may lead them to minimize and/or present with a particularly strong sense of self-blame about their current difficulties, as well as about having "allowed" themselves to be sexually harassed or assaulted in the first place. Although clinicians may also encounter this dynamic in working with civilian sexual trauma survivors, this sense of disbelief about, or reluctance to admit, the impact of their experiences seems to be particularly strong and intractable for many Veterans. Veteran survivors often also evidence noticeable difficulties in monitoring or identifying their emotions, which can complicate both Veteran and clinician attempts to make sense of what might be underlying certain reactions or behaviors. In addition, although many sexual trauma survivors struggle with issues related to power and control, survivors of sexual trauma in the military seem particularly likely to have difficulties with hierarchies, systems, and institutions, as well as with interpersonal interactions in which one person has power over another, such as employee–employer or client–healthcare provider relationships.

Few research studies address potential explanations for these differences between survivors of sexual trauma in civilian and military contexts, but examining the actual experience of sexual trauma in the military provides some insight into them—as we do next. Throughout, we provide case vignettes to illustrate how survivors might talk about their experiences.

Factors Affecting Impact

Military Environment and Ongoing Contact with Perpetrator

> I felt like there was no escape. Everywhere I went, I saw him or his friends and every time it would bring it all back. They'd taunt me when they saw me, say horrible things about how I'd gotten what I deserved. I tried to create little pockets of safety—at work, I'd always make sure to have my back to the wall and to lock the entrance door—but there was nowhere that really felt safe to me. I started carrying a knife everywhere I went and even now I still sleep with my gun under my pillow.

Particularly when deployed, military personnel may have few boundaries between "work life" and "home life," and in both spheres find themselves interacting almost exclusively with the same small group of individuals. As perpetrators are frequently other military personnel, this often creates a situation where the victim must continue to live, work, and socialize with his or her assailant. This can leave victims feeling trapped and helpless and, not surprisingly, increase their psychological distress. Ongoing exposure to the perpetrator can also leave them at risk of additional experiences of sexual harassment or assault or revictimization in other forms. For example, in cases where perpetrators are in a position to influence performance evaluations or promotion decisions victims may find themselves in the difficult position of "consenting" to sexual experiences or risking consequences to their career. In other cases, perpetrators with influence over work assignments may threaten to detail a victim to dangerous patrols or hazardous work environments, meaning a victim's physical safety may also be at stake.

Given the chronic stress, profound sense of powerlessness, and realistic fear associated with living in this type of environment, it is not surprising that sexual trauma in the military is associated with the host of health conditions and psychosocial difficulties outlined earlier. Although individuals vary in their responses, this type of environment has many parallels with environments of childhood abuse and can similarly be associated with some more pervasive deficits in functioning, such as extreme emotional lability and significant issues with interpersonal boundaries, particularly among survivors with a pre-military trauma history (Briere, Kaltman, & Green, 2008; Fergusson, Boden, & Horwood, 2008; Ullman, Filipas, Townsend, & Starzynski, 2007). This may account in part for the empirical findings referred to earlier suggesting an even stronger association between sexual trauma in military settings and negative mental health consequences than for sexual trauma in other contexts (Himmelfarb et al., 2006).

Military Culture and Values

> *I just feel like I'm going crazy, getting angry, getting scared, wanting to take off running at the drop of a hat. I don't know what's going on, why I'm acting like this. I don't even feel like a real man anymore. I'm so mad at myself for not fighting back harder. I mean, I must have appeared weak or not been "man enough" then and led him on somehow, why else would this have happened?*

Another reason that sexual harassment and assault in the military may be particularly damaging relative to civilian sexual trauma is the dissonance between these experiences and core values promoted by the military. For example, in the military tremendous value is placed upon loyalty, teamwork, and functioning as a cohesive group with a shared mission. Combat situations such as those encountered by many OEF/OIF Veterans may make these values even more salient given the many sacrifices, significant life threat, and urgent need to rely on fellow "soldiers in arms" involved. With this worldview a key operating principle out of both training and necessity, victimization from a fellow service member is made that much more incomprehensible and difficult to resolve. In working with survivors, clinicians will frequently encounter Veterans who struggle profoundly with feelings of self-blame, finding it easier to believe that they may have done something to provoke an attack than to conceive of betrayal at the hands of such a trusted other. Similarly, clinicians may find it takes longer to establish a working alliance with Veteran survivors (see section on Relationship and Process) after being victimized by someone considered a trusted ally, it may be exceedingly difficult for survivors to trust others, even after an individual has repeatedly shown him or herself to be relatively trustworthy.

Another set of values particular to the military context that can complicate survivors' recovery are those related to strength and self-sufficiency. Military culture prioritizes being strong, tough, and physically powerful, and these attributes can become idealized by many military personnel and/or deeply embedded in their self-identity. This may be particularly true for women, given the challenges to and doubts about their toughness they may have encountered as women in the military. Victimization, which involves a sense of being weak, vulnerable, and unable to defend oneself, may be extremely difficult to reconcile with this idealized identity or view of oneself. As a result, some survivors of sexual trauma in the military may be extremely reluctant to acknowledge the impact of their experiences. This reluctance is typically accompanied by strong feelings of blame for what happened, for not having been "strong" enough to prevent the experiences in the first place and for being "weak" to let the experiences continue to affect them. Finding an important piece of their self-identity shattered, some individuals may feel completely defeated and become excessively passive and unassertive. In contrast, some individuals, particularly men, may engage in hypermasculine behavior such as being aggressive, drinking excessively, and engaging in reckless sexual behavior. This may be particularly true for a man whose perpetrator(s) were male, in that he may worry that he may have somehow wanted the experiences to occur or that they indicate he is gay. This hypermasculine behavior may also be driven by concerns that he was singled out because he was perceived to be gay or effeminate, or if "out" (to the extent possible under current military policy), for actually being gay.

Finally, military training places a heavy emphasis on suppressing physical and emotional needs and on disregarding internal experiences and messages. This focus on the external world is often a necessity for survival and endurance in combat settings, but can be less adaptive when survivors return home and begin trying to sort through their emotional reactions to their experiences. In terms of what professionals may see clinically, Veterans may present with noticeable difficulty in tolerating distress, with this manifesting itself in physical agitation, impulsivity, angry outbursts, or other behaviors. This may simply be due to lack of practice in experiencing emotions (i.e., impoverished skills) but is undoubtedly complicated by the intense emotional reactions and general emotional dys-regulation (i.e., genuinely overwhelming and out of control feelings) they may be experiencing as a result of their traumatic experiences. Being disconnected from their internal experiences, Veterans may be bewildered by some of their behavior and even with assistance, struggle to identify how what they are thinking or feeling may be contributing to their reactions.

Limited Social Support

> I felt so alone. He threatened to hurt me if I told anyone about what had happened and I believed him. How could he not find out in such a small unit? Plus, what am I going to do—say something, cause problems, and distract from what we're here in Afghanistan to do? Even now that I'm home, I still feel all alone—who can I tell? People don't know what to say and they don't want to hear about it. Part of me tells myself it's not a big deal, anyway; the guys serving in combat, now they're the ones who really deserve the help. But then I get so incredibly angry—at him, at me, at the military and the government. No one understands.

The availability of social support is the most consistent and best predictor of recovery after traumatic experiences (Bliese, 2006; Flannery, 1990; Griffith & Vaitkus, 1999). It is thus crucial to recognize the ways in which limited social support both at the time of the trauma and in the months and years afterwards may increase sexual trauma survivors' risk for subsequent health and psychosocial problems. Aspects of the military environment, culture, and values just described are among the factors contributing to limited support. For example, survivors may tell themselves to be tough and "soldier on," rejecting any suggestion that they might benefit from support from others. They may also remain silent because of concerns about unit cohesion and fears of being ostracized for speaking out about a peer.

Aware of the significance of this issue, the Department of Defense's (DoD) Sexual Assault Prevention & Response Office has established victim advocacy programs that provide support and information to sexual assault survivors and has conducted awareness campaigns specifically tailored to the military context and values (Department of Defense, 2009). Recent DoD policy reforms have similarly targeted this issue by seeking to increase survivors' ability to access healthcare and treatment without having to initiate a criminal investigation. The support available and general climate for OEF/OIF sexual trauma survivors is thus markedly different from those of survivors in previous eras. That said, some survivors may feel there is a code of silence around these issues. They may choose not to report their victimization experiences or not to seek help because they believe that nothing will be done or that they will experience repercussions for speaking up (Pershing, 2003).

Perceptions aside, objective limitations to support may genuinely exist as well. For example, OEF/OIF survivors who are deployed are typically far from family and friends who might otherwise provide support. Even at homecoming, social support may continue to be limited as sexual trauma survivors may believe, or be told by others, that their traumatic experiences and associated mental health struggles are not as "legitimate" as those secondary to experiences of combat. Veteran sexual trauma survivors may also be reluctant to disclose their experiences to loved ones due to intense feelings of shame and an attendant desire for secrecy, and as a result end up foregoing the support friends and family might be able to provide. They may similarly be disinclined to seek help from treatment and benefit programs targeted at returning Veterans because of a belief, accurate or inaccurate, that these programs will not recognize or address their specific needs (Murdoch, Hodges, Hunt, et al., 2003).

Developmental Issues

> I think maybe I misunderstood things and they were just flirting. The guys are always joking around ... It didn't feel right when he put his hands on my hips but still, it's not like he hurt me or anything. And I'm sure he was just kidding about some of the things he said about me, just treating me like one of the guys. I just think I'm hypersensitive around others, I never really feel like I know what to do or how to fit in.

Another significant contributor to the particular toxicity of sexual trauma occurring in military contexts is that survivors are often relatively young at the time of their experiences. This creates complexities for several reasons. First, sexual harassment and assault are interpersonal traumas—perpetrated by another human being, often by a close friend or intimate partner—that involve a profound violation of boundaries and personal integrity. Particularly for individuals that are young, these types of experiences send confusing messages about what is acceptable and expected behavior from a trusted other, what rights and needs people have in relationships, and what is "theirs" versus publicly accessible. Confusion about boundaries may be further exacerbated by the military context where individual needs are often secondary to those of the larger unit.

As such, sexual trauma often has significant implications for survivors' subsequent relationships and understanding of themselves, and thus their functioning on a daily basis. Second, many survivors (regardless of age) find their prior ways of managing distress inadequate when faced with the intense emotions and other reactions associated with experiencing trauma. This is particularly likely to be true for survivors who are young adults in their late teens or early 20s, or those who are survivors of childhood experiences of abuse or other trauma, as they often do not have a fully developed repertoire of coping strategies. Without effective strategies for maintaining internal homeostasis, these individuals are especially vulnerable to developing mental health and other subsequent difficulties. They may also find themselves drawing on less developmentally advanced coping strategies such as dissociation, behavioral acting out, cutting or other forms of self-harm, which can themselves further impair functioning and health.

Interaction with Other Experiences of Trauma

> *It's just the way life is, you know? Bad thing after bad thing. The military was supposed to be my escape. I mean, sure, I knew I might go to Iraq or Afghanistan but who knew I was going to get raped? It makes it hard to believe in anything. I just keep waiting for the other shoe to drop—because it will, eventually.*

Finally, studies of both treatment-seeking and non treatment-seeking samples have found high rates of childhood and pre-military trauma among individuals who enter the military, with these experiences being particularly prevalent amongst those who go on to experience sexual trauma in the military (Rosen & Martin, 1996; Sadler, Booth, Cook, & Doebbeling, 2003). Individuals deployed as part of OEF/OIF who experience sexual harassment and assault may also have had concurrent exposure to combat; even those Veterans not directly exposed to extensive combat trauma during deployment were likely confronted with the generalized decreased sense of safety that accompanies deployment to a warzone. This is salient because evidence from civilian samples indicates that exposure to multiple types of trauma increases the risk of negative mental health outcomes (Cloitre, Scarvalone, & Difede, 1997; Follette, Polusny, Bechtle, & Naugle, 1996), and studies of OEF/OIF Veterans have shown that prior exposure to sexual or physical assault increases the risk of mental health problems following combat exposure (Smith, Wingard, Ryan, et al., 2008). There are a variety of potential explanatory mechanisms for these findings but, in general, the effects of trauma appear to be dose-specific, suggesting that Veterans with pre-military trauma histories and/or with experiences of both combat and sexual trauma during deployment are likely to be at particular risk of readjustment difficulties and/or more chronic, complex problems (Vogt, King, & King, 2007).

Providing Care

In this section, we focus on translating the information just discussed into general principles to assist clinicians in their work with sexual trauma survivors.

Screening and Assessment

Given the significant numbers of both women and men who have experienced sexual trauma in the military and the serious health and psychosocial impact of these experiences, providers should always consider whether sexual trauma may be playing a role in a Veteran's presentation. If it is appropriate to the setting and the provider role, questions about sexual trauma (military or otherwise) should be included as part of all intake interviews, as survivors will rarely disclose their experiences unless asked directly (Crowell & Burgess, 1996; Fisher, Daigle, Cullen, & Turner, 2003). Readers looking for more information about how to screen for sexual trauma and/or related assessment issues are urged to consult Street, Bell, & Ready (in press). In brief, however, questions about sexual trauma are often most smoothly introduced in the context of asking about a Veteran's developmental or military history; sample language is presented in Table 5.1 or can be drawn from standardized self-report questionnaires such as the Sexual Experiences Survey (Koss, Gidyez, & Wisniewski, 1987). Given the potential sensitivity of the topic, it is crucial for providers to establish an environment that is conducive to disclosure and to respond to disclosures in an empathic, supportive manner. Strategies for doing so are also presented in Table 5.1.

TABLE 5.1 Screening for sexual harassment and assault

Steps	Key elements	Example
Establish a comfortable climate for disclosure	Conveying comfort with the topic and your sense that this is an important issue	Private setting without interruptions; non-judgmental stance; unhurried speech; good eye contact
Provide a rationale for asking	Normalizing the topic	*"Many of the Veterans I've worked with have had upsetting experiences in their lives that may still bother them today."*
Ask the question	Use of behaviorally-based language that avoids jargon (e.g., rape, sexual assault) and negative phrasing (e.g., "nothing like that has ever happened to you, right?")	*"During your deployment or at any other time in your life, did you experience any unwanted sexual attention?"* *"During your military service or at any other time in your life, were you ever forced or pressured into having sex? Did someone ever threaten you in order to have sex with you when you did not want to?"*
Respond to disclosure	Provision of support	Validation and empathy: *"I'm sorry this happened to you while you were serving our country but I'm glad you felt you could tell me about it today."* Education and normalization: *"Many Veterans have had experiences like yours and for some it can continue to affect them even many years later. It's important to know that people can and do recover, though."*

Steps	Key elements	Example
Ask essential follow-up questions	Assessment of current impact	Assess current difficulties: *"How much does [use survivor's words about experiences] continue to affect your daily life today? In what ways?"* Assess social support: *"Have you ever been able to talk with anyone about this before? How did they respond?"* Assess coping strategies: *"How do you deal with [use survivor's words about current difficulties] when it happens? Does that help? What happens next?"* Implications for care: *"How do you think this might affect our work together?"*
As appropriate, conduct or refer for more comprehensive assessment	Gathering of information about the experiences and their impact, the Veteran's current functioning, and implications for care	*"It sounds like this experience continues to affect you a great deal today, which is understandable. It makes me think that it would be good for me to have a better understanding of how this fits into your life. Would it be okay to spend a bit more time talking about how it has affected you?"* *"We should definitely think about whether there are things we need to do to address this in our work together. I'm also thinking that it might be useful for you to speak to someone with particular expertise in these issues. She or he might have thoughts about other services that might be helpful or things that we should consider in our own work."*

At a minimum, disclosures should lead the provider to ask follow-up questions about the extent to which the sexual trauma continues to impact the Veteran's current functioning, the extent to which he/she has access to sources of support, and his/her typical coping strategies. It can also be useful for providers to ask survivors how they think their experiences may affect or show up in their work together. If a Veteran reports currently having significant difficulties secondary to his/her sexually traumatic experiences, providers may also wish to conduct—or refer the Veteran for—a more thorough psychosocial assessment. Street, Bell, and Ready (in press) describe some of the areas that should be reviewed during this assessment.

Throughout the screening and assessment process, however, clinicians should carefully balance the need for detailed information with respect for the Veteran's willingness and readiness to disclose at that point in time. In these conversations, it is important to be explicit about wanting to respect the Veteran's boundaries yet also wanting to ensure he/she knows it is okay to talk about difficult and upsetting topics, or topics the Veteran may feel are shameful during their work together. Statements to this effect will help prevent the survivor from attributing the curtailed discussion to clinician lack of interest, reticence about the topic, or negative reactions to the disclosure.

Evaluating the Need for Referral and/or Consultation

Not all sexual trauma survivors will want or need specialized or in-depth psychotherapeutic treatment; but in this area, as in all others, providers need to be aware of the limits of their competency and be prepared to refer out and/or seek consultation when necessary. This is particularly true when a Veteran exhibits pervasive interpersonal deficits, experiences profound emotional lability, or engages in significant self-harm behavior. It can be helpful to make connections with your nearest VA Medical Center (www.va.gov) or community-based Vet Center (www.vetc.enter.va.gov) to learn about expertise and services available locally through the VA or elsewhere. As noted earlier, the VA provides free care for all mental and physical health conditions related to military sexual trauma; Veterans do not need a VA disability rating or proof that the sexual trauma occurred, and this free care is potentially available even to Veterans not eligible for other VA care. Some survivors may be reluctant to seek services through VA due to it being a government agency and/or its perceived ties to the Department of Defense. However, exploring VA resources should be considered as an option— as Veterans, these individuals made sacrifices to serve their country and they deserve to take advantage of the benefits available to them for having done so. Although VA is by no means the only place Veterans can make connections with other Veterans, settings and treatment options that involve contact with other Veterans and even other Veteran sexual trauma survivors can help address some survivors' sense of being alone in their experiences of recovery and homecoming. Even if Veterans are not interested in treatment, it may be helpful to explore disability, educational, or other VA benefits that may help them pursue goals meaningful to them.

Case Conceptualization

Damon often oscillates between being very aggressive and angry and being overly passive. He's given up trying to hold down a job after getting fired numerous times for arguing with his supervisors. He has some ongoing conflict with his neighbors over trivial matters which has several times erupted into physical confrontations.

His "road rage" reactions can be extreme. Yet, he often fails to stand up for himself in interpersonal relationships and is at the beck and call of a girlfriend who treats him very poorly. He's indecisive when confronted with even minor decisions and has even avoided taking action on important financial matters that have left his ownership of his home in jeopardy. He recently began drinking heavily, which has further complicated his situation. During his intake interview, the clinician wonders whether these seemingly incompatible behaviors indicate that Damon is struggling to reconcile a sense of helplessness secondary to being sexually assaulted with societal beliefs about what it means to be a man. Or, whether his questions about some decisions he made at the time of the assault—including the sense that he should have "fought back harder"—might underlie his current hypersensitivity to threat and strong self-doubt. With these hypotheses in mind, she plans to explore with him in future sessions what might be driving these behaviors.

Regardless of a clinician's particular role with a Veteran survivor, there are certain themes that are likely to arise during the course of their work together. Some themes flow very clearly from the factors reviewed earlier in the section on "Factors Affecting Impact," such as difficulties with trust, concerns about being seen as weak, or confusion about identity or relationships. Others may seem more difficult to understand.

In thinking about confusing themes and behaviors, one useful frame to consider is that, by definition, traumas present a challenge to our view of ourselves, others, and the world. In the aftermath of such severe disruptions, normal coping strategies may prove inadequate, leaving survivors uncertain about how to meet basic needs for safety, connection with others, and a sense of control. From this perspective, symptoms and extreme behaviors can be conceptualized as a form of self-protection and of coping—an attempt to manage the unmanageable, to establish safety in what has been proven to be an unsafe world, and to find stability in the midst of emotional dysregulation and cognitive confusion.

It is also important to realize that survivors face a number of double binds during the process of recovery. Some of these binds have been alluded to earlier, such as whether to trust others when you know that even the most trustworthy-seeming others may prove untrustworthy, whether to trust yourself when you know the consequences of being wrong, whether to form relationships and meet your needs for connection and affiliation when you know how profoundly others could hurt you, and whether in general to prioritize safety or freedom, among others. Survivors of sexual trauma in the military face the additional task of reconciling what are often conflicting feelings about their military service, particularly if they continue to believe in the ideals that led them to enlist in the first place.

Interpreting behavior through this lens can assist providers in understanding some of the dilemmas facing survivors even in what appear to be the simplest of choices. The stance clinicians adopt in these conversations is important, not assuming that they know (or that there exists) a "right" answer or even that they know what the worst part of a survivor's experience was (or is). Sorting through these complexities is a key, albeit often painful, part of the recovery process and one that survivors must ultimately resolve for themselves.

Relationship and Process

Several months into some case management work, Julie begins arriving late to appointments and suddenly begins asking questions about her provider's (Martha) personal life; Martha also feels that it has become more difficult to keep their sessions focused on the work at hand. Reflecting back, Martha remembers that this shift began shortly after Julie presented with some time-sensitive housing needs. At the time, Martha felt the need to be more directive in session in order to address all of Julie's concerns. Although Julie's case management needs have now returned to baseline, Martha realizes she has nonetheless remained relatively directive during their meetings. When she checks in with Julie about how she is feeling about their work, Julie initially says she feels things are going okay. Martha responds, "I'm glad to hear that; I've wondered if something was going on for you, because I've noticed you've arrived late a few times and haven't always seemed interested in focusing on your case management needs when we meet. I realized that ever since you received that eviction notice about a month ago, I've been feeling more pressured to make movement on some of these issues and that perhaps I've been more controlling of our sessions than usual. How has that felt for you?" Julie admits that she has been feeling a bit "lost" in their sessions, feeling like the emphasis is on her housing needs without much attention to how she is dealing emotionally with the stresses of moving. Together they develop a plan to spend the first five minutes of each session setting priorities for their time together, and to make sure to spend some time each session talking about how Julie is doing. Based on this conversation, Martha hypothesizes that when Julie is feeling controlled or helpless, she may have a tendency to "push back," resisting direction from others and attempting to cross interpersonal boundaries. Martha makes note of this, both to assist in negotiating future interactions and also as an observation she may want to share with Julie in the future, highlighting how this is an understandable reaction given her sexual trauma history. Regardless, she plans to check in with Julie during their next session to hear her reaction to today's conversation.

As noted earlier, sexual assault is an interpersonal trauma. Regardless of a provider's role, his/her relationship with the survivor thus invariably not only involves complexities, but also offers the potential for therapeutic, healing encounters. For this reason, it is important not only to pay close attention to the working alliance initially, but also to continue to monitor it over time. One helpful strategy can be for the provider to acknowledge at the outset that it may take time for the survivor to feel safe in the relationship. This conveys the provider's interest in the Veteran's perspective and his/her readiness to discuss difficult topics; both important elements in establishing a strong working alliance.

Finding ways to make the provider-survivor relationship itself a component of care, not just a foundation for it, is also important. For example, as noted in the previous section, many symptoms exhibited by survivors may be attempts to regain a sense of control that has been lost. As such, finding ways to structure the therapeutic relationship to promote a sense of control for survivors—such as by having a collaborative discussion at the beginning of sessions about agenda items for the day—can provide a powerful counterbalance to feelings of powerlessness and helplessness they may be feeling in life more generally. These experiences may not only help Veterans restore some sense of control over daily life but, in modeling power-sharing and positive regard in interpersonal relationships, they stand in stark contrast to Veterans' experiences of sexual trauma. As such, they may be profoundly reparative experiences for survivors.

That said, using the therapeutic relationship to model respect for inter-personal boundaries does not mean surrendering one's own thoughts or expertise. While accepting a survivor's choices, clinicians can still share their own perspective on the situation, explore the thinking and processes leading up to the survivor's decisions, and provide additional insight and psychoeducation about the role some behaviors play in maintaining symptoms. Helping Veterans understand some of the functions their behaviors serve, and providing validation of the underlying emotional experience while exploring whether there are alternative ways to meet these needs, can send a powerful message about the survivor's ability to exercise control over many aspects of their internal and external experiences.

With regard to interpersonal boundaries in the patient–provider relationship more generally, it is important to note that the power differential between patients and providers can intensify the significance of boundary crossings—even those meant to be helpful—that occur in therapy. Some accommodations or deviations from routine care may be entirely appropriate, such as honoring a request for a provider of a given gender or agreeing to a brief phone check-in between sessions. However, when a provider finds him or herself repeatedly making exceptions to standard practice, when "going the extra mile" begins to put strain on the provider or on the patient–provider relationship, or when being responsive to requests seems to only result in continued (or intensified) patient distress, the accommodations have likely become problematic. When—or better yet, before—this happens, it is important for clinicians to gently set limits. Doing so in a way that validates the patient's feelings and is transparent about the clinician's reasoning for acting in certain ways or setting certain boundaries, is essential in preventing survivors from feeling shamed or punished.

Impact on the Clinician

Although rewarding, providing clinical care to survivors of any form of trauma can be very challenging, not only in terms of the skill and sensitivity it requires, but also in terms of the emotional impact it can have on providers themselves. Working with survivors of sexual trauma can, in some ways, be even more complex. Most healthcare providers will at least give lip service to the importance of personal self-care, even if many in reality find themselves in the position of saying, "Do as I say, but not as I do." This is problematic given the emotional demands involved in working with trauma survivors and given that our strengths as providers—our empathy, ability to care genuinely about others, and capacity to go to difficult places emotionally—are what leave us vulnerable to depletion. In session, the ability to be present and see events through survivors' eyes, yet also remain grounded and outside the confusion of the emotional storm, is crucial to providing optimal care, but can also be emotionally draining. This is true regardless of how rewarding the work itself might be. Finding ways in our life to remain grounded in what is meaningful, gratifying, and enjoyable to us is important in that it allows us to maintain the emotional stamina, empathy, and perspective underpinning good clinical care. Recovery can often be a long-term process and may involve many stops and starts, sharp turns, and unexpected detours along the way. Remaining attentive to your emotional and physical reactions both in and out of session, and consistently engaging in replenishing self-care activities, will help ensure your continued ability to remain emotionally engaged over the long haul.

Final Thoughts

Working with survivors of sexual trauma can unquestionably be complex, and healthcare professionals should continuously monitor whether they have the specialized training to work effectively with Veteran sexual trauma survivors in certain roles and on certain content areas. That said, it is at times only in the context of an established relationship that survivors feel comfortable disclosing their experiences of sexual harassment and assault, meaning that even providers without specialized training may sometimes find themselves confronting some of the issues raised in this chapter. Similarly, survivors of sexual harassment and assault in the military, like other patients, may present with a range of difficulties (both related and not related to their experiences of sexual trauma) and, like other patients, may benefit from assistance and services addressing a variety of areas. For these and other reasons, it is important for all providers working with Veterans to have at least some basic working knowledge of issues related to sexual trauma in the military.

Underscoring this point, we feel it is important to state that many of us view our work with Veterans as a small way to honor the sacrifices they have made on our behalf and in the service of this country. Remaining sensitive to the range of issues that may be of concern to them—among them, sexual harassment and assault—so that we can optimally assist in their recovery is a powerful way to begin to repay the tremendous debt they are owed.

Authors' Note

The material and opinions presented here do not necessarily reflect the official position or policy of the Department of Veterans Affairs. We gratefully acknowledge the VA Boston and National Center for PTSD resources that supported this work.

References

APA (American Psychiatric Association) (1994). *Diagnostic and Statistical Manual of Mental Disorders* (4th Ed.). Washington, DC: Joan Beder.

Bliese, P. (2006). Social climates: Drivers of soldier well-being and resilience. In A.B. Adler, C.A. Castro, & T.W. Britt (Eds.), *Military Life: The psychology of serving in peace and combat: Operational stress, Vol. 2* (pp. 213–234). Westport: Praeger Security Intl.

Briere, J., Kaltman, S., & Green, B.L. (2008). Accumulated childhood trauma and symptom complexity. *Journal of Traumatic Stress*, 21(2), 223–226.

Cloitre, M., Scarvalone, P., & Difede, J.A. (1997). Posttraumatic stress disorder, self- and interpersonal dysfunction among sexually retraumatized women. *Journal of Traumatic Stress*, 10(3), 437–452.

Crowell, N.A. & Burgess, A.W. (1996). *Understanding Violence Against Women.* Washington, DC, National Academy Press.

Department of Defense (2009). Fiscal Year 2009 Annual Report on Sexual Assault in the Military. Retrieved February 8, 2012 from http://www.sapr.mil/media/pdf/reports/fy09_annual_report.pdf

EEOC (1990). *Policy Guidance on Current Issues of Sexual Harassment.* Retrieved April 13, 2006, from: http://www.eeoc.gov

Fergusson, D.M., Boden, J.M., & Horwood, L.J. (2008). Exposure to child sexual and physical abuse and adjustment in early adulthood. *Childhood Abuse & Neglect*, 32(6), 607–619.

Fisher, B., Daigle, L.E., Cullen, F.T., & Turner, M.G. (2003). Reporting sexual victimization to the police and others: Results from a national-level study of college women. *Criminal Justice and Behavior*, 30(1), 6–38.

Flannery, R.B. (1990). Social support and psychological trauma: A methodological review. *Journal of Traumatic Stress*, 3(4), 593–611.

Follette, V.M., Polusny, M.A., Bechtle, A.E., & Naugle, A.E. (1996). Cumulative trauma: The impact of child sexual abuse, adult sexual assault, and spouse abuse. *Journal of Traumatic Stress*, 9(1), 25–35.

Frayne, S.M., Skinner, K., Sullivan, L., Tripp, T., Hankin, C., Kressin, N., & Miller, D. (1999). Medical profile of women VA outpatients who report a history of sexual assault while in the military. *Women's Health*, 8(6), 835–845.

Griffith, J. & Vaitkus, M. (1999). Relating cohesion to stress, strain, disintegration, and performance: An organizing framework. *Military Psychology*, 11(1), 27–55.

Hall, K. (2007). Sexual dysfunction and childhood sexual abuse: Gender differences and treatment implications. In S.R. Leiblum (Ed.), *Principles and Practice of Sex Therapy* (4th Ed., pp. 350–378). New York: Guilford Press.

Himmelfarb, N., Yaeger, D., & Mintz, J. (2006). Posttraumatic stress disorder in female Veterans with military and civilian sexual trauma. *Journal of Traumatic Stress*, 19(6), 837–846.

Kang, H., Dalager, N., Mahan, C., & Ishii, E. (2005). The role of sexual assault on the risk of PTSD among Gulf War Veterans. *Annals of Epidemiology*, 15(3), 191–195.

Kessler, R.C., Sonnega, A., Bromet, E., Hughes, M., & Nelson, C.B. (1995). Posttraumatic stress disorder in the National Comorbidity Survey. *Archive of General Psychiatry*, 52, 1048–1060.

Kilpatrick, D.G., Acierno, R., Resnick, H.S., Saunders, B.E., & Best, C.L. (1997). A 2-year longitudinal analysis of the relationships between violent assault and substance use in women. *Journal of Consulting and Clinical Psychology*, 65(5), 834–847.

Kimerling, R., Gima, K., Smith, M.W., Street, A. & Frayne, S. (2007). The Veterans Health Administration and military sexual trauma. *American Journal of Public Health*, 97(12), 2160–2166.

Koss, M.P., Gidyez, C.A., & Wisniewski, N. (1987). The scope of rape: Incidence and prevalence of sexual aggression and victimization in a national sample of higher education students. *Journal of Consulting and Clinical Psychology*, 55(2), 162–170.

Lipari, R.N., Cook, P.J., Rock, L.M., & Matos, K. (2008). *2006 Gender Relations Survey of Active Duty Members*. Arlington, VA: Department of Defense Manpower Data Center.

Murdoch, M., Hodges, J., Hunt, C., Cowper, D., Kressin, N., & O'Brien, N. (2003). Gender differences in service connection for PTSD. *Medical Care*, 41(8), 950–961.

Pershing, J.L. (2003). Why women don't report sexual harassment: A case study of an elite military institution. *Gender Issues*, 21(4), 3–30.

Rosen, L.N. & Martin, L. (1996). The measurement of childhood trauma among male and female soldiers in the U.S. army. *Military Medicine*, 161(6), 342–345.

Sadler, A.G., Booth, B.M., Cook, B.L., & Doebbeling, B.N. (2003). Factors associated with women's risk of rape in the military environment. *American Journal of Industrial Medicine*, 43(3), 262–273.

Smith, T.C., Wingard, D.L., Ryan, M.A., Kritz-Silverstein, D., Slymen, D.J., & Sallis, J.F. (2008). Prior assault and posttraumatic stress disorder after combat deployment. *Epidemiology*, 19(3), 505–512.

Street, A.E., Bell, M., & Ready, C.E. (in press). Sexual assault. In D. Benedek & G. Wynn (Eds.), *Clinical Manual for the Management of PTSD*. Arlington, VA: American Psychiatric Press, Inc.

Street, A.E., Kimerling, R., Bell, M.E., & Pavao, J. (in press). Sexual harassment and sexual assault during military service. In J. Ruzek, P. Schnurr, M. Friedman, & J. Vasterling (Eds.), *Veterans of the Global War on Terror*. Washington, DC: American Psychological Association Press.

Street, A., Stafford, J., Mahan, C., & Hendricks, A.M. (2008). Sexual harassment and assault experienced by reservists during military service: Prevalence and health correlates. *Journal of Rehabilitation Research & Development*, 45(3), 409–420.

Suris, A. & Lind, L. (2008). Military sexual trauma: A review of prevalence and associated health consequences in Veterans. *Trauma, Violence & Abuse*, 9(4), 250–269.

Ullman, S.E., Filipas, H.H., Townsend, S.M., & Starzynski, L.L. (2007). Psychosocial correlates of PTSD symptom severity in sexual assault survivors. *Journal of Traumatic Stress*, 20(5), 821–831.

Ullman, S. & Brecklin, L.R. (2003). Sexual assault history and health-related outcomes in a national sample of women. *Psychology of Women Quarterly*, 27, 117–130.

Van Berlo, W. & Ensink, B. (2000). Problems with sexuality after sexual assault. *Annual Review of Sex Research*, 11, 235–257.

Vogt, D.S., King, D.W., & King, L.A. (2007). Risk pathways for PTSD: Making sense of the literature. In M.J. Friedman, T.M. Keane, & P.A. Resick (Eds.), *Handbook of PTSD: Science and practice* (pp. 55–76). New York: Guilford Press.

Vogt, D., Pless, A.P., King, L.A., & King, D.W. (2005). Deployment stressors, gender, and mental health outcomes among Gulf War I Veterans. *Journal of Traumatic Stress*, 18(3), 272–284.

6

WHEN THEY RETURN FROM IRAQ/AFGHANISTAN

The Needs of the Wounded

Joan Beder and Helen Jones

Introduction

As of January, 2012, over 47,430 service members have been wounded in Iraq and Afghanistan. Over half of these wounded service members have been treated and will return to duty within 72 hours; others have not been physically able to return to duty and are sent to the United States for intensive and often prolonged medical care. Many of the casualties result from use of high-energy explosives (Improvised Explosive Devices—IEDs), which are detonated from afar and will blow up military vehicles or derail/overturn the vehicles, harming those within. These IEDs are loaded with shrapnel that cause injuries, often to the extremities. Unique to the history of war for Americans, 90 percent of soldiers wounded who are participating in Operation Enduring Freedom (OEF) and Operation Iraqi Freedom (OIF), and now Operation New Dawn, will survive their injury. This is due to advances in infection control, body armor and quick evacuation to the United States for care (Hyer, 2006). It is remarkable to note that the average time from battlefield to arrival and care in the United States is now less than four days; in Vietnam it was 45 days (Gawande, 2004). The progress in medical care of the wounded is extraordinary, however it means that more service members return home with grave injuries that can transform their lives. These injuries require extensive levels of care, with soldiers and Veterans needing treatment for many years after their initial injury (Savitsky, Illingworth, & DuLaney, 2009). (NB: Veterans are those in the military who are no longer active duty because of completing their tour of duty and not resigning, retirement, or medical retirement. Soldiers/service members are in the military and are still engaged in active duty.) Another way to understand the impact of these improvements is that for every military personnel killed in these wars, at least 16 wounded will return to the

United States (Frain, Bethel, & Bishop, 2010); this does not take into account the number of soldiers who return with major mental health diagnoses estimated at over 20 percent of our troops (Hoge, Auchterlonie, & Milliken, 2006; Seal, Bertenthal, Miner, et al., 2007). This huge influx of wounded has created a situation in which the traditional systems of care are taxed and the civilian sector has begun to become engaged in the care of those returning from OEF/OIF.

Rehabilitation of injured service members, unable to return to active duty, is geared to restoring patients to their highest level of functioning and takes place in a wide array of inpatient and outpatient facilities across the United States. Once the service member is medically stabilized, the Department of Defense (DoD) can elect to send those with traumatic brain injuries and other complex trauma to specialized centers for intense medical and rehabilitative care. These centers include Brooke Army Medical Center and the Walter Reed Army Medical Center in Washington, DC (Manske, 2006). In some cases transitioning Veterans to Veteran Administration hospitals and Polytrauma Rehabilitation Centers (for those with multiple injuries) is the desired venue for this level of care. While many soldiers who receive rehabilitation services will return to active duty, others who are more seriously injured will likely be discharged from their military obligations, receive financial support from the military based on their injuries, and return to civilian life with major disabilities and limitations which could require life-long medical follow-up (Bascetta, 2007).

Becoming Disabled

Service members returning from combat face a multiplicity of challenges in their personal and family relationships, and work situations. Those who are injured in war face the additional experience of having to integrate their war experience while healing from, and adapting to, their experience of injury (Uomoto & Williams, 2009). The consequences of these traumatic injuries can range from obvious impairments in physical functioning to permanent, life-altering changes for both the soldier and their family.

In the language of rehabilitation counseling, this form of injury—wounding as opposed to an on-going disease process—is considered an "acquired disabling condition" (Livneh & Antonak, 2005). The challenges involved in these disabling conditions are numerous and adaptation becomes the work of rehabilitation. The rehabilitation literature that was generated in the 1970s and 1980s, and that discussed adaptation, generally referred to a model of adaptation/acceptance that included stages: shock, denial, anxiety, anger, acceptance and some form of final adjustment. More recent conceptualizations place greater emphasis on the interaction between the individual and the environment and, more prominently, the family in which he/she lives as factors toward acceptance of disability (Bishop, 2005).

Wounding in war must always be considered traumatic. Some theorize that soldiers live in constant fear of being harmed: there is a defined reality to the possibility of wounding and death; many soldiers report having seen or been near another soldier who has been wounded or died in battle; soldiers are far from home and loved ones; and there is the ever present fear of a permanent and disabling injury. There are anticipated emotional reactions and stages—beyond the challenges that the injury provokes—that one who has been wounded will go through. These reactions are heightened when one is engaged in a war and far from home and has to, because of their injury, leave fellow soldiers with whom deep and abiding relationships have formed. Over and beyond the medical concerns, reactions of fear, heightened levels of stress, loss and grief over the lost body part and one's sense of self, there may be body image concerns that lead to feelings of anxiety and depression and cognitive distortions. In addition there is fear of stigma and societal discrimination, uncertainty and unpredictability, and overwhelming quality of life concerns. Typical emotional responses include shock, anxiety, denial, depression, anger/hostility that can lead to aggressive acts, and apprehension over adjustment issues for the self and family. Many of these reactions will span the time that the soldier is hospitalized for their injury and will permeate relationships with family. This overview of predictable reactions will alert the provider to the complexity of emotional responses typical of war related disability (Livneh & Antonak, 2005).

Coping with disability from war-related injury is nonlinear, unpredictable, and discontinuous. The process of adaptation to disability is essentially a process of self-organization that unfolds through experiences of emotional turmoil, and cognitive and behavioral reorganization. This leads to increased functionality and renewed stability (Livneh & Parker, 2005). While this sounds linear, as noted above, it is not; and there are frequent setbacks and upsets. For the disabled, the medical trajectory of hospitalizations includes surgery(ies), possible long-term therapies, pain, anguish, etc., and the road to adaptation may be marked by uncontrollable medical swings. While feeling as though things might be beginning to move in a more stable direction, a medical misfortune will upend growing feelings of acceptance and adaptation (Livneh & Parker, 2005). The role of the hospital and rehabilitation team—especially the social workers—is important for the wounded/disabled soldier. Their guidance and education toward acceptance of the disability, and toward case and family management while also helping them to deal with emotions resulting from the injury event itself almost simultaneously, is essential as is their support toward a new self-identity. These efforts help transcend the medical complexities while working toward family unification and redefinition.

Systems of Care

Injured soldiers may go through several different phases of treatment before they go home. When a soldier is injured, wounded, has a serious illness, or shows serious symptoms of a mental illness when deployed overseas, they will usually arrive at a military medical treatment facility connected to a military post. Depending on the severity of the illness, they may be triaged and admitted to an inpatient unit, or they may go directly to an outpatient program. There may be some transferring to another facility that has special treatment programs or because of a logistical issue.

While at any one of a number of transition units, soldiers progress through a plan of care. If the plan involves the soldier being returned to active duty, they will most likely transition back to their home unit. There may be exceptions. If the illness or injuries are so great that active duty is most likely not going to continue in the military, then the soldier will be working toward parallel goals of going through treatment and working through the medical retirement process. Retirement usually occurs 2-3 years after the injury/illness

Both DoD and VA social workers are involved in the care of these service members. In addition, civilian social workers in the community are, and increasingly will be, involved in the aftercare; often the long-term emotional and life-management needs will be addressed in the civilian sector while the acute, immediate emotional concerns and medical needs will be addressed by the VA/DoD medical staff.

Care for the severely wounded is managed through a variety of programs in the United States: each branch of the military has its own system of care, and the Veterans Administration works with polytrauma (refers to one who has multiple injuries that need care) centers across the United States. The polytrauma system is designed to address the specialized rehabilitation needs of polytrauma patients. Four regional polytrauma centers exist across the U.S.; they provide the most specialized level of rehabilitation care (Collins & Kennedy, 2008). Typically, a wounded service member is airlifted to the States and goes to a medical treatment facility. He/she may then be transferred to a polytrauma hospital or a specialized unit. The unit works toward helping the service member regain their well-being and return to active duty or to ease the eventual transition to civilian life and aftercare within the VA system. Within the Army, there are also ancillary programs; specifically the Army Wounded Warrior Program (AW2), which provides care to soldiers and their families. AW2 supports the most seriously wounded soldiers who have incurred their injuries since the 9/11 invasion of the United States. One of the roles of the AW2 is advocacy and benefit procurement for the service member and family (Hudak, Morrison, Carstensen, et al., 2009). The severely injured will often need coordinated follow-up with multiple disciplines after discharge from their military role. As such, service providers inside and outside the VA may be called upon to be involved in the continued care of the seriously injured, and to be available to address the multiplicity of needs of the family members (Friedmann-Sanchez, Sayers, & Pickett, 2008; Cozza, Guimond, McKibben, et al., 2010).

A typical scenario of a wounded service member might be the following: service member is injured in Afghanistan/Iraq. He/she is sent to Landstuhl,

Germany, and evacuated to a medical treatment facility. He/she is medically stabilized and spends several months in the hospital for a series of operations or whatever is needed to care for the individual. Family and others are engaged in the effort to emotionally stabilize the injured as well. Then comes outpatient care, rehabilitation, and possibly processing through the Military Medical Retirement Board which can lead to eventual discharge and follow-up with their local VA system. Upon discharge, arrangements are made for extended care and, perhaps, the more difficult chapter begins in the life of the Veteran and their family. This was the case for Roy ...

> *Roy served three deployments to Iraq and Afghanistan (and perhaps other deployments to locations that were not combat zones). His job was as an infantryman and he had reached the rank of Staff Sergeant. He has a wife and two children. While in Afghanistan two years ago, Roy was in a convoy that was ambushed. He was driving and his vehicle took fire and two of his men were severely injured. One later died. Roy was injured as well, having been thrown from the vehicle and hit by shrapnel. He sustained severe back injuries and a severed tendon.*

> *Roy was flown to two different overseas hospitals before being medevaced Stateside. It all happened within a matter of days. His wife met him the day after he was admitted to the inpatient hospital of the Medical Treatment Facility, a polytrauma center. It was clear from the extent of his back injuries that he would suffer some degree of permanent disability.*

> *The couple's children stayed behind with grandparents initially. Roy was in a great deal of pain. He had tendon surgery soon after his admission. He was on medicines for pain and to help him sleep, as well as antibiotics after the surgery. Roy was very tired and he and his wife, Sandy, interacted very little. She had time on her hands to imagine what the couple will be dealing with over the next few weeks. She met other spouses in the hallways and waiting areas. She was resisting the reality that Roy might be permanently disabled and that her life as she knew it was altered. And soon the children came to join them, so Sandy suddenly became very busy making sure Roy got to his appointments, keeping up with meals for the family, and entertaining the children.*

Family involvement in the injured service member's life can begin early on in their treatment. Many family members are flown overseas to be with the injured soldier or join the soldier when they are airlifted to the United States. When a patient begins treatment in a polytrauma center or DoD hospital or is sent to the VA, family members are encouraged to become part of the "treatment team." Providers are in agreement that participation from the family improves patient outcome over the long run; in addition, family members feel the need to be involved. Thus, family members become part of the focus of treatment along with the patient, as he/she begins their rehabilitation process (Friedmann-Sanchez et al., 2008).

Long-term and chronic disability impacts the individual in numerous ways and has the potential to have a profound impact on the family system and way of life. Consider that the returning service member has not only been through the experience of war but has returned in a compromised way; the way they departed at deployment is not the way they have returned home. And the returned service member has specific needs and specific limitations related to their injury; in many instances, there is a co-diagnosis of PTSD. It behooves those civilian social workers and other mental health professionals to work with the family and Veteran in three major areas: resource procurement, development and improvement of problem-solving skills, and reframing disabling conditions for the service member and family members. While both the individual and the family are impacted by the diagnosis of a chronic injury, some studies suggest that the families are even more substantially affected than the individual (Friedmann-Sanchez et al., 2008).

After two years, Roy was medically stabilized and ready to leave the treatment facility. Roy's social worker in the outpatient program had discussed treatment follow-up and recommended that he continue to receive Behavioral Health Services when he returned home at his local VA. There was a Veterans' Administration Hospital about 50 miles from his home, where he would have his follow up medical care for physical therapy, and check-ups at the VA clinic. In his community and nearby, there were limited resources for connecting to other Veterans as Roy lived in a small town. While he was still recovering from his injuries, it was difficult just to ride long distances in the car. In fact, he could not drive at all. It was not clear whether this was due to back pain or his lingering PTSD. So Sandy took him to his appointments, although being with him in the car was dangerous as he might yell or become agitated. She had to return to work, so she could not take off every week to transport Roy. As part of the discharge plan the social worker had encouraged Roy and Sandy to follow up with Military OneSource and if needed they should speak with a representative from Tricare, Roy's health insurance provider. They were referred to a social worker located in a nearby town that accepted their insurance.

Roy continued the counseling he had tentatively begun on post with this local social worker. Her initial assessment was that there were many unresolved issues that Roy must address based on his level of disability, his war experiences and the symptoms of PTSD. There was clearly the need for couples counseling as well to help Sandy and Roy find ways to communicate and work toward family reunification. Many adjustments had to be made, as Roy was unable to return to any form of work he had experience in and, because of his back problems, he was limited in what help he could provide at home. His injuries were considered a permanent disability and it is unlikely that he will live without chronic pain, or be able to walk long distances, or do any sort of physical labor. And there are the common issues long present of the changed roles due to Roy's training and multiple deployments over the years.

Psychosocial Goals of Care

Disabling conditions require not only familial and economic adaptations but also psychosocial adaptations for the patient and family. These psychosocial adaptations are summarized into three areas: basic concepts, triggered reactions, and disability related coping strategies. Each will be explored below (adapted from Livneh & Antonak, 2005).

Basic Concepts

These reactions are to be anticipated by those working with the war disabled and include: increased levels of stress to deal with daily challenges in the areas of body integrity; independence and autonomy; and economic stability. There is the experience of the disability as a crisis with loss and grief over the permanency of the disabling condition and the constant reminder of the disparity over the past and present level of functioning; there are major issues concerning body image and self-concept; concern over stigma; and major quality of life issues for the injured and the family members.

Triggered Reactions

These emotions are the most frequently experienced psychosocial reactions to disability and include: shock, anxiety, denial, depression, anger/hostility, and hoped-for adjustment. It should be noted that both the injured service member and the family members experience these reactions as well. The family must learn how to deal with the triggered reactions, especially the anger and frustration experienced by all members of the family, and more frequently by the disabled member. Once these have been mastered, it suggests that there has been some reorganization, reorientation and levels of compromise toward the disabling condition.

Coping Strategies

These are behaviors that decrease, modify or defuse the intensity of the disabling condition. In the case of those disabled through war injury, it suggests that the injured service member and the family have developed strategies that minimize the stressful situations that they encounter through active, direct and goal-oriented activities. These behaviors lead to levels of well-being and acceptance of the disabling condition.

> *For Roy and Sandy and their children, many things had changed and still had to change to reunite this family and bring family cohesion around Roy's disability. First, the family, and especially Roy and Sandy, had to learn the extent of Roy's limitations and understand what he was able to do and not able to do. Educating to the scope and extent of the injuries is an essential starting place for all counseling. Adaptations*

*to his limitations had to be made both in areas of expectations of what he could do
and adaptations to the living space/home of the family. It was very difficult for Roy
to climb steps, so Roy and Sandy had to have their bedroom moved to the ground
floor of the house. Lifting was very difficult for Roy, which meant that they had to
find someone in their community to do yard work and other manual chores. Roy had
numerous bouts of anger and frustration over his limitations that provoked trigger
reactions and outbursts that he had to learn to manage more effectively. His anger was
often directed at Sandy and he had to understand that this was a distancing behavior
that moved Sandy even further from him. In terms of coping strategies, Sandy and
Roy had to schedule time together with the goal of jump-starting and increasing
communication. The counselor, during sessions with the couple, had to teach Roy to
express his frustration in a way that did not set up Sandy to feel responsible for his
upset; she too was angry at what had happened and he had to be able to hear her
anger as well. Slowly, the couple began to reunite, helped by the parallel care Roy was
getting for his PTSD.*

Clinical Intervention Strategies—For the Service Member

To Address the Disability

These clinical interventions are designed to help move the service member
forward in the adaptation to their injury. The goal of intervention is to offer
emotional, cognitive and behavioral support. The first area, and perhaps the most
available area of intervention, is to provide the soldier/Veteran and the family
with relevant medical information regarding the extent and trajectory of their
disability and the extended prognosis. As the relationship evolves between the
counselor and the client, the soldier/Veteran is encouraged to vent their feelings
about their altered body image, frustrations in functioning, and to ultimately
express their grief/depression/mourning over loss of their previous functionality.
Soldiers and Veterans are to be encouraged to meet with like others who have
sustained similar war related injury, with the goal of increasing social support and
to learn new coping skills. It behoves the counselor to be aware of the venues for
Veterans to connect with, and to establish links to available VA services in the
Veteran's community (Livneh & Antonak, 2005). While there may not be local
resources, it may be necessary for the civilian practitioner to begin group
interactions as his/her caseload develops.

Clinical Intervention Strategies—For the Family

"Family members of injured service members experience intense emotions as
they try to come to terms with the loved one's injuries and the long-term
implication of this for their family" (Friedmann-Sanchez et al., 2008, p. 175).
The family is challenged to accept and adapt to the altered physical and emotional

needs of the disabled war Veteran. Many feel that the family, and its resiliency and ability to accept and adjust to the Veteran's disability, are critical factors in the rehabilitation process. The family has to make significant adjustments to the immediate and long-term life. As many of the injured are young and in young marriages, the stability and resilience of longer-term marriages and the willingness to make needed adaptations may pose a significant challenge. In addition, families have sources of stress beyond the immediate grief and loss posed by the injury: financial problems, work interruption and child-care may become pressing issues (Friedmann-Sanchez et al., 2008).

The overarching goal of all rehabilitation efforts is to optimize the quality of life of the disabled and to maximize the quality of life for the family. Toward this end, education and support become vital to assist the family in managing their internal transition. Using a solution-focused approach that emphasizes necessary adaptations to the most pressing needs of the disabled service member can be useful with the family. The overriding question in this approach is: What is it that the family and the Veteran must do to help the Veteran (each other) function as fully as possible?

The family members will go through a set of intense emotional responses similar to the injured service member. These will include denial, depression, despair, shock, confusion, and anxiety. A suggested approach—Medical Family Therapy— combines a biopsychosocial and family systems perspective to address the role of illness and injury in the personal life of the patient and the family. Three aspects of medical family therapy that apply to the situation of the war injured are: soliciting the illness story, respecting defenses, and accepting unacceptable feelings. Soliciting the illness story is a technique to access the family's history with illness and loss, and to help them realize their strengths in the face of these challenges. Respecting defenses and accepting unacceptable feelings includes encouraging the family—if they have these feelings—to express their anger at the military, the deployment experience, and any feelings of guilt and shame they may have regarding the injury. Respect for the family defenses means appreciating whatever means they have devised to not upset the injured service member with their emotional needs.

For the Disabled Veteran Who Has a Co-Diagnosis of PTSD

Citing recent in-depth research, the military endorses three treatment modalities as potentially effective for PTSD. These include Prolonged Exposure therapy, Cognitive Processing Therapy, and Eye Movement Desensitization and Reprocessing (adapted from U.S. Dept. of Veterans Affairs, 2011). Two of these strategies can be easily adapted by the civilian social worker/counselor. The third, EMDR requires special training that a civilian social worker can obtain. (As far as is known, the military requires providers to be formally trained in each of these modalities by a certified program—not just the EMDR. Even at Department of State, the PE providers have to be formally trained.)

Prolonged Exposure (PE) is a form of behavior therapy characterized by gradually re-experiencing a traumatic event through remembering it and engaging with, rather than avoiding it. It is a structured modality with prescribed steps to be taken in each visit with the recommended time frame of 90-minute sessions. The main goal of PE is to reduce the toxicity of the remembered event while instilling a sense of mastery and confidence in the client. The techniques of PE are designed to help trauma sufferers to confront frightening objects, situations, memories, and images. There is continued recounting of the traumatic memory (imaginal exposure) (Nacasch, Foa, Fostick, et al., 2007) and gradual exposure to the fear-evoking object (in vivo exposure). Treatment progresses in four main parts:

- PE starts with education about the treatment. The service member (client) learns about common trauma reactions and PTSD. Education allows the client to learn about their symptoms and understand the goals of the treatment. This education provides the basis for the next sessions.
- Breathing retraining is a skill that helps the client to relax. When people become anxious or scared, their breathing often changes. Breathing retraining helps the individual to keep their airways open longer as they breathe out. As they breathe out stale air they make room for fresh air when they breathe in. Learning how to control breathing can help in the short-term to manage immediate distress and calm oneself.
- Exposure practice with real-world situations is called in vivo exposure. In vivo exposure is the repeated confrontation with situations and objects that cause distress but are not inherently dangerous. The client practices approaching situations that are safe but which they may have been avoiding because they are related to the trauma. An example would be a client who avoids driving since he/she experienced a roadside bomb while deployed. The client would be encouraged initially to drive short distances, and increase them as time goes by and safety is reassured. This type of exposure practice helps trauma-related distress to lessen over time. When distress goes down, the client gains more control.
- Talking about the trauma memory over and over with their counselor is called imaginal exposure. Talking through the trauma repeatedly helps the client to get more control of their thoughts and feelings about the trauma and learn that they do not have to be afraid of their memories. This may be hard at first and it might seem strange to think about stressful things on purpose. Many people feel better over time, though, as they do this. Talking through the trauma helps the client make sense of what happened and have fewer negative thoughts about the trauma.

A round of PE therapy most often involves meeting alone with a counselor for about 8–15 sessions. With time and practice, the client will be able to see that he/she can master stressful situations. The goal is that YOU, not your memories, can control what you do in your life and how you feel.

Another approach to treatment is *Cognitive Processing Therapy* (CPT) that is fairly structured, and has homework (writing about the traumatic event) and points to be addressed in each visit. CPT helps one learn how going through a trauma changed the way you look at the world, yourself, and others. Typically this is done in 12 sessions. The way we think and look at things directly affects how we feel and act.

CPT has four main parts:

- CPT begins with education about specific PTSD symptoms and how the treatment can help.
- Next, CPT focuses on helping the client become more aware of their thoughts and feelings. When bad things happen, we want to make sense of why they happened. An example would be a client who thinks to himself or herself, "I should have known that this would happen." Sometimes we get stuck on these thoughts. In CPT, the client learns how to pay attention to their thoughts about the trauma and how they make a person feel. They are then asked to step back and think about how their trauma is affecting them now. This will help the client to think about their trauma in a different way than they did before. It can be done either by writing or by talking with the counselor. A tool to bring awareness is the writing assignment that the client is instructed to read aloud during their session and outside of the session.
- After the client become more aware of their thoughts and feelings, they will learn skills to help them question or challenge their thoughts. This is done with the help of worksheets that monitor thoughts and reactions. The client will be able to use these skills to decide the way YOU want to think and feel about your trauma and with other problems in your day-to-day life.
- Finally, the client will learn about the common changes in beliefs that occur after going through trauma. Many people have problems understanding how to live in the world after trauma. Beliefs about safety, trust, control, self-esteem, other people, and relationships can change after trauma. In CPT a client will get to talk about their beliefs in these different areas while learning to find a better balance between the beliefs they had before and after the trauma.

The client and their counselor work together to help him/her learn a new way of dealing with trauma. In CPT, the client works closely with their counselor to reach their goals, usually on a regular basis with practice sessions in between.

Eye Movement Desensitization and Reprocessing (EMDR) is another type of therapy for PTSD. Like other kinds of counseling, it can help change how a person reacts to memories of their trauma. While thinking of or talking about their memories, they'll focus on other stimuli such as eye movements, hand taps, and sounds.

EMDR requires specialized training on the part of the counselor. This training is offered in many places across the U.S. It also requires the therapist to receive supervision by a certified trainer while working with the first few clients.

> *To address some of Roy's PTSD symptoms, the social worker began a program of Prolonged Exposure therapy with him. As Roy had focused so much on his physical healing, he did not disclose everything about his war experiences at the MTF. He had a lot of "bottled up" emotions, memories and feelings about his general war experience and the particulars of his injury and care after being wounded. The soldier who died after the explosion in which Roy was injured was a dear friend and someone who went through basic training with him. This loss was particularly painful to him and, because Roy was driving the truck, he felt even more responsible for the injuries and death. He was having nightmares remembering the incident and was encouraged to recall the details of the bombing incident in his counseling sessions (PE prefers that the client selects the worst memory and deals with that one event over and over and over). Slowly, Roy was able to relate the story of the IED bombing with less and less emotion and began to realize that his memories are just that, memories. He was not actually re-experiencing the events each time he thought about them. He gained empowerment over his memories instead of them controlling him. In time, and as part of his homework, Roy was encouraged to be a passenger in a car—he was not able to drive yet because of his back problems—and slowly became more comfortable. It took many weeks of counseling with Roy alone and Roy with Sandy to bring about the needed adaptations to Roy's disability and PTSD. In this case, civilian social workers were engaged in the treatment of this family. At the time of this writing, the family is about 60 percent of what it had been in terms of cohesion and unity. Couples counseling continues as do frequent sessions with Roy as he confronts his PTSD with his counselor. Roy is working with the VA to find work he can do given his physical limitations. The family is hopeful …*

Conclusion

The care of the wounded and disabled poses great challenges to behavioral health providers. The dual view of care for the injured service members and the "injured" family makes the work especially difficult. There are many strategies that can be used to engage the service member and the family in counseling. The counselor has to be able to understand the common personality traits and thought processes of a soldier, the military culture and the demands it makes on those who serve. For those who counsel the wounded, it can be seen as an opportunity to help heal those who have been injured and to bring families into a "new normal" way of functioning and loving.

References

Bascetta, C. (2007). *DoD and VA Health Care: Challenges encountered by injured service members during their recovery process*. GAO-07-606T. Washington, DC: Government Accountability Office.
Bishop, M. (2005). Quality of life and psychosocial adaptation to chronic illness and acquired disability: A conceptual and theoretical synthesis. *Journal of Rehabilitation*, 71(2), 5–13.
Collins, R. & Kennedy, M. (2008). Serving families who have served: Providing family therapy and support in interdisciplinary polytrauma rehabilitation. *Journal of Clinical Psychology*, 64(8), 993–1003.
Cozza, S, Guimond, J., McKibben, J., Chun, R., Arata-Maiers, T., Schneider, B., Ursano, R. (2010). Combat-injured service members and their families: The relationship of child distress and spouse-perceived family distress and disruption. *Journal of Traumatic Stress*, 23(1), 112–115.
Frain, M., Bethel, M., & Bishop, M. (2010). A roadmap for rehabilitation counseling to serve military Veterans with disabilities. *Journal of Rehabilitation*, 76(1), 13–21.
Friedmann-Sanchez, G., Sayer, N., & Pickett, T. (2008) Provider perspectives on rehabilitation of patients with polytrauma. *Archives of Physical & Medical Rehabilitation*, 89, 171–178.
Gawande, A. (2004). Casualties of war—Military care for the wounded from Iraq and Afghanistan. *New England Journal of Medicine*, 24(351), 2471–2475.
Hoge, C., Auchterlonie, J., & Milliken, C. (2006). Mental health problems, use of mental health services and attrition from military service after returning from deployment from Iraq or Afghanistan. *Journal of the American Medical Association*, 295, 1023–1032.
Hudak, R., Morrison, C., Carstensen, M., Rice, J., & Jurgersen, B. (2009). The U.S. Army Wounded Warrior Program (AW2). A case study in designing a nonmedical case management program for severely wounded, injured and ill service members and their families. *Military Medicine*, 174(6), 566–571.
Hyer, R. (2006). Iraq and Afghanistan producing new pattern of extremity injuries. Conference proceedings from American Academy of Orthopaedic Surgeons 2006 Annual Meeting. Retrieved from: http://www.medscpe.com/viewarticl;e/528624
Livneh, H. & Antonak, R. (2005). Psychosocial adaptation to chronic illness and disability. *Journal of Counseling and Development*, 83, 12–20.
Livneh, H. & Parker, R. (2005). Psychological adaptation to disability: Perspectives from chaos and complexity theory. *Rehabilitation & Counseling Bulletin*, 49(1), 17–28.
Manske, J. (2006). Social work in the Department of Veterans Affairs: Lessons learned. *Health and Social Work*, 31(3), 233–238.
Nacasch, N., Foa, E., Fostick, L., Pollack, M., Tzur, D., Levy, P., & Zohar, J. (2007). Prolonged exposure therapy for chronic combat-related PTSD: A case report of five Veterans. *CNS Spectrums*, 12(9), 690–695.
Savitsky, L., Illingworth, M., & DuLaney, M. (2009). Civilan social work: Serving the military and Veteran population. *Social Work*, 54(4), 327–339.

Seal, K., Bertenthal, D., Miner, C., Sen, S., & Marmar, C. (2007). Bringing the war back home: Mental health disorders among 103,788 U.S. Veterans returning from Iraq and Afghanistan seen at Department of Veterans Affairs facilities. *Archives of Internal Medicine*, 167, 476–482.

Uomoto, J. & Williams, R. (2009). Post-acute polytrauma rehabilitation and integrated care of returning Veterans: Toward an holistic approach. *Rehabilitation Psychology*, 54(3), 259–269.

U.S. Department of Veterans Affairs (2011). Retrieved from: http://www.ptsd.va.gov/public/pages/prolonged-exposure-therapy.asp

7

HELPING THE COMBAT MEDIC AND CORPSMAN

Adapting to Both Primary and Secondary Traumatic Stress Down Range and Beyond

David Cabrera, Charles R. Figley, and Jeffrey S. Yarvis

"I will never leave a fallen comrade" is the final of four commitments in the Combat Medic Field Reference, the bible of medical care for those responsible for it in combat: the combat medic. The purpose of this chapter is two-fold:

1 to provide a wake-up call for practitioners working with, or hoping to work with, combatants who may be either medics or corpsmen, as they are significantly different from other combatants;
2 to offer a proper orientation to working with and understanding these combatants and their families in order to bond with them and facilitate healing.

With the number of combat Veterans steadily growing from the past ten years of war, it is likely that most civilian practitioners either have encountered, or will treat combat Veterans in the near future. Case material will highlight critical concepts.

Background

Combat medics and corpsmen are some of the most important and oldest specializations within the military units who are involved in combat. They are the front line of medicine and possess the military training equivalent to an Emergency Medical Technician (EMT) in the civilian arena. The primary role of the combat medic (Army and Air Force) and corpsmen (Navy and Marines) is to provide medical treatment to the wounded, often one per platoon or equivalent sized unit (especially combat units). They are required because of their importance to the success of the unit's mission, especially when they are expected to perform their medical responsibilities under combat conditions.

However, the work ranges widely depending upon their unit and job, but can include, for example: identifying the need for administering and completing paperwork for immunizations; obtaining vitals and initial information from patients; and treating physical and psychological trauma, collecting fluid samples, surgical assistance and suturing. During wartime, their war-related duties as combat medics include entering combatant homes with their assigned team, patrols, and house clearing operations within small units, and covering for members of the fighting unit. As such, they are performing "regular" military duties. Medics and corpsmen are also responsible for providing continuing medical care of any kind, as needed and train others in their unit in basic first aid and how to assist her or him in performing certain combat-related medical operations that are common for combat units.

History of Medics

According to Nestor (2003), the French combat surgeon Dominique Jen Larrey is credited with persuading Napoleon to adopt policies and procedures in 1790 that would save more lives and limbs by bring medicine to the battlefield. In 1862, an American combat surgeon, Jonathan Letterman, initiated an improved, integrated medical treatment and evacuation system for the miltary. In 1917, General Order No. 75 of the War Department established the U.S. Army Ambulance Services. However, it took an act of Congress in 1947 to create our current Medical Services Corps. Although the medical corps serve as non-combatants and enjoy Geneva Convention protection, modern warfare creates a unique combat situation in which such rules do not apply in protecting combat medical personnel. Individuals who served as non-combatant healers in previous wars were seldom targeted by enemy forces and were recognized as a protected group. Though many lost their lives in the line of duty, this was more often as a result of indirect fire (non-intentional) by either of the opposing forces. Beginning with Vietnam, an insurgent style enemy no longer followed international law of warfare, and medics became targets along with their combatant counterparts. This has proven to hold true in the current conflicts in Iraq and Afghanistan; medics no longer maintain any level of protection from the enemy and therefore have been forced to actively defend themselves and their team.

Medics Today

Most medics and corpsmen carry a personal weapon to be used to protect themselves and the wounded or sick in their care. According to the Geneva Accords, established to protect medics and corpsmen, carrying or using offensive weapons disqualifies them from such protection. Due to the nature of the insurgent wars being waged in Iraq and Afghanistan, a medic no longer has the ability to perform his/her mission without being equipped with the equivalent small arms weapons provided to combatants in the unit. It is now common practice among U.S. medical personnel attached to combat units that they carry the same weapons as their team. They are first warriors, and must remain capable of protecting themselves and the members of their team. (NB: The first page of the Combat Medic Field Reference (Bond, 2005) is the Warrior Ethos: "I will always place the mission first. I will never accept defeat. I will never quit. I will never leave a fallen comrade.") This distinction is vital in the understanding of combat medics since the nature of combat has changed to the degree that combat medics are now more likely to face circumstances where they must defend themselves through returning fire on enemy combatants as well as maintain their primary role of saving lives. This often has implications for both primary and secondary stress reactions.

The primary role of the combat medic or "*68W*" (military occupational status) in the U.S. Army is to provide medical treatment to wounded soldiers. These medics are sometimes considered the staple of Army combat functionality, as every platoon (approximately 40 Soldiers) is required to have a Medic along for any hazardous mission. They are found in every stage of medical treatment in a combat zone. Medics initiate medical treatment at the accident or injury location, maintain medical treatment during evacuation to healthcare facilities, and provide medical treatment in the medical facilities. Combat medics are trained to perform medical duties in hazardous and challenging environments. The *68W*, often, must work in the absence of other medical professionals in Basic Life Support (BLS) performance, monitoring and maintenance.

Review of the Research Literature

As with medics and corpsmen, in addition to the daily grind of providing medical care, there is the requirement to be compassionate; to listen to patients with the mind and with the heart to better serve them. In this role, secondary traumatic stress can result from the pressure to be empathic and sensitive to the emotional needs of patients. Needless to say, the additional stress of constant exposure to terrible injury and death takes a toll as well.

Secondary traumatic stress (STS), without proper management, leads to stress reactions. Secondary trauma is an extreme state of tension and preoccupation with the suffering of those being helped to the degree that it is traumatizing for the helper (Figley, 1995a, 2002), and is high in individuals providing care or treatment to traumatized populations (Bride, Radey, & Figley, 2007; Yarvis & Bordnick, 2003). More specifically, Figley (1995a, p. 7) defined STS as "the natural and consequent behaviors and emotions resulting from knowing about a traumatizing event experienced by a significant other—the stress resulting from helping or wanting to help a traumatized or suffering person". Combat medics are a core element in combat teams and maintain close bonds with each unit member. Every injury or death within this unit is likely to be perceived as a secondary trauma.

As with burnout, STS symptoms are associated with emotional exhaustion but, in addition, the condition is also similar to post-traumatic stress disorder (PTSD) in the same way that nurses with secondary trauma are traumatized by their work in treating the suffering. Secondary trauma is the condition of being overwhelmed and unable to effect positive change (Figley, 2002; Collins & Long, 2003a, 2003b; Sabo, 2006), and is also associated with a sense of confusion, helplessness, and a greater sense of isolation from supporters than is seen with burnout (Figley, 1995a, 2002).

Research by Yarvis and Schiess (2008) predicted poorer health and mental status in Veterans, such as combat medics, who present in what are often classified with sub-clinical presentations. Most clinical researchers recognize that STS is comparable to PTSD symptoms and emphasize the need for similar treatment for STS. Yet, it is believed that STS is underidentified, underassessed, underdiagnosed, and undertreated in many treatment settings (Coffey, Dansky, & Brady, 2003; Dansky, Roitzsch, Brady, & Saladin, 1997; Ouimette, Moos, & Brown, 2003). However, because there has recently been more attention to this issue in the research and professional literature, it may be that more medical practitioners are now recognizing the deleterious effects of vicarious exposures to the traumata of medics and corpsman. This highlights the need for offering a range of trauma-focused services specifically for combat caregivers. To date, there has been little in the way of systematic study of the current state of the field in this regard.

Secondary Trauma in Other Professions

Caregivers like combat medics, who work with people in crisis, report secondary traumatic stress reactions. This includes first responders (Salston, 2002); child protection workers (Bride, Radey, & Figley, 2007; Nelson-Gardell & Harris, 2003; Meyers & Cornille, 2002); military Veteran counselors (Munroe, Shay, Fisher, et al., 1995); mental health counselors (Brady, Guy, Poelstdra, & Fletcher-Brokaw, 1999; Pearlman & Mac Ian, 1995); domestic violence counselors (Bell, 2003); sexual assault counselors (Ghahramanlou & Brodbeck, 2000; Schauben & Frazier, 1995); and, various healthcare services (Cunningham, 2003; Dane & Chachkes, 2001). This research clearly indicates that caregivers of the traumatized are at risk of experiencing symptoms of traumatic stress, disrupted cognitive schema, and general psychological distress as a result of their work (Bride, Robinson, Yegisdis, & Figley, 2004).

Burgeoning research has begun to document an occupational hazard that is unique to clinical social work and medicine with traumatized populations. One could infer that medics, given their constant exposure and proximity to those soldiers in harm's way, are at greater risk than their civilian counterparts in emergency response systems. Medics who provide services to traumatized casualties may themselves experience similar trauma reactions (termed secondary traumatic stress) as well as related mental health problems that impact their personal well-being. In addition to its effect on the mental health of medics and corpsman, there is also concern that STS may affect the quality of care provided by those of them who experience it; and may increase the likelihood of attrition from military service. However, to date research has not investigated this phenomenon in combat medics and corpsman who have served in the Global War on Terror. The social work academic, scientific, and clinical communities are faced with meeting the needs of these wounded warriors with unseen wounds through education, research, and intervention.

Case Study

War trauma today no longer comfortably fits into the traditional paradigm of a combat solider exposed to a single event, a paradigm in which the individual might survive an explosion or see a "battle buddy" shot on patrol. Of course these issues continue in today's conflicts. The soldier must negotiate very complex psychological terrain: sexual traumas, spiritual conflicts, TBI and military-induced family separation are among the many things that affect the psyche of the warrior. Today's soldier must exhibit tremendous emotional restraint and never have the locus of control issues contributed to secondary trauma. Arguably, the most challenging duties where these problems are at the psychological fault lines with respect to combat duty and the journey home are with the combat medic or corpsman.

The following is a case that illustrates the complex psychological landscape described above. "Jose" a 29-year-old U.S. Navy Reserve Corpsman (Medic) with three combined tours in Afghanistan and Iraq, self-referred for treatment for "PTSD." Jose, a California native, refused to relinquish his status as a military corpsman and return to his civilian profession (demobilize) until he and his fellow marines received the treatment they deserved. Jose's command did not feel the same way and wanted him to leave active duty and Walter Reed for home. For Jose this mission of self-care and advocacy for others was not just a mission, it was a personal mandate. Though he faced serious punitive measures for disobeying orders, Jose had decided that he must fight this perceived injustice regardless of the personal cost.

Jose presented with an intimidating and angry affect. Physically he was a small yet muscular man standing about 5 ft 6 in. He walked in with a cane and presented with his non-commissioned officer-in-charge (NCOIC) in tow. Jose's NCOIC was berating him for wasting the unit's time and money for making a mental health appointment and saying horribly, as he checked in, "Get the sand out of your vagina and get back to work." After dismissing the NCOIC, Jose took his anger out on the custodial staff and the front desk of the clinic alarming everyone in the room. Jose was escorted into his first session by the chief of the clinic.

Jose presented that he felt betrayed by his superior for the losses he was left to process for his platoon mates on behalf of the commanders he served in combat. He expressed what traumatologists know all too well, that with trauma (secondary or primary) comes a betrayal. For example, betrayal of one's body, mind, or in this case his perceived betrayal by his superiors. He expressed anger toward the clinic chief as a reflection of those who let him down.

His mental status exam revealed a pattern of affective instability and intensity consistent with PTSD. He described patterns of avoidance, dissociation and numbing, and re-experiencing. He spoke powerfully about how he had to "hold it together" and remain calm when he was holding a buddy he knew was "expectant" (a triage category that tells evacuation or treatment personnel that the wounded is expected to die). He recalled that on numerous occasions young officers ordered his comrades into harm's way without listening to the advice of others more senior in service time in combat, but lower in rank. Many of his fellow marines died in his arms, and he describes how, with the wounded man's eyes on him and his mates' eyes on him, he had to cast a shadow of re-assurance to all involved to keep everyone calm and mission-focused. His method was to internalize the sights, sounds and smells, and the anger and grief to all those around him. He was their corpsman, their "doc." He was the platoon's therapist, healer, and steadying force. Yet for Jose, these experiences twisted around his psyche and organs like a secret burning thread that cut him inside.

Over the next few weeks, he received psychotherapy and hypnotherapy as well as SSRIs and hypnotics to help him dull the symptoms of anxiety, depression and restlessness and assist with his erratic sleep. He was beginning to look like the man he saw himself as: strong and calm. Yet, unpredictably, he would have intense angry outbursts.

He still felt out of control and was suggesting he should just "drink away his anger." There was still the issue of his current command and the feeling of betrayal. While he was struggling with all of his own issues, he was expected to forego formal treatment because the unit knew he "knew what his problems were." He was expected to be present for duty, caring for the psychological and physical needs of his peers. The constant re-visitation of war through the eyes of his comrades, the perceived denial of his care needs by his command, and a perception that leaders used him and denigrated the meaning of his combat experiences by focusing on "silly and insignificant base missions" re-victimized or re-traumatized him.

In the end it was not his combat tours or the exposures to horrible things in combat that Jose needed help with. In fact he was keen to serve and return to combat with great resilience each time. Jose denied having these symptoms until he had to endure the trivializing of his experiences and the exposure to the traumata of others, which fueled his anger.

Once the treatment focus shifted to managing the locus of control issues he experienced in garrison, and the powerlessness he felt over his own care and the care of his comrades, his PTSD symptoms began to disappear. Interestingly, his need for a cane also faded. It seems his cane was a visible means to "show" sickness so that his chain of command would allow him to seek medical, or in this case psychological, treatment. During treatment he was able to use his therapist as a surrogate leader at which he could direct his hostilities. After processing this through, he not only made his peace with himself and his leadership, but together they were able to advocate for the care needs of his platoon mates. Jose was able to return home shortly thereafter. He had feared "coming home half a man" and feeling his Latino family would reject him if they saw him as "broken." Feeling whole, he rejoined his family and his unit; healing the scars he had picked up vicariously from his mates and secondarily from his insensitive and combat inexperienced rear detachment command.

Jose's case represents the systemic and individual secondary traumatic stress. He had always had enough psychological capability to manage the war-induced stress. What had been traumatic for him was revisiting the war through the eyes of others during impromptu counseling sessions and debriefings, combat medic training, and the denial of an uninformed command. He had reasons to be in control in combat. He could heal and protect others from the evils they witnessed. At home he had no way to protect his mates from their re-experiencing process, or protect by giving meaning or reason to the seemingly insensitive actions of the NCOIC and leaders around him. His case was clearly one of secondary trauma induced spectrum disorder. As this examination explores strategies for practitioners, it is important to note that many of the clinicians saw Jose's intense reactions as "inappropriate" rather than consistent with his experience, suggesting a lack of cultural sensitivity and awareness about life in the military, combat experience, and how they might contribute unwittingly to a re-victimization process.

Strategies for Practitioners

Practitioners will find that medics and corpsmen hold a deep commitment to duty and fellow warriors. It is primarily the depth of the attachment that makes the Medical Corps, and especially medics and corpsmen, more like family. Ultimately, the fighting unit is "like family," and there is a closeness about the Marine Corps units and how it competes for time and attention with the real families (families of origin). The family of origin system operates in a tightly structured feedback network in which members are simultaneously influencing and reacting to each other (Watzlawick, Beavin, & Jackson, 1967; Watzlawick, Weakland, & Fisch, 1974).

Therapists dealing with the interface between family and fighting unit must also accept many aspects of the unit's influence as givens and not amenable to intervention. The interplay of influence most amenable to change still occurs between family members. If the family maintains emotional safety, then problems can be addressed as they occur. But if emotional safety is lacking, the family will not operate well as a group and may even be dysfunctional. Safety is typically lost in a circular fashion. One member says or does something that another member perceives as a threat in one of the two realms (attachment and esteem), and the second member's reaction creates a reciprocal threat for the first member (or for another member, who reacts in turn). That impact is reflected in unit discipline, mental, physical and emotional toughness, doing what is necessary to survive, and mission accomplishment. The impact is also visible in the avoidance of feelings of grief and vulnerability that are often detected by family members or members of the fighting unit.

What Social Workers Need to Know About Combat Medics

Like other helping professions, medics may experience guilt and will present reluctantly. Usually, seasoned combat medics will be able to deal with combat casualties on some level without decompensating. What may affect them uniquely is locus of control issues and the context of trauma, for example was the casualty they were treating a unit member?

PTSD and guilt commonly co-occur. People who have experienced traumatic events may experience something called *trauma-related guilt*.

What is trauma-related guilt? It refers to the unpleasant feeling of regret stemming from the belief that you could or should have done something different at the time a traumatic event occurred. For example, a military Veteran may regret not going back into a combat zone to save a fallen soldier. A rape survivor may feel guilty about not fighting back at the time of the assault. Combat medics and corpsman may feel they did not "do enough" to save someone. Trauma survivors may also experience a particular type of trauma-related guilt, called survivor guilt. Survivor guilt is often experienced when a person has made it through some kind of traumatic event while others have not. A person may question why he survived. He may even blame himself for surviving a traumatic event as if he did something wrong. Understanding trauma-related guilt is the key to providing intervention for the client.

Trauma-related guilt can be treated through cognitive behavioral therapy. Trauma-related guilt may originate in the ways that medics think about or revisit or reinterpret a combat situation.

For instance, a survivor may feel that she should have seen the attack on her comrades coming, even though it was impossible for her to predict that the assault would occur. Likewise, she may think to herself that she should have done something different to prevent the death of a fellow soldier even though the event may have been completely out of her control, and feel betrayed by the leadership that put the soldiers in that spot at that time on the battlefield.

Cognitive-behavioral therapy for trauma-related guilt would focus on helping warriors become more aware of the thoughts or beliefs that underlie feelings of guilt, such as through self-monitoring. The therapist would then help the person come up with more realistic interpretations of the situation.

For example, lessen your guilt by realizing that the traumatic event was completely out of your control, and you acted in the best way you could given the situation. By reducing guilt, cognitive-behavioral therapy may also help increase self-compassion and acceptance.

In addition to cognitive-behavioral therapy, psychodynamic/psychoanalytic approaches can also be helpful in addressing trauma-related guilt. Psychodynamic and psychoanalytic approaches would aid the patient in exploring her early life experiences (for example, relationships with significant others, early childhood traumas or fears, or previous sexual traumas) in order to identify experiences and factors that may make someone more likely to feel trauma-related guilt and shame.

Traumatic Events and Guilt

The experience of trauma-related guilt does not seem to depend on the type of traumatic event experienced. Combat exposure for medics and corpsman is not unlike other types of trauma in terms of impact. As with survivors of physical abuse and/or sexual abuse, the loss of a loved one has been found to be associated with the experience of trauma-related guilt. Therefore, dealing with trauma-related guilt in medics should not be too foreign if the social worker has conducted grief-related work before with other populations. What will be unique is the combat medic's view of himself or herself who is there to be the helper and re-assuring force of a unit, not to be helped. Providers can deal with this initial resistance by utilizing the same skills as when dealing with any other type of resistant patient. In this case, however, time and rapport (i.e., trust) are the provider's best approach to breaking through. A provider in uniform (active duty) with combat experience maintains an initial rapport and trust with a patient who is initially resistant to care, because the provider "has been there" and is perceived to understand some of what the patient has experienced. A civilian provider may face an initial vetting by a Veteran or active duty Soldier while the individual assesses the clinician's ability to relate to the Soldier's stories of loss, combat, and pain.

Returning Medics and Anger

Researchers have described three components of posttraumatic anger that can become maladaptive or interfere with one's ability to adapt to current situations that do *not* involve extreme threat:

1   *Arousal:* Anger is marked by the increased activation of the cardiovascular, glandular, and brain systems associated with emotion and survival. It is also marked by increased muscle tension. This can cause a person to feel frequently

on-edge, keyed-up, or irritable and can cause a person to be more easily provoked. Anger may not be directed at any particular traumatic event. In fact, anger is often brought about by the state of arousal necessary for surviving the long hours of operation in combat. This displaced anger is often a tremendous source of confusion for the medic. To subdue anger, or dull arousal symptoms, medics often turn to alcohol and drugs to reduce overall internal tension.

2   *Behavior:* Often, the most effective way of dealing with extreme threat is to act aggressively, in a self-protective way. In addition, combat medics and corpsmen are expected to run into areas receiving enemy fire when others are holding their positions. For social workers treating medics, they must understand that many people who were traumatized at a relatively young age do not learn different ways of handling threat, and tend to become stuck in their ways of reacting when they feel threatened. While aggressive tendencies can be adaptive in certain threatening circumstances, individuals with PTSD can become stuck in using only one strategy when others would be more constructive. Social workers can play a pivotal role in helping medics find new strategies for coping during or after combat. Cognitive behavioral strategies, role playing, and helping the individual achieve a new coping skill(s) to gain as positive a resolution to the perceived threat as possible are a few of the methods available to initiate change. Behavioral aggression may take many forms, including aggression toward others, passive-aggressive behavior (e.g., complaining, "backstabbing," deliberately being late or doing a poor job), or self-aggression (self-destructive activities, self-blame, being chronically hard on oneself, self-injury). Those close to the medic often misinterpret these behaviors as misconduct behaviors. Though direct intervention with a client's peers is often not possible (or practical), a clinician can address the internalized thoughts and beliefs held by the medic in order to effect change in their behaviors.

3   *Thoughts and beliefs:* The thoughts or beliefs that people have to help them understand and make sense of their environment can often overexaggerate threat. Often the individual is not fully aware of these thoughts and beliefs, but they cause the person to perceive more hostility, danger, or threat than others might feel is necessary. One evidence-based method to initiate change is cognitive behavioral therapy. The basic tenet of CBT is that one's thoughts cause feelings and behaviors. By helping the medic understand that it is not the event that causes behaviors, but what they think the event means, he/she can begin to shift their thought patterns as well as their behaviors.

How Can Individuals With Posttraumatic Anger Get Help?

In anger management treatment, arousal, behavior, and thoughts/beliefs are all addressed in different ways. Cognitive-behavioral treatment, or exposure therapy, are commonly utilized therapies that show positive results when used to address anger. It applies many techniques to manage these three anger components:

1   For *increased arousal*, the goal of treatment is to help the person learn skills that will reduce overall arousal. Such skills include relaxation, self-hypnosis, and physical exercises that discharge tension.
2   For *behavior*, the goal of treatment is to review a person's most frequent ways of behaving under perceived threat or stress and help him or her to expand the possible responses. More adaptive responses include: taking a time out; writing thoughts down when angry; communicating in more verbal, assertive ways; and changing the pattern "act first, think later" to "think first, act later."
3   For *thoughts/beliefs*, individuals are given assistance in logging, monitoring, and becoming more aware of their own thoughts prior to becoming angry. They are, additionally, given alternative, more positive replacement thoughts for their negative thoughts (e.g., "Even if I am out of control, I won't be threatened in this situation," or "Others do not have to be perfect in order for me to survive/be comfortable"). Individuals often role-play situations in therapy so that they can practice recognizing their anger-arousing thoughts and apply more positive thoughts.

There are many strategies for helping individuals with posttraumatic issues deal with the frequent increase of anger they are likely to experience. Most individuals have a combination of the three anger components listed above, and treatment aims to help with all aspects of anger. One important goal of treatment is to improve a person's sense of flexibility and control so that he or she does not feel re-traumatized by his or her own explosive or excessive responses to anger triggers. Treatment is also meant to have a positive impact on personal and work relationships (Chemtob, Novaco, Hamada, et al., 1997.)

Conclusion

The dual and sometimes contradictory pressures placed on the medic—between a culture and a "family"—must be challenging for everyone in the family of origin. The values underlying survival, mission accomplishment, and anticipating more deployments are central to understanding medics. The competition for time and resources of the medic between career and family is inevitable.

As noted throughout this chapter, providing care for our current and past Service Members is a complex set of challenges due to the intensity of circumstances encountered in multiple years of war, and the special context inherent in the "subculture" of the Armed Forces. There continues to be a growing need for effective services for war Veterans and their families; and these services need to be provided by a variety of behavioral health practitioners. These issues need to be faced with candid discussion, attention on the specific needs of this population, and the vigor of agencies to meet the needs of the growing military population.

Studies are underway to identify and address the protective factors for medics, though at this time the best clinical interventions lie with treating the Service Member and his/her family for presenting problems. A brief overview of combat medics was provided in this chapter to help providers better understand this growing population of clients as well as specific treatment recommendations for working with this group. Rapport has been shown to be a significant indicator of treatment success, and this chapter provided tools to better understand this unique clientele (rapport building) as well as methods offering recommended intervention options.

Long honored for their bravery and the importance of their work, combat medics, and other critical Service Members who risk their life to care for others in and after combat, deserve far more attention toward their own care. Our efforts and the efforts of other social work professionals are beginning to help design programs tailored to their specific circumstances in order to promote resilience among medics and their families and to alert a grateful nation about their important service.

References

Bell, H. (2003). Strengths and in family violence work. *Social Work*, 48(4), 513–522.

Bond, C. (2005). *Combat Medic Field Reference*. Burlington, MA: Jones & Bartlett Learning.

Brady, J.L., Guy, J.D., Poelstra, P.L., & Fletcher-Brokaw, B. (1999). Vicarious traumatization, spirituality, and the treatment of sexual abuse survivors: A National survey of women psychotherapists. *Professional Psychology: Research and Practice*, 30, 386–393

Bride, B.E., Radey, M., & Figley, C.R. (2007). Measuring secondary trauma. *Clinical Social Work Journal*, 35(3), 155–163.

Bride, B.E., Robinson, M.M., Yegidis, B., & Figley, C.R. (2004). Development and validation of the tic stress scale. *Research on Social Work Practice*, 14(1), 27–36.

Chemtob, C.M., Novaco, R.W., Hamada, R.S., Gross, D.M., & Smith, G. (1997). Anger regulation deficits in combat-related posttraumatic stress disorder. *Journal of Traumatic Stress*, 10(1), 17–35.

Coffey, S.F., Dansky, B.S., & Brady, K.T. (2003). Exposure-based, trauma-focused therapy for co-morbid posttraumatic stress disorder-substance use disorder. In P.C. Ouimette & P.J. Brown (Eds.), *Trauma and Substance Abuse: Causes, consequences, and treatment of comorbid disorders* (pp. 127–146). Washington, DC: American Psychological Association.

Collins, S. & Long, A. (2003a). Too tired to care? The psychological effects of working with trauma. *Journal of Psychiatric and Mental Health Nursing*, 10(1), 17–27.

Collins, S. & Long, A. (2003b). Working with the psychological effects of trauma: Consequences for mental health-care workers—a literature review. *Journal of Psychiatric and Mental Health Nursing*, 10(4), 417–424.

Cunningham, M. (2003). Impact of trauma work on social work clinicians: Empirical findings. *Social Work*, 48, 451–459.

Dane, B. & Chachkes, E. (2001). The cost of caring for patients with an illness: Contagion to the social worker. *Social Work in Health Care*, 22(2), 31–51.

Dansky, B.S., Roitzsch, J.C., Brady, K.T., & Saladin, M.E. (1997). Posttraumatic stress and substance abuse: Use of research in a clinical setting. *Journal of Traumatic Stress*, 10, 141–148.

Figley, C.R. (Ed.) (1995a). *Secondary Trauma: Coping with tic stress disorder in those who treat the traumatized*. London: Brunner-Routledge.

Figley, C.R. (2002). Secondary trauma: Psychotherapists' chronic lack of self care. *Journal of Clinical Psychology*, 58(11), 1433–1441.

Ghahramanlou, M.A. & Brodbeck, C. (2000). Predictors of secondary trauma in sexual assault trauma counselors. *International Journal of Emergency Mental Health*, 2, 229–240.

Meyers, T.W. & Cornille, T.A. (2002). The trauma of working with traumatized children. In C.R. Figley (Ed.), *Treating Compassion Fatigue* (pp. 17–55). New York: Brunner-Routledge.

Munroe, J.F., Shay, J., Fisher, L., Makary, C., Rapperport, K., & Zimering, R. (1995). Preventing secondary trauma: A treatment team model. In C.R. Figley (Ed.), *Secondary Trauma: Coping with tic stress disorder in those who treat the traumatized* (pp. 209–231). New York: Brunner/Mazel.

Nelson-Gardell, D., & Harris, D. (2003). Childhood abuse history, tic stress, and child welfare workers. *Child Welfare*, 82(1), 5–26.

Nestor, P. (2003). Baron Dominique Jean Larrey. *Journal of Emergency Primary Health Care*, 1(3-4). Retrieved on December 16, 2011 from: http://www.jephc.com/uploads/990004.pdf

Ouimette, P., Moos, R., & Brown, P. (2003). Trauma and substance abuses: Causes, consequences, and treatment of comorbid disorders. In *Substance Use Disorder-Posttraumatic Stress Disorder Morbidity: A survey of treatments and proposed guidelines* (pp. 91–110). Washington, DC: American Psychological Association.

Pearlman, L.A. & Mac Ian, P.S. (1995). Vicarious traumatization: An empirical study of the effects of trauma work on trauma therapists. *Professional Psychology: Research and Practice*, 26, 558–565.

Sabo, B.M. (2006). Secondary trauma and nursing work: Can we accurately capture the consequences of caring work? *International Journal of Nursing Practice*, 12(3), 136–142.

Salston, M.D. (2002). *Secondary Trauma: Implications for mental health professionals and trainees*. A defended dissertation at Florida State University.

Schauben, L.J. & Frazier, P.A. (1995). Vicarious trauma: The effects on female counselors of working with sexual violence survivors. *Psychology of Women Quarterly*, 19, 49–64.

Watzlawick, P., Beavin, J.H., & Jackson, D. (1967) *Pragmatics of Human Communication*. New York: Norton.

Watzlawick, P., Weakland, J., & Fisch, R. (1974). *Change: Principles of problem resolution*. New York: Norton.

Yarvis, J. & Bordnick, P. (2003) Psychological intervention for 9/11 military mental health responders, *The U.S. Army Medical Department Journal* (Jan–Mar.), Fort Sam Houston, TX.

Yarvis, J.S. and Schiess, L. (2008) Subthreshold PTSD as a predictor of depression, alcohol use, and health problems in soldiers. *Journal of Workplace Behavioral Health*, 23(4), 395–424.

Websites about medics: http://home.att.net/~steinert/

[There are at least a dozen others if you include corpsmen and medics of all branches.]

8

THE BATTLE WITHIN

Understanding the Physiology of Warzone Exposure

Victoria E. Bruner and Pamela Woll

> *It was as though my body had a mind of its own after I came back. No matter what I did, I couldn't stop the crazy excitement that I felt—the rushes, the craving for something, my heart racing, sweats, hitting the ground, looking for flash glare in windows, and—worst of all—feeling like I would jump out of my skin.*
>
> Marine, three tours in Iraq and Afghanistan

> *Strange things began to happen. My blood pressure went through the roof. Why? I was a fighting machine over there. Now I can't sleep. I feel exhausted, as though my body has aged like an old man.*
>
> Army Major, three tours in six years

> *I was a crack ER nurse. Nothing shook me there. Now I barely have energy to get though the day. The slightest sound sets me off. Doing blood draws causes me to shake. The smell of wounds causes me to want to run the other way, leaving my patients. Am I crazy? What's wrong with me?*
>
> Army Nurse, two tours, aid station, Afghanistan

"Am I crazy?" "What's wrong with me?" "Why?" These are among the questions that haunt so many men and women who have returned from Iraq and Afghanistan with post-deployment stress effects.

Since the attacks of 9/11, our military men and women have endured increasing numbers of deployments and increasing duration of exposure to stress and threat. Insurgency wars such as those in Iraq and Afghanistan have no "front lines" that one might safely stand behind, and no relief from the need for 360-degree, 24/7 tactical awareness and vigilance. In the words of one former Marine reconnaissance officer, "Even when it's safe, it's not safe." As the troops have mobilized to meet the demands of two wars, so have their neuroendocrine systems (systems that control emotions, reactions, and drives by regulating hormones through the pituitary gland in the brain) kept them moving, functioning, fighting, thinking, reacting, saving one another's lives, and enduring great hardship.

The human body's adaptive powers are nothing short of miraculous, but survival comes at a price. Each warrior who deploys will experience some degree of altered physiology, ranging from mild and temporary stress reactions to conditions such as posttraumatic stress disorder (PTSD) and depression. Along with their physical symptoms, many service members and Veterans struggle with cognitive, emotional, social, and spiritual challenges that often baffle them and tear at the fabric of the supportive relationships that are crucial to their recovery and reintegration.

The most common explanations for these phenomena range from the moral to the psychiatric. The less enlightened still interpret them as signs of weakness, cowardice, or lack of moral fortitude—all of which are conditions that are absolutely incompatible with the military mission and culture. Even the more accurate and more humane diagnoses of mental illnesses, including PTSD, are easily confused with having "emotional problems" or being "crazy," and are still stigmatized within much of the military culture, despite progress in the Department of Defense's efforts to normalize and destigmatize combat and operational stress effects.

An estimated 19 percent of Iraq and Afghanistan Veterans suffer from symptoms of PTSD but, of those who qualify for this diagnosis, only half have been evaluated or sought treatment (Tanielian & Jaycox, 2008). Shame and the fear of reprisal still keep many service members and Veterans from endorsing their symptoms and seeking or accepting help (Hoge, Castro, Messner, et al., 2004), while their post-deployment stress effects grow steadily more complex and chronic.

According to Farris Tuma, ScD, chief of the traumatic stress program at the National Institute of Mental Health, the idea that PTSD is merely a psychological disorder is one of the most common myths concerning this condition. In reality, PTSD is a biologically based disorder in which the stress system functions in overdrive (Elias, 2008).

Charles Hoge, MD, one of the nation's leading authorities on the mental health impact of war, agrees.

> Although PTSD is considered a mental disorder, it's actually a physical condition that affects the entire body, and is best understood through the emerging science of stress physiology, which describes how the body normally response to extreme stress ... PTSD is a contradiction, a paradox—a collection of reactions that are both normal and abnormal depending on the situation—and there is debate as to where to draw the line.
>
> (Hoge, 2010, p. 2)

This is not to say that the cognitive, affective, relational, and spiritual dimensions of warzone effects are not of critical importance, but rather that these experiences have also been encoded in the body and take much of their intensity from the ways in which the body responds to extreme stress.

Until recently, very few who have suffered from PTSD and other post-deployment stress effects have received the simple, empowering, and destigmatizing message that:

1   The overwhelming intensity of their post-deployment symptoms comes from a physical core, from powerful but perfectly normal and adaptive changes in brain/body functioning in response to conditions in the war zone.
2   There are concrete things they can do to bring their bodies back in balance, creating a level playing field on which they can address the other human reactions to the experience of war.

For the clinician seeking to help returning and transitioning service members, Veterans, and their families, two essential roles are those of student and teacher of the physiology of warzone stress and the skills of resilience. Not only will such an education give both clinician and client effective tools for stress management, emotion regulation, and perspective, but it will also answer that agonizing question—"Am I crazy?"—with a resounding "No!!"

This chapter provides a brief discussion of ways in which the body and brain adapt to warzone stress, resulting challenges, and implications for clinical services and ongoing recovery. Included will be tools and concepts from the first author's "Combat Brain and Body" curriculum, delivered for more than five years to warriors with combat stress injuries; and from the second author's workbook for service members and Veterans (*Resilience 101: Understanding and optimizing your stress system after deployment*, Woll, 2010). These are by no means the only such tools that exist; nor is stabilizing the stress system a sufficient response to serious stress injuries and illnesses like PTSD, other anxiety disorders, or depressive disorders. However, when more help (e.g., medication, exposure therapy, EMDR, psychotherapy) is needed, modulation of the stress system can be an important foundation for safety and success in those interventions, and the tools described here were designed to take the approach the authors are suggesting.

The Autonomic Nervous System: From Adaptation to Dysregulation

In the words of one Iraq/Afghanistan combat Veteran with three deployments under his belt, "You gotta do what you gotta do, and then you have to live with it." The same could be said for the human body, its adaptation to life in the warzone, and the burdens it carries back home. A little information about the autonomic nervous system (ANS) and its role in human survival can help service members and Veterans understand that:

- They did not choose their bodies' reactions to the stress, threat, tragedy, and moral conflict they have encountered in the war zone.
- The body will do what the body must do to keep going, regardless of the strength, skills, courage, and knowledge of its occupant.
- The reactions that cause problems back home are the natural results of adaptations that keep people alive and functioning in the field of war.
- As evidence of the body's incredible capacity to adapt and survive, these reactions are signs of strength, rather than weakness.
- The individual can retrain his or her ANS to respond in ways that are more adaptive outside the warzone.

The human brain/body is hard-wired for survival, responding rapidly to perceived threat in ancient and primitive ways. Our automatic "fight, flight, and freeze" responses have all the power we might need to slay or escape from a predator, or to "play dead" until the predator loses interest. These responses are initiated by, and mediated through, the action of various brain structures and the release of various neurotransmitters, neuropeptides, and hormones. The brain and body are designed to adapt swiftly to temporary stress and threat, and then return to normal after the stress and threat are gone.

To understand how all this works, keep in mind the basic human instinct to stay in balance. The ANS has two arms or branches, the sympathetic (fast system—fight or flight) and the parasympathetic (slow system—rest, reset, and "freeze"), each with its own chemical messengers (e.g., adrenaline, norepinephrine, and dopamine on the sympathetic side; and cortisol, serotonin, and endorphins on the parasympathetic). One might think of the sympathetic system as the gas pedal and the parasympathetic as the brake, both necessary for effective functioning. One way to keep their names straight is to think of the sympathetic response as a "surge" of energizing chemicals, and the parasympathetic as a parachute, bringing the body down gradually.

These two systems are designed to keep us in balance—the way we tilt our arms and bend our bodies to stay in balance as we walk a narrow board—by pumping out more or less of their signature chemicals in response to environmental demands. Feedback loops between the two systems allow high levels of one chemical to trigger the release of its opposite, bringing the body and brain a little closer to balance or "homeostasis" through a process called "allostasis," the use of change to achieve stability (McEwen & Wingfield, 2003). This balancing act contributes to our resilience, our ability to "bounce back" during and after adversity.

What happens, then, in the warzone, where intense and prolonged stress and threat are the very fabric of service members' lives and occupations? The intensity of the combat experience can lead the brain's alarm system to override its natural feedback loops. The sympathetic processes and chemicals can overpower the parasympathetic, providing counterbalance to the experience of war by throwing the body and brain out of balance. Over time, the brain and body find ways of staying "wired" for action but shutting down all emotion, for the sake of survival and effective functioning.

In *Generation Kill*, author Evan Wright (2004) described the reactions of Marines from the First Recon after two months of heavy combat in the 2003 invasion of Iraq:

> In combat, the change seems physical at first. Adrenaline begins to flood your systems the moment the first bullet is fired. But unlike adrenaline rushes in the civilian world—a car accident or bungee jump, where the surge lasts only a few minutes—in combat, the rush can go on for hours. In time, your body seems to burn out from it, or maybe the adrenaline just runs out. Whatever the case, after a while you begin to almost lose the physical capacity for fear. Explosions go off. You cease to jump or flinch. In this moment now, everyone sits still, numbly watching the mortars thump down nearby. The only things moving are the pupils of their eyes. This is not to say the terror goes away. It simply moves out from the twitching muscles and nerves in your body and takes up residence in your mind. If you feed it with morbid thoughts of all the terrible ways you could be maimed or die, it gets worse. It also gets worse if you think about pleasant things. Good memories or plans for the future just remind you how much you don't want to die or get hurt. It's best to shut down, to block everything out. But to reach that state, you have to almost give up being yourself.
>
> (Wright, 2004: 300–301)

The body's reaction to life in the warzone is absolutely normal, natural, automatic, and adaptive; but the prolonged nature of this experience places an enormous burden on the body and the brain—and on the human being who lives there. During deployment, many warriors' bodies stay in survival mode for days, weeks, or months at a time. After their return home or deployment in safe locations, the removal of that constant threat puts the body off balance once more, and the sheer physical toll of constant stress and arousal begins to become apparent.

This can range from the more common and temporary stress reactions to disorders such as PTSD. In *Once a Warrior—Always a Warrior*, Charles Hoge writes that:

> Neurobiological research has helped us to understand that PTSD is not an "emotional" or "psychological" disorder, but a physiological condition that affects the entire body, including cardiovascular functioning, hormone system balance, and immune functioning. PTSD can result in physical,

cognitive, psychological, emotional, and behavioral reactions that all have a physiological basis.

(Hoge, 2010, p. 3)

Service members, commanding officers, family members, friends, employers, and co-workers are often baffled and frightened by the mysterious symptoms that seem to arise "out of nowhere." Fear of being labeled "defective," losing the trust of their comrades and commanders, and losing important opportunities can keep many service members and Veterans from acknowledging and seeking help for their symptoms (Hoge et al., 2004).

CAPT Sandy Davis is a 34-year-old Emergency Room (ER) Nurse who served two tours in Afghanistan with her Army National Guard unit. She is married, with a six-year-old daughter, and worked in an ER for eight years before her first deployment. In Afghanistan, CAPT Davis attended to wounded and dying Soldiers and Marines, and earned a reputation for her ability to function with skill and compassion even under the most stressful, painful, and sometimes tragic circumstances. As the fighting in Afghanistan accelerated during her last tour, her unit saw more and more casualties and set up a makeshift morgue next to her quarters. On a daily basis, she was exposed to severe burns, amputated limbs, and death. Through it all, CAPT Davis remained a highly effective member of her unit, providing comfort and care and saving many lives.

Six months after her return home, CAPT Davis began to awaken at night, shaking, often following intense nightmares. She found herself growing irritated with her husband and her child over little things, and she began to take less pleasure in activities she had always enjoyed, feeling "numb" and separate from these experiences. She lost all desire for sexual activity with her husband, though their marriage had always been a peaceful and supportive one. She wanted to return to civilian employment in the ER, but somehow kept thinking of reasons not to apply. She also found it harder and harder to find the motivation to go anywhere or do anything.

On one level, CAPT Davis knew she was experiencing problems, but she felt ashamed of and defeated by her symptoms. She had an unspoken belief that these challenges meant that she was weak, or that she was losing her sanity. Fearing that something was terribly wrong, she pretended nothing was wrong. She dismissed her husband's repeated suggestions that she seek help, until a mandatory routine screening process brought her in for an assessment. She arrived at the assessment ready to defend herself against evidence that she was "crazy."

It is precisely this fear, this misunderstanding of post-deployment effects, that the educational component of treatment is designed to remedy. At the Deployment Health Clinical Center, a Department of Defense agency that is a tenant at Walter Reed Army Medical Center, Soldiers with PTSD, depressive disorders, and other post-deployment conditions are given extensive, user-friendly psychoeducation on the body's reactions to war. In the *Combat Brain and Body* curriculum developed for that program five years ago, combat and post-combat effects are explained in non-stigmatizing terms as Autonomic Nervous System Reactivity Syndrome, or ANSRS (pronounced "answers"). The following "Blood, Sweat, and Fear" chart developed for *Combat Brain and Body* summarizes some key ANS adaptations, their benefits to functioning in combat, and their toll on the body.

TABLE 8.1 Blood, sweat, and fear: natural responses to stress

Response	*Natural stress/combat benefit*	*"In the now" drawback*
Release of cortisone from adrenals	Protection from instant allergy	Chronic elevation leads to: • the destruction of the body's resistance to stresses of cancer/infection/illness/surgery; • lymph glands atrophy; • immune response weakened; • increased acidity leading to ulcers, colitis, IBS; • bones brittle/osteoporosis; • panic, hypertension, sodium retention
Thyroid release	Hypermetabolism, extra energy	Intolerance to heat Hyper-alert Insomnia, leading to exhaustion, leading to burnout
Endorphin release from hypothalamus	"Feel-good" hormone—potent pain killer Wisdom of body	Stress depletes endorphins/enkephelins Chronic immune system activity
Reduction of stress hormones—Testosterone/progesterone	Decreased fertility	Decrease in libido leading to anxiety, sexual dysfunction
Shutdown of digestive tract	Blood diverted to muscles/heart/lungs	Decrease in secretions—dry mouth, abdominal discomfort
Release of sugar in blood, increasing insulin to metabolize it/Glucogenesis	Quick, short-distance energy supply Hyperinsulinimia	Increased demand on pancreas for insulin—leads to diabetes, hypoglycemia
Increase of cholesterol—mainly from liver	"Long-distance" fuel	Chronic—leading to Chol in blood vessels, CAD/Coronary
Increased heart rate	Pumps more blood to muscles and lungs (increased O_2)	Increased allergy, asthma, sensitivity to cigarette/secondary smoke

(Continued)

TABLE 8.1 (*Continued*)

Response	Natural stress/combat benefit	"In the now" drawback
Blood thickens	Increased O$_2$, fight infection, stop bleeding	CVA, emboli, heart attack
Skin "crawls"	Increased sensitivity, reduces blood loss, sweat leading to coolness	Sweaty palms, pallor, hotsweats, sensitivity to pain
Heightened awareness—all senses	Peak function: Optic—pupils dilate; Olfactory—acute; taste/smell—enhanced	Leads to crash, overload

Source: *Combat Brain and Body*, developed by Victoria Bruner, LCSW, RN, BCETS, Deployment Health Clinical Center, Walter Reed Army Medical Center.

The Brain: Safety, Control, and Complication

As the body slams into overdrive, pulls back on the throttle, or shuts down its capacity to feel emotion, the brain functions as the driver of this process. Information about the brain under stress and threat can be a powerful force in destigmatizing post-deployment stress reactions. Such information shows how automatic and powerful these processes are, and how far beyond the reach of conscious intent they tend to operate.

When extreme threat is combined with helplessness—as often happens in the overwhelming circumstances of war—the brain can send out signals that tell the body to shut down or "freeze." Heart rate slows, blood pressure lowers, body temperature drops, and movement stops. In the warzone, this reaction might be momentary or temporary, because much of military training has focused on staying in fight mode and avoiding the freeze. However, even a brief freeze response that is not discharged through physical movement or emotional release may result in the storage of the sensory experience of trauma in the body (Levine, 1997).

Threat, Trauma, and Memory

To the service member, Veteran, or family member, the most frightening and humiliating reactions to combat and operational stress often include the many effects of these processes on memory. The experience of trauma can leave people with absent or incomplete conscious memory of important events and/or lead to flashbacks (re-lived sensory experiences of traumatic events and emotions), vivid nightmares, or intrusive memories (van der Kolk & Fisler, 1995). Without an understanding of the way the brain stores memory in trauma, people often conclude that they are "blocking out" memories because they are too weak or cowardly to face them, that they are hallucinating or "making up" experiences that never happened, or that they have lost all control of their minds.

One of the most liberating gifts to service members, Veterans, and their families may be straightforward information about the way the brain consolidates and retrieves memories and the effects of stress chemicals on this process.

While the primitive amygdala is storing unconscious fragments of survival-related emotional memory, the more sophisticated hippocampus is storing conscious, narrative, "context" memories. Under threat, though, the combination of stress chemicals can signal the hippocampus to stop storing narrative details in long-term memory. So vivid unconscious memories of battle can be "burned" into the service member's brain and body, but conscious narrative memories of the same event may never be consolidated or stored properly (van der Kolk & Fisler, 1995). The gaps in memory, flashbacks, and intrusive memories that can seem so much like evidence of "insanity" are in reality the function of natural and adaptive chemical processes, designed to protect us.

The same can be said for the body's reactions to environmental cues that resemble sights, sounds, odors, and sensations associated with danger at war. The most common examples include fireworks (which the survival brain may interpret as explosions), the smell of meat on the barbecue (which the survival brain may connect with the smell of burning human flesh), or encountering roadside litter (which the survival brain may see as a possible improvised explosive device, or IED). In and of itself, the act of driving can trigger alarm responses, given the high rates of casualties on the roads in Iraq and Afghanistan. Even strong emotions can set off a cascade of survival reactions within the body, resulting in behavior that can be baffling to civilians, e.g., driving recklessly at high speed through residential areas.

Take, for example, the Army Sergeant who had survived numerous IED attacks in which he saw flashes, smelled smoke, and was shaken to the core. Back in his home town, as he walked down the street, the Sergeant saw a large truck, which simultaneously rolled loudly over a metal grate and discharged a large plume of black smoke. Despite his conscious knowledge that this was a commercial truck in a safe community, the combination of sight and sound triggered a freeze response. He stood there, speechless and unable to move.

One additional challenge is the fact that these automatic reactions can grow more intense over time, rather than fading. Unlike the narrative memories stored by the hippocampus, the amygdala's emotional memories do not degrade over time. Each time the brain and body react to an innocent stimulus as if it were a remembered war-time threat, the emotional memory is learned and encoded even more deeply. The body's reaction becomes a source of alarm in and of itself, triggering even stronger reactions over time. This "kindling" process is one reason why untreated post-trauma effects can continue to grow more severe long after exposure to the war zone.

The sometimes progressive nature of war-zone stress effects makes effective outreach, screening, intervention, and assessment—tailored to the Military experience—all the more critical. When CAPT Davis was screened for the severity of her post-deployment effects, she was administered the PCL-M

(Weathers, Litz, Herman, et al., 1993), the version of the PTSD Checklist used to measure symptoms that arise following "stressful Military experiences." Used for diagnosis and symptom monitoring in active duty service members and Veterans, the PCL-M uses a self-report format to assess 17 items, organized within the three major symptom categories identified in the Diagnostic and Statistical Manual of Mental Disorders (DSM-IV-TR): re-experiencing, avoidance, and hyperarousal (APA, 2000). Each item is scored on a Likert scale from 1 to 5, with totals ranging from 17 to 85, and a cutoff score of 50. CAPT Davis had an overall score of 60 and endorsed "quite a bit" of hyperarousal, feeling upset by reminders, and feeling emotionally numb. However, she had been screened relatively early in the progression of her symptoms, and her concern for family relationships had left her willing to answer the questions honestly and consider treatment options.

The Whole Human Being

For service members, Veterans, and their families, information about the brain and Autonomic Nervous System Reactivity Syndrome might ring hollow if it seems to discount the complex psychological, social, and spiritual experience of the individual and family. It is essential to remember that the experience of war—like other experiences—affects us simultaneously on a number of levels, including the body in general, the brain, thoughts, feelings, the spirit, the family, and the human community (including the military Unit). These levels are connected, not only in a psychological or spiritual sense, but also in some very concrete physical ways. For example, the depth and quality of human relationships—from early caregiving relationships to camaraderie at war or family support back home—can have profound effects on people's physical, neurological, and emotional ability to regulate their stress reactions (Siegel, 1999).

As Evan Wright (2004) described so eloquently in *Generation Kill*, common responses to combat stress include an adaptive tendency to compartmentalize and feel separate from areas of experience that might hold intolerable levels of emotion. The recovery process includes exploration of and reconnection with the neglected realms of the self, as it becomes safe to do so. The following chart (Table 8.2), called "Stress and Survival Systems at a Glance," is reprinted from *Resilience 101: Understanding and optimizing your stress system after deployment* (Woll, 2010), a workbook for service members and Veterans. The chart summarizes some common reactions to war on multiple levels, showing at each level a few typical automatic responses, the adaptive power of these responses in the war zone, the possible impact later, and suggestions for restoring balance.

TABLE 8.2 Stress and survival systems at a glance

	1. Common automatic responses	*2. Power of these responses*	*3. Possible impact afterwards*	*4. Suggestions for restoring balance*
The Body	Powerful chemicals go into "overdrive"—heart racing, "super-human" strength; if helpless, go into "freeze" responses, tensing protective front core muscles.	In combat, speed and strength help you feel confident, react quickly and decisively, fight, save lives, escape harm. "Freezing" can save lives.	After these chemicals go into overdrive, the body has some unfinished business. It may be shaky, "jumpy," or very tired or weak (feeling "paralyzed") for a while.	Use the Virtual Tranquilizer® and Grounding Exercises to relax and release energy from front core muscles. Good diet (whether or not you feel hungry), rest, exercise, vitamins and minerals, and medical care to help the body handle stress and learn to make stress chemicals again. Patience with the time it takes the body to "normalize."
	In constant threat, these systems can stay on overdrive for a long time.	You can stay ready for battle at all times, for long periods of time.	Constant stress makes the body jumpy, weak, vulnerable to chronic illness.	
The Brain	Some chemicals speed up thoughts, raise feelings of alarm and fear.	Speedy thoughts help you take action. Alarm and fear help you judge threat.	"Speedy" chemicals cause jittery nerves, anger, feeling threatened, sleep trouble.	Understand that these are normal chemical reactions to sometimes unimaginable events. Use Grounding and Mindfulness skills to become an observer of your own reactions. Watch your reactions to things that seem like threats or insults, and question whether they really are, or if it's just your brain chemicals talking. Avoid alcohol, drugs, and caffeine, and get medical advice if you think you might need help. Get help for depression and any other reactions that last more than a month.
	Some chemicals calm you down, help you control your actions/reactions; keep your moods stable, even in unstable situations like combat.	These calming chemicals help you think more clearly, make better decisions, react in more effective ways, cooperate better, be a better leader.	Calming chemicals can "wear out" after they've been needed too much, causing anxiety, depression, urges to drink or use drugs, higher risk of getting addicted.	
	Some chemicals relieve pain and sometimes help you forget what you experienced under intense stress.	Pain relief during the crisis—and forgetting the pain afterwards—helps you keep going in spite of the pain.	You might lose important memories later, or memories might "come at you out of nowhere," even long after combat is over.	

(Continued)

TABLE 8.2 *(Continued)*

	1. Common automatic responses	2. Power of these responses	3. Possible impact afterwards	4. Suggestions for restoring balance
Thoughts	"This isn't happening. It isn't so bad."	Makes it easier to cope and function.	You might neglect signs you need help.	Talk about what happened, how it really was. Question the thoughts that sound self-critical or self-destructive. Balance helping others with getting the support or professional help you need. Let trust grow back slowly. Question blame, and put it in context. Talk about responsibility.
	"I'm strong; other people need me."	Brings more hope, courage, action.	You might see needs as weaknesses.	
	"I can't trust anyone outside the Unit."	Helps you spot danger and react to it.	You might not trust anyone outside the Unit.	
	"This is all happening for a reason."	Helps you accept pain and move on.	You might blame yourself or others.	
Feelings	Not feeling emotions (numbing them).	Less pain/fear, more decisive action.	You might not grieve important losses.	Practice noticing what you feel, putting a name to it, and feeling whatever it is. Use skills like Grounding and Mindfulness to help you notice and manage your feelings. Let the grieving happen in whatever form or timetable it seems to want to take. Remember: It takes great courage to feel.
	Feeling only "safe" emotions (anger).	Helps you focus on fighting and winning.	You might take feelings for weakness.	
	"Projecting" your feelings onto others.	Helps you not notice/feel your feelings.	You might resent, damage relationships.	
	Giving in to just feeling overwhelmed.	Lets people know you need help.	You might ignore real strength/courage.	
The Spirit	Connecting with your spiritual beliefs.	Strength in safety, connection, meaning.	You might reject others' help or beliefs.	Know that there's plenty of room for your beliefs, others' beliefs, and human help.
	Questioning or rejecting your beliefs.	Helps explain painful and unfair things.	You might lose connection, meaning.	Use questioning to strengthen your beliefs and get closer to what you really believe.
	Finding new spiritual feelings/beliefs.	Brings in new spiritual strength/hope.	You might lose beliefs when crisis is over.	Balance acceptance with need for action.
	Accepting and transcending events.	More clarity, calm, sense of purpose.	You might accept things you should change.	

The Unit	Military discipline, high expectations.	Standards promote strength, discipline.	You might be ashamed of reactions to stress.	Know that it's not weak or disloyal to get help for the body's and brain's reactions to warzone stress. Make and keep deep friendships with others who have served.
	Staying alert for danger at all times.	You're ready to react to any emergency.	Toll on body and brain (see above).	
	Sense of unity within the Unit.	Cooperation saves lives, wins battles.	You might feel lost/alone after deployment.	
Home	Keeping in contact from the warzone.	Sense of connection brings strength.	Stronger feelings of stress, loss, missing them.	Accept that you've changed, and those at home have changed, too. Learn who you all are now. Use resources for re-learning trust, communication, and relationships.
	Not talking about bad experiences.	Protects loved ones from pain and fear.	You might feel disconnected from home.	
	Remembering your home as ideal.	Reminds you what you're fighting for.	Nobody can live up to an ideal in real life.	

Reprinted from *Resilience 101: Understanding and optimizing your stress system after deployment*, developed by Pamela Woll, MA, CADP (2010).

Implications for Clinical Services and Ongoing Recovery

Between stimulus and response there is a space. In that space is our freedom and power to choose our response. In our response lies our growth and our freedom.

Viktor Frankl (1961, p. 122)

As powerful and automatic as the body's responses to war may be, their hold is not absolute:

- An understanding of these responses can make them less frightening and remove the stigma that stands as a barrier to help-seeking, access to services, and retention in treatment. Service members, Veterans, family members, and friends can all benefit from user-friendly psychoeducation on the adaptive power of the human brain and body. The goal is to spread the understanding that these symptoms make sense and the people who struggle with them are neither "defective" nor "crazy."
- Trustworthy relationships with caring friends, mentors, family members, and clinicians can strengthen the brain's ability to modulate stress responses, while they feed the human need for connection and community. Services that prepare and support families and communities are essential to the wellbeing of service members and Veterans. Civilian clinicians who study and respect important elements of the military culture and the experience of war can help bridge the gap between the military and civilian cultures.
- Identification of the environmental cues that trigger traumatic memories and stress reactions can keep these cues from taking service members and Veterans by surprise and give them time to formulate coping strategies. Plans for anticipating and navigating triggers can increase both the perception and the reality of psychological safety.
- Skill training in methods of regulating the stress system (e.g., grounding, breathing, Mindfulness, Yoga, qi-gong, physical exercise) can prepare service members and Veterans for safer and more effective self-management during redeployment overseas, reintegration at home, and participation in treatment processes designed to heal the body's relationship with the memory of war. If the number of sessions is limited and the clinician accomplishes nothing else, these self-regulation skills can help service members and Veterans achieve higher levels of physical and psychological safety. Skill training is also highly compatible with military values and the military culture's emphasis on physical training and resilience. Many service members and Veterans will be more likely to gravitate toward something called "skill training" than toward something called "therapy."
- Therapeutic models and practices that involve or focus on the body can help discharge and release stored responses to trauma. Used carefully, models and practices that integrate emotional and narrative memories of traumatic events

can effectively defuse the power of traumatic memories. Models that address both the body and the integration of memories (e.g., EMDR, Modified Exposure Therapy with Somatic Pacing) often combine the best of both approaches. Without a somatic component, "talk" therapies may fail to reach the trauma where it lives.

- A holistic focus on understanding the whole human response to stress, threat, and trauma can help service members and Veterans understand the intensity of their reactions on a variety of levels, and begin to reintegrate areas of life they might otherwise be tempted to compartmentalize.

- The need to encourage hope and change—countering the temptation to believe these symptoms are inevitably chronic and permanent—brings us full-circle, back to an emphasis on psychoeducation and skill training. (A number of tools are available, including materials from the *Combat Brain and Body* curriculum from Walter Reed Army Medical Center and the *Resilience 101: Understanding and optimizing your stress system after deployment* workbook and pocket booklet, available for free download at http://sites.google.com/site/humanprioritiesorg/home/resilience-101).

Driven by the ancient instinct to survive, the body responds to threat in ways that can save lives but sometimes come at a high price. The service member or Veteran is free to choose less painful responses, but first must understand the programmed physical responses, learn how to retrain the body, and work toward bringing the body and mind back into balance. Often this freedom to choose is found in partnership with a skilled clinician who is willing to listen, learn, care, respect, teach, train, process, and believe in the individual and his or her sources of strength and support.

After her assessment, CAPT Davis was assigned to a therapist who understood deployment stress and the military culture and slowly established a relationship of rapport and trust. The psychoeducational program that began her treatment helped CAPT Davis realize that the symptoms she was experiencing made sense, given the ways in which her body had reacted to the extreme stress she experienced in Afghanistan. She received skill training in managing her breathing, recognizing her body's reactivity, and modulating her stress system. She learned that some of her symptoms indicated moderate depression and was encouraged to begin a course of antidepressant medication. At first she declined the medication, but a few weeks later she decided that medication would be a good temporary measure.

After she had undergone enough skill training to feel confident facing her memories, CAPT Davis began a short course of Eye Movement Desensitization and Reprocessing (EMDR), a therapeutic process that combines memory de-sensitization with a somatic component. Her nightmares and high levels of arousal began to subside, and her interactions with her family became more harmonious.

Through the skill training and group discussions with other women who had been deployed, CAPT Davis came to understand and accept the fact that it would take a while for her stress effects to go away completely, but that this said nothing negative about her strength or her character. Over the next year and a half, her symptoms gradually diminished, and she tapered off the antidepressant, with no ill effects. Six months after she began treatment, CAPT Davis returned to work in the local ER and found that her stress-management skills helped her cope, even with situations that reminded her of the carnage and death she had seen in Afghanistan.

CAPT Davis is not the same person she was before her first deployment—and understands she will never be that person again—but her life is a fulfilling one, and she is able to take joy in her surroundings, her work, her family, and her friends. For CAPT Davis and others who have served, there may be no real safety in the warzone, but the willing clinician can help construct real safety—and real freedom—in the heart, mind, and body of the service member or Veteran who has risked all and sacrificed so much.

References

APA (American Psychiatric Association) (2000). *Diagnostic and Statistical Manual of Mental Disorders, DSM-IV TR* (4th Ed.). Arlington, VA: American Psychiatric Association.

Ellis, M. (2008). Post-traumatic stress is a war within for military and civilians. *USA Today*, 10/27/08. Retrieved March 18, 2010 from: http://www.usatoday.com/news/health/2008-10-26-PTSD-main_N.htm

Frankl, V.E. (1961). *The Harvard Lectures.* Vienna: Viktor Frankl Archives.

Hoge, C.W. (2010). *Once a Warrior, Always a Warrior: Navigating the transition from combat to home—including combat stress, PTSD, and mTBI.* Guilford, CT: Globe Pequot Press.

Hoge, C.W., Castro, C.A., Messner, S.C., McGurk, D., Cotting, D.I., & Koffman, R.L. (2004). Combat duty in Iraq and Afghanistan: Mental health problems and barriers to care. *New England Journal of Medicine*, 351(1), 13–22.

Levine, P.A. (with Frederick, A.) (1997). *Waking the Tiger: Healing trauma.* Berkeley, CA: North Atlantic Books.

McEwen, B.S. & Wingfield, J.C. (2003). The concept of allostasis in biology and biomedicine. *Hormones and Behavior*, 43(1), 2–15.

Siegel, D.J. (1999). *The Developing Mind: How relationships and the brain interact to shape who we are.* New York: The Guilford Press.

Tanielian, T. & Jaycox, L.H. (Eds.) (2008). *Invisible Wounds of War: Psychological and cognitive injuries, their consequences, and services to assist recovery.* Santa Monica, CA: The Rand Corporation.

van der Kolk, B.A. & Fisler, R. (1995). Dissociation and the fragmentary nature of traumatic memories: Overview and exploratory study. *Journal of Traumatic Stress*, 8(4), 505–525.

Weathers, F., Litz, B., Herman, D., Huska, J., & Keane, T. (1993). *The PTSD Checklist (PCL): Reliability, validity, and diagnostic utility.* Paper presented at the Annual Convention of the International Society for Traumatic Stress Studies, San Antonio, Texas.

Woll, P. (2010). *Resilience 101: Understanding and optimizing your stress system after deployment* (Version 3). Chicago, IL: Human Priorities.

Wright, E. (2004). *Generation Kill: Devil dogs, iceman, Captain America and the new face of American war.* New York: G.P. Putnam's Sons.

PART III
Clinical Challenges

9

THOSE WHO HAVE SERVED IN AFGHANISTAN/IRAQ

Coming Home

Joan Beder

Imagine your life: You have a family, a spouse, parents and friends. You are active duty military. You are 25 years old. You receive notice that you are to deploy in three weeks. The family has been expecting this for some time but now the time has come. You start to make ready for the long-awaited experience. You have been in training for many months and are really eager to deploy. Domestic issues at home have been addressed and goodbyes said. Off you go for 12–15 months. You arrange to make contact with the family as often as possible. While in Iraq/Afghanistan, you are exposed to sights, sounds, and experiences that are consistent with war: people shooting at you, soldiers being shot, people dying in battle, killing. You've lost buddies in battle. Soldiers have been sent home but you remain, having suffered only a minor wound from shrapnel. Fifteen months goes by—holidays, birthdays, anniversaries, sicknesses, problems at home, intense loneliness, terror, and anguish—have marked the time away. And now imagine returning home. Reintegration means to integrate again, restore to unity. What awaits you?

Reentry—Returning Home—Background

War changes people. One can argue whether these changes are positive or negative, but the fact that combat deployed soldiers change cannot be argued. War changes everyone, the warriors and their families, their siblings, parents and grandparents (Hall, 2008). These changes potentially influence the quality of relationships with family, friends, coworkers and others. For those who are wounded, the experience is that much more complex as health and medical concerns dominate the return experience. An uncertain future marked by anxiety over physical disabilities and the subsequent medical care can be daunting for the returning military member and their family (Blaise, Thompson & McCreary, 2006). While the challenges can be great for any soldier returning from combat, many who return from Iraq/ Afghanistan experience positive reintegration and report being enhanced through their military experience. But the fact remains, that participating in war can have a lasting impact on the soldier and their family that can ultimately strengthen the individuals or deplete them. It is best to understand that "When a soldier deploys, the whole family serves. When a soldier returns from combat, the whole family is affected" (Darwin, 2009, p. 433). This suggests that deployment does not happen in a vacuum; the experience and the subsequent reintegration to home and family touch many.

Unique to the history of war for Americans, 90 percent of combat Veterans wounded in Iraq and Afghanistan will survive their injury. Service members injured in battle are surviving injuries that would have been fatal in previous conflicts thanks to improved armor and battlefield medical treatment (Hyer, 2006). Many of these service members are treated in a military facility and will return to active duty within weeks of their injury. Some of these soldiers will even return to their unit and reengage in combat. Because so many military members survive, their care has become extremely complex and protracted. It is not just the physical wounds that cause strife. Psychologically there is much to be concerned about as well since "... for the first time in recorded warfare, psychological morbidity is likely to far outstrip physical injury associated with combat" (Sammons & Batten, 2008, p. 921). "The complications of psychological injury (may be) disastrous and fatal ... Complications wreck the capacity for a flourishing life not only of the Veteran but of the whole family, sometimes their workplace, sometimes their local community" (Shay, 2009, p. 292). Because of the potential for psychological injury, the process of coming home and the reintegration with family deserves particular attention on the part of social workers and other mental health providers.

This chapter provides an overview of some of the issues involved in reintegration and offers suggestions for intervention. Case material will highlight the salient issues faced by reintegrating service members and their families. The material in the chapter is designed to offer practical information related to the experience of reintegration because "whether you have a private practice or work in a university counseling center or a community mental health clinic, you may be encountering military members who had returned from Iraq and/or Afghanistan" (Shaw & Hector, 2010, p. 128).

> David R. came from a military family and there was no question but that he was headed to Iraq. David's wife, Sue, was left for months and although they had frequent contact, she struggled much of the time with intense loneliness and anxiety. In the seventh month of his deployment, he was shot in the leg. The wound was serious and he was shipped back to the States, suffered an amputation and was fitted for a prosthetic leg. He has nightmares daily, is angry and depressed, cannot be in large crowds, and is socially

withdrawn. There is the strong possibility of a co-diagnosis of Post Traumatic Stress Disorder (PTSD). Home is essentially dysfunctional and relates more to David's state of mind more than anything else. Sue is struggling to accept the marriage and home situation.

The Service Member Experience

As a combat Veteran—one who has served in Iraq or Afghanistan—there are certain "givens" based on what a service member does and what he/she experiences as well as the subsequent burdens they bear. Active participation in war is synonymous with fear, aggression, loss, anguish, and confronting both visual and emotional challenges. Stress is the most common part of military life and, while the most immediate stressor that comes to mind is active combat, service members also face stress from other sources.

The stressors of deployment are most frequently cited as combat related and include being attacked, high levels of alertness and arousal, being fired upon, being wounded, seeing others sustain injury or death, witnessing destruction etc. Research on recorded warzone experiences by members of the military found that 60 percent reported being attacked or ambushed, 86 percent received incoming fire, 50 percent were shot at, 36 percent discharged their weapon, 63 percent saw dead bodies, and 79 percent reported knowing someone seriously wounded or killed (VA National Center for PTSD, 2010). Additional stressors include job demands (the job of being a soldier) which include long work hours, heavy work loads, conflicts with supervisors and no option to leave the job; work–family conflicts which include long separations and fears; sexual harassment; and perceived threat, the fear of harm that a service member may experience in the warzone. Perceived threat impacts not only the service member but also those who are at home as well (Kelly & Vogt, 2008).

In a recent study of over 40,000 participants, those men and women that had combat exposure had the highest rate of onset depression, followed by those not deployed and those deployed without combat exposure (Wells, Leardman, Fortuna, et al., 2009). In addition, further stress is experienced as a result of difficult living conditions, lack of privacy, climate issues, lack of sleep, unpredictable situations and overall anxiety regarding safety. Based on all of the above stressors, it is reasonable to assume that "... returning home from combat may present considerable challenges for service members ... Many will easily make the adjustment back to living and working in noncombat environments; others will have more difficulty" (Conoscenti, Vine, Papa, & Litz, 2009, p. 139).

Reintegration

Segal (1986), a sociologist, described an on-going conflict between the military and the family. She saw the military and the family as "greedy institutions" each vying for the individual's time and energy and their exclusive and undivided loyalty. As greedy institutions, Segal contends, "... they (greedy institutions) are characterized by the fact that they exercise pressures on component individuals to weaken their ties, or not to form any ties, with other institutions or persons that might make claims that conflict ..." (1986, p. 11). As greedy institutions, there is often an underlying tension between the needs of the military and the family. As a result, when service members return home after their service, tensions and allegiances that have been shelved while deployed are frequently destined to surface as the service member has to potentially embrace conflicting "institutions" and shift allegiance from one to another to successfully return to home life. For many, this struggle cannot be accomplished successfully and redeployment becomes an option/choice. Nevertheless, the "greedy institutions" will often vie for the allegiance of the service member creating tensions for the service member or family members or both.

Returning from military service in wartime has challenges and the impact of reentry permeates many aspects of the service member's life. There are several factors that may influence the reintegration process: the length of the deployment, the number of deployments, the age of the service member, the level of combat exposure, the strength of the marriage/family situation pre-deployment. The length and impact of deployments has been noted in research by Beder, Coe, & Sommer (2011). Findings in this study showed that those who had had multiple deployments were negatively impacted in their personal sense of self and in their family lives; those with three or more deployments were the most negatively impacted. Those who had deployments that lasted more than six months were negatively impacted in their personal and work lives (sense of productivity and industry). Similarly, those who had direct combat experience experienced a negative impact on their family life upon reintegration. Age could be a factor in the reintegration experience, as younger service members may not have been in marriages that are of long duration and may have joined the military to leave lives that were not fully established. It is estimated that 47 percent of the active duty enlisted force is between the ages of 17 and 24 (Tanielian & Jaycox, 2008).

Assuming the service member has been deployed for a period of months—typically the service member is deployed from 12-15 months—home may be a different place than what they remember it to be. During this time, everyone has been changed by the passage of time. There have been developmental changes in children, the acquisition of new skills and the exposure to new things. Spouses and their children will have created new and different routines, behavioral patterns and different personal and family alliances. For the service member, relationships with others in their unit may have ended abruptly due to injury and relocation, and the constant support of military relationships is no longer available. Soldiers who have been in a battle zone with danger all around must tone down their nervous system that has been tuned to fight or flight in the face of danger and realize the safety of home (Darwin, 2009). The shift from camaraderie with other soldiers to the reengagement with family and friends may be initially welcomed, but the soldier may still feel isolated. Service members may have a lack of clarity regarding the next steps in their life; apprehension over the return to their civilian jobs, schools or community can be overwhelming.

Another aspect of reintegration that may promote confusion for the returnee relates to the level and frequency of communication that occurred while the service member was overseas. With advances in cellular technology, wider email and Internet access and the use of social networking sites, troops in combat zones can be in close communication with those at home, daily or even more frequently. However, what has been communicated to the service member, and what has the service member communicated to home? How much of the difficult aspects of wartime have been edited out of communication? How much of home-to-soldier information has been edited? What are both sides of the communication leaving out, "cleaning up," and omitting to prevent worry and anxiety of the other? What then will the service member encounter upon return and vice versa? Staying in touch with home for the duration of the deployment will surely promote gaps in information that could provoke anguish and confusion when the service member returns. Another area of difficulty to anticipate is that the returning service member may feel marginalized and superfluous to the running of the household. Also, the emotional and physical state of the returnee may have to be considered and time needed to adjust to home and household obligations.

As the typical deployment has been 15 months (due to have been reduced by President Bush in 2008) many marriages will have suffered and been destroyed. A report by the Army Mental Health Advisory Team (MHAT) in 2008 surveyed mental health specialists working with soldiers in Iraq and Afghanistan, noting that 15-month deployments frequently destroy marriages. The report further noted that by the 14th or 15th month, 20 percent of marriages were planning divorce. For younger soldiers, in younger marriages, the number was closer to 30 percent.

These and many other readjustment challenges should be expected as non-parallel experiences have occurred between the family and the service member. The challenges of successful reintegration, defined by a family being able to readjust to a new and stable homeostasis, are many.

SR joined the military at 20, soon after high school. He was in a two-year marriage with an 18-month-old son when he received his notice to deploy to Iraq. He was in Iraq over a year during which time his son was walking, talking and had begun a day care program so Mary, his wife, could work to keep the family finances on an even keel. SR's deployment was very difficult for Mary; she had few friends and her family was several states away and she had limited contact with SR's family. SR returned looking fit and well. The couple had had weekly telephone and email communication during the deployment and while much had gone on for both Mary and SR, they imagined that the reunion and safety of home would insure a smooth reintegration.

SR's sleep patterns were very irregular, and he seemed edgy, nervous, and generally, according to Mary, difficult to be around.

What Can Families Expect—What is "Normal/Typical"?

In the following discussion, it is important to note that the majority of returning service members and their families will successfully readjust to life back home; it may take some weeks or months but, for most, life will stabilize and become the "new normal."

There are a number of expected/common reactions that can be anticipated for the returning service member (see Table 9.1). Each of these reactions is to be anticipated and is to be considered within a "normal" range. They are typical reactions to the trauma of war and military life and typical of reactions upon returning home. Over time, most will abate and eventually disappear as the service member makes the needed adjustments to the routines at home and their departure from the military life. As with most of these reactions, if they do not abate over time, if they become more intense and disruptive, if they interfere with family and social relationships, or if the individual is persistently severely depressed or angry, or even suicidal, then help must be considered. In general, as described by Hutchinson and Banks-Williams (2006, p. 67), "in many instances, a traumatized soldier is greeting a traumatized family and neither is 'recognizable' to the other". Time, and frequently intervention, is needed to address these struggles.

David R.'s situation is characteristic of a marriage in which there has been major disruption not only due to the deployment but the aftermath of serious injury and possible PTSD. Several of David's responses to his situation fall outside of what would be considered "normal" reactions and suggest that this

TABLE 9.1 Normal/common reactions that can be anticipated for the returning service member

Physical reactions	Mental/emotional reactions	Behavioral reactions
Trouble sleeping	Bad dreams, nightmares	Trouble concentrating
Trouble eating	Flashbacks, unwanted memories	Jumpy, easily startled
Headaches	Nervous, fearful, helpless	Being on guard
Health problems may worsen	Feeling sad, rejected, abandoned	Avoiding people
Agitated, easily upset	Irritated	Too much smoking, drinking, or drug use
Lack of exercise	Being numb	Aggressive driving

Source: Adapted from *Returning from the War Zone* (VA National Center for PTSD, 2010).

family/marriage will need intervention. David's behavior strongly suggests PTSD and, as well, he and Sue are struggling with adaptation to his injury. Couples counseling would surely be in order and whatever support programs are available to ease the acceptance and the adaptation to a prosthetic leg would be advised. A PTSD group might also be considered for David. David's wife is uneasy, scared, and worried. Support for each member of this family would be helpful.

SR's situation is somewhat more optimistic. He is struggling to make the transition to home and is having common and predictable reactions to the transition. His sleep is disrupted and he is edgy a good deal of the time; slowly, he is reengaging with their son who initially did not know or recognize him. As SR is in a relatively new marriage, some of the needed stability of a longer-term marriage is not fully there. Nevertheless, Mary is eager to have things work out and wants to restore the family to a more comfortable homeostasis. Mary and SR have discussed counseling as an option and both are tentative but willing.

How Can We Help?

When working with service members and their families a thorough assessment of current functioning and needs is important. Within the assessment, issues around substance abuse, presence of traumatic brain injury, depression and symptoms of an anxiety disorder, suicidality, and changes in social, occupational and family functioning should be evaluated. A PTSD screening is often needed to rule out or rule in this disorder. Since impulse control and aggressive behavior are common in many returnees, domestic violence, child abuse and other aggressive behaviors need to be evaluated. Within the assessment process, education of service members and family members is helpful regarding typical reactions to combat and normalizing many of the reintegration experience struggles.

The following assessment used a strengths based perspective for David/Sue and SR/Mary.

David, because of his wounding and subsequent amputation, has gone through a very difficult time. He is not considering suicide. One of David's strengths is that which he may struggle with the most—being in a military family. However, as part of a military family, David can be seen as a hero and supported by his family's tradition of having served. Sue is his strongest advocate and despite the struggles, says she will be with him "through thick and thin." Her commitment to him is strong and must be seen as a positive in the reintegration effort. Another strength is that David has acknowledged his PTSD and is willing to address this with support group and individual counseling intervention. David is determined to be able to walk with his "new leg" and resume most of his pre-deployment athletic activities. His and Sue's spirits are strong. In terms of intervention, it is timely and welcomed by both David and Sue.

SR does not have the stressor of physical injury. He does have greater emotional depletion than had been initially expected. He claims to feel somewhat marginalized as Mary has been running the home and managing childcare for the last 15 months. Mary was so glad to have SR home and safe but has been struggling to adapt to his moods. The strength of this marriage is being tested in these first few weeks of return. However, the fact that the couple has sought counseling this early speaks of an openness to explore the difficult areas and work toward enhanced communication. Mary is willing to be patient with SR as he reconnects to their son—her patience is a strong part of the marriage. SR is not suicidal and while he exhibits some of the physical and emotional reactions mentioned above, they are slowly abating, also seen as a positive. SR has contacted some of his buddies who served with him and are at home and has enjoyed the contact. SR's ability to connect and reconnect is a strength and has helped take "some of the heat off Mary."

Bowling and Sherman (2008) have defined four major tasks facing service members when reintegrating following deployment: redefining roles; managing strong emotions; abandoning emotional constriction and creating intimacy in relationships; and creating a sense of shared meaning surrounding the deployment experience (p. 452). During deployment, roles for the remaining spouse/partner are significantly impacted, as she/he has to assume full responsibility for managing all things related to the running of the home. Similarly, the role of soldier casts the person in a watchful, vigilant, order-bound environment in which danger and killing is an everyday occurrence. Upon return, these often-disparate roles have to be redefined; this requires a degree of flexibility on the part of both parties and the ability for the couple to be able to communicate their struggles. Counseling can be helpful in this process of redefinition, encouraging discussion about the time apart, how it has impacted both of their lives and exploring the needed adjustments on both sides to the deployment/reintegration experience.

Managing strong emotions and abandoning emotional constriction and creating intimacy suggests almost opposite goals. Service members may return with a complex emotional range based on experiences in war. There may be a sense of pride and accomplishment laced with anxiety and uncertainty about the future. As roles are being redefined and a future mapped out, some of the service member's emotional responses may have to be de-escalated to be able to engage with the family. This creates a constriction of emotions. At the same time, there may well be the hunger to reconnect emotionally and physically. Being numb may be effective to diminish some of the more powerful emotions but creates barriers to intimacy. Clinicians are urged to educate to this phase, normalize the need to hold back while seeking closeness. Keeping communication open is the best method for helping couples to engage and reengage. Couples may need to be encouraged to learn how best to care for and about each other, and may benefit from simple strategies such as making time each day for each other, scheduling "dates" each week, and spending quiet companionable time together.

Shared meaning suggests that a couple/family needs to understand the experiences of deployment and create a narrative that incorporates how each was impacted by the deployment. The creation of the narrative can highlight how each has grown from the experience, stressing strengths that become empowering to the family unit. Children can be involved in the creation of the narrative, stressing their contribution to the deployment period and how they worked together to help the remaining parent.

Overall, the short-term goal of intervention is to address the most pressing problems and to help the family members in communicating their struggles and accomplishments. The longer-term goal is to "… afford families the opportunity to learn additional communication skills and coping skills, new roles, and enhance a sense of cohesion and shared purpose" (Bowling & Sherman, 2008, p. 456).

Using the Bowling and Sherman Task Model, How Might David and SR Fare?

David and Sue agreed to couples counseling. Their need to "vent" was obvious from the first encounter. David had terrible guilt over having "failed" while in Afghanistan. He saw his wounding as a blot on his military duty and obligation to his unit, and he felt guilty because he came home "not a complete man." As David had come from a military family, this was even more potent as a source of anguish. Due to his injury, David's military obligation was finished and he was uncertain what he could do with the rest of his life and how he might be able to support his wife and hoped-for children with his disability. David acknowledged that he had PTSD and agreed to seek help with managing his symptoms. This would hopefully allow David the ability to express, in a safe environment, some of the more intense emotions related to his war experiences. As the emotional constriction eases he would ultimately be freer to be more empathic with Sue and reengage at a stronger intimate emotional level. The idea of shared meaning was elusive, as David was not able to really see Sue's struggles as equal to his own. The aspect of shared meaning may eventually be realized but that was not attained through the tenure of the counseling. The marriage still appears fragile despite gains made by David especially in managing his PTSD.

SR and Mary experienced a more protracted and complex reintegration than initially would have been anticipated as so many of SR's reactions seemed to fall in the "normal" or expected range. The most pronounced issue between SR and Mary revolved around their son, Tony. As noted, Tony did not recognize SR when he returned. The bond between Mary and Tony was so intense that there did not seem to be a place for SR in the household. Mary would not leave Tony with a baby sitter or with SR. SR had the strong feeling that he was not only superfluous in the home but that Mary would rather be with Tony than with any one else, SR included. The situation spoke to a redefinition of roles for Mary and SR. SR now had to become a husband and father, and Mary a wife and mother. This necessitated several sessions to bring understanding to the situation, as well as to begin the process of reinforcing the marital bond. SR was relatively unscathed by his war experience and, while glad it was completed, he did not seem deeply troubled by events overseas. As such, this freed the couple to explore who they were to each other without some of the more intense emotional barriers which create emotional constriction. The family was encouraged to spend time with SR's family and attempt to see Mary's family as well. The overall aim was to de-intensify the relationship between Sue and Tony and realign the relationship with SR. In addition, SR and Tony had to forge a new bond.

Conclusion

We have been at war for over 10 years. Thousands of service members have served in Iraq or Afghanistan and returned home. For most the experience of reintegration is a joyful reunion and life resumes a familiarity and comfort with a few bumps in the road. For others, it is not as seamless. Many of our service members are young and in young marriages. Some marriages and families are troubled before the strains of deployment and will falter and fail. Many will return with profound disability and emotional and mental health problems. Many private sector social workers and mental health providers are beginning to see couples and families in their offices and agencies. The goal of this chapter was to inform these providers of some of the salient struggles that families and marriages would encounter as they reintegrate to civilian life. Perhaps the biggest struggle will not take place in the counselor's office but in motivating families and couples to seek counseling. Nevertheless, our work with these couples and families, while challenging, can make a substantial contribution to those who have served our country.

References

Beder, J., Coe, R., & Sommer, D. (2011). Women and men who have served in Afghanistan/Iraq: Coming home. *Social Work in Health Care*, 50(7), 515–526.

Blaise, A.R., Thompson, M., & McCreary, D. (2006). The post-deployment reintegration scale: Associations with organizational commitment, job related affect, and career intentions. *Defence R & D Technical Report DRDC Toronto TR* (2-6-192).

Bowling, U. & Sherman, M. (2008). Welcoming them home: Supporting service members and their families in navigating the tasks of reintegration. *Professional Psychology: Research and Practice*, 39(4), 451–458.

Conoscenti, L., Vine, V., Papa, A., & Litz, B. (2009). Scanning for danger: Readjustment to the noncombatant experience. In S.M. Freeman, B.A. Moore, & A. Freeman (Eds.), *Living and Surviving in Harm's Way* (pp. 123–145). New York: Routledge.

Darwin, J. (2009). Families: "They also serve who only stand and wait." *Smith College Studies in Social Work*, 79(3/4), 433–442.

Hall, L. (2008). *Counseling Military Families*. New York: Routledge.

Hutchinson, J., & Banks-Williams, L. (2006). Clinical issues and treatment considerations for new Veterans: Soldiers of the wars in Iraq and Afghanistan. *Primary Psychiatry*, 13, 66–71.

Hyer, R. (2006). Iraq and Afghanistan producing new patterns of extremity war injuries. *Medscape Medical News*. Retrieved February 23, 2011 from: http://www.medscape.com/view article/528624

Kelly, M. & Vogt, D. (2008). Military stress: Effects of acute, chronic, and traumatic stress on mental and physical health. In S.M. Freeman, B.A. Moore, & A. Freeman (Eds.), *Living and Surviving in Harm's Way* (pp. 85–106). New York: Routledge.

Mental Health Advisory Team (2008). *Final Report*. Washington DC: Office of the Surgeon General of the Army.

Sammons, M. & Batten, S. (2008) Psychological services for returning Veterans and their families: Evolving conceptualizations of the sequelae of war-zone experience. *Journal of Clinical Psychology*, 64(8), 921–927.

Segal, M. (1986). The military and the family as greedy institutions. *Armed Forces and Society*, 13(1), 9–38.

Shaw, M. & Hector, M. (2010). Listening to military members returning from Iraq and/or Afghanistan: A phenomenological investigation. *Professional Psychology: Research and Practice*, 41(2), 128–134.

Shay, J. (2009). The trials of homecoming: Odysseus returns from Iraq/Afghanistan. *Smith College Studies in Social Work*, 79(3/4), 286–298.

Tanielian, T. & Jaycox, L.H. (2008). *Invisible Wounds of War: Psychological and cognitive injuries, their consequences, and services to assist recovery*. Santa Monica, CA: Rand.

VA National Center for PTSD (2010). *Returning from the War Zone: A guide for military personnel*. VA National Center for PTSD.

Wells, T., Leardmann, C., Fortuna, S., Smith, B., et al. (2009). A prospective study of depression following combat deployment in support of the wars in Iraq and Afghanistan. *American Journal of Public Health*, 100(1), 90–99.

10

FAMILY RESILIENCE AND THE FORTUNES OF WAR

Mark Chapin

Introduction

> *Clarice was an active duty Army Major who was also a single mother of four children aged ten and younger. She was deployed to Iraq in 2005 with only 30 days' notice to fill in for another soldier who became medically disqualified at the last minute. It was extraordinarily stressful, because most soldiers are given 90 days' notice of impending deployment and Clarice had to relocate her children and their live-in nanny to her hometown 600 miles away at her own expense. Also stressful was that the children's biological father was also on active duty and deployed to Iraq. Five months into the deployment, Clarice was medically evacuated to Landstuhl Army Regional Medical Center in Germany and flown immediately back to Walter Reed Army Medical Center for emergency abdominal surgery which required two full months of recovery.*

Military families prepare for deployment in the way that civilian families prepare to welcome a new baby or get ready for moving or retirement: with some degree of excitement, adventure and anguish. These are considered normative reactions to a major change in the life of the family. In this chapter a theoretical framework for understanding, assessing, and reinforcing family resilience related to wartime stressors will be explored. It is intended to provide social workers and other mental health practitioners with a strengths-based approach to working with families impacted by war.

Since the military's involvement in Operation Enduring Freedom in Afghanistan in 2002 and Operation Iraqi Freedom in Iraq in 2003, the vast majority of military families have experienced the deployment of their service member.

For families in the military, deployment is a developmental, or "normative," crisis. Deployment and serving in a war effort is part of a soldier's job. Service members are expected to go wherever they are needed either for combat, peacekeeping, or humanitarian missions (Chapin, 2009). Deployment will often impact the family in diverse ways, and place psychological and emotional strain on the family system. If a family is one that has a strong sense of cohesion and meaning, good coping and problem solving skills, both material and emotional resilience, effective communication, and an extended support system then deployment presents stresses that challenge the family. The outcome can be growth and strength.

> *Clarice got through the deployment with help from her extended family in her hometown, a nanny who literally became a part of their family, and her boyfriend who supported her through the deployment and post-operative period. They were later married and both said that the deployment experience taught them incredible lessons about patience, communication, support, and commitment very early in their relationship.*

This example shows how the "normative crisis" of a military deployment, complicated by single parenthood and a serious health issue, challenged Major Clarice's problem solving, coping, and social support resources; yet resulted in stronger relationships and an enhanced sense of personal competence.

Even an "uneventful" deployment stresses families, who must face dislocation, alteration of family roles, fears about the safety of the deployed service member, and the loneliness of separation from loved ones. This chapter will look at issues faced by families where the service member returns with PTSD, severe disabling injuries, or is killed in action. In these instances, the family is further challenged to adapt to circumstances that will test their resilience and ability to handle stressors caused by the service member's war experience.

Resilience Model of Family Functioning

Hamilton McCubbin was an Army Social Work Officer during the Vietnam War who worked for five years with families of Vietnam era Prisoners of War (POW). He has researched and written extensively about this most extreme form of stressful deployment: families not knowing whether their deployed soldier is alive or dead or when they might come home. The basic model is presented in Figure 10.1.

This model describes how stressor events pile up and are processed by a family. Basically, the adaptation to the stressors is influenced by the family's resources and coping abilities. The role of the family in the adjustment to disability and/or chronic illness is crucial to rehabilitation. Events—in this case, disabilities or death due to participation in the wars in Iraq/Afghanistan—are filtered through

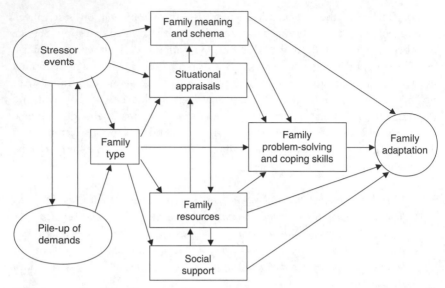

FIGURE 10.1 Family resilience model

Source: McCubbin, Thompson, & McCubbin, 1996.

a family's appraisal of the situation, the type of family, how the family internalizes the event, availability of social supports, and coping and problem-solving skills. These strategies for dealing with change make up the family's components of resilience; it emphasizes and builds on the functional abilities within the family system to strengthen and bolster resilience. As such, it builds on the strength within and around the family. Figure 10.1 shows numerous arrows with multiple connections, indicating different relationships between these concepts. The relative strengths of the relationships between components influence how these arrows connect. For example, situational factors (like deployment) may affect the strength of the relationships between components of the model.

The three most important family factors that influence adaptation to disability/ death are a family's social supports, their appraisal of the disability, and their coping and problem-solving abilities. These areas are central to developing and sustaining resilience within the family. In working with families in which a member has sustained serious injury, these three attributes—social support, appraisal and coping strategies—can be assessed and are helpful in identifying areas of intervention for a social worker/mental health professional. The goal is to foster and build on the family's resiliency.

An additional area to describe is the component labeled "Family Meaning and Schema." This component represents how a family develops an identity and meaning, such as a sports family or identification as a "military family." This identification can be a source of strength in the face of wartime stressors. The family schema lends meaning to different activities and how they may be valued (or devalued). A family schema that gives meaning to deprivation, struggle, separation, or violence can be one protective factor adding resilience and determination to a family stressed by changes and events. The opposite may also apply—if a family has conflict about whether the soldier should stay in the Army, opposes the war, or does not see the effects of deployment separation, then the meaning that the family assigns to deployment can create stress rather than resilience.

The interaction of these processes yields an adaptational outcome either in a positive or negative direction. The adaptational outcome refers to the family's efforts to achieve a new balance after a family crisis. Positive movement is termed by McCubbin as "bonadaptation" (McCubbin & Thompson, 1994) and shows changes moving towards growth and maturation. Bonadaptation is demonstrated by the family's continued ability to maintain and support the intactness of the family unit in the face of disability and accompanying stress. Essentially, the family is utilizing their resources and coping mechanisms, and accepts and understands the crisis.

Negative adaptation, termed "maladaptation" is also possible, creating movement toward further disability, divorce, suicide, crisis, or mental illness (Lavee, McCubbin, & Olson, 1987). An example is the Willis family, seen for marital counseling.

> *The Willis family very quickly had problems getting the husband/father reintegrated into the family. He can't adapt after homecoming and denies he might have PTSD despite numerous outbursts and episodes that are consistent with a diagnosis of PTSD. His wife says that they were better off without him, since the "well-oiled machine" that was their family during the deployment has been disrupted since his return. The husband has volunteered to deploy again and has received orders to return to Iraq on short notice. The wife is disgusted and talking about divorce.*

In working with the Willis family described above, interventions to improve family resilience would include helping the husband recognize and address his irritability (situational appraisal) and helping the couple utilize more effective and less destructive conflict (family problem solving and coping skills). Because the husband took unilateral action to deploy again on short notice, the family's resolution could be considered maladaptation since they did not successfully reintegrate the husband into the family. However, as they continued counseling prior to the deployment, the worker was able to re-frame this unilateral action as "pushing the pause button" on the family, and plans were made to resume counseling prior to his next return home. So this time-out for the family could be seen as one form of bonadaptation that will allow them to reset their system dynamics when he returns again.

Deployment Cycle

Previous work by the author applied the family resiliency model to the three phases of the deployment cycle (Chapin, 2009), where both individuals and entire units are rotated from their training base (Pre-Deployment) in the U.S. into a combat theater of operations (Deployment), and then brought home for reconstitution, replacements and retraining (Re-Deployment).

Looking sequentially at each phase of the deployment cycle, the Resiliency model was applied to the soldier—family issues that typically occur in that phase. Some of these transitions include: changed roles and responsibilities, the children's reactions to war, open-ended deployment schedules, single to mutual decision making, glad and resentful attitudes toward help, single parenting and loneliness. Each of these transitions has the potential to "pile up" and erode resilience.

Traumatic Events and Deployment

It is important to emphasize that the above example—the Willis family—reflects a relatively "uneventful" deployment. The same resilience model can be applied to deployments that go horribly wrong: when a soldier returns with Posttraumatic Stress Disorder (PTSD), when a soldier is medically evacuated from the combat theater with severe injuries, or when a soldier is lost in battle as killed or missing in action. The remainder of this chapter will describe how the family resilience model can be used to understand the impact on a family when the fortunes of war are traumatic and tragic.

Family Resilience and Post-Traumatic Stress Disorder

All soldiers are affected in some way by deployment to a combat zone. In addition to the stresses imposed by separation and family changes during deployment, Castro and McGurk (2007) report that currently deployed soldiers are exposed to hostile fire (82% exposed to incoming artillery, 62% exposed to small arms fire), know someone seriously injured or killed (66%), and have seen dead or seriously injured Americans (42%). The length of deployment over 180 days also increased levels of PTSD. Reported in the results for the Mental Health Assessment Team, (MHAT)-IV, the percentage of soldiers with behavioral health symptoms (anxiety, depression, acute stress) were progressively higher for those exposed to low, medium and high levels of combat, respectively (Castro & McGurk, 2007).

Reporting results from the MHAT-V the following year, Hoge, Castro, Messer, and colleagues (2007) noted that 18 percent of soldiers return with diagnosable PTSD, depression, or anxiety disorder. Many more are affected by deployment, but do not meet full diagnostic criteria. Soldiers typically minimize symptoms on the Post Deployment Health Assessment (PDHA), knowing that endorsing symptoms upon arrival back in the USA will delay their reunion with their families.

PTSD in returning soldiers affects couples and families on multiple levels. A common clinical presentation in distressed couples is a complaint from the non-deployed spouse: "He/She just isn't the same person as before."

Hector, a 37-year-old Hispanic Staff Sergeant had a moderate Traumatic Brain Injury (TBI) and compound fracture of his Tibia and Fibula from an Improvised Explosive Device (IED) blast on his second deployment to Iraq. After several surgeries in Germany, he was sent to Walter Reed for extensive reconstructive surgery. His wife and 14-year-old daughter came along, but were not supportive emotionally. A referral from his case manager for marital counseling revealed that undiagnosed and untreated PTSD after the soldier's first Iraq deployment manifested by the husband withdrawing from his family, excessive drinking, engaging in high risk behaviors, and having an extramarital affair. His wife said she was done with the marriage and was only staying to be supportive while he got his surgeries and rehab completed. After that, she said, "I don't know, but I'm not feeling hopeful."

Applying McCubbin's Family Resilience Model to families where the soldier returns with PTSD, we can assess which components of this model may be affected. They include: caregiver burden (financial, emotional, or physical stress experienced as the result of caring for a loved one with an illness or injury); the spouse acting as a buffer; withdrawal from intimacy; the "not quite right" syndrome; family meaning; and impaired family problem solving and coping skills. Interventions would focus on finding sources to strengthen and relieve Hector's wife from overwhelming responsibilities, trying to help the couple find meaning for Hector's service in the military, and developing coping strategies for management of Hector's PTSD.

In addition to the traumatic events which precipitated the PTSD, the reactivity, irritability, and disproportionate emotional reactions can be stressor events in the family. Examples from clinical practice include: "He crosses four lanes of traffic on the beltway if he sees a car parked on the side of the road," "We can't go to the fireworks on 4th of July ... he gets too jumpy," "His nightmares have him yelling and tossing in his sleep—it keeps me awake too." Further, the intrusive memories and unexpected reactions characteristic of re-experiencing symptoms can cause the combat Veteran to act in frightening and high-risk ways that may cause accidents or injuries. PTSD-related behaviors can be significant stressors, especially if they involve violent outbursts, high-risk behaviors, or result in law-enforcement involvement (e.g. driving infractions, intimate partner violence, embarrassing reactions in public settings) or lower intensity social consequences, such as strained friendships, broken items in house, neighbor kids not allowed to come over to play.

PTSD affects marital intimacy in several ways. First if the PTSD symptoms are severe enough to impact daily functioning, then family roles may shift from the adult dyad being partners who care for each other, share household tasks, both bring income into the family from outside work, and share child care. If PTSD imparts significant social and occupational disability, the spouse may transition from partner to caregiver. Psychological, social and physical demands sum up to "burden," adding caregiver burden to the "pile-up of demands" accumulation of stressors.

As Riggs and colleagues (1998) reported, the most significant source of marital stress among couples with PTSD was the avoidance symptom cluster with concomitant emotional numbing and distance that impacted feelings of closeness and intimacy. Clinical reports from work with couples where PTSD is a factor include statements like: "He just won't talk about it; he won't 'connect' with me emotionally," "He keeps to himself much more, he won't play with the kids." A current study of recent combat Veterans showed that sleep problems, dissociation, and sexual dysfunction had the greatest impact on relationship dissatisfaction (Nelson-Goff, Crow, Reisbig, & Hamilton, 2007).

Further, the arousal cluster of symptoms usually are accompanied by irritability and emotional reactivity associated with hypervigilance, poor sleep, and activation of the Hypothalamic–Pituitary–Adrenal neural axis. This increases risk for domestic violence (Kulka, Schlenger, Fairbank, et al., 1990), as well as impacting family problem solving when minor conflicts and disagreements escalate into angry exchanges that don't resolve the issue at hand (Sayers, Farrow, Ross, & Osliln, 2009). Clinical practice quotes include: "He gets angry at the smallest things and flies off the handle" and "It's hard to have a discussion about issues without it turning into a fight."

Family resources are highly impacted if the Veteran's PTSD impacts employment and employability when considering financial resources and the increased options that affluence affords. PTSD also impacts parenting ability, usually increasing withdrawal of the parent with PTSD, and reluctance to re-engage children at new developmental stages. There is increased likelihood of angry outbursts and physical violence. Very recent studies of returning OIF/OEF Veterans also show that PTSD symptoms are associated with parenting impact including lack of warmth towards children and children being afraid of the parent with PTSD (Sayers et al., 2009).

Sense of meaning and family "schema" can either be a source of support and resilience or create conflict and confusion if the service member's deployment is dystonic with the family's identity. After return from a combat deployment, a family's sense of identity as a military family and their coherence with the current national mission can be protective by providing a sense of meaning for combat experiences and even psychological sequelae such as PTSD. In contrast, a family that does not have a strong identity as a military family may see combat deployments as unfair intrusions into their life or, if they do not support the political agenda of the current conflicts, the family reaction may raise doubts about the meaning of combat experiences that can be de-stabilizing.

The family schema and sense of meaning will also impact the family's current situational appraisal. The normal process of a "honeymoon" phase immediately after return from deployment evolving into a growing awareness of changes in family members that create conflict can alter a family's appraisal of the situation.

A family's sense of "We're back together again and everything is great" may change to "We're together but things aren't right."

Often, the role shifts include the non-PTSD partner acting as a "social buffer" between the combat Veteran with PTSD and the children or outside social contacts. The buffer partner may pre-screen errands or outings to minimize encounters with known re-experiencing triggers (e.g. crowds, traffic), explain or apologize for PTSD-related behaviors, and even intervene to remove the partner from an escalating situation. These "shifts" potentially undermine the resiliency of the family and can create more serious rifts as time goes on.

While many families adapt to PTSD related behaviors, others are able to recover from their PTSD with support from their families. Riggs and colleagues (1998) found that the mean number of marriages in their sample of Veterans with PTSD was three, indicating that long-standing PTSD may have a profound effect on marital stability and longevity. So, family adaptation can be either positive, such as post-traumatic growth; or negative, such as transmitting psychopathology to children or not surviving as a family unit.

The Army has helped soldiers and families adapt in numerous ways. "Battlemind" training has been useful to help soldiers re-orient their thinking from a combat environment back to a family environment, contrasting combat survival skills with their opposite counterpart in marital and family functioning. Spouses engaged in caregiving and social buffering can benefit from the continued support offered by Family Readiness Groups, which may continue to meet after the deployed unit has returned home. Military units like the 4th Infantry Division at Ft. Hood ran a "family school" in the month after return from deployment, with classes for soldiers and families such as "Getting to Know My New Baby" and "My Child Became a Teenager While I Was Gone." These are community based educational interventions—offered at most VA hospitals—that can help families boost their resilience as they go through a time that is recognized as being stressful. For families that are dealing with more severe stresses, marital and family counseling which helps families address and cope with changes, learn better communication and problem solving skills, and provide a gateway to more intensive services (if warranted) can help a family rebound from challenges to their level of functioning brought about by PTSD or other mental health issues in the returning soldier or family member.

Family Resilience and Severe Injury

One of the bittersweet fruits of medical progress is that soldiers who are injured in Iraq or Afghanistan have a much higher survival rate than those injured in previous conflicts. Lighter, more effective body armor that soldiers will actually wear, and battlefield treatments such as quick-clot, result in fewer mortal combat wounds. Also, the rapid evacuation to definitive care available in forward-deployed field hospitals and rapid movement back to the specialized military medical facilities abroad and in the U.S. have greatly improved survival rates for severely injured soldiers. However, this has resulted in a huge influx of combat wounded and a huge increase in soldiers with long-term disabilities such as limb loss and traumatic brain injury.

Family members have a number of initial stressor events: the initial trauma of notification of the injury, usually incomplete details about the injury and the soldiers condition (which may be changing hourly), unplanned travel to a distant hospital, and the initial shock of seeing a loved one so badly hurt. In the following days, the family must deal with the crisis of whether the soldier will survive or not, and the family may be faced with some difficult decisions to make if the soldier's level of consciousness is compromised and can't make decisions for him/herself. There have been some family conflicts where a young spouse who was very recently married to the soldier was not in agreement with the soldier's parents' wishes about whether to maintain life supports for a soldier whose injuries left him in a vegetative state.

If the soldier recovers consciousness, one of his/her first concerns is usually the level of disability the injury will impose and how much recovery is possible. For soldiers who lose a limb, are blinded, or who have TBIs there is also a crisis of meaning: "Can I still be a soldier?" In families with a schema and meaning oriented toward being a military family, this can be a crisis for the whole family involving loss of community, housing, and benefits.

As the initial crisis of survival is resolved and soldiers become involved in the recovery and rehabilitation aspects of care, the "pile-up of demands" starts to accumulate. Some of the family consequences of disruption and dislocation during recovery begin to occur. For the soldier, being away from his/her unit feels alien and uncomfortable. Unanswered questions about the injury event, who else may have been hurt or killed, or how the unit is doing without the soldier are pre-eminent, as well as a frequently expressed wish to get back to the unit as soon as possible. Often, this is distressing to family members, who expect the soldier would be grateful for being back with family and not want to go back to where they were so badly injured. Family members may have to contend with using up all vacation and sick time, and whether they must quit their job back home to stay and care for the soldier. Also, after a month, bills need to be paid, and "temporary" childcare arrangements made hastily during the initial emergency may need revision. The spouse may be torn between duty to help the recovering soldier in the hospital and duty to young children left at home on the other side of the country. The social workers serving as case managers for severely injured soldiers are also available to help spouses navigate these difficult decisions and provide psychosocial support, access to resources available from the military and voluntary organizations, and help facilitate the implementation of their chosen solutions.

One example is the Rogers couple, which was in residence at Walter Reed for almost three years.

Husband Bill was a sergeant serving in Iraq as a Military Policeman when an Improvised Explosive Device (IED) blast left him with severe traumatic brain injury (TBI), including shrapnel imbedded in his brain. Bill was in a coma almost six weeks. He also lost two fingers and suffered multiple injuries to one leg. He underwent 21 surgeries for wound closure, physical and cosmetic reconstruction, and shrapnel removal. Bill also suffered multiple pulmonary emboli from clots breaking loose from injury scar tissue-each one life threatening. He experienced recurrent anxiety attacks. Bill and his wife Nora were referred for marital therapy at the two-year mark at Walter Reed: other families at the on-post Fisher House residence were complaining about the volume of their arguments. Bill continued to drink alcoholic beverages, even though he was brain injured and was taking prescribed opiate analgesics, benzo-diazepines, and SSRIs. Even though his commander referred him to the Army Substance Abuse Program (ASAP) and gave him an order not to consume alcoholic beverages, he persisited. Nora wanted some acknowledgement of her participation in his care, including bedside vigil during the six weeks of his coma but none was forthcoming.

At the beginning of their third year at Walter Reed, Bill had made large gains in recovering his basic functioning (dressing himself, speech and ambulation). However in some areas, he was still dependent on Nora and this dependency was tinged with hostility. As a non-commissioned officer (NCO), he would spend lots of free time coaching and counseling other brain-injured soldiers. One of those was a young female soldier with TBI who was at Walter Reed without any family member support. Nora became very suspicious and jealous of the time her husband spent with this young female and this became a major source of conflict. The arguments between them became so frequent and intense that the medical treatment team held a multidisciplinary team meeting with everyone including his primary care physician to the chaplain, commander, and the Fisher House manager to address the impact that this conflict was having on Bill's rehabilitation. They decided to fund Bill to go home to California (where Bill's family lives) for convalescent leave at Christmas, but insisted his wife Nora go to her home in Texas because the level of conflict was seen as "detrimental to the soldier's recovery."

Not all journeys through the family resilience model result in growth and positive adaptation. Some, like the Rogers family, are unable to problem-solve conflicts and may not be able to count on social supports that are out of state or with conflicted in-laws. In these situations, families may engage in maladaptive behaviors that can accelerate dysfunction and further decrease adaptation. Nora and Bill were referred to marital counseling very late in this cycle, where the couple had discussed divorce and the command was ready to withdraw financial support for the wife's presence as a non-medical attendant since she seemed to derail his recovery. Earlier intervention may have helped the couple understand

and articulate feelings about their changing roles–especially in normalizing the changes they were experiencing. Further, open communication about transitioning from an invalid back to being an independent, fully functioning adult (Bill), and concerns about giving up the control inherent in the caregiver role (Nora), may have avoided some of the actions that provoked their worst arguments.

As weeks of recovery become months of rehabilitation, the spouse or caregiver will likely experience shifting caregiver responsibilities. In contrast to many care-giving scenarios (e.g. elders with Alzheimer's, stroke recovery), the caregiving curve is usually the opposite for families where there has been a severe injury: it starts out with intense caregiving and lessens as the soldier recovers and begins to regain functioning and learns to work around any permanent disabilities, like a severed limb. For family members assisting recovering soldiers, there is a delicate balance between protective nurturing and pushing for maximum rehabilitation. The lingering impact of TBI and posttraumatic stress issues may result in cognitive changes, emotional lability, irritability and depression, which may not have any visible markers like missing limbs or shrapnel scars. As with the Rogers example cited above, sometimes the soldier, who is anxious to become as independent and autonomous as before the injury, resents the residual dependence an injury leaves. Also observed in this population are some soldiers who become quite comfortable with dependency and need to be encouraged to re-engage in selfcare behaviors after they have become accustomed to having a spouse or parents provide.

Restoration of marital intimacy after disability is an area that is not often discussed, either in the literature or even in clinical settings. An unspoken co-occurrence is that explosions powerful enough to sever limbs often do significant damage to genitalia as well. Restoration of intimate relations between partners is often neglected as a topic addressed by health care providers. A group of spouses of amputees participating in Project Comfort, a caregiver skills workshop provided by the Social Work department at Walter Reed, addressed the topic with amazing candor, grateful that any provider would raise the issue. Experiences varied from physical damage to genitalia that made sexual functioning difficult, intact biological equipment but libido or performance impaired by the side effects of multiple medications, residual effects of trauma activation, and loss of self-esteem from body image alteration with amputation. The sub-culture of paraphilia where sex with amputees is the source of arousal and the solicitations that injured soldiers were getting on-line were highly disturbing to spouses. Providers are urged to initiate these discussions to open a familiar area of comfort between spouses to foster coping and resilience. While spouses of severely injured soldiers found that open and frank discussion of this topic was helpful to begin a supportive dialogue among caregivers, having trauma informed therapists on board who could discuss sexual changes, alternative and options, and the intense emotions surrounding this topic is essential to help couples work through these changes.

Family Resilience and Soldiers Killed in Action

Families of soldiers killed in action receive support both through the military as well as from volunteer organizations outside the military. The military has established procedures and rituals that are designed to ease the pain of notification as well as the family's bereavement and adjustment to the loss of the soldier.

All soldiers make some preparations for death in combat, including wills prepared for free by military attorneys, low-cost life insurance ($400,000 of Service-member Group Life Insurance—SGLI) available for about $20 per month; however few soldiers (and fewer families) expect this to occur. The notification of a soldier's death is a recognized traumatic event, and those who have researched and worked in this clinical area recommend a theoretical approach that blends crisis intervention and trauma treatment as well as standard bereavement counseling methods (Wright, Burrell, Schroeder and Thomas, 2006). Recognizing the traumatic nature of death notification to a soldier's next of kin, the military makes great effort to make this notification in person by an officer accompanied by a chaplain at the person's home (both have had special training for this duty).

The combination of an unexpected death and the trauma of notification begin a cascade of stressor events for the family experiencing the death of their soldier. Families must also come to terms with the meaning and context of the soldier's death. These may include family opinions about the politics of the conflict in which the soldier lost his/her life, whether the soldier suffered greatly, whether there were heroic circumstances (especially if the soldier sacrificed his/her life to save others), or whether there are lingering questions about friendly fire, or circumstances "unknown" about the death. It is frequently difficult for surviving family members to move on in the grief process until these details are resolved (Worden, 2009). Balancing these stressors are the acknowledged effects of military funeral rituals, including an honor guard, flag-draped casket, a 21 gun salute, and presentation of the folded casket flag to the widow or parents of the deceased soldier. These rituals which honor a soldier's sacrifice for his/her country's ideals allow a formal and public acknowledgement of loss accompanied by a highly formal sense of honor which can help the surviving family members put doubts and concerns about the meaning of the soldier's death to rest, and then get on with the process of grieving (Wright, 2006).

For families with a schema and identity as a military family, the death of the soldier can precipitate a crisis of meaning that begins with the requirement to move out of military housing after the soldier's death. While the family can remain in military housing for an additional 365 days or continue to receive the military's housing allowance if living in a nearby community, at some point the family will be required to move their household. This involves children changing schools, losing social and community supports in the local area, and finding roots in a new community at a time of great stress and vulnerability. Also, when a combat death occurs in a young adult family with small children, there are few models for grieving among peers; the survivors may feel isolated by their unusual (for the young adult age group) and unique experience of loss, and many other daily responsibilities for child care which can interfere with the process of grieving (Walsh–Burke, 2006).

Fortunately, recent financial improvements in compensation for soldiers killed in the line of duty do not produce financial hardship. Most soldiers carry the maximum $400,000 SGLI life insurance, so there is a large infusion of financial support. In addition, there is a $100,000 tax-free "Death Gratuity" paid immediately upon the soldier's demise. Spouses can continue to receive medical care at military medical treatment facilities for three years. After that, surviving spouses and children are eligible to use Tricare medical insurance according to the same plan offered for retirees or until the children reach age 21 (23 if in college) or until the spouse remarries. As a military survivor, the spouse and children retain eligibility to use on-post facilities (Post Exchange, Commissary, recreation, etc.) in perpetuity. They also retain continued eligibility for Military One Source counseling, as well as bereavement counseling provided through the VA's network of 300 Vet Centers (Readjustment Counseling Services).

Cultural background of the surviving family members may provide rituals that are comforting, beliefs that provide transcendence in grief, or may impose burden on a family removed from extended family supports (Rosenblatt, 2008). Cultural practices around mourning and rituals for memorials may dovetail well with military traditions or might clash in painful ways, which is why it is important for anyone working with a grieving military family to understand not only the military culture, but also the ethnic and religious cultural context in which this family is experiencing their grief.

After the initial months of funeral and memorial services, processing paperwork, making a geographical move away from the soldier's permanent duty station, the family must re-organize its schema and situational appraisal, asking themselves, "How do we go on?" Provost (1989) suggests that for deaths occurring in combat, the socio-political climate surrounding the conflict can either provide a vehicle for support among community contacts or can create an atmosphere of silence and disenfranchisement, such as that experienced by survivors of Vietnam era casualties. Ongoing support for military bereavement is provided by a highly effective non-profit organization called Tragedy Assistance Program for Survivors (TAPS, www.taps.org), which provides connections to on-line and in-person counseling, support groups, and summer camps for children grieving the loss of a parent or sibling. Many local hospice organizations provide grief counseling and social activities for surviving spouses and children, and welcome survivors of military losses (who may not have been clients of the hospice). Also, as mentioned earlier, one essential mission of the VA's Vet Centers (www.vetc.enter.va.gov) is to provide bereavement counseling to families of military personnel who die while on active duty at no charge to the family.

Conclusion

With approximately 18 percent of combat deployed service members returning from Iraq or Afghanistan with PTSD (Hoge et al., 2007), over 40,000 service members wounded in action and over 5,000 killed in action (U.S. Dept of Defense, 2010), the fortunes of war have profoundly affected many families. As these families return to Reserve and National Guard units scattered across the country, separate, or retire from military service, or surviving family members return without their soldiers to their home communities to grieve and build new lives; social workers will be there to provide both direct and indirect care. While Department of Defense and VA health care facilities will continue to provide care for some Veterans and military retirees, many will relocate into areas far from federal health care facilities. These Veterans will access care in local communities and will need case management, medical social work, and behavioral health services on all levels.

Also important is to be aware of the many organizations that provide support to service members, Veterans, retirees and their families. Table 10.1 provides a partial listing of some of the most widely used support agencies and non-profit organizations.

TABLE 10.1   Organizations supporting soldiers

Military Resources
- DVBIC (Defense Veterans Brain Injury Center) www.brainline.org
- DHCC (Deployment Health Clinical Center) www.pdhealth.mil
- Military One Source www.militaryonesource.com
- National Resource Directory

Veteran's Administration
- VA Med Centers—inpatient treatment centers, Polytrauma centers www1.va.gov/health/index.asp
- Readjustment Counseling Services: community based http://www.vetc.enter.va.gov

Private Organizations (just a few examples)
- SOFAR: (Strategic Outreach to Families of All Reservists) www.sofarusa.org
- DSUSA (Disabled Sports USA) www.dsusa.org
- TAPS (Tragedy Assistance Program for Survivors) www.taps.org
- Canine Companions for Independence www.cci.org
- Give an Hour Foundation www.giveanhour.org
- Iraq and Afghanistan Veterans Association www.communityofVeterans.org
- Disabled American Veterans www.dav.org

Partnerships
- Intrepid Fallen Heroes Fund with the Defense Centers of Excellence for Psychological Health and TBI to fund the National Intrepid Center of Excellence
- VA "Seamless Transition" social workers placed in DoD Medical facilities
- National Demonstration Program for Citizen-Soldier Support (University of NC, Chapel Hill & NC National Guard Bureau & Department of Defense)

Finally, members of our profession need to familiarize themselves with yet another cross-cultural competency: understanding the culture of the military, the meaning of military service, and the unique dynamics of military families. The Family Resilience Model used to describe how families are affected by the fortunes of war is a useful tool that can guide practitioners in a culturally-competent, multi-dimensional assessment which can quickly identify strengths and areas of need.

Author's Note

All names used in this manuscript are fictitious. Detail has been changed to prevent identification of the real individuals and circumstances described.

References

Castro, C.A. & McGurk, D. (2007). The intensity of combat and behavioral health status. *Traumatology*, 13(6), 6–23.

Chapin, M.G. (2009). Deployment and families: Hero stories and horror stories. *Smith College Studies in Social Work*, 79, 263–282.

Hoge, C.W., Castro, C.A., Messer, S.C., McGurk, D., Cotting, D.I., & Koffman, R.L. (2007). Combat duty in Iraq and Afghanistan, mental health problems, and barriers to care. *New England Journal of Medicine*, 351, 13–22.

Kulka, R.A., Schlenger, W.E., Fairbank, J., Hough, R., et al. (1990). *Trauma and the Vietnam War Generation: Report of findings from the National Veterans Readjustment Study*. Philadelphia, PA: Brunner/Mazel.

Lavee, Y., McCubbin, H.I., & Olson, D.H. (1987). The effect of stressful life events and transitions on family functioning and well-being. *Journal of Marriage and the Family*, 49(4), 857–873.

McCubbin, H.I. & Thompson, E.A. (1994). Preserving family values in the age of technology. In D. Malcolm (Ed.), *The family in the aquatic continent: Cultural values in the age of technology* (pp. 25–33). Kapalua, Maui, HI: Maui Pacific.

McCubbin, H.I., Thompson, A.I., & McCubbin, M.A. (1996). *Family Assessment: Resiliency, coping and adaptation—inventories for research and practice*. Madison, WI: University of Wisconsin.

Nelson Goff, B.S., Crow, J.R., Reisbig, A.M.J., & Hamilton, S. (2007). The impact of individual trauma symptoms of deployed soldiers on relationship satisfaction. *Journal of Family Psychology*, 21, 344–353.

Provost, P.K. (1989). Vietnam: Resolving the death of a loved one. *Archives of Psychiatric Nursin*, 3(1), 29–33.

Riggs, D.S., Byrne, C.A., Weathers, F.W., & Litz1, B.T. (1998). The quality of the intimate relationships of male Vietnam Veterans: Problems associated with posttraumatic stress disorder. *Journal of Traumatic Stress*, 11(1) 87–101.

Rosenblatt, P.C. (2008). Grief across cultures: A review and research agenda. In M.S. Stroebe, R.O. Hansson, H. Schut, & W. Stroebe (Eds.), *Handbook of Bereavement Research and Practice* (pp. 207–222). Washington, DC: APA Press.

Sayers, S.L., Farrow, V.A., Ross, J., & Oslin, D.W. (2009). Family problems among recently returned military. Veterans referred for a mental health evaluation. *Journal of Clinical Psychiatry*, 70, 163–170.

U.S. Department of Defense (2010). Daily summary casualty report. Accessed on 15 March, 2010 from: http://www.defense.gov/news/casualty.pdf

Walsh-Burke, K. (2006). *Grief and Loss: Theories and skills for helping professionals.* Boston, MA: Allyn & Bacon.

Worden, W.J. (2009) *Grief Counseling and Grief Therapy: A handbook for the mental health practitioner* (4th Ed.). New York: Springer.

Wright, K.M., Burrell, L.M., Schroeder, E.D., and Thomas, J.L. (2006). Military spouses: Coping with the fear and the reality of service member injury and death. In T.W. Britt, A.B. Adler, & C.A. Castro (Eds.), *Military Life: The psychology of serving in peace and combat* (pp. 64–92). Westport, CT: Praeger.

11

ASSESSING AND RESPONDING TO SUICIDAL RISK AMONG OIF/OEF VETERANS

Christie Jackson and Yvette Branson

At a recent suicide prevention outreach training, a social worker from the audience voiced a concern that many clinicians have—"If I ask my clients about suicide, I will alienate them. It's awkward to ask people if they want to kill themselves. I sometimes worry that if I mention suicide I may put the idea into the head of a client and I am afraid to do so." On the other hand, Veterans and other clients report they will not volunteer information about suicidal thinking or planning because it is embarrassing and difficult, and might make their providers uncomfortable. If we as mental health professionals do not ask about suicide, who will? Suicide risk assessment must be an essential aspect of our work with clients, including Veterans. In this chapter, we will present salient issues pertaining to Veterans and suicide, detail a comprehensive suicide risk assessment procedure, and provide treatment recommendations and resources for suicidal individuals.

Stigma and Help-Seeking

Veterans are especially reluctant to ask for help. While the stigma of seeking help from any mental health service is widespread in our society, military culture is entrenched with this unfortunate attitude. Indeed, often the individuals who need help the most are the ones least likely to get it. According to Hoge, Castro, Messer, et al. (2004), OIF/OEF Veterans who met criteria for a mental disorder were twice as likely to report stigma and barriers to care than those who did not meet criteria.

The suicide prevention hotline and chat line, available 24/7, was designed by the VA in part to address the difficulties some Veterans may have in asking for help. Public announcements for the hotline adorn VA waiting areas and are carried on buses around the country. The pertinent message encourages the use of the hotline, "*It takes the courage and strength of a warrior to ask for help … if you are in emotional crisis call 1-800-273-TALK (8255); Press 1 for Veterans.*" This is a relevant resource that all Veterans and providers should be aware of. The call is routed to a Veterans Suicide Hotline Call Center located in Canandaigua, New York, where trained professionals will help the caller and assess risk. The hotline personnel can arrange for emergency medical or police dispatch, and can make direct referrals to the Veteran's local Suicide Prevention Coordinator. More recently, a corresponding website with a chat line has been established as an effort to appeal to OIF/OEF and other technologically sophisticated Veterans (www.suicidepreventionlifeline.org).

As providers, we should echo the sentiments of the VA public announcement and reassure Veterans that admitting to emotional difficulty is not a sign of weakness (Hoge et al., 2004). Veterans may also resist seeking treatment because of perceived concerns relating to non-military mental health providers. We can address such issues of estrangement due to being civilian providers (not military personnel) by being honest about our experiences, but also offering professional expertise and psychoeducational information. Clinicians might say something like, "Despite the fact that I am not a Veteran, I have been trained to work with the kind of problems that Veterans are dealing with, and together we can develop tools to address your difficulties." This ambivalence regarding seeking help can sometimes lead to poor adherence to treatment, and clinicians would do well to address these issues at the outset of their work to ameliorate potential therapy-interfering behaviors.

Veterans and Suicide Risk Factors

Veterans are thought to comprise as much as 20 percent of all suicides (Posey, 2009). This is partially because of the difficulties of surviving the challenges of a warzone coupled with the particular strains a soldier must face in his/her transition back to civilian life. Clinicians can begin to address these difficulties by obtaining a clear picture of the Veteran's military experiences. Assess whether s/he has been in combat, has been the target of military sexual trauma (pertinent for both males and females), or has any war-related injuries, physical as well as emotional. Each of these variables has been linked to suicidal ideation and attempted suicide in the Veteran population. It is important to note that, even if a Veteran was not involved in direct combat, surviving the theater of war can be just as draining for some.

Clinicians should educate themselves about the nature of the conflicts in Iraq and Afghanistan, as well as other factors pertinent to this group of Veterans. For example, OIF/OEF Veterans may be particularly sensitive to driving and crowds, as this war was distinguished by the constant threat of suicide bombers and roadside explosives. In Iraq and Afghanistan, marketplaces and any other crowded areas, as well as motor vehicles, were frequent targets and some soldiers may find similar situations at home especially difficult to navigate. Traveling through tunnels or over bridges and overpasses may be especially triggering. Other reminders may even include conditions such as extreme heat, sand, and city noises. It is also not uncommon for returnees to experience distress when dealing with individuals of Muslim or Middle Eastern origin, and some individuals have expressed extreme guilt for these reactions. Other Veterans have noted that prayer calls often preceded warzone attacks, and so now even walking past a mosque can be frightening for them. It is important for clinicians to normalize these reactions as learned behavioral responses that can be "unlearned" over time as the Veteran safely confronts these stimuli under the supervision of his/her therapist.

Difficulties with relationships, career plans, housing, and financial stressors are common for returning/retiring service members. Veterans sometimes feel that civilians could never understand their wartime experiences and subsequently isolate themselves more and more over time. Providers can normalize these feelings while simultaneously helping the Veteran find appropriate, encouraging sources of social support. Indeed, having strong social support and a sense of connectedness are associated with reduced risk for suicide (Resnick, Bearman, Blum, et al., 1997; Stroebe, Stroebe, & Abakoumkin, 2005). It may be helpful to urge a Veteran to attend local Veterans Organizations, a support group, or a Vet Center in the community. Vet Centers, part of the Veterans Administration and located throughout the United States, offer confidential counseling and support where individuals can connect to other Veterans and learn about resources. Often, family members and significant others are encouraged to participate as well.

Disappointments while transitioning home can be compounded by psychiatric symptoms such as insomnia, hyperarousal, and guilt or confusion about their roles while in service or during deployment. It is helpful to normalize the fear and frustration the Veteran may be experiencing relative to his/her symptoms by explaining how combat-ready skills can interfere with readjustment to civilian life (see *Battlemind Training*, Castro, Hoge, Milliken, et al., 2006). The very skills that kept them alive and safe during combat may be creating problems for them at home. Often these problems are related to the hesitation to allow one's guard down and the difficulties of actually doing so. Surviving in combat requires emotional control, focused aggression, and hyperawareness. Relating to loved ones, controlling anger, and relaxing one's defenses to life as usual is challenging for many (Maguen, Cohen, Cohen, et al., 2010). Risky and thrill-seeking behaviors, including reckless driving and unprotected sex, as well as impulsivity and overreacting, may be common. Since research reflects that impulsivity increases risk for suicide (Brent, Johnson, Perper, et al., 1994), clinicians should be careful to assess for these factors. Maguen et al. (2010) recommended that clinicians educate returning Veterans about these adjustment issues, perhaps by providing a handout such as the one developed by James Munroe of the Boston VA Healthcare System, "Adjustment Issues in OEF/OIF Veterans: War Zone Skills That May Interfere with Readjustment." Normalizing and dealing with these symptoms and stressors directly can ease a Veteran's transition back home and reduce the risk of accidental death or suicide.

Certain demographic factors are also important to keep in mind. Male Veterans are twice as likely to kill themselves as male civilians (Kaplan, Huguet, McFarland & Newsom, 2007). Female Veterans are also at a higher risk for suicide than non-Veteran females. One recent study suggested that young female Veterans, aged 18–34, are *three* times more likely to commit suicide than their non-military peers (McFarland, Kaplan, & Huguet, 2010). As in the civilian population, Veterans who are male, over 65 or 18–25 years old, living alone, white or American Indian/Alaska Native may be particularly at risk (Pearson, Conwell, Lindesay, Takahashi, & Caine, 1997; Centers for Disease Control and Prevention (n.d.)).

For Veterans and civilians alike, the single most important predictor of suicidal behavior is past suicide behavior (Nordstrom, Asbert, Aberg-Wistedt, & Nordin, 1995; Paykel & Dienelt, 1971). Other factors that increase risk include a family history of suicide (Moscicki, 1995), hopelessness (Beck, Rush, Shaw, & Emery, 1979), and stressful life events. It is a disturbing fact that many of the same issues that returning Veterans face—interpersonal conflict or loss, work difficulties, financial or legal problems, major illness, and chronic pain—are listed as precipitating events linked to suicidal behavior.

Chronic pain is common among those returning from military service, and has been linked to elevated risk for suicide (Tang & Crane, 2006). Chronic pain is also a frequent complication of Traumatic Brain Injury (TBI) (Nampiaparampil, 2008). Service members are at high risk for TBI resulting from blast injuries, motor vehicle accidents, falls, or gunshots (Warden, 2006). TBIs further exacerbate suicidal risk because of their propensity to increase impulsivity, thought to be due to damage to the frontal lobes (Banasik, 2005), especially among those with a concussion, cranial fracture, or a cerebral contusion and hemorrhage (Teasdale & Engberg, 2001). Taking all of these factors into consideration, it is not surprising that a Veteran's suicide risk increases along with the number of deployments, the length of deployments, and the number of injuries sustained.

Whereas morale and support for the troops was fairly high during the beginning of the conflict, over the years enthusiasm has waned. At the same time, resilience in the face of multiple deployments and multiple stressors is ever harder to maintain. The Army's divorce rate and suicide rate used to be lower than the civilian population but, since 2008, military divorce and suicide rates supersede civilian rates. In fact, at least as many soldiers are dying by their own hand as are dying in combat. In a recent New York magazine article detailing the psychological sequellae of our nation's longest war, Jennifer Senior quotes an Army suicide report:

At 24 years of age, a Soldier, on average, has moved from home, family, and friends and resided in two other states; has traveled the world (deployed); been promoted four times; bought a car and wrecked it; married and had children; has had relationship and financial problems; seen death; is responsible for dozens of Soldiers; maintains millions of dollars' worth of equipment; and gets paid less than $40,000 a year.

(Senior, 2011, p. 30)

Suicide Risk Assessment

It is encouraging to note that clinicians, armed with the right knowledge and tools, can help to prevent suicide. A comprehensive suicide risk assessment should be performed on every Veteran that is new to one's practice, and an abbreviated assessment should be conducted at periodic intervals as needed, depending on the Veteran's diagnosis, functionality and current stressors. Immediate warning signs for suicide include threatening to hurt or kill oneself, looking for ways to kill oneself; seeking access to pills, weapons or other means, and talking or writing about death, dying, or suicide (Knox & Kemp, 2009). The presence of any of these signs requires immediate attention and further evaluation, which may include hospitalization and/or involving local emergency services as needed.

Other warning signs indicate that the Veteran may be at increased risk for suicide, alerting the clinician to put precautions in place to protect his or her safety. These signs include:

* hopelessness;
* rage, anger or seeking revenge;
* acting reckless or engaging in risky activities (including driving recklessly);
* feeling trapped;
* increasing alcohol or drug abuse;
* withdrawing from friends, family, or society;
* anxiety, agitation, unable to sleep or sleeping all the time;
* dramatic changes in mood;
* no reason for living, no sense of purpose in life;
* giving away valued possessions.

We recommend that clinicians ask the following types of questions to assess suicidal ideation:

* Have you been feeling so sad lately that you were thinking about death or dying?
* Have you been thinking that life is not worth living?
* How often are you thinking about suicide?

- What kind of thoughts have you had about hurting yourself?
- Do you feel you have control over the thoughts and/or responses to them?

These questions are helpful at determining suicidal plan and intent:

- Have you thought about how you would kill yourself? What would you do?
- Have you thought about when and where you might do it?
- Do you have access to (guns, knives, pills, whatever means the Veteran identifies)?
- How much do you want to die right now?
- How likely are you to kill yourself today? This week?
- Have you ever rehearsed how you might commit suicide?
- You mentioned shooting yourself, have you ever practiced?

As noted above, previous suicidal behavior is an important risk factor and should be assessed next. Clinicians can ask:

- Have you ever tried to commit suicide before? Where? When? How? Did you get medical treatment? What happened? Were there any injuries?
- Did you attempt to avoid discovery or rescue?
- What triggered the crisis?
- What was your perception of the lethality of the behavior?
- How did you feel about the fact that you were still alive?
- Have you ever started to kill yourself but stopped? What happened?

A comprehensive suicide risk assessment will include other factors such as history of mental illness, recent losses (financial, emotional, or physical), family history of suicide, and sexual orientation. The assessment should also include protective factors that may decrease risk, such as positive social support, spirituality, dependents, and positive coping skills (APA, 2003). Ascertaining the severity of risk depends on consideration of relevant risk factors, present symptoms, social support (or lack thereof), and the Veteran's current behavior (i.e., is the effect and behavior congruent with what s/he is reporting). Clinicians should not hesitate to seek consultation or supervision, and risk will need to be reassessed throughout treatment, as risk level will wax and wane. Often, it is not enough to ask just once about suicidal behaviors and risk factors. People sometimes report conflicting information at different time points to the same mental health provider or to different individuals. The value of obtaining consent to get collateral information and consult with all members of the treatment team cannot be overstated. In Appendix A, we offer a Comprehensive Suicide Risk Assessment for clinicians to utilize. We also provide a Brief Suicide Risk Assessment Template in Appendix B for periodic re-assessment of suicidal risk.

Interventions and Resources

If a Veteran endorses wanting to kill him or herself, has specific plans with the intent of acting on those plans, has already made or begun to make an attempt, or otherwise leads the clinician to feel s/he is at imminent risk, emergency action should be taken. In this case, clinicians should either hospitalize the Veteran or involve emergency services. Clinicians can call 911 to assist in bringing the Veteran to a local hospital, preferably a VA hospital if feasible, or dispatch local emergency responders to the Veteran's location. Another option is to call the local police precinct, explain the situation and request a "wellness check." Finally, there may be mobile outreach services available to check on a patient whose safety is in question. These units are available in most metropolitan areas and can usually be found either with a quick internet search using the patient's residential zip code or through the local hospital. Mobile crisis units have a 24–48 hour window in which they will go to a Veteran's home, evaluate the patient for suicidal risk, and then report back to the provider. Clinicians can also access the VA's 24-hour Suicide Prevention Lifeline to request immediate assistance.

If a Veteran is willing to be hospitalized, it is imperative that s/he never be left alone. The mental health provider should escort the Veteran to the hospital and not leave him or her until another mental health professional has taken over. Depending on the Veteran's preference and situation, it may be helpful to involve family members or significant others during the hospitalization process. If the Veteran is not willing to go to the hospital and it is determined s/he is at imminent risk, then s/he will need to be hospitalized involuntarily.

It is recommended that an emergency contact person be assigned for every patient during the first session, so that in the event family or others need to be involved, the information is available. Whenever safety is in question, err on the side of caution. In other words, it is better to break confidentiality and risk therapeutic rupture if it means saving a Veteran's life. Veterans and all clients should be warned that in the event that their safety or that of someone else is threatened, confidentiality may be broken.

It is important to note the steps for appropriate care for suicidal Veterans before a crisis occurs. It is recommended that community therapists working with Veterans make contact with their local Suicide Prevention Coordinator (SPC). Every VA Medical Center has at least one SPC, and these individuals can share valuable resources as well as offer support and consultation. Contact with the VA has shown to be a protective factor in Veteran suicidality (Maze, 2010) and does not preclude outside care; it is a way to enhance Veteran support. It is also helpful to know that not every VA Medical Center has an emergency department or inpatient unit. Additionally, if there is no VA Medical Center nearby, identify the closest community hospital in case of emergency.

If a Veteran is not at imminent risk and declines hospitalization, then s/he and the therapist will need to work together to determine ways in which the

Veteran can remain safe. This collaborative effort should include the development of a suicide safety plan, described below. Other options include increasing the number of therapy contacts and/or telephone check-ins over the next few weeks or as needed. Continuing to work on building the Veteran's coping strategies and distress tolerance skills, assisting him/her in regaining control and a sense of balance, involving social supports, and removing or securing lethal means of self harm should be the focus of treatment during this time.

It is essential to realize that a patient continues to be at heightened risk once an acute risk subsides. In fact, individuals are most vulnerable to making a suicidal attempt during the first month following an inpatient stay. Clinicians should be attuned to all the risk factors articulated above and continue to check in regarding suicidal ideation and safety throughout treatment. For further information and resources, see Appendix C.

Suicide Safety Plans

The "No-Suicide Contract" is not recommended for use with suicidal individuals, Veterans or otherwise (Rudd, Mandrusiak, & Joiner, 2006). Experts contend that suicide contracts on their own are insufficient to prevent suicide, should never be used in lieu of a formal suicide assessment, and provide a false sense of security if a patient is willing to sign one. Rather, clinicians should work with clients to develop a Suicide Safety Plan (Stanley & Brown, 2008). A suicide safety plan is a hierarchical list of coping skills that can be used to manage distress or suicidal crises, and is designed so that any clinician working with a Veteran may implement it as part of an overall treatment package. Safety plans include six basic steps. When the first step fails to decrease the level of suicide risk, the Veteran is instructed to move on to the next step, and so forth. The steps of a safety plan are as follows:

1   recognizing warning signs;
2   using internal coping strategies;
3   socializing with family members or others who may offer support or distraction from the crisis;
4   contacting family members or friends who may offer help to resolve a crisis;
5   contacting professionals or agencies;
6   reducing access to means.

Clinicians should establish a working rapport with the Veteran and explain that the safety plan is a list of strategies to help him/her tolerate suicidal feelings and other times of extreme distress. It is recommended that plans be written out on paper in a collaborative fashion using the Veteran's own words. A copy should always be given to the Veteran, and efforts made to increase the likelihood the Veteran will actually use the plan when needed (i.e., recommend the plan be put on the refrigerator or carried in a wallet, problem-solve ways to overcome obstacles to its implementation, encourage sharing the plan with trusted significant others).

Clinicians should generate no more than five responses at most for each step of the plan. Listing too many options can be just as overwhelming as not having any skills to draw from during a psychiatric emergency. In short, the plan should be clear, written in the words of the Veteran, and easily accessible. Although the plan is brief and concrete, much can be learned through the process, such as an individual reporting s/he has no social support, or what mental health professionals they feel most connected to or would call upon in a time of crisis. The safety plan should accompany patients as part of overall treatment or life circumstances and evolve, with ongoing refinements as new skills are learned and personal contacts change. Clinicians should inquire about its use and efficacy, problem-solving barriers, and reinforcing its implementation. Safety plans should be the focus of any mental health visit when safety is in question.

Case Study

Will is a young male, white, non-Hispanic OIF Veteran who came into the outpatient clinic because his wife said if he did not get better control of his anger, she would leave him. During the first session, he expressed suicidal ideation and said he frequently had the thought, "I don't want to be here," but he denied having a plan of how he would kill himself or any intent that he would act on those thoughts. Will denied any previous suicide attempts or current access to firearms. He also denied abusing drugs or alcohol. When asked if there was a family history of mental illness or suicide, the Veteran stated that a maternal uncle had died by suicide before he was born and his younger sibling had made several suicide attempts over the past decade. He also said his mother was "crazy." Will endured several military traumas, but denied any traumatic brain injury. He also denied having a history of interpersonal traumas.

Although Will had some significant risk factors (suicidal ideation, family history of suicide attempts and mental illness, military trauma, and demographic risk factors), he had no current plan or intent, and it was determined that he was not an acute risk for suicide. However, he told his clinician that he was grateful someone had asked him to talk about his suicidal feelings, and he felt relieved he could discuss these "embarrassing things" with his therapist. He was happy to collaborate on a Suicide Safety Plan to use as a way to cope with distress, and to assure himself and his clinician that he would take appropriate steps if his suicidal ideation increased. He was eager to share his Suicide Safety Plan with his wife, and thought she would be relieved as well because she had been worried about him.

Will's Suicide Safety Plan

Step 1—Warning Signs

Fighting with his wife
Feeling trapped
Remembering IED blast that killed his friend
Having the thought "I don't want to be here"

Step 2—Internal Coping Strategies

Listen to music
Go for a run
Focus on school work

Step 3—Social Contracts Who May Distract from the Crisis

Skype with good friend who is abroad this semester
People watch downtown
Go to the movies

Step 4—Family Members or Friends Who May Offer Help

Call wife XXX-XXXX
Call friend XXX-XXXX

Step 5—Professionals and Agencies to Contact for Help

Call therapist XXX-XXXX
Call Veteran Suicide Hotline 800-273-TALK (8255)

Step 6—Making the Environment Safe

Has no guns. Agrees to clear medicine cabinet of all extra OTC and prescription drugs

---

After this initial meeting, Will's clinician assessed suicidal ideation, risk, and intent at every session and reinforced the use of his Safety Plan. He learned several effective coping skills for dealing with his suicidal thoughts, and began to address his anger and his relationship with his wife. Will discovered that his anger was in fact related to his military traumas and a symptom of PTSD, and as therapy progressed and his symptoms improved, his clinician reduced the frequency of suicide risk assessments.

Conclusion

Suicidal behavior can occur before, during, or after military service and may or may not be directly related to deployment. It is imperative that clinicians working with returning Veterans identify those at risk and provide effective interventions (Martin, Ghahramanlou-Holloway, Lou, & Tucciarone, 2009). Cognitive-behavior therapy (CBT) and dialectical behavior therapy (DBT) (Linehan, 1993) are two types of empirically supported treatments recommended as first-line interventions for suicidal individuals. Cognitive therapy for suicidal patients (Wenzel, Brown, & Beck, 2009) is a particular type of CBT that follows a 10-session protocol focusing on suicidal ideation and strategies to deal with suicidal crises. The authors purposefully developed a relatively brief protocol that could easily be adopted by community mental health centers. DBT is another form of CBT that was specifically developed to treat chronically suicidal individuals. DBT typically includes individual and group therapy as well as telephone coaching for the patient, and a consultation team for therapists. It explicitly organizes treatment to focus first on suicidal and self-harm behaviors and incorporates four modules: mindfulness, distress tolerance, emotion regulation, and interpersonal effectiveness. DBT's underlying principle is to help individuals "build a life worth living." Finally, since numerous studies point to a strong link between interpersonal traumas (e.g., rape, sexual assault, domestic violence, child abuse) and suicidal risk both male and female Veterans (Belik, Stein, Asmundson, & Sareen 2009; Tuet, Finney, & Moos, 2006), may wish to consider other forms of therapy that address these issues directly, such as Skills Training in Affective and Interpersonal Regulation (STAIR) (Cloitre, Cohen, & Koenen, 2006), a type of CBT specifically developed to treat complex trauma. No matter what type of treatment is utilized, clinicians should remind themselves and their clients that "Safety is Always Number One."

Appendix 11.A

Comprehensive Suicide Risk Assessment

1 Ideation
2 Plan
   Intent
3 Previous Attempts
   Describe:
4 Impulsivity (e.g., Are you the kind of person who might get into fights? Risk-taker/thrill seeker?)
   Violence
   Verbal Aggression
   Impulsive Behaviors
   Head Injury
5 Psychiatric Illness
   None
   Depression
   PTSD
   Bipolar Disorder
   Substance Abuse
   Alcohol Abuse
   Psychosis
   Personality Disorder

6   Physical Problems
     Pain: (*Note*: Tang and Crane (2006) recommend ascertaining helplessness and hopelessness about the pain, the desire for escape from pain, pain catastrophizing and avoidance, and problem-solving deficits related to the pain.)
     Chronic Illness (Clinicians should be aware that medical conditions, such as hepatic encephalopathy, unstable diabetes mellitus, and renal failure can contribute to altered mental status.)
     Acute Illness
     Describe:
7   Acute Symptoms
     Psychic Pain
     Anxiety
     Panic
     Hopelessness
     Insomnia
     Obsessionality
     Recent intoxication
     Hallucinations
8   Adherence to Medication
     Reliable, Poor, Other
9   Firearms
     Available, Restricted
     Other Means—medications, heights, razors, extra extension cords, sharp knives, etc.
10   Protective Factors
     Religious/spiritual beliefs
     Hopes and plans for the future
     Positive/explicit reasons for living
     Dependent others
     Living with others
     Regular contacts with supports
     Psychic toughness

Appendix 11.B

Brief Suicide Assessment

1   Are you feeling hopeless about the present or future?
2   Have you had thoughts about taking your life? Or, have you had thoughts of killing yourself? Or, have you had thoughts of suicide?
3   Do you have a plan for how you would kill yourself?

Appendix 11.C

Resources for the Clinician, Veteran, and Family

CLINICIAN

1   Suicide, Guns and Public Health
    www.meansmatter.org
2   Complete list of VA health care facilities
    www.va.gov
3   The Veterans Mental Health Coalition of NYC
    www.mha-nyc.org/advocacy/Veterans-mental-health-coalition.aspx
4   American Association of Suicidology (AAS)
    www.suicidology.org/
5   The American Foundation for Suicide Prevention (AFSP)
    www.afsp.org/
6   The Suicide Prevention Resource Center
    www.sprc.org
7   VA Mental Health Suicide Prevention
    www.mentalhealth.va.gov/MENTALHEALTH/suicide_prevention/
    index.asp
8   VISN 19 MIRECC Clinical Services
    http://www.mirecc.va.gov/visn19/clinical/clinical_vets.asp
9   Department of Defense
    http://www.defense.gov/home/features/2010/0810_restoringhope/
    http://www.realwarriors.net/
10 Clinical Records Initiative: Military Addendum
    http://www.mtmservices.org/NYSCRI_2010F/Program_Pages/All_
    Forms.html

VETERAN/FAMILY

1   U.S. Airforce Suicide Prevention
    http://www.af.mil/suicideprevention.asp
2   Department of Navy—Minding Your Mental Health™
    www.nehc.med.navy.mil/Healthy_Living/Psychological_Health/Mental_
    Health/mmh_mentalhealth.aspx
3   U.S. Army Suicide Prevention
    http://chppm-www.apgea.army.mil/dhpw/Readiness/SPTRG/
    GoodCharlotte2.wmv
4   Army Behavioral Health
    http://www.behavioralhealth.army.mil/sprevention
5   Marine Corps Veterans and families
    www.usmc-mccs.org/suicideprevent/index.cfm?sid=fl&smid=1

6 TRICARE Military Healthcare Program: Suicide Prevention
www.tricare.mil/mybenefit/ProfileFilter.do?&puri=2Fhome%2FMent alH
ealthAndBehavior%2FConditions%2FSuicidePrevention
7 United States Coast Guard—Suicide Prevention
www.uscg.mil/worklife/suicide_prevention.asp
8 Military OneSource
A 24-hour, 7-days-a-week, toll-free information and referral telephone
service.
www.militaryonesource.com/
9 Affordable readjustment services and reintegration support
www.homeagainVeterans.org
10 Veterans Suicide Prevention Hotline and Chatline
www.suicidepreventionlifeline.org/
1-800-273-TALK (8255), and press "1"
11 Defense Centers of Excellence for Psychological Health and Traumatic
Brain Injury (DCoE) http://www.realwarriors.net/

References

APA (American Psychiatric Association) (2003). *Practice Guidelines for the Assessment and Treatment of Patients with Suicidal Behaviors. Quick Reference Guide.* Arlington, VA: American Psychiatric Publishing, Inc., PsychiatryOnline.

Banasik, J.L. (2005). Acute disorders of brain function. In L.C. Copstead & J.L. Banasik (Eds.), *Pathophysiology* (3rd Ed., pp. 1093–1123). St. Louis, MI: Elsevier.

Beck, A.T., Rush, A.J., Shaw, B.F., & Emery, G. (1979). *Cognitive Therapy of Depression.* New York: Guilford Press.

Belik, S.L., Stein, M.G., Asmundson, G.J., Sareen, J. (2009). Relationship between traumatic events and suicide attempts in Canadian Military personnel. *Canadian Journal of Psychiatry*, 54(2), 93–104.

Brent, D.A., Johnson, B.A., Perper J., Connolly, J., Bridge, J., Bartle, S., et al. (1994). Personality disorder, personality traits, impulsive violence, and completed suicide in adolescents. *Journal of the American Academy of Child and Adolescent Psychiatry*, 33, 1080–1086.

Castro, C.A., Hoge, C.W., Milliken, C.W., McGurk, D., Adler, A.B., Cox, A., Bliese, P.D. (2006). *Battlemind Training: Transitioning home from combat.* Paper presented at the Army Science Conference, Orlando, FL. Abstract retrieved from: http://oai.dtic.mil/oai/oai?verb=getRecord&metadataPrefix=html&identifier=ADA481083

Centers for Disease Control and Prevention, National Center for Injury Prevention and Control. Web-based Injury Statistics Query and Reporting System. (n.d.). *Injury Prevention and Control: Data and statistics.* Retrieved from: http://www.cdc.gov/ncipc/wisqars

Cloitre, M., Cohen, L.R., & Koenen, K.C. (2006). *Treating Survivors of Childhood Abuse: Psychotherapy for the interrupted life.* New York: Guilford Press.

Hoge, C.W., Castro, C.A., Messer, S.C., McGurk, D., Cotting, D.I., & Koffman, R.L. (2004). Combat duty in Iraq and Afghanistan: Mental health problems and barriers to care. *New England Journal of Medicine,* 351(1), 13–22.

Kaplan, M.S., Huguet N., McFarland B.H., & Newsom, J.T. (2007). Suicide among male Veterans: A prospective population-based study. *Journal of Epidemiology and Community Health*, 61, 619–624.

Knox, K. & Kemp, J. (2009). *Operation S.A.V.E.: Suicide Prevention. Education, Training, and Dissemination.* Canandaigua, NY: VISN 2 Center of Excellence.

Linehan, M. (1993). *Cognitive Behavior Therapy for Borderline Personality Disorder.* New York: Guilford Press.

Maguen, S., Cohen, G., Cohen, B.E., Lawhon, G.D., Marmar, C.R., & Seal, K.H. (2010). The role of psychologists in the care of Iraq and Afghanistan Veterans in primary care settings. *Professional Psychology: Research and Practice*, 41(2), 135–142.

Martin, J., Ghahramanlou-Holloway, M., Lou, K., & Tucciarone, P. (2009). A comparative review of U.S. military and civilian suicide behavior: Implications for OEF/OIF suicide prevention efforts. *Journal of Mental Health Counseling*, 31(2), 101–118.

Maze, R. (2010). Eighteen Veterans commit suicide each day. Retrieved from: www.armytimes.com/news/2010/04/military_Veterans_suicide_042210w

McFarland, B.H., Kaplan, M., & Huguet, N. (2010). Self-inflicted deaths among women with U.S. military service: A hidden epidemic. *Psychiatric Services*, 61(12), 1177.

Moscicki, E.K. (1995). Epidemiology of suicidal behavior. *Suicide and Life-Threatening Behavior*, 25, 22–35.

Nampiaparampil, D.E. (2008). Prevalence of chronic pain after traumatic brain injury. *Journal of the American Medical Association*, 300(6), 711–719.

Nordstrom, P., Asberg, M., Aberg-Wistedt, A., & Nordin, C. (1995). Attempted suicide predicts suicide risk in mood disorders. *Acta Psychiatrica Scandinavia*, 92, 345–350.

Paykel, E.S. & Dienelt, M.N. (1971) Suicide attempts following acute depression. *Journal of Nervous and Mental Disease*, 153, 234 –243.

Pearson, J.L., Conwell, Y., Lindesay, J., Takahashi, Y., & Caine, E.D. (1997). Elderly suicide: A multi-national view. *Aging and Mental Health*, 1(2), 107–111.

Posey, S. (2009). Veterans and suicide: A review of potential increased risk. *Smith College Studies in Social Work*, 79(3), 368–374.

Resnick, M.D., Bearman, P.S., Blum, R.W., Bauman, K.E., Harris, K.M., Jones, J., et al. (1997) Protecting adolescents from harm. *Journal of the American Medical Association*, 278(10), 823–832.

Rudd, M.D., Mandrusiak, M., & Joiner, T.E. (2006). The case against no-suicide contracts: The commitment to treatment statement as a practice alternative. *Journal of Clinical Psychology*, 62(2), 243–251.

Rudd, M.D., Berman, A.L., Joiner, T.E., Nock, M.K., Silverman, M.M., Mandrusiak, M., Van Orden, K., & Witte, T. (2006). Warning signs for suicide: Theory, research and clinical applications. *Suicide and Life Threatening Behavior*, 36, 255–62.

Senior, J. (2011). *The Prozac, Paxil, Xoloft, Wellbutrin, Celexa, Effexor, Valium, Klonopin, Ativan, Restoril, Xanax, Adderall, Ritalin, Haldol, Risperdal, Seroquel, Ambien, Lunesta, Elavil, Trazodone War* (pp. 26–30, 83–84). New York: Byliner, February 14, 2011.

Stanley, B. & Brown G.K. (2008). *Safety Plan Treatment Manual to Reduce Suicide Risk: Veteran version.* Washington, DC: United States Department of Veterans Affairs.

Stroebe, M., Stroebe, W., & Abakoumkin, G. (2005). The broken heart: Suicidal ideation in bereavement. *American Journal of Psychiatry*, 162, 2178–2180.

Tang, N. & Crane, C. (2006). Suicidality in chronic pain: A review of the prevalence, risk factors and psychological links. *Psychological Medicine*, 36, 575–586.

Teasdale, T. & Engberg, A. (2001). Suicide after traumatic brain injury: A population study. *Journal of Neurology, Neurosurgery & Psychiatry*, 71, 436–440.

Tuet, Q., Finney, J., & Moos, R. (2006). Recent sexual abuse, physical abuse and suicide attempt among male patients seeking psychiatric treatment. *Psychiatric Services*, 57(1), 107–113.

U.S. Department of Veterans Affairs, Office of Mental Health Services, Suicide Prevention Program (2010). *Preventing Veteran Suicide: Fact sheet*. Retrieved from: http://www.mentalhealth.va.gov/college/Veteranfamilies.asp

Warden, D. (2006). Military TBI during the Iraq and Afghanistan wars. *Journal of Head Trauma Rehabilitation*, 21, 398–402.

Wenzel, A., Brown G.K., & Beck A. (2009). *Cognitive Therapy for Suicidal Patients: Scientific and clinical approaches*. Washington, DC: American Psychological Association.

12

OPERATION IRAQI FREEDOM/ OPERATION ENDURING FREEDOM

Exploring Wartime Death and Bereavement

Jill Harrington LaMorie

The stories shared by survivors are from actual OIF/OEF surviving families and service members. The author had obtained permission from each individual survivor interviewed to quote him or her directly. Each wanted their personal names and names of their deceased service member to be shared in this chapter. They all strongly believed it would honor their grief and their service member's life. However, it was determined that, even though consent was provided, it was in the best interest of survivors to remove their names. Pseudonyms were used in place of survivor and service member names.

> *My dear Sir and Madam, In the untimely loss of your noble son, our affliction here is scarcely less than your own. So much of promised usefulness to one's country, and of bright hopes for one's self and friends, have rarely been so suddenly dashed, as in his fall … In the hope that it may be no intrusion upon the sacredness of your sorrow, I have ventured to address you this tribute to the memory of my young friend, and your brave and early fallen child. May God give you that consolation which is beyond all earthly power.*
> *Sincerely your friend in a common affliction,*
> *Abraham Lincoln (May 25, 1861), 16th President of the United States*
> *Letter to Ephraim D. and Phoebe Ellsworth, Mother and Father of Colonel*
> *Elmer E. Ellsworth, United States of America, Union Army, died at 24 years old.*

Since 2001, the U.S. has been involved in wars on two global fronts. There have been over 43,000 men and women casualties associated with these wars. This has put the families and survivors of those killed under tremendous stress and pain. This chapter will focus on the needs of those families and survivors, will explore some of the unique stressors endured by family members and those close to the deceased, and will suggest intervention approaches to help those who work with the traumatized and bereaved.

> *The nature of war is destruction, both from property and human life. It has always been known that combat takes the lives of warfighters on the battlefield and, later, through wounds that are too serious to heal.*
>
> Charles R. Figley, Ph.D, MSW and William P. Nash, M.D.
>
> From *Combat Stress Injury: Theory, Research and Management* (Figley & Nash, 2007, p. 1)

OIF/OEF Deaths: Behind Every Flag-Draped Coffin

> *On October 15, 2004 at 6:38 in the morning our doorbell rang. Robert was just getting his first cup of coffee. I leaped from the bed and ran into the closet to get a robe. As I rounded the corner, Robert was turning on the lights and reaching for the door. I yelled at him NOT to open the door. He looked bewildered, but he opened it anyway, allowing the soldiers to enter. They removed their berets and one of the soldiers was turning his around and around in his hands. The other asked if we were Robert and Ellen Bixby. At that point, as they seemed to freeze in time, I asked loudly, "Is Brian dead?" Instead of answering, the Sergeant said, "Mr. Bixby, Mrs. Bixby, the Secretary of the Army has asked me to express his deepest regrets that Specialist Brian Scott Bixby was killed in action on October 14, 2004 in Ar Ramadi, Iraq." We just stared. Our daughter came down the stairs and Robert told her, "Brian is dead." I slid down the wall and sat on the floor.*
>
> **Surviving Mother** *of Specialist, U.S. Army, 2nd Battalion, 17th Field Artillery Regiment, 2nd Infantry Division, Camp Red Cloud, Korea, K.I.A at 22 years old, Iraq, October 14, 2004*

There are few images that strike at the heart of the American public and provoke a more powerful range of emotions than that of a flag-draped coffin being escorted to burial by the U.S. military. Behind every flag-draped coffin are individuals, families, fellow comrades and communities affected by the death of a military service member.

Given the age (18–30) of most troop casualties associated with the wars in Iraq and Afghanistan, the typical profile of a surviving family of a service member may include a young spouse, infants, pre-adolescent and adolescent children, young-adult siblings, young parents (who may be young-adult themselves), and a generally younger group of extended family members and friends.

The "typical" Primary Next of Kin (PNOK) of a service member is a spouse (if married) or partner or parent (if unmarried), and the "typical" Secondary Next of Kin (SNOK) is a parent (if married) and sibling/other close relation (if unmarried). The military formally focuses its resources and support on the Primary Next of Kin (PNOK) and Secondary Next of Kin (SNOK) listed by the service member on their personnel paperwork. However, the death of the service member can affect all who have felt an attachment to this service member and are either outwardly or silently grieving their loss. These disenfranchised grievers may include siblings, cousins, friends, stepparents, aunt/uncles, grandparents, fiancés, significant relationships, ex-spouses/estranged couples, lovers and same-sex partners.

Another vastly unrecognized population who are at risk for direct exposure to traumatic grief are fellow uniformed service members. The attachments shared by soldiers has been compared to that of kinship and the sudden death of a fellow comrade can produce an ensuing grief of a most deeply felt familial relationship. The attachments generated by soldiers, particularly in combat, "call forth a passion of care among men who fight beside each other" and whose grief can not begin to be understood if "we do not know the human attachment which battle nourishes and then amputates" (Shay, 1994, p. 39).

> *At this point in our tour, 3-509th lost several soldiers and I had known most of them. Two of my close friends had been killed only a month earlier and I remember just feeling extremely numb about Toby's death, as if I didn't want to hear it or cope with the loss of another friend. After all, I was still dealing with the loss of my friends from the previous month.*
>
> **Sergeant**, *3-509th, Airborne Infantry, U.S. Army, OIF Veteran 2006–2007, 28 years old*

The Rippling Effects of Wartime Deaths

> *I want you to know you do not mourn alone today. All across America from Virginia to Delaware to Pennsylvania and Minnesota, Montana and Wyoming, people are thinking of you and praying for you. You should know that Chance has touched many people.*
>
> From the HBO movie *Taking Chance*

The film is based on the journal kept by Lt. Col. Michael Strobl, USMC Escort for PFC Chance R. Phelps, 3rd Battalion, 11th Marine Regiment, 1st Marine Division, 1st Marine Expeditionary Force, Camp Pendelton, CA. K.I.A. at 19 years old, Al Anbar Province, Iraq, April 9, 2004.

The death of a U.S. service member as a result of war can cast a broad net that captures survivors affected by the impact of its rippling wake, leaving them susceptible to the effects of primary, secondary and vicarious grief and traumatization. The death of each individual impacts multiple micro, mezzo and macro systems: from the members of the unit in which they served; their immediate and extended families by whom they are survived; the casualty and mortuary affairs personnel who tend to their burial and remains; military families living on the posts/bases from which they are deployed; communities in which they may have lived and/or been raised; the greater military community at large; and the American public. Providers of care must be sensitive to the multi-systematic impacts of trauma and how best to support the individual and collective grief of these communities (Zinner & Williams, 1999).

The Intersection of Trauma and Grief

I was 23 years old and pregnant with our first child when my husband was killed in action by a suicide bomber in Fallujah, Iraq. His convoy was lost on an unmarked road when a suicide car bomb attacked, killing him and seven of his fellow Marines. Jack was 23 years old and we had fallen in love in Hawaii and had recently been married. When you asked if I could briefly describe what the experience of being notified about Jack's death was for me, it would never be possible to briefly describe this experience, as I am still experiencing it everyday. If I were to try and "briefly" describe it, I would say painful, traumatic and horrifying.

Surviving Spouse *of Lance Corporal, U.S. Marine Corps, 1st Battalion, 3rd Marine Regiment, 3rd Marine Division, III Marine Expeditionary Force, K.I.A. at 23 years old, Fallujah, Iraq, October 30, 2004*

Deaths associated as a result of U.S. military service in Iraq and Afghanistan are overwhelmingly sudden, traumatic and violent in nature and often involve the death of an adolescent or young adult.

Grief and bereavement following loss through death is a normative human process (Worden, 2009). How each individual responds to loss is a highly individualized and subjective experience. There is no definitive, prognostic response to death; loss and bereavement reactions vary among individuals in their meaning, presence, intensity, frequency and duration (Bonnano, 2004). Intense emotions, including sadness, anger, longing, guilt, fear and sorrow, accompanied by somatic sensations in the stomach, shortness of breath, profound fatigue, agitation, difficulties in swallowing and perceived helplessness are common in the first few months of grieving. Loss of interest, lack of motivation and social withdrawal are also frequent. Nonetheless, distress and an adaptive course of adjustment is often a common response to loss, as is the ability of the majority of survivors to integrate the loss into their lives and to accommodate with resilience (Bonnano, 2004; Neimeyer, Burke, MacKay & van Dyke Stringer, 2009). However, research suggests that 10%-20% of bereaved persons suffer from more complicated grief reactions (Shear, Frank, Houck, & Reynolds, 2005).

Loss by traumatic means predisposes the survivor to the combined synergistic influences of loss and trauma. Although we have only recently begun to explore the intersection of trauma and bereavement (Kaltman & Bonnano, 2003), the literature suggests that those affected by sudden, violent deaths caused by accidents, suicide, homicide, acts of terrorism and war are highly vulnerable to psychological trauma (Doka, 1996; Green, 2003) and the potential of developing complicated grief (Rando, 1993; Prigerson & Jacobs, 2001). The survivor is confronted with mourning the loss, but also the personal traumatization of the unforeseen psychological onslaught resulting from the circumstance of the death (Figley, Bride & Mazza, 1997; Rynearson, 2006). Often, the violence of the death eclipses the memories of the deceased, which can further heighten psychological distress and impair mourning (Rynearson, 2006).

Sibling Survivors

The pain was very raw. I remember feeling like I was on the edge of crying a lot. I had a hard time sleeping and had very serious insomnia for probably about a month after my brother died. It took me a little over a year to get back to a normal sleep pattern and nearly two years before I was consistently dreaming while sleeping. I think I was scared of what I might see if I dreamed about my brother, and so it was easier not to dream at all.

> ***Surviving Sibling*** *of Specialist, U.S. Army, 1st Battalion,*
> *18th Infantry Regiment, 2nd Brigade Combat Team,*
> *1st Infantry Division, Schweinfurt, Germany, K.I.A. by*
> *I.E.D at 22 years old, Baghdad, Iraq, August 6, 2007*

Bereaved siblings are often an unrecognized group of survivors, who cope to survive in the shadow of their service member sibling's death. Even though bereaved siblings experience profound loss, they are often overlooked in their grief (Godfrey, 2006). When adults and young adults lose a sibling, they often feel abandoned by society. Society often does not recognize siblings as primary grievers, nor acknowledge the death of an adult sibling as a significant loss (Godfrey, 2006). The sympathy, condolences and offers of support usually go to the parents, and siblings are implicitedly expected to "get over it" quickly so they can support their parents. When society fails to validate the loss and sadness of surviving siblings, they can often feel disenfranchised in their grief. Grieving siblings can retreat into hiding their feelings and suffer from complications in a healthy grieving process.

Since the military focuses it resources and supports on the PNOK and SNOK, who are typically spouses and parents, siblings who are not these designees may feel further marginalized in their grief from both the military and society at large. Social and emotional supports for siblings who have lost a young adult brother or sister are limited.

As with all mediating factors, how the sibling died, the nature of the sibling relationship, and the dynamics of the family are also important influencing factors in working with siblings. If the death is deemed heroic, the sibling must contend with the influence this has on their role and status in the family. The "hero child" who dies young may eclipse the attachment, roles and status of other children in the family. Anecdotally, it has been observed that sibling survivors may not be able to share in holidays (especially national holidays) that were once celebrated because surviving parents may not wish to celebrate holidays after one of their children has died. Siblings may have difficulty processing their own feelings about their sibling's involvement and service in the war. If the death is stigmatized, this can further compound grief for siblings.

Complicated Versus Uncomplicated Grief

In practice, one of the major problems with distinguishing between uncomplicated and complicated grief is the lack of operationalized criteria, including the inability to separate complicated grief from other syndromes, such as anxiety, depression or post-traumatic stress disorder. Traumatic loss can be a causal factor in the development of PTSD, especially when there are traumatic circumstances surrounding a death, such as the sudden, unexpected and/or violent death of a loved one, friend, co-worker or family member. Otherwise known as traumatic grief, characteristics of normal grief and PTSD may coexist and may be difficult to differentiate. Sometimes the effects of the trauma or PTS/PTSD may dominate and it becomes necessary for survivors to work through the trauma before grieving can begin.

Currently, very little is known about the sequelae of bereavement following violent death. Pivar (2004) documented grief symptoms in 70 percent of Veterans and discovered that these could be differentiated from symptoms of depression and PTSD. This works suggests that violent bereavement is a powerful stressor.

Grief, following the death of a loved one, is a normal process of adapting emotionally, cognitively, physically, psychologically and socially to the loss and absence of a loved one or attached relationship. Grief will unavoidably disturb the mental functioning of the bereaved survivor. While grief really never ends, from time to time the intensity of an individual's grief may be overwhelming and persistent over time. Complicated grief has been described as a form of grief in which the acute reactions to a loss continues with the same intensity with no abatement or integration of the loss over time (Shear & Shair, 2005).

Traumatic grief may predispose survivors to physical, psychological, social, emotional and behavioral problems that may complicate bereavement. Currently, there is no diagnostic criteria for traumatic grief; however, assessment of symptoms needs to be recognized by professionals and by traumatic grief survivors, because complicated grief is treatable. These symptoms may include:

- preoccupation with the deceased;
- pain in the same area as the deceased;
- upsetting memories;
- avoiding reminders of the death;
- death is unacceptable;

- feeling life is empty;
- longing for the person;
- hearing the voice of the person who died;
- drawn to places and things associated with the deceased;
- seeing the person who died;
- feeling anger about the death;
- feeling it is unfair to live when this person died;
- disbelief about the death;
- bitterness about the death;
- feeling stunned or dazed;
- envious of others;
- difficulty trusting others;
- feeling lonely most of the time;
- difficulty caring about others.

Although there is no timeline for grief, acute grief reactions commonly will begin to ameliorate and become more bearable as time progresses. When grief becomes complicated, affected survivors can remain intensely distressed for years post-loss, interfering with their ability to achieve the tasks of mourning and "find an enduring connection with the deceased in the midst of embarking on a new life" (Worden, 2009, p. 50). It has been suggested that assessment for complications in bereavement should begin around six months post-loss, although there is no current consensus in the bereavement field, and circumstantial complexities involved with certain types of losses, such as a military death, may actually predispose survivors to complicated bereavement/mourning.

Worden (2009) suggests using a paradigm to describe complicated mourning which includes:

1 *Chronic grief reactions.* An example can be that of a wartime bereaved parent who presents to a clinician 2–5 years after the death and feels "stuck in their grief" due to having extreme difficulty living daily with the reality that their child has died and will never return.
2 *Delayed grief reactions.* An example is that of a military wife whose husband dies while deployed overseas in a combat zone and whose bodily remains cannot be found due to the circumstance of the death. Even though a memorial service may be performed, the wife's grief may be suppressed until the unit in which her husband served arrives home and the reality of his death is recognized and reinforced to her by his absence upon their homecoming.
3 *Exaggerated grief reactions.* An example is that of a surviving sibling whose brother was captured and killed in combat and has begun "cutting" himself, driving at excessive speeds and abusing substances.

4   *Masked grief reactions.* An example is of a Marine Corps Lance Corporal who loses a fellow marine to suicide and has difficulty expressing his grief, but keeps showing up at medical clinic with vague symptoms of pain.

Serious Bereavement Complications

While maintaining that grief is highly personal and each individual copes with loss in their own unique way, it is essential that anyone working with the bereaved, especially those impacted by war, be aware of signs and symptoms of potentially serious complications in bereavement. Examples include a persistent inability to perform acts of daily functioning for many weeks and months after the death, abuse of drugs or alcohol, symptoms of major depression and/or PTSD, medical neglect, failure to thrive, engagement in high-risk and self destructive behaviors, and suicidal ideation and intent. Warning signs and symptoms should all be addressed immediately and professionally and should not be dismissed by the clinician as "just part of the grieving process," as they can be potentially life threatening to the survivor.

Routine assessments of all traumatic loss survivors should include a careful evaluation of suicidal ideation, suicide in the family, and a past history of suicide attempts. If the clinician assesses risk factors for suicidal behavior, this should become the immediate clinical focus and precautions must be put into place to protect the griever.

Clinicians should receive supervision and continuing education on suicide, sub-intentional suicide, suicide risk assessment, and suicide intervention. For more information on suicide education, training prevention, and postvention, resources include the American Foundation for Suicide Prevention (www.afsp.org), and the American Association for Suicidology (www.aas.org).

Complicating Factors and Distinct Issues for Survivors Surrounding a Loss in the U.S. Armed Services

> *In that moment and still today, the reality that Kevin, my best friend and father to our little girls is no longer in this world is not fathomable. And the coffin we witnessed being so honorably removed from the airplane was his. Months later he really was not at the airport with all the rest of his unit. The men he left with returned home and I could see them stepping out of the plane. Kevin was a coffin, no smiling face, no hug or hand to hold. A flag-draped coffin came home. I know what was left of him was in there, yet I can't accept that the bigger than life man I loved, came home to me that way.*
>
> **Surviving Spouse** *of Chief Warrant Officer 4, U.S. Army 1st Battalion, 227th Aviation Cavalry Regiment, 1st Cavalry Division, Fort Hood, Texas. Died of wounds sustained when his Apache helicopter was forced to land during combat operations at 41 years old, Taji, Iraq, February 2, 2007*

The death of a loved one in the U.S. Armed Services is fraught with complexities unlike those seen in the civilian world (Carroll, 2001; Steen & Asaro, 2006) lending itself to a potentially prolonged, distressing and complicated grief process for many survivors.

Factors surrounding a death in the U.S. military which may compound the loss and predispose survivors to complicated grief include: the sudden, traumatic and violent nature of the death; geography of the death; age of the decedent; age of survivor/s; condition of bodily remains; their commitment to duty; military casualty and burial rites and rituals; and media involvement. Traumatized and acutely grief-stricken survivors, especially if they are the PNOK, are also immediately confronted with the task of making complex decisions in the face of complex loss and trauma. The PNOK must navigate through the intricate bureaucratic process involved with the disposition of the remains of a service member; deal with personal effects of the service member; and attend to a substantial amount of paperwork associated with entitlements for survivor benefits. These tasks often involve multiple systems within the larger macro systems of the Department of Defense and Department of Veterans Affairs.

If a service member is killed during wartime, it may be difficult for the survivor to obtain specific information about the death. If the circumstances of the death involve an unattended body (e.g., a soldier's dead body is found in the house and appears to be a suicide) or warrants further investigation, survivors are also subjected to the burden of a death investigation, which involves more layers of bureaucracy within the military. Death investigations can be prolonged (extended over a year or more); can be chronically re-traumatizing to the survivor; and can be performed by criminal investigators who often may not work in tandem with victim assistance providers.

Interpersonally, the survivor is coping with their own response to the service member's death. Often, they are also having to negotiate a roller coaster of emotions and complex factors within the context of multiple, intrapersonal familial, military and organizational interactions. The aftermath of a military death does not exist in a vacuum, nor does the survivor. This is especially relevant for spouses and children who not only lose a family member, but a way of life. The social changes that death may bring to the survivor may come very unexpectedly.

To help understand some of the prominent factors and differences affecting military families, several areas need explication.

Age of Survivors

When John and I met, I was a Freshman in college and he was a Junior at the time. I was training to be a Marine Corps Officer and he was an enlisted Marine going for his degree so he could be an Officer as well.

Surviving Spouse of U.S. Marine 1st Lt., 1st Battalion, 6th Marines, 24th Marine Expeditionary Unit, II Marine Expeditionary Force Accident, Non-Hostile Action died at 29 years old, Garmsir, Afghanistan, July 17, 2008

Since the majority of deaths of service members are those of young adults, survivors are often young adults themselves. The vast majority of deaths in OIF and OEF have been of young men in their twenties and thirties. Young adult widowhood is often an indelible marker of war. Young widows and widowers have also unexpectedly become single parents, as many newly budding military families have young children.

Parents are also a profoundly affected group of survivors, as well as young adult siblings. The unexpected, tragic and untimely death of a young adult places the survivor in a position that is out of sync with their developmental phase.

Case example: Maria Garcia had given birth to her only son, Jorge when she was twenty years old. She had raised Jorge as a single mother in a two-bedroom apartment, worked most of her life as a medical secretary at a local hospital and felt fortunate to have the help of good friends throughout the years as Maria did not have much family in the United States. Jorge and his mother had a very close relationship throughout his childhood years and when he decided to enlist in the Marine Corps after his high school graduation, Maria supported his decision with reserved concern as her son had always wished to serve in the U.S. military, especially as a Marine. He dreamed of one day being the best Marine he could be, having the ability to learn a skill and trade, meeting and marrying a wife he could share this dream with. and being able to see parts of the world he had only imagined. Maria shared Jorge's hopes and dreams for the future and did not want to discourage him from pursuing them, but was concerned that he was joining the Marine Corps when the U.S. was at war with both Iraq and Afghanistan.

Jorge's unit was deployed to Fallujah, Iraq in 2004. Maria only had the opportunity to see her son once at boot camp graduation before he left and she prayed for him every day. Approximately two months into his deployment, at 6:38 pm on a Thursday evening, Maria received a knock at her apartment door. When she opened the door, two men dressed in U.S. military uniform greeted Maria. They were both officers; one wore a cross and neither one was her son. They asked if she was Maria Garcia and when she answered "Yes, the last words she remembered hearing were "We regret to inform you ...".

Her only son, her boy, the child she had nursed when sick, raised on her own, and loved unconditionally had been killed by a suicide bomber in Fallujah. She didn't know what to feel because at that moment she couldn't feel anything at all.

As Maria stood over the closed, flag-draped coffin of her son, her boy, her heart yearned to be able to see him, even if it was just his body, one more time. The circumstances of his death did not afford her that opportunity to be able to hold her son, her boy, just one more time and say "goodbye." As she stood in front of his coffin, weeping, she threw herself with sorrow over his casket, grabbing onto the American Flag Jorge so proudly served. At 38 years old, she was burying what was left of her only son as well as the past they shared and all the hopes and dreams of his future. There would be no future career in the military, no wife for him to come home to, no other foreign places in the world he dreamed to see, and no family with children he dreamed of having. For Maria, she supported these hopes and dreams for her son, and her hopes and dreams of living, loving and sharing life together with her only child and only family were now shattered, broken and gone forever. She struggled to breathe, to move, to cry. She struggled to imagine how to go on living. Maria was the parent; children are not supposed to predecease their parents—this death was developmentally "incorrect."

Geography of the Death/Geography of the Survivor

Wartime deaths typically occur in "theater," either in Iraq or Afghanistan, or in support of missions attached to OIF/OEF. The service member may have been deployed for a short time when the death occurred or could have been finishing the end of a deployment cycle. Whatever the situation, family members may not have seen their loved one for an extended period of time.

When the death occurs, spouses and significant others are often living on or around the base/post where their service member was deployed. Their primary support system may be their military or community in which they live, or they could be stationed far away from their own family members and lack the ability to have their immediate support. Last words and last moments spent together may have been few and far away. Distance from family imposed by military life may make the grief even more potent. Surely the military community is present and supportive, but the grievers may yearn for immediate family members to support them in their grief.

Circumstances of the Death and Condition of Bodily Remains

> *Violent, traumatic, sudden, devastating. The issues these survivors are dealing with include burnt dog tags, bent wedding rings, and mangled body parts. These are not quiet deaths between clean sheets. These are sudden, violent losses in often horrid conditions a long way from home.*
>
> **Bonnie Carroll**, *Surviving Spouse, Brigadier General Thomas Carroll,*
> *killed in a C-12 plane crash in Alaska, 1992. Founder and*
> *Executive Director, Tragedy Assistance Program for Survivors (T.A.P.S.)*
> From *Living with Grief After Sudden Loss* (Doka, 1996, p. 74)

The manner in which someone dies can have a deeply profound and enduring impact on survivors. Conceptually, a majority of war-related deaths have a human against human element with strong elements of violence.

The psychological and emotional impact of violent death to the survivor is a synergistic experience of both grief and trauma (Neria & Litz, 2004). Anxiety, fear, shock, isolation, numbness, blame, betrayal, anger, guilt, shame, powerlessness, revenge fantasies, depression, personality changes, obsessive-compulsive thoughts, and emotional regression are generalizable emotional experiences of traumatic death survivors (Spungen, 1998; Harris-Lord, 2006). In addition, violent deaths during war often leave trauma to the body. Bodily remains may be fragmented, retrieved bit by bit, never found or, due to circumstance, not viewable. If not viewable or received by the survivor, this can further complicate their grief or ability to grieve as the survivor can deny or delay the existence of the death. Recent evidence suggests that there may be benefits to being allowed to view a loved one's body after a sudden death (Chapple & Ziebland, 2010). The ability for the survivor to get up close to the deceased affords them the opportunity to orient themselves to the reality of the death and recognize the loss. When bodily remains are not viewable, the survivor is robbed of this opportunity. It can add to a heightened sense of denial, promote a preoccupation with the circumstance of the death, and be a further causal factor in chronic reenactment of the traumatic event by intrusive imagery.

Sometimes additional bodily remains are found months after the initial remains were returned home to the family and laid to rest. This may be very difficult for survivors, who struggle with complications in their grief as each part of their loved one's remains represents the presence of their death and loss. Each time a set of remains is found, the next of kin may be formally notified by the military. This can be extraordinarily re-traumatizing to the survivor and set them back on a path as emotionally powerful as the day of the initial notification. Family members and society may have difficulty recognizing how difficult it is for a survivor who deals with missing remains to fully detach from the possibility that pieces of their loved ones may be lost and may or may not be found. With the ambiguity of the loss, the detachment which is necessary for closure is difficult to achieve (Boss, 2000). The uncertainty not only complicates the loss, it also complicates bereavement.

> *I remember the day the Marines came to formally notify me that they had found a second set of Jason's remains. There was that knock at the door again and it all came back to me as if I was reliving being notified of his death for the first time.*
> **Surviving Spouse** *of Marine Gunnery Sgt., Explosive Ordinance Device (EOD) Technician, 8th Engineer Support Battalion, 2nd Marine Logistics Group, II Marine Expeditionary Force, Camp Lejeune, N.C., K.I.A disarming I.E.D. at 28 years old, Anbar province, Iraq, March 8, 2006*

Their Commitment to Service

> *The mix of emotions: feeling pride and anger, knowing the true price of freedom and seeing so many people take it for granted. It hurts.*
> **Surviving Army Spouse**

> *I am proud still, but the memories make my heart ache.*
> **Surviving Marine Corps Spouse**

One of the most important things we can do is honor their service and sacrifice.
Surviving Army Mother

The reasons for commitment to service may be a risk for further complication to the survivor or a protective, healing factor as they grieve. The survivor's viewpoint of the service member's military career is an essential determining factor. Some may be angry at their choice to join, especially during a time of war. They may also feel abandoned and cheated if their service member chose to re-enlist or voluntarily go to war. The public label of "hero" may add to a sense of emotional confusion for the survivor. Often times anger at the deceased, rational or irrational, is a common emotion after sudden death, even knowing the death was no fault of their own (Harris-Lord, 2006). Survivors may feel guilty for their anger at a hero. Helping the survivor to understand where the anger is coming from can help facilitate these complex emotions.

To begin this discussion in a counseling situation, start by asking questions such as: "What makes you angry about your loved one's death?" "What was their relationship at the time of their death?" There is often the possibility of blame, maybe toward the military or blame toward the service member for joining the Armed Services. Anger needs a reason and a target to exist. The reason for the anger is clear to the survivor—someone they love, or had a relationship with, has died suddenly and/or violently. The target of their anger can be at someone specific such as "the enemy," the military, the deceased, other family members, their friends, themselves. God is a common target. If a specific target cannot be identified, the bereaved can walk around like time bombs waiting to explode on the first person or situation that crosses their path—displacing their anger on any target they can find.

It is very important to process this anger with the survivor so that they can begin to gain insight, understanding, and sometimes validation for their anger. Knowing why they are angry, and who or what the anger is aimed at, helps the bereaved control their anger rather than continuing to allow it to control them. A trusted therapeutic relationship can provide a safe place for survivors to release their anger and help them to understand that, although they may never get rid of it, they can better understand it, express it and manage it. Helping the survivor understand that they may not always be able to control how they feel, but that they can control how they act, can begin to foster healing.

Death Notification

For many survivors, especially the next-of-kin, their lives are indelibly altered by a knock at the door. The U.S. military formally notifies the primary and secondary next of kin that their service member has died in the line of duty by an official death notification process. The military usually arrives by an official government vehicle, wearing sharply cleaned and decorated uniforms and come in pairs—a notifier and a chaplain.

Receiving and delivering this news is painful and difficult for both the survivor and notification team. However, even with the best training and sensitivity, notifying a family that a service member has suddenly died can be a "primary" traumatic event. When the death is sudden, traumatic and/or violent, the shock of the news can overwhelm the internal resources of the survivor, triggering a variety of individual responses.

Shutting down, screaming, acting numb, crying hysterically, behaving with intense rage, can all be responses to hearing the news. For mental health practitioners, survivor's recall of the event can be as varied as their emotional reactions, they can remember nothing, vague details or with pinpointed accuracy every detail of the moment.

The Casualty Officer

Unlike the civilian world, where the details of the death and paperwork are often the sole responsibility of an executor of a will, the military assigns a casualty officer to be the point of contact for the PNOK for weeks or months after the death.

The Casualty Officer is assigned to a family for guidance and support during one of the most difficult and challenging times of their lives. Many military widows or grievers, who are far away from home and without support, rely heavily on their casualty officers for practical and emotional support. The officers assist the primary next of kin in making complex, major life decisions during a time of intense trauma, grief and confusion.

The Immediate Impact to Survivors

The practical and emotional demands on the individual survivor and family who are suddenly notified of a service member's death are extraordinary. From the moment the casualty officer walks in the door, the complex decisions regarding the death begin.

Dignified Transfer of Remains

Designated family members of the fallen are invited to attend the dignified transfer of remains at Dover Air Force Base, Delaware. In many cases, the family must decide quickly if they want to attend the transfer, as well as whether or not to allow the media to film them.

What to Tell the Children?

Any parent that has young children struggles with words about death, especially if it involves the death of a parent or family member. Grief counselors and therapists have been invaluable in assisting families with this process. But when the death is unexpected, traumatic and violent, there is limited real-time opportunity to obtain immediate assistance to a critical need. Because of the circumstances of the death, the condition or lack of bodily remains, and the coping skills of the surviving parent, some may delay relating detailed information to their children and may need assistance in the next few days, weeks, months or years after the death. Some questions are: "What is developmentally appropriate for each child?" "How much should I tell them?" "What is helpful information?" "What is hurtful information?" "Should I tell them the circumstances of the death?" Answering these questions is an individual, difficult, process for parents of young children. Organizations, such as The Dougy Center, The National Child Traumatic Stress Network and TAPS can be helpful resources for parents and general practitioners needing further training.

> *Because the death is so public—the family needs help working through how to handle that public role, and how to handle the media.*
>
> **Surviving Army Sibling**

Complex Decisions Under Complex Trauma and Grief

Immediate complex, life-altering decisions need to be made within hours, days and the short weeks following a service member's death. The experts in grief suggest that you do not make any life-altering decisions within six to twelve months after the death of a loved one or significant relationship. The military is beginning to recognize this best practice suggestion, but often times, survivors, especially spouses, are faced with relatively immediate, life-altering decisions on where to move, financial considerations/monetary benefits, handling personal effects and household goods, and schooling for children all within the first three to twelve months after a service member has died and depending upon where they are stationed.

Secondary and Multiple Losses

The death of a loved one in active duty military service confronts the family member with a series of losses associated with their death. These losses include the actual death, a loss of their way of life and identity associated with this life (e.g., military spouse, military mom, military child), loss of their housing (if on base/post), and loss of their greater military community. For spouses and children, it is an "involuntary transition" from military family to civilian family. These often sudden, multiple and compounding losses may bring with them a profound sense of isolation, loneliness and disenfranchisement for the surviving family.

Issues for Clinicians

I had just delivered a baby on my own. My beautiful, young husband, the love of my life, had been killed in Iraq a few months ago. I was driving down the turnpike in tears and realized I needed someone to talk to. I called the military all-source hotline number given to me by my CACO. When I explained to the counselor on the phone how John died and my situation, her first response was "Oh My God." I immediately hung up the phone.

Surviving Marine Corps' Spouse

First, it is vitally important for the general practitioner in community-based care to monitor their own feelings about the current wars, military service, the military and how this may or may not create issues for them within the context of a clinical relationship.

A key factor in working with any one in the midst of grief, loss and transition is being mindful of the cultural factors of the target population. There is a unique culture to the military that is definitely an unfamiliar concept to most civilian mental health providers. The culturally competent provider will self-assess for their own biases, values, preconceived ideas and personal boundaries in working with military clients and their families. In choosing to work with this population, the practitioner should become informed as much as possible and learn from the client about the military culture.

Second, "do no harm!" General practice clinicians may see military loss survivors who either integrate or are part of the American community as part of their local practice. These cases can be quite complicated, graphic in nature, and involve an intense amount of complex grief and trauma. As a reminder, if the client's presenting problems are beyond one's skill set ... refer, refer, refer. Referrals to grief therapists and trauma counselors in your area can found through the Association for Death Education and Counseling (www.adec.org), the International Society for Traumatic Stress Studies (www.istss.org), or Tragedy Assistance Program for Survivors (www.taps.org).

Finally, what you are most likely to see among survivors is the intersection of grief and trauma. The knowledge base on the effects of combined trauma and grief is limited. Practitioners who seek to become more skilled in working with this population should seek further training and continuing education on both grief and trauma. Professional organizations, such as the ADEC, ISTSS and TAPS are excellent sources of education, training and further resources of support.

Suggested Resources and Interventions for Care

The definition for a survivor affected by a wartime death is broad. Social workers and therapists may encounter a civilian, uniformed personnel and their families, as well as war Veterans, survivors and surviving families in multiple settings of care.

The short- and long-term psychosocial care needs for surviving families is an area of concern that is beginning to be addressed through the military. In the absence of such services, Veteran service organizations, such as TAPS, provide care and community support to military survivors who often feel disenfranchised from the military. Since there are so many concrete needs and issues survivors face, social workers and therapists may need to work concurrently to help the survivor to meet these needs or process the stressors around them.

Whether uniformed, civilian, Veteran or survivor, for those seeking counseling or treatment, it is extremely important for the provider to perform a comprehensive biopsychosocial assessment to "meet the survivor where they are" in their process as well as to assess for co-morbid conditions. Some questions to ask, may include: Date of Death; Branch of Service; Age of Decedent at Death; Your Relationship to the Deceased; Their Circumstances of Death; Where were they when they died? Are you the Primary or Secondary Next of Kin? Where do you live? Who lives with you? What support systems do you have? What kind of relationship do you have with your family? Have you needed to move since your loved one's death? What are some of the practical matters you have needed to deal with? Can you tell me about your loss and trauma history? Have you been in therapy before? (Yes: Can you explain a little further. Why? What was going on at that time? How did your therapy end?) Have you ever been diagnosed with a mental health condition? Have you ever struggled with substance abuse? Have you ever been self-destructive? Have you ever been prescribed psychotropic medication? How have you coped through any previous challenges you have had in your life?

Grief may be secondary, primary or co-equal to a presenting organic depression, substance abuse, lack of social support, familial distress, financial difficulties, relationship problems, or acute/post traumatic stress reactions. In trying to gauge where they are in their grief, the counselor can use Worden's (2009) "Tasks of Mourning" and assess if the survivor is working on: Task I (To Accept the Reality of the Loss); Task II (To Process the Pain of Grief); Task III (To Adjust to a World without the Deceased); or Task IV (To Find an Enduring Connection With the Deceased in the midst of Embarking on a New Life). In using this model, they can also look for complications in grief that may warrant further grief therapy and more prolonged interventions.

If a survivor is a parent, spouse or child of a U.S. Armed service member, reservist or National Guardsmen who die in the line of duty, they are eligible for bereavement counseling through the Department of Veteran's Affairs Vet Center (www.vetc.enter.va.gov). If a survivor is close to a Vet Center, is eligible and wants to attend, then Vet Center individual and group counseling can be an excellent source of psychological and social support. Also, many will seek care from civilian social workers or other mental health providers.

The power of peer support is an under-utilized, and an empirically under-recognized, area of healing and comfort to bereaved survivors, especially those incurring a loss due to a military death. Peer support programs, including mutual support groups, peer chat rooms and peer-to-peer programs and conferences can provide to survivors what individual therapy and the therapist often cannot. They can also provide that instillation of hope, feeling of universality, altruism and information sharing that Yalom (1995) believes is a benefit of the peer process.

The workplace and cultural connection among the military and Veteran community is strong. The mission-oriented life of the military requires a reliance on peers for both the service member and their family for survival. This peer connection and occupation-related connection may be beneficial to the survivor. Peer support is not for everyone but, for many who are connected to the U.S Armed Services, it is beneficial in their ability to cope and heal. A military widow may provide this type of comfort and care to bereaved military survivors, but the only designated Veterans service organization providing this type of aftercare is TAPS, founded in 1994. Practitioners should consider them as a resource for beginning a support group for these types of military losses.

Conclusion

What are we doing as a nation and as a profession whose history is steeped in working with the vulnerable to "bind up the wounds" for those who have borne the battle? It was a promise to a nation and its people so nobly endeared and made into law by a President over 145 years ago. This is the question our society and our profession, as instruments of change in the social world, must ask.

The study of complex trauma and grief has implications not just subject to bereaved survivors, but also to wounded warriors and their families who live with the lifelong wounds of trauma, loss and life transitions. Social workers play a pivotal role as one of the largest groups of mental health providers in the DoD and VA health systems, as well as being the largest group of providers of mental health care in the United States.

References

Bonanno, G.A. (2004). Loss, trauma, and human resilience: Have we underestimated the human capacity to thrive after extremely aversive events? *American Psychologist*, 59(1), 20–28.

Boss, P. (2000). *Ambiguous Loss: Learning to live with unresolved grief*. Princeton, NJ: Harvard University Press.

Carroll, B. (2001). How the military family copes with a death. In O.D. Weeks & C. Johnson (Eds.), *When All the Friends Have Gone: A guide for aftercare providers* (pp. 173–183). Amityville, NY: Baywood Publishing Company.

Chapple, A. & Ziebland, S. (2010). Viewing the body after bereavement due to a traumatic death: Qualitative study in the UK. *British Medical Journal*, 340, c2032.

Doka, K. (Ed.) (1996). *Living with Grief after Sudden Loss: Suicide, homicide, accident, heart attack, stroke*. New York: Routledge.

Figley, C.R. & Nash, W.P. (Eds.) (2007). *Combat Stress Injury: Theory, research, and management*. New York: Routledge.

Figley, C.R., Bride, B.E., & Mazza, N. (Eds.) (1997). *Death and Trauma: The traumatology of grieving.* Washington, DC: Taylor & Francis.

Figley, C.R. & Nash, W.P. (Eds.) (2007). *Combat Stress Injury: Theory, research, and management.* New York: Routledge.

Godfrey, R. (2006). Losing a sibling in adulthood. *The Forum: Association of Death Education and Counseling,* 32(1), 6–7.

Green, B.L. (2003). *Trauma Interventions in War and Peace: Prevention, practice and policy.* New York: Kluwer Academic/Plenum Publishing.

Harris-Lord, J. (2006). *No Time for Goodbyes: Coping with sorrow, anger, and injustice after a tragic death* (6th Ed.). Burnsville, NC: Compassion Press.

Kaltman, S. & Bonanno, G.A. (2003). Trauma and bereavement: Examining the impact of sudden and violent deaths. *Anxiety Disorders,* 17, 131–147.

Neimeyer, R.A., Burke, L.A., Mackay, M.M., & van Dyke Stringer, J.G. (2009). Grief therapy and the reconstruction of meaning: From principles to practice. *Journal of Contemporary Psychotherapy,* 40(2), 73–83.

Neria, Y. & Litz, B.T. (2004). Bereavement by traumatic means: The complex synergy of trauma and grief. *Journal of Loss and Trauma,* 9, 73–87.

Pivar, I.L. & Field, N.P. (2004). Unresolved grief in combat Veterans with PTSD. *Journal of Anxiety Disorders,* 18, 745–755.

Prigerson, H.G. & Jacobs, S. (2001). Traumatic grief as a distinct disorder. In M.S. Stroebe, R.O. Hansson, W. Stroebe, & H. Schut (Eds.), *Handbook of Bereavement Research: Consequences, coping and care* (pp. 613–645). Washington, DC: American Psychological Association.

Rando, T.A. (1993). *Treatment of Complicated Mourning.* Champaign, IL: Research Press.

Rynearson, E.K. (Ed.) (2006). *Violent Death: Resilience and intervention beyond crisis.* New York: Routledge.

Shay, J. (1994). *Achilles in Vietnam: Combat trauma and the undoing of character.* New York: Scribner.

Shear, K. and Shair, H. (2005), Attachment, loss, and complicated grief. *Developmental Psychobiology,* 47: 253–267.

Shear, K., Frank, E., Houck, P.R., & Reynolds, C.F. (2005). Treatment of complicated grief: A randomized controlled trial. *Journal of the American Medical Association,* 293(21), 2601–2608.

Spungen, D. (1998). *Homicide: The hidden victims.* Thousand Oaks, CA: SAGE Publications, Inc.

Steen, J.M. & Asaro, M.R. (2006). *Military Widow: A survival guide.* Annapolis, MD: Naval Institute Press.

Worden, J.W. (2009). *Grief Counseling and Grief Therapy: A handbook for the mental health practitioner* (4th Ed.). New York: Springer Publishing Co.

Yalom, I.D. (1995). *The Theory and Practice of Group Psychotherapy.* New York: Basic Books.

Zinner, E.S. & Williams, M.B. (Eds.) (1999). *When a Community Weeps: Case studies in group survivorship.* Philadelphia, PA: Brunner/Mazel.

13

SPOUSES AND THEIR FAMILIES IN THE MODERN MILITARY SYSTEM

Problems, Assessment, and Interventions

Blaine Everson and C. Wayne Perry

Throughout the history of military conflict, female significant others (wives, lovers, or consorts) have played an ongoing part in the lives of warriors (Hobbes, 2003). Indeed, some of our more memorable myths and legends have involved the departure, lengthy absence, and return of warriors to the ones who have loved them in spite of their absence and waited anxiously for their return. The Greek poets, philosophers, and historians were able to make a compelling case for the difficulties associated with military lifestyles. Both of Homer's major works, the *Iliad* and the *Odyssey*, remind us of the travails associated with long-term, war-related separations and the warrior's arduous journey to a home that no longer existed as they once knew it (Buxton, 2004). Most often overlooked is Penelope, the wife of Odysseus, who must contend with both the loneliness associated with his lengthy absence (and perilous return), hope for the best (while preparing for the worst), and resist the unwanted temptations of a persistent suitor in the form of the lecherous Eurymachus.

In the *Illiad*, the spouses of warriors await the news from the battles as their children, who were infants when their fathers left for a decade-long war with Troy, have grown into adulthood (e.g., Odysseus' son Telemachus) without having known their fathers. (NB: Spouses is used generically and refers to wives, partners, and those who cohabitate.) Fate was, and is, often unkind to families of soldiers and sailors, in other ways as well. One can hardly imagine the horror of Andromache as she watched her beloved Hector fall to the spear of Achilles on the plains of Troy (Martin, 1991). Even today, many spouses of combat troops dread each and every knock on their door for fear that it may bring news of their loved one's injury or death in the line of duty. Shay (2002), however, argues that dying in battle, as mighty Achilles succumbed to the cowardly Paris' well-placed arrow, is sometimes easier than, although certainly not preferable to, the arduous emotional journey that awaits those returning from war and those who await their return.

An increasing number of female military spouses are experiencing this kind of anxious waiting. In 2009, The U.S. Department of Defense established the number of military dependents at 1,864,427, far exceeding the 1.36 million active duty service members at that time. Military spouses comprised 681,679 of this total with 1.72 children per household (Office of the Deputy Under Secretary of Defense for Military Community and Family Policy, 2007). In fact, the number of military spouses increased dramatically from the time the Carter Administration ended the practice of conscripting service members in the late 1970s, in favor of an all volunteer force (Segal, 1986). Prior to this time, service members were either single, serving for a short period of time in the military before their resumption of civilian life, had married prior to conscription with families remaining at their longtime residences, or career oriented individuals who began families with the expectation of long-term military service. In any case, the number of military spouses in the U.S. was historically much smaller and their numbers were often confined to higher ranks of the armed services (i.e., officers and non-commissioned officer spouses) prior to the 1980s. What is unique about the modern American military system are the lengths to which all four branches of the armed services have gone, with varying degrees of success, to create a more stable and harmonious environment for dependents of service members. However, several basic problems remain associated that may never be surmounted: long-term separations, the threat of danger to a loved one, and the stability of the family unit in light of the strains associated with a military way of life. The purpose of this chapter is threefold:

1   To provide a brief overview of recent practice-related information and research;
2   To inform practitioners about issues facing modern military spouses and their families;
3   To elaborate on a unique therapeutic approach to the stressors that military spouses and families experience as a part of their ongoing lives.

Demographic and Statistical Overview

Not only can a military way of life be stressful for spouses, Warner, Breitbach, Yates, et al. (2007) reported that stressors related to family life were a consistent concern for soldiers serving in Iraq as deployments increased to beyond six months in length. The average deployment, in both the Iraqi and Afghan conflicts, has increased to over a year creating an almost unbelievable amount of emotional strain for spouses, as well as service members in many cases (Gibbs, Martin, Kupper, & Johnson, 2007). In an effort to address family related issues associated with longer deployments and separations, the Department of Defense has commissioned a number of surveys across all branches of military service during the past decade (e.g., *The 2008 Surveys of Military Spouses* (DMDC, 2009); and *Survey of Army Families V* (U.S. Army Morale, Welfare, and Recreation Command, 2006). Other studies have been untaken by private foundations and nonprofit organizations in order to provide improved information about military families outside of the purview of the executive branch of the U.S. government (e.g. *Military Families Survey* (Kaiser Family Foundation, 2004); and *The Military Family Lifestyle Study* (Blue Star Families, 2009)). The information in this section focuses on data derived from several of the more well known surveys conducted by both public and private entities with military families in recent years.

The results from *The 2008 Surveys of Military Spouses* (DMDC, 2009), included both active duty (28% response rate; n = 14,210) and reserve (30% response rate; n = 16,200) components across all branches of the armed forces. This large scale survey focused primarily on the impact of deployments on spouses and their children. Some major findings associated with the SMS include higher levels of loneliness during deployments, greater readjustment problems after the service member's return, and more disruption in children's lives than previously reported among military spouses.

A second source of data is *The Military Family Lifestyle Study*, published in 2009 by Blue Star Families, a nonprofit organization whose mission is to support military families and raise public awareness of issues related to the military lifestyle. The 2,794 participants in this on-line survey included military spouses across all branches of the armed services, including members of the Army National Guard (20% of respondents) and Air National Guard, and across multiple geographic regions and those spouses stationed overseas (6% of respondents). The results of the MFLS have been cited frequently by First Lady Michelle Obama as evidence of the need for enhanced support for military families.

For an understanding of spouses and families of members of U.S. ground forces, results from the *Survey of Army Families V* (SAF-V) (U.S. Army Morale, Welfare, & Recreation Command, 2006) are included in the discussion of problems associated with recent military lifestyle. SAF-V was unique in that it was the first survey fielded at the behest of the U.S. Army's Morale, Welfare, and Recreation Command (MWRC) after September 11, 2001. Data were gathered from 24,793 spouses of soldiers who were deployed at the time, recently returned from deployment, or had not deployed since 9/11. The SAF-V included information from four major areas associated with Army life: demands and way of life, deployment, career plans, and leadership. According to the Strategic Resources Incorporated website (www.sri-hq.com) included 75,000 randomly selected U.S. Army spouses.

The *Military Families Survey* (Kaiser Family Foundation, 2004) included 1,053 randomly selected U.S. Army spouses, who were interviewed in order to ascertain the extent of their experiences during deployments since September 11, 2001 (444 currently experiencing deployment; 342 who had experienced deployment since September 2001; 256 of spouses who had not experienced a deployment since September 2001).

An Elaboration of Stressors Associated with Military Lifestyle

Figure 13.1 provides a graphic representation of these stressors on spouses of members of the military.

Although there are a number of stressors associated with military life, we have chosen to briefly discuss the seven that we consider to be the most prominently observed among clients presenting for psychotherapy with mental health professionals: deployments, wellbeing, parenting, work–life balance, relational quality, fear of harm to service member, and financial problems. Financial stressors and fear of harm for the service member are discussed within the wellbeing and relational quality sections, and the deployment section.

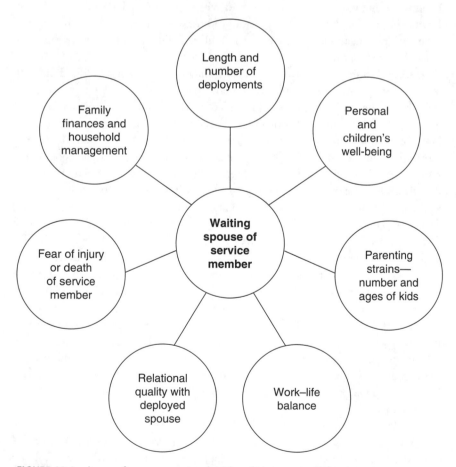

FIGURE 13.1   Array of sensors associated with military spouses' lifestyle

Deployments

There is no other stressor that negatively impacts female military spouses and their families in the way that long-term deployments do. The problems experienced by families of military personnel stem from the unique emotional adjustments required by all family members at each phase of the deployment process. There are three primary phases of a deployment: pre-deployment, the actual separation caused by the deployment, and the post-deployment or reunification of the service member with the family (Doyle & Peterson, 2005). The pre-deployment phase usually begins at the time when the active duty spouse "unit" (often a battalion sized [300-1300 personnel] contingent in the U.S. Army or USMC; "wing" in the USAF; or "task element" in the U.S. Navy) receives orders to mobilize as part of a larger force generally. For those spouses who have experienced previous deployments, there is often a sense of normalcy in that they are familiar with the events that are about to transpire. Some spouses even report the occurrence of emotional detachment between themselves and the service member, as well as the increase in apprehension in their children (Burrell, Adams, Durand, & Castro, 2006). For those who have not experienced previous deployments, there are often feelings of confusion, exasperation, and helplessness associated with this phase of deployment. While the pre-deployment phase not only signals the beginning of a long-term separation for military families, it also signals the end of the post-deployment phase in which the service member has returned from a previous deployment. In many cases, reunification is successful with families effectively reintegrating the service members back into the household; yet there is some indication that the repeating cycle of deployments is negatively impacting military families as nearly two-thirds of spouses (63%) recently surveyed reported problems with post deployment adjustments (*Surveys of Military Spouses*, DMDC, 2009).

Extended absences are commonplace in today's military, but have grown longer and more frequent in recent years due primarily to a limited number of active duty service members and war planners operating within budgetary constraints. Of U.S. Marine and U.S. Army units serving in Iraq or Afghanistan, many spend more than a year at a time away from their families within the theater of operation (Gibbs et al., 2007). These limitations have created the need for the mobilization of military reserves and National Guard forces. Unfortunately, the utilization of these components has resulted in a disparity between the regular service members and their families, and reservists, as well as guardsmen, and their families. In the *Surveys of Military Spouses* (DMDC, 2009), 69 percent of active duty spouses had experienced a deployment within the past three years, while 80 percent of reservist and National Guard spouses had seen loved ones deployed within the past 24 months. In addition to the strain of extended separations, guardsmen and reservists often have limited combat training prior to their change to active duty status, and may therefore be more vulnerable to combat related stress injuries that impact their post-deployment familial experience (Hoge, Castro, & Eaton, 2006). When compared with the risks associated with occupations in the general population, the hazards of military duty become particularly noticeable (Hall, 2008). The fear of death or injury of the service member is a common stressor associated with combat related deployments. Deployments are nonetheless a never-ending concern among military spouses of active duty service members (Springle & Wilmer, 2010).

Wellbeing

Personal and family wellbeing before, during, and after deployments are a primary concern for military spouses (Booth, Segal, Bell, et al., 2007). Wellbeing, as a psychological concept, can be defined as a sense of personal satisfaction with life and is often measured by both physical and psychological standards. It may also give one a sense of how well they are coping with major stressors in their lives at that time or over a long-term life course. It is closely related to quality of life, in that both indicate a general sense of overall health and an appraisal of functioning for those individuals in question. For spouses in military systems, their own sense of wellbeing is often related to how they perceive their family members to be functioning at any given point in time. Within the military context, these appraisals are related quite often to where the family may fall in the deployment cycle. The wellbeing of the military spouse may be the lynchpin holding the entire military family together, and has been shown to be a crucial factor in the career length of the service member (Hall, 2008). A lack of personal and/or family member wellbeing may be the most common factor that brings the military family into the clinicians' office for initial consultation.

Parenting

The daily stress and emotional strains associated with parenting children within a military family is a primary factor affecting interpersonal relationships and quality of life for family members. In addition, to become single parents for the duration of a deployment, military spouses often find themselves under strain as a result of the number and ages of the children in their households (Gibbs et al., 2007). They may also experience difficulty due to the presence of children who are not biologically related to them within their homes (i.e., step-parenting), and/or the conflict with an ex-spouse of the deployed service member over the parenting styles and techniques (Everson, Herzog, & Haigler, 2010). During the past decade, our concern over the experience of parenting in the military context has increased, especially surrounding the issues of childcare and family member wellbeing (Cozza, Chun, & Polo, 2005). The provider is encouraged to see this experience as a unique opportunity for observing successful, or perhaps unsuccessful, parenting in often extreme circumstances.

Work–Life Balance

Many spouses of service members work outside of the home in various jobs varying from hourly jobs to professional occupations, and ranging in number of hours per week from part-time to full-time. Given the multiple other strains associated with daily life, it is often difficult for military spouses to balance their own personal needs with those of their family members (McFadyen, Kerpelman, & Adler-Baeder, 2005). This work–life balance is often made more difficult during periods of time when the service member spouse is deployed. Not only may absenteeism increase and work place productivity suffer, but the spouse may experience a negative impact on quality of life as a result of the role strain between being a successful worker, a parent, and spouse of a deployed service member (Gibbs et al., 2007).

On occasion, the mental health professional will see a spouse of a service member who is active duty themself or who recently ended their term of service in the military. This represents a life transition and a loss of identity—for the spouse was formerly in the military, but now is simply a military spouse. Mathewson (2010) points out that the primary difficulty in achieving military work-life balance is experienced as a result of the conflict between being a parent, a spouse of service member, and an active duty service member themselves. While we are generally speaking of non-active duty military spouses, the practitioner should be aware that the military spouse may be (or may have been) affiliated with a branch of service themselves. Regardless, the social work professional should be prepared to assist with the improvement of symptoms related to this common problem set (Herzog, Boydston, & Whitworth, 2010).

Financial matters are a common source of disagreement for all couples and families, but in the case of military families, monetary stressors are particularly problematic, since the non-military spouse may be the financial manager for the family as well. The stress associated with managing limited resources, due to higher debt and lower pay, may also create tension between the members of the military couple, influence the spouse's personal sense of wellbeing, and negatively impact the quality of their marital relationship (Burrell et al., 2006). Decisions on what to spend, how much to spend, and when to spend money is at times an ongoing source of conflict between military couples in therapy.

Relationship Quality

A great deal of attention has been paid to military marriages in recent times, given the fact that the divorce rate among military couples has outpaced the rate among the general population since the middle of this past decade (Sneath & Rheem, 2010). There are five common phenomena experienced by military couples during their marriages:

1   emotional distance, disinterest, or disengagement between the couple;
2   the development of extramarital interests by one or both members of the couple;
3   difficulties related to a remarriage situation;
4   conflict due to financial stressors and strains;
5   domestic discord or violence stemming from unresolved conflict or substance use.

(Hall, 2008; Everson & Herzog, 2010)

The mental health professional may observe all of these problems within a single military couple, even though they may have only presented with one admitting complaint. The experience of extramarital affairs is typically the most common reason that military couples seek therapy and, as with civilian couples, may create some very volatile moments in therapy, but it should be noted that in our experience these couples are more likely to present with multiple infidelities or infidelities on the part of both spouses (Sneath & Rheem, 2010). As with any couple, re-establishing fidelity, rebuilding trust, and enhancing intimacy are the primary goals of working with these couples to create an affair proof marriage (Solomon & Teagno, 2006). Ensuring continued fidelity and reducing mistrust within military couples in therapy are extremely difficult given the frequent and lengthy separations caused by deployments. Many practitioners note the long-term effects of unresolved infidelity in the quietness of emotional distance or disinterest experienced through the suffering of both spouses in the military couple. Sadly, many will not get the chance due to the continued separation caused by deployment, and the marriage may only end when the service member leaves the military (ETS) (Catherall, 2010).

The above detailed areas of concern for military spouses are well documented. How broad based are these areas, and how many spouses actually are challenged thus? One research study of 940 military spouses showed that 17 percent reported moderate to severe emotional, alcohol or family problems, 19 percent state that they were interested in receiving help with these problems, and 22 percent noted that the stress and their emotional problems were impacting negatively on their quality of life and work. Of the spouses who screened positive for emotional problems, over half the sample of 940 sought care for their mental health problems. The researchers further noted that stigma, often a reason offered for not seeking care, was a minor issue for the spouses surveyed in the study (Eaton, Hoge, Messer, et al., 2008). The *Surveys of Military Spouses* (DMDC, 2009) reported that upwards of 60 percent of wives surveyed were struggling with emotional problems related to deployment.

Coping Strategies

Many wives/spouses employ a variety of coping strategies to manage their emotional lives during deployment and after. These coping strategies can be divided into two areas: problem-focused coping (PFC), and emotion-focused coping (EFC). Problem-focused coping strategies include acceptance (I accept the reality of what is happening), planning (I keep thinking about the next steps), religion and using religious support while emotion-focused strategies include self-distraction (I keep busy with other work), venting (I express my negative feelings), humor, self-blame and denial (I say to myself that this is not real). Both coping strategies have been noted to be effective in managing deployment stress (Dimiceli, Steinhardt, & Smith, 2010).

Therapeutic Intervention for Spouses and Family Members of Service Members

Quite often the spouse of a service member, U.S. Army or Marine spouses in particular, will seek counseling for herself (himself, in some cases) or her (his) children during a long-term deployment (Everson, Herzog, & Haigler, 2010). Family therapy is frequently the method of choice with families seeking services for a child or adolescent, especially during the conceptualization of the problem stage of therapy. From that point, the practitioner may choose to see the family and the child separately at times, or together, as the situation dictates. There are other times during which military couples will seek assistance also. Often the couple will utilize counseling services because of readjustment problems they experience upon the service member's return from their area of operations, or they may experience an increase in their anxiety in anticipation of an upcoming deployment due to problems experienced in previous deployments (Hall, 2008).

Correct assessment and evaluation of the military spouse and their family situation is critical and must be systemic for our standpoint as practitioners, since psychopathology often stems from dysfunctional relational patterns. A thorough evaluation and understanding of current anxiety or depressive symptoms is also crucial given that these symptoms may require immediate medical attention as a part of the ongoing treatment plan. A genogram that includes several generations of analysis, along with detailed personal, family, and symptomological history, are important as a basis for systemic interventions (Kerr & Bowen, 1988). Any approach to the military family should be taken with the spouse and family with the family life cycle in mind (Carter & McGoldrick, 1998), although it should be noted that military families tend to experience life cycle transitions in a variety of ways different to those families in the general population (Everson & Camp, 2010).

Recent attention has been given to the development of treatment protocols within emotional focused couple therapy (Johnson & Denton, 2002) for military couples experiencing problems at various phases in the deployment cycle (Sneath & Rheem, 2010). Solution-focused approaches are currently taught within a number of social programs around the U.S., and can also be very successful in helping these couples with their problems given the short time frame they may have before their next transition period (deployment, moving, etc.). Given these circumstances, some form of couple therapy is often indicated.

We prefer a metasystemic model of family therapy that is multi-theoretical in its focus and multidisciplinary in its scope. Metasystems, as a paradigm, draw upon the fields of psychology, sociology, social work, and family therapy as their sources, while integrating key aspects of these fields into one cohesive model for helping individuals and families. One such model is the Metasystems Model (Perry, 2008). Fundamentally grounded in the Individual Psychology of Alfred Adler (1999) and the dramatological analysis of Erwin Goffman (1956), the Metasystems Model provides the therapist with a trans-theoretical model for providing flexible, integrated care of the client. The model is called Metasystems because it considers the individual as well as the multiple systems in which the individual's life is embedded. In that sense, it is similar to Nichols' "self-in-the-system" concept (Nichols, 1987). The individual is meta (literally from the Greek, alongside of) the systems. Both levels are important.

Humans first find themselves as part of a system *in utero*. During fetal development and following birth, the person is part of a larger system called the family of origin. In this system, the person begins to form his or her personal life script, based on the meaning the family of origin gives to facts such as gender, birth order, the socioeconomic status, cultural and subcultural rules, etc. As the person grows and the circle of influence begins to expand, second order family becomes important, at times more so than the family of origin. Second order families are those who are emotionally significant to the person, even though they are not biologically related. Some examples of second order family include teachers, scout leaders, gangs, and military units. Obviously from this list, second order family may be a positive or a negative influence, but it is an influence to be considered.

Some of this life script development takes place on the "front stage," that is, in the sphere of life of which the individual is consciously aware and which others could become aware of if they chose. Other parts of the script are developed and maintained "back stage," which includes what traditional psychotherapy has called the "unconscious" and also "things forgotten but not lost," such as secrets, repressed memories, and collusion (Imber-Black, 1998). Education, including psychoeducation, takes place on the front stage. Depth therapy, including a brief depth therapy like Metasystems, also addresses the back stage.

From all of these life experiences, the individual develops some emotional "baggage" for the journey of life. These are the beliefs, and they may be front stage or back stage. As the travel metaphor implies, some baggage is necessary for the journey. The issue of therapy is to determine whether the baggage the client brings is appropriate for this current stage of the journey. Structuring the actions of life are the various rituals, including family rituals, societal rituals (e.g., national holidays), and religious rituals. Once again, these may operate on the front stage or the back stage. Finally, following the social constructionist idea that all behavior is relational (Gergen, 1999), ghosts may exist on the front stage or back stage. Ghosts are those people, living, dead, or fictitious, who influence the person's behavior as though they were present even though they are not. They are part of the audience to which the person is constantly playing. According to the Metasystems Model, change happens as the person changes his or her life script. This change in the script is measured through changed behavior and a changed teleology (end goal) of their life.

The model of therapy depends greatly on the practitioner, but it should be systems oriented, strengths focused, and tailored to the military culture in order to maximize the effectiveness of the therapeutic experience. In some cases, multiple modalities with co-therapy provided by colleagues with different family members may best benefit the military family in need (i.e., couple therapy in addition to individual work). With this said, we now focus on the case of a military spouse negatively impacted by the recent combat experience of her soldier in Afghanistan.

Case Illustration

Sgt. and Mrs. Love

Sgt. Love made an appointment at our private counseling center at the insistence of his wife, who threatened to serve him with a notice of legal separation if he did not do so immediately. They came together for the first session, after he had made the appointment as requested. They were both African American and reported having been married for five years. It was their first marriage. She had two children from a previous relationship, with her oldest in college. He had one child. Her youngest child was a permanent resident, whereas his son visited for weekends and holidays in their home. They were both oldest children in their sibling sets (from genogram in first session). She was a self-confessed news talk and cooking show "junkie," who spent most of her evenings after dinner alone watching CNN, MSNBC, or Fox News, while he watched sports in the living room until bedtime.

He had returned early from a yearlong deployment with his National Guard unit in Afghanistan. He had been injured as the result of an IED detonation, in which a close comrade (Staff Sergeant Franco), who was riding in their MRAP near Kandahar Province, was mortally wounded in September of 2009. After convalescing, he returned to his full time job as a foreman at a local factory and trained with his National Guard unit one weekend a month. He had been diagnosed with post-traumatic stress disorder (PTSD) subsequent to his stay at Walter Reed Army Hospital, but had taken no medication since returning home, although he had attended group sessions at the local V.A. center. His wife owned and operated a beauty salon. She related that she had been anxious and somewhat depressed during the past several months, for which she had been prescribed Lexepro by her family physician. The background information offered here was obtained from the first two sessions. Present for the sessions were the client couple, the first author, and a doctoral intern from University of Georgia's graduate program in Marriage and Family Therapy.

Session Excerpts—3rd session

Co-therapist: You were going to tell us last time about how you came to need our assistance. If I may recap, we talked a little about the affair, the disappointment in the relationship, you (*to wife*) withdrawing in response to him, and about the trauma diagnosis. Is that about right? (*Checking in initially with couple.*)

Wife: He hasn't been the same since he's been back and he quit going to the groups at the V.A. a few months ago. He had a rough time when he first got back and he almost ruined everything by having that affair early last year. I can't imagine what he's been going through, but he has a hard time talking about it.

Therapist: What was that like for you (*to husband*)? I mean the experience of his being sent home wounded, dealing with his subsequent emotional problems, and his inability to connect with you?

Wife: It hasn't been easy. I knew that he would be gone from time to time with the military when I married him. He was in Iraq the second year of our marriage, but Afghanistan and his trying deal with Franco's death—there's been nothing like it before in my life. He won't let me help, though.

Therapist: Some of that (*his emotional withdrawal*) may be symptom related (*PTSD*). He has to learn to move beyond those restrictive ways of relating and coping. What's going on with you, Sarge? You okay to talk about some of these things with us?

Husband: Yea, I'm okay. Losing Franco was rough. We did everything together. When you get there, you find somebody to hang with—someone who's gonna have your back. We started hanging out behind the dining hall after chow and we'd smoke (*cigarettes*). That day it happened, I wasn't supposed to go, but they needed a driver. I'm a sergeant—I'm not even supposed to be driving. That's real strange to me. I almost got killed doing something I didn't have to do because they wanted me to ride with them. We had just found our ETD from over there the day before (*projected timeframe for the end of deployment*).

Therapist: So what actually happened to Franco?

Husband: We were returning from a supply run when our lead vehicle activated an IED in a car beside the road. These things are so powerful in Afghanistan. It slammed the entire vehicle into our MRAP on Franco's side and flipped us completely over into the ditch, so that my door (*driver's side*) was lying against the ground—essentially I'm pinned in the vehicle and Franco's on top of me— dead, but I don't know yet. Of course the rest of the guys are trying to put out the fire in our vehicle for what seems like forever. (*Very tearful, but continues talking in a low monotonous voice.*)

Co-therapist: How long was it actually?

Husband: I don't know, five minutes maybe. I kept shouting at Franco, but he wouldn't respond, nor would our gunner, who was riding up top. I didn't know until later that he was decapitated by the blast. It all happened so fast. It's like I couldn't stop crying after they told me later on that he (*Sgt. Franco*) was dead. I still see Franco in my dreams and I catch myself talking to him, like he's really here, but I know he's not. Nothing bad—he's always alive. They just said it was the PTSD out at the V.A., but those groups made it worse. (*Wife begins crying softly as a he relates this experience with Franco's "ghost"*).

(*He continues to relate the details of the experience of Franco's death and his return home for another 15 minutes in the session.*)

Therapist: Do you sometimes feel that other people will never understand what you've been through? I mean, that's a hell-of-a-lot to carry around with you. (*Referring to the presence of emotional baggage associated with his experience.*)

Wife: It's like he's "in his head" a lot, but I've never heard him say all that before, nor has he ever talked to me this much about it. I'll hear him talking to himself in the other room sometimes.

Husband: That's Franco.

Wife: Talking to you? (*surprised*)

Husband: Naw, just me talking to him.

Co-therapist: It doesn't sound like hallucinations or delusions, since you know he's not really there, but he is present in a sense.

Husband: It's okay that he stays around I guess. You know, I never even talked that much about it in group. It's like they wanted me to talk about it in a certain way, but not like just now.

Therapist: They may have been using a particular technique that didn't meet with your needs or experience. Also, it may not have been the right time for it yet. I also think it's okay for him to stay for a while—he's kind of family that way. (*Referring to second order family status of the deceased soldier and acknowledging his importance to the system.*) Let's check with your wife though.

Wife: I wish I could have met him. They were very close and he was a good friend. I want to be that close to him (*Sgt. Love*) again at some point in the future. We have started talking and spending more time together since the last two sessions, so I am very hopeful.

Therapist: I think that may happen sooner than later.

This couple continued in therapy for two more sessions and he attended alone twice in between. They began to move toward reconciliation and became more trustful of each other, as she was able to see that his affair was a backstage ploy to reconnect emotionally to something and damage the relationship at the same time, and as he was able to experience her ability to listen without fear of her rejection because of what had happened to him in Afghanistan. They discontinued therapy after six sessions, but felt that they had improved enough to know if and when they needed to return to therapy. Although the husband initially sought treatment, he did so at the behest of his wife who became the focus of the therapy in relation to his problems with the ongoing influence of complex PTSD.

Summary

In this chapter, we have attempted to provide social workers and other mental health professionals with an overview of military life and have offered a clinical approach for therapeutic work with this unique population. In addition to providing an overview of the problems frequently experienced by these families, we have proposed several approaches which we feel are successful with military spouses and their family members in various branches of the uniformed services before, during, and after deployments. The metasystems family therapy approach continues to be validated, and research is ongoing to provide more empirical support for its effectiveness. Regardless of the therapeutic approach, however, any work with military families and service members should be guided by an understanding of their branch of service, rank with the military hierarchy, and an understanding of the cultural uniqueness of their situations, along with the application of tested techniques to maximize therapeutic outcomes.

References

Adler, A. (1999). *The Practice and Theory of Individual Psychology*. New York: Routledge.
Blue Star Families Military Lifestyle Study (2009). *Military Family Issues Survey*. http://www.bluestarfam.org/drupal/study
Booth, B., Segal, M.W., Bell, D.B., Martin, J.A., Ender, M.G., Rohall, D E., & Nelson, J. (2007). *What We Know About Army Families: A 2007 update*. Fairfax, VA: Caliber.
Burrell, L.M, Adams, G.A., Durand, D.B., & Castro, C.A. (2006). The impact of military lifestyle demands on well-being, Army, and family outcomes. *Armed Forces & Society*, 33, 43–58.
Buxton, R. (2004). *The Complete World of Greek Mythology*. London: Thames & Hudson.
Carter, E.A. & McGoldrick, M.M. (Eds.) (1998). *The Expanded Family Life Cycle: Individual, family, and social perspectives* (3rd Ed.) New York: Allyn and Bacon.
Catherall, D. (2010). Systemic therapy with families of U.S. Marines. In R. Everson & C. Figley (Eds.), *Families Under Fire: Systemic therapy with military families* (pp. 99–114). New York: Routledge.
Cozza, S., Chun, R., & Polo, J. (2005). Military families and children during Operation Iraqi Freedom. *Psychiatric Quarterly*, 76, 371–378.
DMDC (Defense Manpower Data Center) (2009). *The 2008 Surveys of Military Spouses*. U.S. Department of Defense: Washington, DC.
Dimiceli, E., Steinhardt, M., & Smith, S. (2010). Stressful experiences, coping strategies, and predictors of health-related outcomes among wives of deployed military servicemen, *Armed Forces & Society*, 2, 351–373.

Doyle, M.E. & Peterson, K.A. (2005). Re-entry and reintegration: Returning home after combat. *Psychiatric Quarterly*, 76, 361–370.

Eaton, K., Hoge, C., Messer, S., Whitt, A., et al. (2008). Prevalence of mental health problems, treatment need, and barriers to care among primary care-seeking spouses of military service members involved in Iraq and Afghanistan deployments, *Military Medicine*, 173(11), 1051–1057.

Everson, R.B. & Camp, T.G. (2010). Seeing systems: An introduction to systemic approaches with military families. In R. Everson & C. Figley (Eds.), *Families Under Fire: Systemic therapy with military families* (pp. 3–30). New York: Routledge.

Everson, R.B. & Herzog, J.R. (2010). Structural-strategic approaches with army couples. In R. Everson & C. Figley (Eds.), *Families Under Fire: Systemic therapy with military families* (pp. 55–78). New York: Routledge.

Everson, R.B., Herzog, J.R., & Haigler, L.A. (2010). Systemic therapy with adolescents in army families. In R. Everson & C. Figley (Eds.), *Families Under Fire: Systemic therapy with military families* (pp. 79–98). New York: Routledge.

Gergen, K.J. (1999). *An Invitation to Social Construction*. Thousand Oaks, CA: SAGE Publications.

Gibbs, D.A., Martin, S.L., Kupper, L.L., & Johnson, R.E. (2007). Child maltreatment in enlisted soldiers' families during combat related deployments. *Journal of the American Medical Association*, 298, 528–535.

Goffman, E. (1956). *The Presentation of Self in Everyday Life*. Garden City, NY: Doubleday.

Hall, L.K. (2008). *Counseling Military Families*. New York: Routledge.

Herzog, J.R., Boydston, C., & Whitworth, J. (2010). Systems approach with Air Force members and their families. In R. Everson & C. Figley (Eds.), *Families Under Fire: Systemic therapy with military families* (pp. 115–125). New York: Routledge.

Hobbes, N. (2003). *Essential Militaria*. London: Atlantic Books.

Hoge, C.W., Castro, C.A., & Eaton, K.M. (2006). Impact of combat duty in Iraq and Afghanistan on family functioning: Findings from the Walter Reed Army Institute of Research Land Combat Study. In *Human Dimensions in Military Operations: Military leaders' strategies for addressing stress and psychological support* (pp. 5–1—5–6). Neuilly-sur-Seine, France: RTO.

Imber-Black, E. (1998). *The Secret Life of Families: Truth-telling, privacy and reconciliation in a tell-all society*. New York: Bantam Books.

Johnson, S.M. & Denton, W. (2002). Emotionally-focused Couple Therapy: Creating secure connections. In A. Gurman & N. Jacobson (Eds.), *Clinical Handbook of Couple Therapy* (3rd Ed.). New York: Guilford Press.

Kaiser Family Foundation (2004). *Military Families Survey*.

Kerr, M.E. and Bowen, M. (1988). *Family Evaluation: An approach based on Bowen theory*. New York: W.W. Norton.

Martin, R.P. (1991). In T. Bulfinch (ed.) *Bulfinch's Mythology*. New York: Harper-Collins.

Mathewson, J. (2010). In support of military women and families: Challenges facing community therapists. In R. Everson & C. Figley (Eds.), *Families Under Fire: Systemic therapy with military families* (pp. 215–236). New York: Routledge.

McFadyen, J.M., Kerpelman, J.L., & Adler-Baeder, F. (2005). Examining the impact of workplace supports: Work-family fit and satisfaction with the U.S. military. *Family Relations*, 54, 131–144.

Nichols, M.P. (1987). *The Self in the System: Expanding the limits of family therapy*. New York: Brunner/Mazel.

Office of the Deputy Under Secretary of Defense for Military Community and Family Policy (2007). *Profile of the Military Community: Demographics Report.* Fairfax, VA: IFC International.

Perry, C.W. (2008). *Basic Counseling Techniques: A beginning therapist's toolkit* (2nd Ed.). Bloomington, IN: Author House.

Segal, M.W. (1986). The military and the family as greedy institutions. *Armed Forces and Society*, 13, 9–38.

Shay, J. (2002). *Odysseus in America: Combat trauma and the trials of homecoming.* New York: Scribner.

Sneath, L. & Rheem, K.D. (2010). The use of emotionally focused Couples Therapy with military couples and families. In R. Everson & C. Figley (Eds.), *Families Under Fire: Systemic therapy with military families* (pp. 127–152). New York: Routledge.

Solomon, S. & Teagno, L. (2006). *Intimacy after Infidelity.* Oakland, CA: Harbinger Publications.

Springle, C.K. & Wilmer, C.M. (2010). Painting a moving train: Preparing civilian community providers to serve returning warriors and their families. In R. Everson & C. Figley (Eds.), *Families Under Fire: Systemic therapy with military families* (pp. 237–257). New York: Routledge.

U.S. Army Morale, Welfare, & Recreation Command (2006). *Survey of Army Families-IV.* Washington, DC: U.S. Department of Army.

Warner, C.H., Breitbach J.E., Appenzeller G.N., Yates. V., Grieger, T., & Webster, W.G. (2007). Division mental health: Its role in the new brigade combat team structure Part I: Pre-deployment and deployment. *Military Medicine*, 172, 907–11.

14

SUBSTANCE USE DISORDERS IN VETERANS

A Clinical Overview of Assessment and Treatment of Substance Use Disorders in Veterans and Service Members

Monica Roy and W. Christopher Skidmore

Substance use disorders have been called "the most serious public health concern in the United States," (Schneider Institute for Public Health Policy, 2001). The costs of substance use disorders (SUDs) are enormous, with epidemiologic studies estimating that one-seventh of all civilian healthcare dollars spent in the United States are attributable to substance use (Merrill, 1999). Substance use is also a serious issue for some military Veterans and active duty soldiers. For example, the National Survey on Drug Use and Health found that almost 60 percent of Veterans reported recent alcohol use and 7.4 percent reported heavy use (Wagner, Harris, Federman, et al., 2007). These rates were higher than those found in civilians, although rates of substance abuse and dependence diagnoses were similar to civilian rates. Wagner and colleagues also found that rates of marijuana use (3.5%) or other illicit substance use (1.7%) were also higher than civilian rates, although rates of abuse and dependence were not higher. More recent data on service members returning from Iraq deployments (Santiago, Wilk, Milliken, et al., 2010) indicated that 27 percent of Army soldiers had positive responses to an alcohol screening measure, were likely to engage in risky behaviors (e.g., drunk driving), and had experienced negative consequences (e.g., missing work). These data suggest that professionals providing care to Veterans in a variety of settings need a basic familiarity with substance use issues.

SUDs are strongly associated with many other psychiatric and health conditions in the general population, including posttraumatic stress disorder (PTSD), major depressive disorder, bipolar disorder, other anxiety disorders, personality disorders, and physical health problems (Merikangas, Mehta, Molnar, et al., 1998), in addition to physical traumas (Fox, Merrill, Chang, & Califano, 1995). Comorbidity issues are also relevant to Veterans for several reasons. First, Veterans seeking care for conditions such as anxiety or depression outside of substance abuse settings should still be routinely assessed for substance use. Second, Veterans seeking specialty care for SUDs are also likely to require assessment of, and interventions for, issues such as PTSD or depression. Third, treatment of the underlying or comorbid mental health issue, which is often a stated cause for urges to use substances, may be an important part of a successful case conceptualization and substance use treatment plan.

This chapter summarizes basic assessment and treatment issues relevant to working with Veterans and service members with a variety of issues related to substance use. Care should be taken in the use of terms and diagnoses when discussing military service or when addressing substance use issues due to the stigma in this area. For example, we will use the term "Veterans" as an umbrella term to refer to individuals who are Veterans, reservists, or active duty service members, although each group is unique; and even individuals from the same group may have different needs. Due to space limitations, we also use the term "substance use disorders," or "SUDs" to encompass a range of substance use problems, from hazardous use to a diagnosable disorder of abuse or dependence, and for a range of substances from alcohol to tobacco to illicit substances. Further consultation and education about specific substances will be necessary for readers who are interested in further information. Finally, we strongly recommend careful review of the *Diagnostic and Statistical Manual of Mental Disorders* (DSM-IV-TR) (APA [American Psychiatric Association], 2000) when diagnosing Veterans with SUDs. Familiarity with diagnostic criteria can aid providers in making accurate diagnoses and appropriate referrals for services, which will be discussed below.

Brief Overview of Theories of Substance Use Disorders

The etiology of SUDs can be conceptualized in several ways. Due to space limitations, we will briefly review genetic/biological and social learning theory models, as they may have particular relevance when working with Veterans. For a more detailed discussion of theoretical models, diagnostic issues, and special clinical considerations on this topic, we refer readers to Skidmore and Roy (2011), an earlier version of this report.

Hereditary Factors. Data on the impact of heredity on substance use have indicated a strong hereditary component to SUDs. This relationship may be stronger for men than for women, however (NIAAA, 1993). The effects of hereditary factors are also complex. The interaction between environment and heredity may be even more salient for Veterans given the high-stress environment of the military and that many Veterans enter the service during such a developmental period, when risk for problematic use is at its peak (e.g., SAMHSA, 2008).

Social Learning Theory and Cognitive-Behavioral Models. Several theories emphasize the importance of one's social environment, cognitions, and behavioral factors in the development of SUDs. Bandura (2001) argued that social and cultural values, which are gained through observation (i.e., vicarious learning), influence people's future actions. Along with heredity and the influence of the social environment, social control theory (Petraitis, Flay, & Miller, 1995) considers the use of alcohol and drugs to be caused by a lack of social bonds as well as rebellion against age-related restrictions.

Cognitive-behavioral models of SUDs focus on cognitions related to substance use as well as to heredity. These cognitions may be related to positive expectancies of substance use, which can lead to further use. For example, if a person learns that alcohol is a socially acceptable mode of coping with stress, then the likelihood of continued use of alcohol as a method of coping is increased. This may in turn lead to decreased self-efficacy or attempts to use alternative coping strategies.

Self-Medication. The most supported model of SUD development is the "self medication" hypothesis, which argues that substances are often used to cope with or avoid emotional and physical symptoms of pain (Hein, Cohen, & Campbell, 2005). In our clinical experience, some Veterans report use of substances such as alcohol or marijuana to treat insomnia, as well as to numb anxiety and other emotions (or conversely, to aid in accessing them). Alternatively, cocaine may appeal to some because of its ability to relieve distress associated with depression, hypomania, and hyperactivity (Khantzian, 1985). We have found that the self-medication model may appeal to clients as a non-stigmatizing conceptualization that can increase motivation for treatment and aid in identifying other factors that may also contribute to substance use.

Military Factors. There are several ways in which military-specific factors illustrate the theories described above. In terms of environmental and cognitive factors, Veterans may encounter both rewarding and punishing situations for early problematic use in the military. This may be due partly to the juxtaposition of military culture, which honors strength, independence, self-control, and reliability, alongside the normal stressors and duties of active duty service (both in and out of combat). These may include periods of acute and chronic stress alternating with periods of down time. This is further compounded by multiple and longer tours of duty (APA, 2007; Eibner, 2008; Nash, 2007). In terms of social bonds, service members may face loss of prior bonds along with initiation of very strong new ones. Most importantly, in terms of self-medication, exposure to stressors such as military sexual trauma, combat, and frequent losses of friends and peers may be associated with increased risk for anxiety, depression, trauma, or PTSD (Gradus, n.d.). The development of such symptoms may lead to increased use of substances for self-medication, often starting very soon after discharge.

Other military-specific factors may also play a role in SUD development. Differences in the conflict or era in which a Veteran served may result in differential exposure to specific substances. During the current conflicts in Iraq and Afghanistan, for example, returning Veterans have reported increased exposure to opioids, given that Afghanistan is one of the leading producers of opium in the world (United Nations Office of Drugs and Crime, 2009). This is compounded by a greatly increased rate of severe injury, leading to more individuals coping with chronic pain and injury (Clark, Bair, Buckenmaier, et al., 2007). Given that narcotics may be used to treat such injuries, this may result in the development of opioid abuse and dependence in some individuals. Another unique factor of the current conflicts is exposure to improvised explosive devices (IEDs), which has led to an increase in traumatic brain injuries (TBIs). TBIs may lead to increased vulnerability to developing SUDs in some Veterans, although this relationship is likely to be complex (e.g., Corrigan & Cole, 2008).

In our experience, Veterans presenting for substance abuse treatment report one of two general pathways of SUD development. Some report an early onset of substance use or behavioral problems during their school-age years, which then worsens during or shortly after military service. The second pathway involves a later onset of alcohol and/or drug problems, when Veterans are exposed to substances in the military and begin using to cope with military-specific stressors, particularly alcohol, since it is more culturally and socially acceptable than other substances. In both pathways, substance use tends to become more problematic in later stages of military service and after discharge due to worsening mental health concerns or the normal difficulties of transitioning back to civilian life (e.g., Armstrong, Best, & Domenici, 2006; Hoge, 2010).

Case Illustration: Frank

Frank is a 62 year old, single, Anglo-Caucasian Vietnam combat Veteran who has been diagnosed with PTSD. Frank was referred by his housing case manager for outpatient treatment of his alcohol use. Frank had been sober for almost three years and living at the local Veteran's shelter where he received assistance for finding independent housing. He secured an apartment and after living there for one month began drinking. He initially began drinking after he experienced some difficulty falling and staying asleep as a result of nightmares about his combat experiences in Vietnam. Frank's drinking began with having two to three beers during the late evening until he fell asleep. After a few weeks drinking only three beers was no longer helping him to fall asleep and his drinking increased. Soon, Frank began experiencing memories about his combat experiences during the day. The distress that resulted from his memories in combination with the increased pressure to maintain his apartment and pay bills and rent led Frank to feeling overwhelmed. In turn, his drinking began earlier and earlier in the day. It had been two years since Frank had experienced this level of stress and he knew that in the past drinking had helped to cope with this stress.

Case Illustration: Isabella

Isabella is a 23-year-old Puerto-Rican–American Iraq war combat Veteran. She recently attended a medical appointment and requested a prescription for pain medication from her primary care provider, a nurse practitioner in her local clinic. On further questioning, she reported that she has been buying Percocets off the street for the past year to manage chronic pain from back and knee injuries that she sustained during her military service. She has considered buying Oxycontin but denies having done this yet. She noted anxiety about the costs and risks of this behavior and is interested in a safer way to manage her pain, although she does not feel she has any other options. She also noted some increased drinking with friends that was "no big deal."

Assessment of Substance Use Disorders

The multiple factors that influence risk for substance use suggest that treatment providers should actively screen for SUDs when working with Veterans. The assessment of SUDs is an essential but complicated process. Thoughtful assessment can be critical in informing treatment planning, referrals, and goals. Conducting a proper functional assessment of a Veteran's substance use and identifying patterns of use and drugs of choice can provide essential information for choosing the appropriate intervention.

Initial screening and self-report. An assessment should begin with a basic screening to identify the specific substances being used and the quantity and frequency of a Veteran's substance use. Self-report measures can be given in conjunction with a comprehensive interview. Brief screening questionnaires such as the *Alcohol Use Disorders Identification Test* (AUDIT) (WHO, 2001), the Drug Abuse Screening Test (DAST-10) (Skinner, 1982), and the Alcohol, Smoking, and Substance Involvement Screening Test (ASSIST) (WHO ASSIST Working Group, 2002) have been found to provide accurate information about a patient's substance use if a patient is ensured that the results are confidential and if the information is collected when the patient is not under the influence of a substance (Brown, Kranzler, & Del Boca, 2006). In general, brief screening that is used to provide individualized feedback and a nonjudgmental menu of recommendations to clients may be an effective intervention in and of itself (Madras et al., 2009), particularly for those with less severe SUD-related problems.

Frank's Self-Report Assessment

To better assess his substance use, trauma, and anxiety symptoms, Frank was given the AUDIT, the DAST-10, the Coping Behaviors Inventory (CBI) (Litman, Stapleton, Oppenheim, & Peleg, 1983), and a Brief Situational Confidence Questionnaire (BSC) (Breslin, Sobell, Sobell, & Agrawal, 2000) upon his arrival at the clinic. He then met with a licensed social worker for a 60-minute interview, and the social worker reviewed his questionnaire responses prior to the meeting. Frank reported an AUDIT score of 19 indicating that, at minimum, brief counseling and further monitoring of his drinking would be warranted (WHO, 2001). On his BSCQ he indicated low confidence in areas related to unpleasant emotions, urges and temptations, interpersonal conflict, and social pressure. On the CBI Frank indicated that the coping skills that he uses to cope with urges to drink included isolating and staying indoors and finding activities indoors. Finally, on the DAST-10 he received a score of zero indicating that he had not used any other substances other than alcohol over the past twelve months.

Interview and history. After a brief screen, a more extensive interview may be needed to develop a functional assessment of an individual's substance use and co-occurring problems that may need to be addressed in treatment. An assessment should begin with a basic biopsychosocial interview that includes information about a Veteran's pre-military, military, and post-military history. Pre-military history should include information about the Veteran's family of origin, including family history of SUDs and the role of substance use in the household. Questions about family mental health, childhood trauma (emotional, physical, and/or sexual abuse) and neglect, and early behavioral problems should also be included. This can be valuable information for assessing possible co-morbid diagnoses. Patterns of pre-military substance use, if any, should also be assessed, since this can provide information about age of onset, a potential indicator of SUD chronicity and severity (Hein et al., 2005).

Frank's Pre-Military History

During the interview, Frank reported that he was raised in the inner city of a major metropolitan area. His mother and father had divorced when Frank was ten years old as a result of Frank's father's alcohol dependence. While growing up, Frank described himself as the "class clown" in elementary school. When Frank was 13 years old he had his first drink of alcohol and by the time he was 15 years old, he and his friends eventually were drinking before and after school. Frank was suspended several times from school for intoxication. By the time Frank was 16 years old, he was on the verge of being expelled from school for truancy and fighting. When Frank turned 17 years old, he dropped out of high school, took his GED, and his mother agreed to sign permission for him to enlist in the Army.

Isabella's Post-Military History

When asked about her pre-military history, Isabella denied any major physical injuries, learning problems, or emotional or behavioral difficulties prior to enlisting in the service.

Regarding military history, assessment should include benefits of military service and reasons for enlisting, in addition to degree of exposure to combat, sexual harassment or assault, and other traumas or losses during one's enlistment. However, detailed accounts of military stressors are neither necessary nor recommended during an initial assessment. Information regarding substance use or the presence of reprimands (e.g. Article 15s, etc.) during enlistment can also provide important information about the extent and duration of the problems that a Veteran may have encountered due to their substance use.

Frank's Military History

> Frank reported that he was stationed in Vietnam for 14 months as an infantry soldier, very quickly after boot camp. After a particularly stressful firefight not too long after he arrived in Vietnam, Frank noticed feeling shocked and numb for several hours and he soon noticed having even more difficulty sleeping and feeling intense anxiety during down time and numb at other times. Frank soon began smoking marijuana regularly with other soldiers during their down time and tried smoking opium on several occasions when he and other soldiers went into town. He noticed that smoking opium was immensely helpful for decreasing his anxiety. When Frank returned to the U.S., he was stationed at an Army base for approximately one year before he was discharged and returned to his hometown. During this year he and other soldiers drank excessively.

Isabella's Military History

> Isabella described an automobile accident while in the military in which her vehicle ran off the road into a ditch following a nearby IED explosion. She suffered a mild lower back injury and brief loss of consciousness, but had not been formally evaluated or diagnosed with TBI. Despite exposure to moderate combat and losing two close friends during her deployment, she reported that she enjoyed the excitement of her service and is proud of what she accomplished. She also told the interviewer that she wanted to continue with a career in the military, but her physical injuries made this difficult, and she has felt depressed by this loss.

Information regarding post-military history and recent substance use should include questions regarding the types of substances used since one's discharge from the military, the function of substance use (i.e., social functioning, sleep aid, avoidance or numbing of trauma-related cues, etc.), and possible problems related to use (e.g., legal, financial, interpersonal, medical, etc.). Questions should also establish the date of the Veteran's last use of any substances and the quantity, frequency, and effects of use. Perceptions of negative effects and goals for changes in substance use patterns should also be discussed. Finally, particular attention should be given to asking about all classes of substances during an interview for a full understanding of the range of substance use. This information may also provide an understanding of changes in drugs of choice over a Veteran's lifetime.

Frank's Post-Military and Substance Use History

When he returned to home to live with his mother, Frank began to experience symptoms of PTSD. The only time he would leave his home was to meet friends at the local bar, where he continued to drink excessively. Then, a friend taught him about snorting heroin, which would dampen his anxiety, similar to smoking opium when he was in Vietnam. He began using IV heroin soon thereafter and felt an immediate decrease in his anxiety and anger. He also began to be able to tolerate being around people, and was soon using on a daily basis. While this helped to decrease his anxiety and anger, it also brought legal problems (two convictions for possession of an illegal substance), interpersonal problems (e.g., turbulent relationships with girlfriends), and occupational problems (e.g., being fired from ten jobs).

As part of his comprehensive assessment, Frank was also asked to provide information about his first and last use of the following drugs: alcohol, cannabis, cocaine, benzodiazepines, barbiturates, opiates (including heroin), hallucinogens, and designer drugs. He was asked about the route of administration for several drugs such as cocaine (e.g. intranasal, intravenously, or by being smoked). Frank was asked about past substance abuse treatment including any detoxification admissions, residential treatment admissions, and outpatient treatment, including self-help groups that he may have attended. He reported numerous years of struggling with attempting to quit heroin, including over 50 detoxification admissions and several episodes of outpatient treatment. Most recently, Frank was able to maintain abstinence after completing a one-year residential treatment program.

Isabella's Post-Military and Substance Use History

Isabella reported that she was first prescribed an unknown pain medication by a military doctor two years ago because of significant difficulties with back and knee pain from daily wearing and carrying of heavy equipment. She reported that she had tried to obtain records of this but had not been able to. She reported that she first used alcohol during the first week after her honorable discharge from the military as a way to celebrate with friends. However, her drinking had slowly escalated in the past year, and now she admitted to sometimes drinking to feel good or forget about her problems "for a while." She reported drinking two to four beers a night at least three times per week and "a few" shots of whiskey when out with friends to "blow off steam." She also felt that drinking alcohol sometimes helped her physical pain. She denied any specific legal, physical, or relationship difficulties stemming from her substance use, although she appeared somewhat guarded and concerned when discussing it. She denied problematic use of any other substances but asked during the interview about obtaining medications for ADHD due to trouble concentrating.

Although she initially denied any other post-military difficulties, Isabella described in later sessions irritability, trouble concentrating, and moderate symptoms of depression.

She denied symptoms of PTSD or other anxiety disorders. However, she did report ongoing worry about finances and keeping her job as a security guard. She also admitted that she had not been getting along as well as she would like with old friends and family members since returning from her deployment, and has found the transition back to civilian life painful and disappointing.

Assessment of strengths and skills. An assessment of a Veteran's strengths and current coping skills will provide additional valuable information. A provider can then help the patient to maximize, enhance, and generalize these skills. This can be done in a variety of ways including via biopsychosocial assessment and self report. For example, one can ask explicitly about the strengths that a Veteran has that may help move toward treatment goals, particularly strengths cultivated in the military. Veterans can also be asked about situations when they have experienced urges to use substances but have chosen to abstain. This can lead to a discussion of skills a Veteran may be utilizing to make this choice. Such an assessment may also help to reinforce self-respect for a client who may have suffered many years of shame and guilt about substance use (Najavits, 2002). The Coping Behaviors Inventory (Litman et al., 1983) is a 36-item self-report measure that can be used to identify coping skills such as "Calling a friend," or "Working harder," to prevent acting on urges to use. Such measures can identify skills that are being used as well as skills to be developed in treatment.

Assessment of risk. Substance abuse is considered a risk factor for suicide, violence, and homicide (Waller, Lyons, & Costantini-Ferrando, 1999; Rivara, Mueller, Soames, et al., 1999), so risk level should be thoroughly evaluated at any initial encounter, when completing a comprehensive assessment, and during periods of increased substance use or increased stress. Notable risk factors for suicide completion are gender (male), race (Caucasian and Native American), substance abuse, the recent experience of loss or death of a loved one, and a first degree relative who committed suicide (Cheng, Chen, & Jenkins, 2000). Veterans and their families may also contact the National Suicide Hotline at 1-800-273-TALK (8255), 24 hours a day, seven days a week for any mental health crisis. By pressing "1" when prompted, the hotline directs a Veteran's call to a special call center dedicated to assisting Veterans. The lifeline also runs a website with live chat capabilities for those in need.

Frank's Risk and Mental Health Assessment

Frank was asked detailed questions about his history of suicidal or homicidal ideation, intent, or plans. Asking about Frank's substance use history as well as his mental health history provided a means of creating a functional analysis of potential high risk situations for relapse and areas on which to work with him; e.g., building skills for maintaining sobriety and ultimately for keeping him alive.

Treatment of Substance Use Disorders

Levels of care. A comprehensive assessment results in treatment recommendations, beginning with recommendations regarding the appropriate level of care. The substance abuse field, including clinics within VA Medical Centers, has moved from a "one size fits all" approach to a stepped care model of treatment (Sobell & Sobell, 2000). In a stepped care model, the first level of care received by a person entering into a clinical setting is based on research findings, clinical judgment, and her or his specific needs. Three core concepts of stepped care are: (1) individualized treatment (2) that is evidence-based, and (3) is the least restrictive but still likely to work for the client (Sobell & Sobell, 2000). Types of treatment steps range from self-help, to outpatient treatment, to inpatient programs.

Often, treatment may need to begin with the most intensive step, an inpatient admission for detoxification with medical observation, where clients can be monitored closely for withdrawal symptoms and treated appropriately. The remaining steps in the delivery of care are defined by different intensities of treatment contact. The next most intense step is residential treatment. This includes patients living and receiving treatment together within the same facility. Patients attend several group therapies and safe activities per day and are monitored by trained staff 24 hours a day. Residential programs can vary in the length of admission from two weeks to six weeks on average. The next least restrictive step is intensive outpatient treatment programs (IOPs). IOPs require patients to commute to a facility up to five days per week to attend several group therapy sessions per day. In IOPs, patients continue living at home while still receiving intensive treatment. The next step down is standard outpatient treatment consisting of weekly group or individual therapy focusing on SUDs and associated symptoms. This is the least restrictive and intensive mode of treatment.

Modalities of treatment. There are several modalities of treatment for SUDs, all of which have been used with Veterans. Group therapy is the most common treatment (Stinchfield, Owen, & Winters, 1994), and would likely be informed by several of the above therapeutic interventions. Group therapy provides support, improves awareness of "triggers" for use, allows for skill acquisition to reduce use or maintain abstinence, teaches healthy relationship skills, may address underlying comorbid mental health problems, and can increase honesty about substance use (e.g., Najavits, 2002). In our experience, although many younger Veterans are less interested in group treatment, it can be a powerful experience for Veterans due to the shared military bond among them.

Marital and family therapy are also potentially useful modes of intervention, since SUDs are influenced both by individuals' family and by social systems, and cause significant disruption in those systems. For example, behavioral couples therapy (e.g., O'Farrell & Fals-Stewart, 2006) teaches clients and their partners to implement a variety of behavioral changes in the system to reduce or eliminate substance use. Interventions include a daily sobriety contract in which clients state their commitment to sobriety and their partner affirms support. Pharmacotherapy is another treatment modality that may be valuable for Veterans with SUDs. Goals of pharmacotherapy include management of withdrawal symptoms, reduction of harms associated with use, decreasing the reinforcing effects of substances, relapse prevention, or prevention/management of complications of prolonged use (Lingford-Hughes, Welch, & Nutt, 2004).

Clinical interventions. As noted above, careful assessment of substance use will be helpful in treatment planning. Assessment data can also be used to prioritize short- and long-term treatment goals (e.g., Kadden & Skerker, 1999), and to make decisions about appropriate levels of care (e.g., Hoffman, Halikas, Mee-Lee, & Weedman, 1991). There is not yet a large body of knowledge about treatment effectiveness specific to SUDs in Veterans. As a result, the following is a brief overview of a selection of therapies for SUDs mainly tested in non-Veteran samples with comments about their use in Veterans where relevant.

Multiple treatments may be helpful in the treatment of substance use disorders in Veterans. As noted above, a client's level of motivation to change may be a critical factor in treatment. Miller and Rollnick (2002) have described Motivational Interviewing (MI) and Motivational Enhancement Therapy (MET) as efficacious interventions. These can be woven into effective assessment and treatment planning to engage clients in therapy and also can be an initial target in treatment. MI and MET involve core components (e.g., being empathic, rolling with resistance, supporting client self-efficacy) and specific interventions, such as providing feedback, encouraging clients to take responsibility for their choices, and eliciting statements that indicate readiness to change (Miller & Rollnick, 2002). These interventions assume that individuals need to be appropriately motivated to make changes and assist Veterans in considering their options.

Other therapeutic interventions also may prove to be effective for SUDs in Veterans. Two of the most frequently used treatments include 12-Step programs and cognitive-behavioral therapy (McCrady, 1994). Most 12-Step programs focus on self-help, support, and spirituality as primary elements of treatment. They also generally subscribe to a model of addiction in which participants accept an "addict" identity and lifetime abstinence as the primary goal (Ouimette, Finney, & Moos, 1997). Cognitive-behavioral therapies (CBT) teach Veterans to actively monitor their own emotions, behaviors, and urges, to become aware of and challenge substance use-related cognitions and urges, and to identify red flags or triggers for potential relapse. They also teach Veterans to identify behavioral coping strategies such as activity scheduling to cope with and distract from urges to use. Relapse Prevention therapy (RP) (Marlatt & Donovan, 2007) is the foremost CBT for SUDs. RP also teaches individuals to explicitly weigh the pros and cons of substance use. Both 12-Step and relapse prevention therapy, and their combination, have been found to be effective for Veterans in a large multisite study (Ouimette, Finney, & Moos, 1997).

Newer cognitive-behavioral therapies have also begun to be implemented for treating Veterans with a variety of difficulties including SUDs. For example, acceptance and commitment therapy (ACT) is currently being applied to work with Veterans in many areas. A central tenet of ACT is that trying to fight off, reduce, or avoid negative emotions or symptoms only leads to more complications. Thus, the goal of ACT is to help patients learn to accept negative states and re-focus on creating a life worth living. Similarly, Dialectical Behavior Therapy (DBT) (Linehan, 1993) teaches individuals skills to tolerate distress without engaging in self-destructive behaviors, to manage emotions regularly in healthy ways, and to successfully negotiate interpersonal relationships. Emotion regulation difficulties and relationship stressors (which may precede, accompany, and result from SUDs) would thus be appropriately targeted by DBT (Linehan, Dimeff, Reynolds, et al., 2002). Some promising initial research has been done on the use of DBT with Veterans (Spoont, Sayer, Thuras, et al., 2003), and some programs are currently using DBT components to help Veterans with SUDs, PTSD, and other problems. Finally, mindfulness techniques, common to several of the above therapies including relapse prevention, ACT, and DBT, also show promise in treating SUDs (Breslin, Zack, & McMain, 2002).

General comments about SUD treatment. An underlying goal of most therapies is to actively understand and address painful emotions or problems rather than avoid them. This is often a difficult, uncomfortable, or anxiety-provoking approach for Veterans, who have been taught the realistic benefits of suppressing emotional reactions while in the military. Furthermore, large reviews (Miller & Wilbourne, 2002) have found that briefer therapies targeting specific skills and case management are more effective than insight-oriented or scare-tactic therapies. It may also be more helpful to view SUDs as chronic vulnerabilities with recurring acute episodes rather than an acute problem that is "cured" by treatment (Merrill, 1999). Thus, relapses to substance use after a period of abstinence may not be seen as failures but rather as expected signs of the disorder to be resolved and learned from. Careful consideration should also be given to short- and long-term goals of SUD treatment. For most Veterans, sustained abstinence may be the primary goal, but developing a structured and meaningful life is also critical. In addition, for a smaller percentage of people with very specific patterns of use, moderated or controlled use (of legal substances) may be considered. We have found this goal to be particularly more appealing to younger returning Veterans, whose peers may be using alcohol in developmentally normative ways. However, careful assessment remains vital for determining the safety of such a goal (see Miller & Muñoz, 2005).

Frank's Treatment

Based on Frank's assessment, alcohol use was identified as the primary focus for treatment. Frank was given feedback regarding the results of his AUDIT score and

BSCQ during his first session. Frank was then asked to self-monitor his urges to use alcohol for two weeks and note the days that he drank and the quantity that he drank. This helped his therapist and Frank to create a more detailed functional analysis of his urges to drink. Frank initially set a goal to work on moderating his alcohol use; however, after two weeks of self-monitoring his use, he and his therapist noticed that he had difficulty controlling his use once he started drinking. Frank and his therapist discussed his moderation goal for approximately three sessions. They discussed the pros and cons, and his therapist utilized motivational interviewing throughout this period. Frank ultimately decided to work towards abstaining from all substance use. He continued to self-monitor his urges for alcohol use and also was asked to identify feelings that led to urges to drink. Over the next four weeks, Frank and his therapist identified that feelings of anxiety related to intrusive memories, stress related to daily hassles such as paying bills, loneliness of being in his own apartment with very little social support, and boredom would trigger urges to use. At times, feelings of stress and loneliness would trigger intrusive memories, and on these occasions Frank would be especially likely to drink.

The next phase of treatment involved Frank's therapist working with him to build new skills to cope with his triggers without alcohol (e.g., Marlatt & Donovan, 2007). During this time, psychoeducation regarding PTSD symptoms was also integrated into Frank's treatment. Over the next four months, Frank was able to build new skills to cope with his feelings and urges. He also worked on building a sober support network, which included attending an aftercare group at the VA, where he met other Veterans experiencing similar struggles. Frank also began attending AA meetings in the community to help expand his network outside of therapy. Eventually, after approximately eight months of individual therapy, Frank's BSCQ increased and his CBI indicated that he was utilizing many more coping behaviors, and he had maintained sobriety for approximately five months when he and his individual therapist decided to consider terminating therapy or referring him for additional PTSD treatment.

Isabella's Treatment

Isabella was referred to a community clinic to help her achieve abstinence from nonprescribed opiates. She did not endorse abstinence from alcohol as a goal even after feedback from her assessment about the negative effects of alcohol. She initially had significant difficulty attending appointments, often missing without calling to cancel. When clinic staff reached her by phone, she reported that work and childcare obligations were making it difficult to make time for therapy. The clinic was able to provide brief case management to help her find more stable childcare and also offered more flexible appointment times, which helped improve her attendance. The case manager discussed whether Isabella should explore a structured buprenorphine program to help manage her urges to use non-prescribed pain medication. However, it *was determined that she would work with her physician to find a safer prescribed medication alternative, and that this would be available to her as long as she participated in therapy and demonstrated abstinence from non-prescribed pain medications via random observed urine screens. Although initially she felt that this meant clinic staff did not trust her, she later agreed after the screens were described as a healthy part of the treatment process that could provide additional motivation for her to "stay on track." To facilitate improved communication, Isabella also eventually signed a release of information form to allow clinic staff to stay in close contact with the physician prescribing her pain medications.*

Isabella was encouraged to try Narcotics Anonymous as part of her initial treatment plan, but she went to a few local meetings and reported that she couldn't connect with the people there. Clinic staff initially encouraged her to search around for other meetings, but she wasn't willing to, so she was referred for individual therapy for relapse prevention, pain management, and depression management. This included behavioral activation to improve her mood and distract from the pain and occasional urges to use. Cognitive therapy also helped her to challenge thoughts such as, "I can't take the pain," "I can just use a little and no one will know," and "There's no point; I'll never get any better." She had several slips initially in which friends gave her pain medications, or she was so stressed by her busy schedule that she felt she needed to buy a small supply of Percocets off the street. Because of the urine screens and the supportive clinic environment, she was able to tell her counselor fairly quickly. This was addressed in a matter-of-fact way by removing her extra supply, helping her tell friends not to offer her medications, discussing triggers for the slips, and identifying alternative coping methods for future triggers. She was thus able to "get back on track" without feeling demoralized or discontinuing her prescribed pain medication. She continued to use alcohol socially, but her use decreased dramatically once her pain, stress, and depression, were under better control. She demonstrated fair compliance with the individual counseling and was transitioned to a biweekly therapy group after she had maintained several months of abstinence for ongoing support.

Special Clinical Considerations

There are several additional factors in the assessment and treatment of SUDs that merit special consideration. To provide additional context for providers who may encounter Veterans with SUDs, we briefly review these clinical considerations below.

Substance use in woman Veterans. Women working in a traditionally male-dominated environment may be at higher risk for alcohol use disorders (AUDs) (Ames & Cunradi, 2004). This is accompanied by other military-related problems faced by women, such as the pressures of performing in a traditionally masculine field, the increased risk for depressive states, and the risk of experiencing negative life events also faced by men, such as physical, sexual, or combat-related trauma.

In particular, those who report military sexual trauma may be two to three times more likely to meet screening criteria for depression and alcohol abuse (Hankin, Skinner, Sullivan, et al., 1999). *Providers should consider the unique needs of female Veterans such as Isabella, who may be outnumbered by men in many clinic settings. Making clinic environments more female-friendly could increase female Veterans' comfort, including leaving out pamphlets about women's issues, overt gestures welcoming women (e.g., "Women are Veterans, too," signs), and attention to the layout and privacy of waiting areas.*

Other sociodemographic factors. The impact of cultural background and age is an important issue in the assessment and treatment of SUDs. For example, cultural background may impact a Veteran's views and expectations of substance use. If a Veteran's cultural background condones the use of substance use as the primary way of coping with stress or celebrating success, this may directly impact the Veteran's expectations of using substances and goals for therapy. The age of the Veteran who presents for treatment may also impact the type of treatment that is recommended. As noted above, younger returning Veterans who present for alcohol abuse treatment with shorter histories of problems related to their alcohol use may be more likely to be candidates for moderation than older Veterans with more longstanding histories (Adamson & Sellman, 2001). *Providers working with younger Veterans such as Isabella would need to carefully determine what is age-appropriate substance use in her family and community.*

Homelessness and substance use disorders in Veterans. Veterans compose a large proportion of our homeless population, with some studies indicating that approximately 32–51 percent are Veterans (Institute of Medicine, 1988). Homelessness is thus an important factor to assess when working with Veterans with SUDs. The daily pressure of trying to maintain a safe place to stay may include significant risks and stress. This may impact treatment attendance, ability to communicate with providers (e.g., by phone), and ability to complete between-visit assignments. Other important considerations include transportation issues and exposure to risky situations (e.g., "wet" shelters, "crashing" with friends or family who also use substances, etc.). We recommend that providers maintain flexibility when possible to assist homeless Veterans in addressing their most immediate needs. This may include identifying resources and services for immediate short-term housing, longer-term sober living environments, and employment opportunities. Helping Veterans to utilize these services to be able to build a healthy, structured lifestyle may reduce the risk of relapse, although obtaining stable housing is only one part of the recovery process.

SUDs and PTSD. Although comorbidity issues are described above, the well documented association between SUDs and PTSD of up to 40 percent for men and 28 percent for women (Kessler, Sonnega, Bromet, et al., 1995) deserves special discussion. This is especially true for providers working with Veterans, as Veterans may have been exposed to multiple potentially traumatic events. Data indicate that individuals may develop PTSD after surviving a traumatic event and then begin using (or increasing the use of) substances in order to avoid or cope with the symptoms of PTSD (Jacobsen, Southwick, & Kosten, 2001). This may work in the immediate short-term, thus reinforcing substance use; however, it unfortunately may worsen and maintain symptoms in the long term, resulting in increased use of substances and associated problems (Ouimette, Moos, & Finney, 2003). Alternatively, Veterans with existing SUDs may also be exposed to additional traumatic events due to the multiple physical, mental, and legal risks that accompany heavy substance use. As a result, providers working with Veterans should familiarize themselves with trauma, PTSD, and related issues. Due to the high rates of comorbidity, we also recommend routine screening for PTSD symptoms in Veterans with SUDs (e.g., Najavits, 2004; Ruzek, Polusny, & Abueg, 1998). *Frank's providers might recommend that he attend a PTSD group in conjunction with his individual therapy. This could allow him to learn more specific skills to cope with his PTSD, help to normalize his experience of trauma related symptoms, and help to prepare him for future trauma-focused work to maximize his recovery.*

Stigma and other barriers to care. There are multiple barriers to care for Veterans with SUDs, including general barriers for Veterans and barriers specific to substance use. A 2007 report by the American Psychological Association identified multiple self-reported barriers to care for returning Veterans with any mental health concerns. Some of the more common responses included not being able to get time off from work, it being difficult to schedule an appointment, and not trusting mental health professionals; however, the three most cited responses involved fears that leaders would blame them, that leaders would treat them differently, or that their units would lose confidence in them (APA, 2007). These highlight the powerful and real impact that military culture has on Veterans. As soon as deemed appropriate, we recommend exploring with tentative clients who are service members what contact with mental health professionals might mean, ways in which civilians might be able to be trusted, the benefits and drawbacks of asking for help, and ways that asking for help is actually a sign of strength.

With regard to SUD-specific barriers, perhaps most devastating is the stigma surrounding SUDs and SUD treatment. Studies have shown that SUDs are among the most, if not the most, stigmatized conditions across numerous cultures (Room, Rehm, Trotter, et al., 2001). Such stigma includes ideas such as substance use: results from choice, from weakness, or from a flawed character; and that individuals with SUDs should be able to "just stop using" whenever they want. This impacts Veterans in multiple ways. First, it may make it extremely difficult for Veterans to disclose substance use or answer questions honestly, especially since military culture is built around strength and independence (Hoge, 2010; Nash, 2007). Veterans may feel that they should "handle it on their own," thus preventing them from asking for help or seeking support. Moreover, there could be increased shame around admitting to difficulties with SUDs. *Stigma might be a particularly difficult barrier for Isabella because of her age, or because her family might believe that mental health treatment is unnecessary, and that the family should deal with her problems internally. Her providers would need to be sensitive to this history but also help her to access her desired care despite her concerns.*

The importance of a strengths-based/recovery-oriented approach. A strengths-based, recovery-oriented approach, which emphasizes client goals, responsibility, self-respect, and realistic hopefulness, may also be particularly helpful for Veterans with SUDs. Another way to apply this approach is through the language used to assess, describe, and treat individuals with SUDs. For example, labels such as "addict" may further stigmatize individuals and undermine their strengths and coping skills, which might otherwise prove critical for recovery (Kelly & Westerhoff, in press). Thus, we strongly encourage readers to raise their awareness of these issues in everyday public and private discourse, and to practice mindfulness of recovery-oriented language when working with Veterans. Finally, these approaches may also help to foster a sense of self-efficacy, increased control, and decreased hopelessness, which may also be important agents for change. *Veterans like Frank and Isabella would be helped in terms of both esteem and motivation by discussing their difficulties as stemming from interrupted recovery processes. One goal of therapeutic interventions could be to help them overcome barriers to recovery and enhance positive life changes.*

General Conclusions

Given the complex difficulties faced by Veterans with SUDs, as well as the mental and physical problems that accompany them, we encourage providers to seek continuing education and consultation about the issues discussed above. Attention to compassion fatigue is also critical for those working with Veterans with SUDs. This issue has been discussed in the general counseling literature and the PTSD literature (see Bell, Kulkarni, & Dalton, 2003, and Munroe, Shay, Fisher, et al., 1995, for examples). However, less attention has been paid to this in the SUD field. This can be emotionally challenging work given the high rates of comorbidity, risk issues, relapse, and dropout rates. Even the most experienced and motivated providers can sometimes feel frustrated or hopeless. However, this work can also be deeply rewarding with proper administrative and interpersonal support (e.g., Bell, Kulkarni, & Dalton, 2003). We thus strongly encourage providers, much like our clients, to actively engage in self-care and to "practice what you teach" to maintain healthy compassion. Providers may also need to negotiate and reinforce therapeutic boundaries, such as not meeting with clients when they are under the influence. Aspects of workload and the work environment can be structured to promote this. We have also found nonjudgmental peer support and consultation (e.g., Linehan, 1993) invaluable for maintaining enthusiasm and fostering a sense of community.

Supporting Veterans with substance use disorders and associated problems remains a critical and unique service that we can provide for those who have sacrificed so much. Veteran clients will come from a range of backgrounds and need a range of services. Regardless of one's role in their care, we encourage readers to view their work with Veterans as an honor and privilege and to be inspired by Veterans surviving and overcoming the issues discussed above. We also believe it is important to convey a sincere sense of hopefulness to Veteran clients, that their service was meaningful, and that there is evidence that they can use their strengths, skills, and training to overcome substance use issues.

References

Adamson, S.J. & Sellman, D. (2001). Drinking goal selection and treatment outcome in out-patients with mild–moderate alcohol dependence, *Drug and Alcohol Review*, 20(4), 351–359.

APA (American Psychiatric Association) (2000). *Diagnostic and Statistical Manual of Mental Disorders* (4th Ed., text rev.). Washington, DC: Joan Beder.

APA (2007). *The Psychological Needs of U.S. Military Service Members and Their Families: A preliminary report*. Washington, DC: Joan Beder.

Ames, G. & Cunradi, C. (2004). Alcohol use and preventing alcohol related problems among young adults in the military. *Alcohol Research and Health*, 28, 252–257.

Armstrong, K., Best, S., & Domenici, P. (2006). *Courage after Fire: Coping strategies for troops returning from Iraq and Afghanistan and their families*. Berkeley, CA: Ulysses Press.

Bandura, A. (2001). Social cognitive theory: An agentic perspective. *Annual Review of Psychology*, 52, 1–26.

Bell, H., Kulkarni, S., & Dalton, L. (2003). Organizational prevention of vicarious trauma. *Families in Society*, 84, 463–471.

Breslin, F.C., Sobell, L.C., Sobell, M.B., & Agrawal, S. (2000). A comparison of a brief and a long version of the Situational Confidence Questionnaire. *Behavior Research and Therapy*, 12(1), 1211–1220.

Breslin, C.F., Zack, M., & McMain, S. (2002). An information processing analysis of mindfulness: Implications for relapse prevention in the treatment of substance abuse. *Clinical Psychology: Science and Practice*, 9, 275–299.

Brown, J., Kranzler, H.R., & Del Boca, F.K. (2006). Self reports by alcohol and drug abuse inpatients: Factors affecting reliability and validity. *British Journal of Addiction*, 87, 1013–1024.

Cheng, A.T., Chen, T.H., & Jenkins, R. (2000) Psychosocial and psychiatric risk factors for suicide. *Journal of Psychiatry*, 177, 360–365.

Clark, M., Blair, M., Buckenmaier, C., Gironda, R., et al., (2007). Pain and combat injuries in soldiers returning from Operations Enduring Freedom and Iraqi Freedom: Implications for research and practice. *Journal of Rehabilitation Research and Development*, 44(2), 179–194.

Corrigan, J.D. & Cole, T.B. (2008). Substance use disorders and clinical management of traumatic brain injury and posttraumatic stress disorder. *Journal of American Medical Association*, 300, 720–721.

Eibner, C. (2008). *Invisible wounds of war*: Quantifying the Societal costs of psychological and cognitive injuries. (Testimony presented before the Joint Economic committee, June 12, 2008). Santa Monica, CA: Rand Corp.

Fox, K., Merrill, J.C., Chang, H., & Califano, J.A. (1995). Estimating the costs of substance abuse to the Medicaid hospital care program. *American Journal of Public Health*, 85, 48–54.

Gradus, J.L. (n.d.). *Epidemiology of PTSD.* Retrieved from: http://www.ptsd.va.gov/professional/pages/epidemiological-facts-ptsd.asp

Hankin, C.S., Skinner, K.M., Sullivan, L.M., Miller, D.R., Frayne, S., & Tripp, T.J. (1999). Prevalence of depressive and alcohol abuse symptoms among women VA outpatients who report experiencing sexual assault while in the military. *Journal of Traumatic Stress,* 12, 601–612.

Hein, D., Cohen, L., & Campbell, A. (2005). Is traumatic stress a vulnerability factor for women with substance use disorders? *Clinical Psychology Review,* 25, 813–823.

Hoffman, N., Halikas, J., Mee-Lee, D., & Weedman, R. (1991). *Patient Placement Criteria for the Treatment of Psycho-active Substance Use Disorders.* Chevy Chase, MD: American Society of Addiction Medicine.

Hoge, C.W. (2010). *Once a Warrior—Always a Warrior: Navigating the transition from combat to home—including combat stress, PTSD, and TBI.* Guilford, CT: Globe Pequot Press.

Institute of Medicine (1988). Committee on Health Care for Homeless People. In *Homelessness, Health, and Human Needs.* Washington, DC: National Academy Press.

Jacobsen, L.K., Southwick, S.M., & Kosten, T.R. (2001). Substance use disorders in patients with posttraumatic stress disorder: A review of the literature. *American Journal of Psychiatry,* 158, 1184–1190.

Kadden, R.M., & Skerker, P.M. (1999). Treatment decision making and goal setting. In B.S. McCrady & E.E. Epstein (Eds.), *Addictions: A comprehensive guidebook* (pp. 216–231). New York: Oxford University Press.

Kelly, J.F., & Westerhoff, C. (in press). Does it matter how we refer to individuals with substance-related conditions? A randomized study of two commonly used terms. *International Journal of Drug Policy.* Advance online publication.

Kessler, R.C., Sonnega, A., Bromet, E., Hughes, M., & Nelson, C.B. (1995). Posttraumatic stress disorder in the National Comorbidity Survey. *Archives of General Psychiatry,* 52, 1048–1060.

Khantzian, E.J. (1985). The self-medication hypothesis of addictive disorders: Focus on heroin and cocaine dependence. *American Journal of Psychiatry,* 142, 1259–1264.

Linehan, M.M. (1993). *Cognitive-behavioral Treatment of Borderline Personality Disorder.* New York: Guilford Press.

Linehan, M.M., Dimeff, L.A., Reynolds, S.K., Comtois, K.A., Welch, S.S., Heagerty, P., & Kivlahan, D.R. (2002). Dialectical behavior therapy versus comprehensive validation therapy plus 12-Step for the treatment of opioid dependent women meeting criteria for borderline personality disorder. *Drug and Alcohol Dependence,* 67, 13–26.

Lingford-Hughes, A., Welch, S., & Nutt, D. (2004). Evidence-based guidelines for the pharmacological management of substance misuse, addiction and comorbidity: Recommendations from the British Association for Psychopharmacology. *Journal of Psychopharmacology,* 18, 293–335.

Litman, G.K., Stapleton, J., Oppenheim, A.N., & Peleg, M. (1983). An instrument for measuring coping behaviours in hospitalized alcoholics: Implications for relapse prevention treatment. *British Journal of Addiction,* 78, 269–276.

Madras, B.K., Compton, W.M., Avula, D., Stegbauer, D., Stein, T., & Clark, H.W. (2009). Screening, brief interventions, referral and treatment (SBIRT) for illicit drug and alcohol use at multiple health care sites: Comparison at intake and 6 months later. *Drug and Alcohol Dependence,* 99, 280–295.

Marlatt, G.A., & Donovan, D.M. (Eds.). (2007). *Relapse Prevention: Maintenance strategies in the treatment of addictive behaviors* (2nd Ed.). New York: Guilford Press.

McCrady, B.S. (1994). Alcoholics Anonymous and behavior therapy: Can habits be treated as diseases? Can diseases be treated as habits? *Journal of Consulting and Clinical Psychology*, 62, 1141–1158.

Merikangas, K.R., Mehta, R.L., Molnar, B.E., Walters, E.E., Swendsen, J.D., Aguilar-Gaziola, J.J., & Kessler, R.C. (1998). Comorbidity of substance use disorders with mood and anxiety disorders: Results of the international consortium in psychiatric epidemiology. *Addictive Behavior*, 23, 893–907.

Merrill, J. (1999). Economic issues and substance use. In B.S. McCrady & E.E. Epstein (Eds.), *Addictions: A Comprehensive Guidebook* (pp. 595–610). New York: Oxford University Press.

Miller, W.R. & Muñoz, R.F. (2005) *Controlling Your Drinking*. New York: Guilford Press.

Miller, W.R. & Rollnick, S. (2002). *Motivational Interviewing: Preparing people for change* (2nd Ed.). New York: Guilford Press.

Miller, W.R. & Wilbourne, P.L. (2002). Mesa grande: A methodological analysis of clinical trials of treatments for alcohol use disorders. *Addiction*, 97, 265–277.

Munroe, J., Shay, J., Fisher, L., Makary, C., Rapperport, K., & Zimering, R. (1995). Preventing compassion fatigue: A team treatment model. In C. Figley (Ed.), *Compassion Fatigue: Coping with secondary traumatic stress disorder in those who treat the traumatized* (pp. 209–231). New York: Bruner/Mazel.

Najavits, L.M. (2002). *Seeking Safety: A treatment manual for PTSD and substance abuse*. New York: Guilford Press.

Najavits, L.M. (2004). Assessment of trauma, PTSD, and substance use disorder: A practical guide. In J.P. Wilson & T. Keane (Eds.), *Assessing Psychological Trauma and PTSD* (pp. 466–491). New York: Guilford Press.

Nash, W. (2007). The stressors of war. In C.R. Figley & W.P. Nash (Eds.), *Combat Stress Injury Theory, Research, and Management*. New York: Routledge.

NIAAA (National Institute of Alcohol Abuse and Alcoholism) (1993). Genetic and other risk factors for alcoholism. In *Alcohol and Health: Eighth Special Report to the U.S. Congress* (NIH Publication no 94–3699, pp. 61–83). Washington, DC: National Institute of Health.

O'Farrell, T.J. & Fals-Stewart, W. (2006). *Behavioral Couples Therapy for Alcoholism and Drug Abuse*. New York: Guilford Press.

Ouimette, P.C., Finney, J.W., & Moos, R.H. (1997). Twelve-step and cognitive-behavioral treatment for substance abuse: A comparison of treatment effectiveness. *Journal of Consulting and Clinical Psychology*, 65, 230–240.

Ouimette, P.C., Moos, R.H., & Finney, J.W. (2003). PTSD treatment and 5-year remission among patients with substance use and posttraumatic stress disorders. *Journal of Consulting & Clinical Psychology*, 71, 410–414.

Petraitis, J., Flay, B. R., & Miller, T.Q. (1995). Reviewing theories of adolescent substance use: Organizing pieces in the puzzle. *Archives of General Psychiatry*, 48, 10–28.

Rivara, F.P., Mueller, B.A., Somes, G., Mendoza, C.T., Rushforth, N.B., et al., (1999). Alcohol and illicit drug abuse and the risk of violent death in the home. *Journal of American Medical Association*, 278, 569–75.

Room, R., Rehm, J., Trotter, R.T. II, Paglia, A., & Üstün, T.B. (2001) Cross-cultural views on stigma, valuation, parity and societal values towards disability. In T.B. Üstün, S. Chatterji, J.E. Bickenbach, et al. (Eds.), *Disability and Culture: Universalism and diversity* (pp. 247–291). Seattle: Hogrefe & Huber.

Ruzek, J.I., Polusny, M.A., & Abueg, F.R. (1998). Assessment and treatment of concurrent posttraumatic stress disorder and substance abuse. In V.M. Follette, J.I. Ruzek, & F.R. Abueg (Eds.), *Cognitive-Behavioral Therapies for Trauma* (pp. 226–255). New York: Guilford Press.

SAMHSA (Substance Abuse and Mental Health Services Administration, Office of Applied Studies) (2008). *Results from the 2007 National Survey on Drug Use and Health: National findings* (NSDUH Series H-34, DHHS Publication No. SMA 08-4343). Rockville, MD: Author.

Santiago, P.N., Wilk, J.E., Milliken, C.S., Castro, C.A., Engel, C.C., & Hoge, C.W. (2010). Screening for alcohol misuse and alcohol-related behaviors among combat Veterans. *Psychiatric Services*, 61, 575–581.

Schneider Institute for Health Policy (2001). *Substance Abuse: The nation's number one health problem*. Princeton, NJ: Robert Wood Johnson Foundation.

Skidmore, C. & Roy, M. (2011). Practical consideration for addressing substance use disorders in Veterans and service members. *Social Work in Health Care*, 50(1), 85–107.

Skinner, H.A. (1982). The Drug Abuse Screening Test. *Addictive Behaviors*, 7, 363–371.

Sobell, M.B. & Sobell, L.C. (2000). Stepped care as a heuristic approach to the treatment of alcohol problems. *Journal of Consulting and Clinical Psychology*, 68, 573–579.

Spoont, M.R., Sayer, N.A., Thuras, P., Erbes, C., & Winston, E. (2003). Practical psychotherapy: Adaptation of dialectical behavior therapy by a VA Medical Center. *Psychiatric Services*, 54, 627–629.

Stinchfield, R., Owen, P.L., & Winters, K.C. (1994). Group therapy for substance abuse: A review of the empirical research. In A. Fuhriman & G.M. Burlingame (Eds.), *Handbook of Group Psychotherapy* (pp. 458–488). New York: Wiley.

United Nations Office of Drugs and Crime (2009). *Afghanistan Opium Survey*. Retrieved from: http://www.unodc.org/documents/crop-monitoring/Afghanistan/Afghanistan_opium_survey_2009_summary.pdf

Wagner, T.H., Harris, K.M., Federman, B., Dai, L., Luna, Y., et al. (2007). Prevalence of substance use disorders among Veterans and comparable nonVeterans from the National Survey on Drug Use and Health. *Psychological Services*, 4, 149–157.

Waller, S.J., Lyons, J.S., & Costantini-Ferrando, M.F. (1999). Impact of comorbid affective and alcohol use disorders on suicidal ideation and attempts. *Journal of Clinical Psychology*, 55, 585–595.

WHO ASSIST Working Group (2002). The Alcohol, Smoking and Substance Involvement Screening Test (ASSIST): Development, reliability and feasibility. *Addiction*, 97, 1183–1194.

WHO (World Health Organization) (2001). *The Alcohol Use Disorders Identification Test: Guidelines for use in primary care* (2nd Ed.). Retrieved from: http://whqlibdoc.who.int/hq/2001/who_msd_msb_01.6a.pdf

PART IV
Services

15

ANIMAL-ASSISTED INTERVENTION

Joan Beder, Laurie Sullivan-Sakaeda, and Tamar P. Martin

This chapter is in four parts with each part describing animal-assisted interventions in working with Veterans and service members: Part 1 will explore the human–animal bond; Part 2 will describe animal assistance with dogs; Part 3 will discuss equine assisted therapy; and Part 4 will discuss angler assisted therapy.

I The Human–Animal Bond

Joan Beder

The American Veterinary Medical Association defines the human animal bond as:

> A mutually beneficial and dynamic relationship between people and other animals that is influenced by behaviors which are essential to the health and well-being of both. This includes, but is not limited to, emotional, psychological, and physical interactions of people, other animals, the environment.
>
> (American Veterinary Medical Association, 1975, pp. 1–5)

What this definition suggests is that the relationship we have with animals/pets is dynamic in that each influences the other in both physiological and psychological ways. As social beings, we need others and we crave attachment, whether it is with other humans or animals/pets or both. These bonds address the fundamental need we all have for contact and connection. The human–animal bond reflects our yearning to form a deep and sustaining attachment with an other (Bowlby, 1969); it provides a focus for caring and has noted social and health benefits (Digges, 2009).

Animals/pets help us to live more energetic lives. Dogs need to be walked, horses need to be cleaned and ridden, cats need to be brushed and fed. In the act of caring for a pet we have to "do" for them and that requires physical effort on the part of the owner.

The role of pets in physical illness has been studied for many years. The focus of most research on the benefits of pet ownership documents their potential to decrease loneliness and depression, reduce stress and anxiety, and provide a stimulus for exercise. Further studies document other heath benefits, including lowered blood pressure and heart rate in pet owners (Friedman, Son, & Tsai, 2010). Pet ownership may protect people from developing coronary heart disease or slow its progression; in several studies owning a pet was related to fewer medical visits, the number of health problems, and functional status (Headey, Grabka, & Kelley, 2002). Oncology patients who were receiving chemotherapy in the presence of an animal had significantly more improvement in oxygen saturation in a room with dogs present than those who did not have dogs present (Orlandi, Trangeled, Mambrini, et al., 2007). Studies of the elderly have shown that older pet owners visit the doctor less and take less medication than non-pet owners. Among the elderly living in an institutional facility, animals have been found to be therapeutic; in a study of two long-term facilities, significant positive changes in mood were recorded in residents who were visited by a volunteer with a dog as compared to those without (Lutwack-Bloom, Wijewickrama, & Smith, 2005). For the psychiatrically impaired, benefits include increased socialization, reduced feelings of stigmatization, and emotional support and connection (Tedeschi, Fine & Helgeson, 2010).

Animal assisted interventions, which build on the human–animal bond, take two basic forms: animals who are companions and animals who work with those who are disabled and often will offer assistive help to perform daily tasks to their owners. Companion animals are usually considered "pets" and offer the owners all the benefits, comfort and companionship mentioned above. Assistance animals are specially trained and serve as guides for those with visual impairment, hearing for the hearing impaired, and perform service functions for those with disabilities. The assistance animals "... represent a truly unique model of enablement for a person with disabilities" (Rabschutz, 2009, p. 59).

While there has been a great deal of study, much more remains to be addressed to further understanding of the human–animal bond. The use of animals in many venues is growing, and scientific rigor will further substantiate the value of the bond between animals and human and their utility in addressing some of the struggles life imposes.

II Animal Assistance with Dogs

In recognition of the strength and utility of the human–animal/pet bond, the Veterans Administration, under Title 38, Section 1705, offers an assistance dog to any Veteran who has been blinded in the service, or has a spinal cord injury or dysfunction or other impairment that limits mobility, or has a mental illness or PTSD. An assistance dog can be trained to help Veterans with daily living activities, pulling a wheelchair, or by picking up or retrieving items. Assistance dogs become a component of independent living for the Veteran by providing the means to control and add predictability to their daily lives (Rabschutz, 2009). As part of the VA benefit, expenses incurred in the training and transport of the dog are reimbursed. All across the United States, there are non-government programs that specialize in training service/assistance/companion dogs and matching them with Veterans who have physical disabilities. One such program is Canine Companions for Independence (CCI) Wounded Veterans Initiative.

Canine Companions for Independence, which was founded in 1975, is headquartered in Santa Rosa, California; there are five regional training centers across the United States. CCI pioneered the concept of the specialized service dog, a dog that has been trained to assist people who have disabilities through performing specific tasks (Tedeschi et al., 2010). The CCI Veterans program began in 2008, and there are specific criteria for military applicants in the CCI program which are typical of most programs in offering service dogs: they must have been disabled as a result of military service, use a wheelchair, are an amputee or paraplegic and have mobility of both arms or upper body strength, have a stable home life, good cognitive and speech ability, have a fenced-in yard, and are one year post-rehabilitation. Dogs—usually golden retrievers, Labrador retrievers or a mixture of both—go through a rigorous training process facilitated by CCI staff and volunteers who take the dogs into their homes for a period of time. Dogs and Veterans are matched based on compatible task requirements, lifestyle, family and personality.

The dogs are taught to perform tasks that a person with a disability may not be able to accomplish on their own. Some of the tasks include picking up dropped articles, pulling wheelchairs, turning on and off lights, opening and closing doors. For the disabled Veteran with PTSD, additional training teaches the dog to wake the Veteran from a debilitating nightmare or hallucination, to be able to recognize changes in the owner's breathing that indicates a panic attack, and to seek help in an emergency. The recipient of the dog also goes through a training process so that the dog and the Veteran form a team. While the dog is a working part of the Veteran's life and helps the Veteran manage, the dog is also a companion and "buddy." The combination of companionship and material assistance creates a bond between the Veteran and the dog that in almost all cases is sustaining and meaningful.

SC joined the New York National Guard right after 9/11. His unit deployed in October 2004, and his yearlong tour was just about over when he was injured by an IED blast on July 4, 2005. The patrol was outside of the Green Zone in Baghdad when they spotted a suspicious object. SC was outside his vehicle with his Captain when the object exploded; and his life was saved by the quick responses of his medic and unit. Since the injury, SC has received over 40 surgeries to help repair some of the damage to his arm and chest. The blast blew out his left side taking with it his brachial artery and almost all of his left bicep and tricep. Because of the amount of nerve loss to his upper arm, SCs hand was now considered a secondary injury. He spent three years fighting a never-ending battle to keep his hand, but his hand and wrist were amputated in 2008. Since then SC has been working to remain as independent as possible and, while a service dog was suggested, he thought it would make him look weak and that others would see him as a "sissy." Another concern was that people would say he was the "poor gimp guy." A friend of SC's, someone who had a service dog, was instrumental in having SC reconsider and, in 2010, SC "accepted the leash" of Gillian, his black Labrador service dog, trained at CCI in New York as part of their Veteran Initiative Program. SC describes Gillian as "my companion."

> Yes, she does things for me. When I drop my keys she gets them, when I need a door opened, she can push it and she carries the groceries from the car to the house. But equally important, she is my companion. Yes, I have my wife and my kids and, of course they help, but I miss the guys. It is very hard to leave the battlefield knowing that you will not return and you may never see the members of your unit again. When I feel down, she is there to give me comfort.

What might help a social worker or mental health provider to do or say to motivate a disabled Veteran to consider a service dog? SC's experience suggests that the service provider must emphasize that the service dog will help increase independence and that it is a sign of strength to accept help. The dog travels everywhere with SC and, as a side benefit, SC noted, "Gillian is the best first class upgrade imaginable when I fly."

Clinicians working with a disabled Veteran need to be aware of the various programs that offer service/assistance animals and the criteria for application and acceptance. While each program will have their own requirements for placement of a service/assistance dog, there is usually a period of training to acquaint the dog and the recipient, and to teach the various commands that are necessary for the "team" to work effectively. The emphasis must be on empowerment and independence; a realizable goal for those who receive a service dog.

III Equine Assisted Therapy (aka Equine Facilitated Therapy)

Laurie Sullivan-Sakaeda

> *There is something about the outside of a horse that is good for the inside of a man.*
> *Winston Churchill*

Equine therapy is a specialized program using horses as the medium for treatment. Rather than agency or office based, therapy takes place in a field, round pen, barn or arena. This venue can be particularly helpful for those who tend to avoid "talk therapy" because their memories are too painful, are concerned about stigma, or do not like being confined in an office setting.

Why a horse? Horses are mirrors of emotions and lie detectors. If a person is nervous, the horse knows it; if the person is angry, the horse reacts to it; if the person is hurting, the horse responds. Also, horses live in the here and now and demand that of others. They have no hidden motives or agendas, they don't engage in passive-aggressive behavior and they thrive on honest direct communication. Combining horses and Veterans for therapy represents a natural relationship.

The basic existence of the horse can provide a calming sensation for the over-stimulated and highly anxious Veteran. The horse does most things in a rhythm that is in complete contrast to the rushing and rumbling of anxiety or the slow dragging of depression. Concentrating on the rhythm of the horse's walk can change the rate at which the person breathes. Brushing a horse in a well-defined pattern can slow the heart rate (observations of clients). Riding a horse is a very rhythmic exercise that involves the entire body. The horse provides a large three-dimensional vehicle for grounding as well. There are several other specific areas in which horses are of particular help; and one area is with Veterans.

Horses are used as tools for military Veterans to gain self-understanding and emotional growth. It recognizes the human–animal bond as a source of emotional healing when a relationship is formed between the two species. The Department of Veterans Affairs provides grants for practitioners to run equine-assisted groups with returning troops. Typically, Veterans take part in standard ground activities with the horses including grooming, feeding, rope work and ground training. Self-awareness comes from direct interaction with the horse and, if done in groups, from interaction with other group members. As part of the therapy, a Veteran is assigned a task and then asked to discuss their feelings or behavior. The clinician then guides the Veteran to expand their self-concept, based on task completion, and discover things about themselves.

Veterans who are dealing with particular issues can attend sessions that are structured to deal specifically with those issues, including those suffering with posttraumatic stress disorder. Military Veterans with PTSD tend to not trust anyone. They don't trust the government, other people, or themselves—but they often trust animals. Since the horse, especially mustangs, have significant trust issues themselves, they become a natural conduit to developing trust in the Veteran. As the relationship develops between the horse and the Veteran, they become more trusting of each other.

One basic exercise designed to facilitate trust with the horse involves picking up a hoof. This seems like an easy exercise because we've all seen pictures of horse tenders holding hooves or people cleaning a hoof. When the Veteran approaches the horse, however, there is a level of confidence and self-assuredness that they need to feel in order to convince the horse they are safe enough to hold the hoof. Sometimes there is little problem with the exercise, depending on the experience of the client and the horse that was chosen; other times it becomes more difficult. One woman who, it was believed, had been pretty severely abused both as a child and in the military was scared to death of the horses. She entered the field hesitantly and was slow and careful in even touching any of the horses. However, when it came to this exercise she decided she was going to do it. She stood next to the horse, shaking like a leaf, reached down slowly, and grabbed the hoof. The horse sensed her anxiety and gave her the hoof more easily than she often did even for those who usually tended to her. The client was overjoyed when she finished the task, and she was amazed that she had done it and was so proud of herself for having confronted her fears and followed through. Several people picked up hooves that day but no one else celebrated it so much. The processing in this exercise focuses on who has to trust whom, and why. Obviously the client has to trust that the horse isn't going to kick them. There is also the chance that the horse will reach around and nip the person as they bend over to grab the hoof. The surprising element is when we talk about the horse needing to trust them. For people who don't trust themselves or others, it is very powerful to realize that a 1,200-pound animal has basically just trusted them with their life.

Communication is another block to re-entry as well as survival for the Veteran. The military has its own language. Many of the survivors are incredibly hesitant to discuss their trauma, they don't want to look weak, they don't think anyone outside of the service will understand, and speaking of it initially reignites all the feelings from the trauma. Often when they shut down from the trauma they lose the ability to read signs in the environment, to pick up on non-verbal cues, or to attend to changes in body language. The horses live on non-verbal communication— ears, tails, shoulders, teeth, and hooves are all immediate and vital forms of expressing themselves. One of the first exercises initiated in the therapy is to put out a small amount of hay in the field and have everyone watch how the horses respond. Often the group is fascinated that there is no verbal interplay but it is quickly clear who is in charge. When a horse pins their ears back to their head, they are angry and contemplating attack. The goal is for the group members to see this so they can be aware later when they are in with the horses as a means of assessing the danger in the environment. The exercise is then used as a metaphor to get the Veterans to start thinking about their anger, what do they look like when their ears are pinned, what makes them feel that way, what do they do. How do they metaphorically pin their ears, or do they?

People with PTSD often have a dysfunctional relationship with anger. Maybe they grew up in a home where the expression of anger was forbidden, or maybe they have a history of anger that they are now trying to tamp down. In working with the combat Veterans, it seems as though many of them deal with the rage by going to the other end of the spectrum and becoming passive, so they have stuffed their awareness of how and when they get angry. To give them an example and set up a metaphor is an attempt to help them start to break down some of those barriers and to better understand their anger.

In order to help facilitate communication, there is an exercise in which the horse is haltered with two lead ropes. One person is on either side holding a lead rope while they take the horse through an obstacle course. The basic rule of the course is to get the horse through it without allowing the horse to step out of the bounds, without knocking anything over, without the horse eating any of the temptations laid out on the course, and without letting go of the lead rope. The idea, of course, is that the two people will communicate with each other about how to do the course. The horse becomes the spokesman for how well the two are communicating, as they will wiggle, walk away, become frightened, or express confusion if the communication is not clear.

Many of the exercises are designed for the group to work as a whole. The common observation during one of these exercises is that people are slow to take charge, they don't work as a group, and there is very little communication. The exercises are about the process, and the goal in itself becomes unimportant; except that when it is accomplished there often is a great sense of excitement for the group as they realize all the limitations they overcame to get to the end. It is ironic that in a group of people who were heavily trained to work as a group and to rely on each other to accomplish tasks, once the PTSD symptoms have set in, these skills are lost. Use of group exercises with gentle intervention helps the Veterans increase awareness of the environment, what it has to offer to help rather than solely as a threat, to build communication skills, and understand how to develop an interdependent relationship with others, including horses.

For confidence building the round pen is a great place (a round pen is typically made of steel panels but can also be formed out of wood panels that form a circle 50-60 feet in diameter). In this setting, one horse and one person are placed. Someone who is insecure and lacks self-confidence can hardly even get the horse to look at him or her. The intervention is to ask what the horse is doing, to whom the horse is attending, and is this typical of his/her life existence? One woman Veteran answered that the horse was attending to everything but her and yes, people in her life typically do not really attend to her and don't listen to her. As she was talking and becoming more in touch with her emotions, the horse's head came slowly around until the horse was fully attending to the woman. The woman's response was mixed because having the attention in real life often means trouble, but at the same time she was able to enjoy a few moments of safe attention from someone. This leads to discussions about whether the person "deserves" positive attention and how they might go about getting it on a more consistent basis.

In concert with "deserving" attention comes the need to set appropriate boundaries, which are often also worked on in the round pen. A woman, Veteran M, was given instructions on how to apply pressure to the horse to move it away from her. She immediately rebelled, stating that people had often applied pressure to her and she didn't like it. She never fully described when and how people had applied pressure but, since she was also a survivor of military sexual trauma, one can safely assume that that was at least part of the issue. She was asked to pick a horse, so she picked the horse in the herd at that time with the most attitude and aloofness. The group and M agreed that the horse's attitude mirrored M's general attitude. Ultimately, she was able to lead the horse around the pen; this achievement enabled M to feel stronger and more confident, better able to resist pressure, and feel in concert with others.

The round pen also teaches the difference between passivity, aggression, and assertiveness. Passivity gets no reward from the horse. Aggression begets aggression but these are often the only levels of communication understood by traumatized Veterans. One of the mustangs is highly sensitive to body language and to movements. He senses any level of aggression before the people do. When the horse is in the round pen, the person has an excellent opportunity to monitor and manage the energy that they are eliciting. The task with him is to move him as slowly as possible in the pen, which takes intense monitoring. People often come away from a session with him with a new awareness of their body language and internal messages. This also works because he is big and he is the alpha horse of the herd. Since he is a mustang, there is a desire to touch him. He is the best representative of the Veterans' own functioning as he is hyper alert, reactive, and very slow and sporadic to trust. There is immediate reinforcement at being able to touch this horse, named Akai. After a session in the round pen with Akai, many people report a significant decrease in anxiety.

Many Veterans have distinct problems with taking on the leadership role as a result of military experience with unquestioned following, the way they were treated by their leaders, or from having made decisions as a leader that put others in harm's way. So taking the leadership role with a horse can be quite challenging directly, as well as dragging out other issues. This is not a process that happens in one session. Most of the Veterans spend several meetings in the round pen working a little at a time getting the horse's attention and then establishing a leadership role. This process also needs to be closely monitored by the horse specialist and the therapist, as people will react strongly to the reactions of the horse. If the horse challenges them too much they may become more passive and set up a dangerous situation, or they may become aggressive.

The people in the groups are the brothers, sons, husbands, and fathers/mothers who have gone to war. When they return home, the shame, humiliation, guilt, and embarrassment may come flooding back. That's when drinking, drugs, violence, avoidance, and anger can set in. To start the process of opening up, the group members are given a grooming tool, told to grab a horse, and are sent to separate areas. Their task is to tell the horse a secret as they groom the horse. This gives the person an opportunity to open up, to hear the secret said out loud with someone listening but not a person. They accomplish several things in this process:

the secret is stated out loud and the world doesn't crash down around them; and the horse listens in a non-judgmental manner. The client is always reminded that the animal they are talking to is highly sensitive to anything or anyone dangerous, or inherently mean or dangerous, so that if they were as "bad" as they believe, or if their behavior was as unforgivable as they interpret, the horse would be the first to leave.

Sometimes, just the presence of the horse propels people to talk about things they never thought they could. It is as though when the horses are around and we are in an arena, as opposed to a sterile office or group room setting, there is an increased atmosphere of caring and support and the ability to let down becomes easier. There is a level of comfort found in the barnyard that cannot be recreated in any kind of office setting, and this is the integral difference for some people in their willingness to share.

The horses help the Veterans understand and confront their fears as well. The horses are fear-based but don't stop their lives out of fear so they set good examples of how to move on. Desensitizing particularly frightened horses leads to discussions of how to desensitize the Veteran.

The interactions with horses continue to teach people how to develop and maintain boundaries, as horses are curious animals and some express a lack of respect by invading the space of others. They help people learn to establish self-respect, confidence, self-esteem, and even humor, as horses have distinct and often very interesting personalities. They can confront their fears, sort out emotions, and play in a way they haven't for years. This is a therapy that requires innovation and flexibility on the part of the therapist since the Veteran and the horse respond differently to each situation. When asked a question about "What is the horse doing/thinking/feeling?", the answer is going to reflect what the person is thinking and feeling and not necessarily what the horse is truly thinking or feeling. Observation, reflection, and careful interpretation are constant companions of the provider.

The therapy does not lend itself to all clients, however. NARHA (http://www.narha.org/resources-education/resources/eaat/203-precautions-and-contraindications) lists several issues that they consider precautions. These include someone with a history of animal abuse, history of fire setting, suspected current or past history of physical, sexual, and/or emotional abuse, history of seizure disorder, gross obesity, medication side effects, stress-induced reactive airway disease, and migraines. These are described as precautions but not distinct prohibitions, although legal standards need to be kept in mind if there is suspicion of ongoing abuse. Physical safety needs to be assessed with fire-starters and the animal abuse history. Medications can affect people's physical and emotional stability. The list of contraindications is much shorter and includes: active danger to self and others; actively delirious, demented, dissociative, psychotic, or severely confused; medically unstable; and actively substance abusing. These are valid concerns and their possible presence needs to be carefully evaluated. People with a history of any type of violent behavior need to be evaluated and carefully observed if allowed in the program. Some people are actually less likely to be aggressive with the horses and in the treatment program than in other situations. Additionally, many Veterans have physical limitations as well as the mental health problems but want to participate in the program anyway. This adds a dimension to the planning of the exercises but should not be seen as immediate elimination.

Assessment and Referral for Equine Therapy

As a civilian therapist, it is recommended that equine therapy be considered throughout one's work with a Veteran. However, it is advantageous to think about referring at the beginning of therapy for someone who has just returned from combat or is just getting out of the service and has issues from other traumas. ET can seem less restrictive and less military than being seen in a formal therapy setting, especially if the setting is at a large VA hospital. Many of the Veterans just enjoy being outside of the city, or away from the rigidity of the hospital, and the atmosphere around the horses can provide a relief from symptoms. Another important time to make the referral is if the client is having a difficult time experiencing and expressing their feelings. The military system is not favorable to strong emotions, and it is hard for someone who has survived in the military by putting aside their feelings to find ways to "suddenly" open up, particularly, again, in a pseudo-military setting like the VA center. The horses are not judgmental as many fear even the therapists will be.

In terms of assessment, the best assessment process is to conduct a session and see how the person reacts to the horses and the horses to them. If the therapy is too intense for them, which it can be, they will have a strong reaction in the situation and/or find an excuse not to come back. If they are fearful of the horses, this provides an opportunity to determine if they are willing to work on the fear or if they are still overwhelmed by it and unable to even make small movements forward. They may not want to get into the arena with the horses the first time, but are they willing to get into the arena in the future? Are they open to working with miniature horses or to at least engage in close observation?

Two groups that can be assessed prior to working with the horses are people who dissociate and people with strong anger issues. Someone with anger issues needs to be carefully assessed as far as their history of aggression and violence outside of a combat zone. This includes a history of domestic violence, animal abuse, child abuse, fighting or assaults in any setting. If the history indicates poor impulse control, multiple arrests for assault of any kind, failure of traditional DV programs, not taking responsibility for their actions, and/or continuing substance abuse, it is best to consider them a high risk and not recommend them for the program. If they defend themselves with an angry demeanor but don't have the legal history, they can be assessed in a one-time ET session and see how they interact with the animals, but close supervision is needed. Since the animals can have such a relaxing effect on some people, ET might be the very place they need to be. Some people will select themselves out if they have a history with horses or own horses and think they don't have anything to learn from the therapy.

Conclusion

This type of treatment is not for everyone but it appears to have meaningful results. In some cases, Veterans who have participated in these programs and have learned to address factors that affect their mental health are able to reduce their medications or may even be able to stop taking them altogether. Many who have been through ET programs also develop a life-long love of horses and continue working with the animals even when their therapy is complete; adding yet anther diversion to their lives. Unfortunately, there is a paucity of rigorous research in this area. With equine therapy, it is difficult to get control groups and find a situation in which there can be randomization of groups. Much of the information is similar to that described in this chapter: stories, reflections, and comments on generalities of how people have responded to the interventions. There are few published clinical studies conducted with Veterans, although research is in progress in Maine and other centers across the country. Preliminary reports are quite positive, and it is suggested that civilian and VA mental health providers become familiar with venues that offer ET as a primary or secondary source of support and treatment for Veterans and service members.

IV Community Reintegration Through the Healing Properties of Fly Fishing

Tamar P Martin

Recent research suggests the need for a broad expansion of services beyond the VA/DoD systems to address the gaps to quality mental health care for Veterans (Burnam, Meredith, & Jaycox, 2009). In addition to professional organizations, local communities need to improve Veterans' access to quality services and utilize evidence-based treatments to support recovery and adjustment. If local organizations do not become more engaged in treating Veterans who are returning to their communities, they can expect the Veterans' pain to affect their families, their ability to contribute to society, and their ability to care for themselves.

Therapeutic recreation has become a prominent modality in mental health treatment programs, although its role may not yet be fully realized. Involvement in active recreational leisure activities has shown a consistent positive relationship in improved self-esteem, self-efficacy, social skills, problem solving, and greater levels of cooperation and trust. Veteran Anglers of New York, Inc. is the local chapter of a national program, Project Healing Waters Fly Fishing, Inc., which was founded in 2006 at Walter Reed Army Hospital. The program has over 90 local chapters in three countries. Veteran Anglers of New York (VANY) is a non-profit volunteer organization dedicated to the recovery and rehabilitation of disabled active-duty military personnel and Veterans through the therapeutic benefits of fly fishing. The goal of VANY and similar programs is to support Veterans with disabilities who have endured the stress of serving in harm's way. Instruction in fly casting, fly tying, rod building and destination trips involves participants in socializing and interacting with volunteer anglers and rehabilitation specialists. All services and activities of VANY-PHWFF are offered at no cost to participants. In several states, the cost of a fishing license has been waived for qualifying Veterans who enter the program. Fly fishing tackle, fly tying materials and equipment are provided, including accommodations for special needs.

Through the therapeutic benefits of fly fishing, military personnel and Veterans with disabilities participate in a recreational activity to aid their emotional and physical recovery. The trout steam's calming qualities, an ecologically pristine environment, with cool water gurgling among boulders shaded by the forest canopy and the total absence of competitive pressure to perform under stress, yields peaceful rewards for all who participate in this sporting activity. The companionship that emerges between those who share the joys of ever-evolving angling skills further enhances the intrinsic value of the fly fishing adventure. The unique, valuable experiences gleaned from fly fishing may enhance community reintegration of Veterans with disabilities, leading to an improved quality of life and greater life satisfaction.

VANY believes fly fishing is a recreational activity that offers numerous benefits to injured soldiers and disabled Veterans as part of the healing process including the following:

- It demands creativity and is highly complex.
- It enhances fine and gross motor skills.
- It enhances cognitive skills and requires attention and focus.
- It reduces stress and enhances self-esteem.
- It assists to improve social skills and develop new relationships.
- It is rewarding and can develop into a lifelong activity.

Fly fishing is a distinct and ancient angling method which uses artificial flies that are cast with a special fishing rod and line. Fly fishing has been referred to as the sport where art meets science. The following outlines the four basic activities of fly fishing: fly tying; fly casting; environmental factors; and the fishing experience.

Fly Tying

Fly tying requires a basic understanding of entomology to create a fly (hook) using a variety of materials including feathers and color fibers that are wrapped with thread to emulate the characteristics of an insect the fish will pursue. Fine motor skills are utilized to create quality fly fishing ties during regularly scheduled instructional group sessions or practicing the techniques privately, and personally; there is a great sense of pride and accomplishment with the successful completion of a realistic fly.

Fly Casting

Fly casting is the art of using 6-10 feet long flexible rods to project the fly to the desired location by creating a smooth front to back repetitive motion with the movement of the forearm. A light-weight line spooled on a reel connects the fly to the reel. Proper casting requires balance, timing, patience and practice to achieve the desired skill. Casting may be practiced in an open field, yard, or in flat or flowing water. Casting helps center the individual and focus efforts, moving them away from intrusive thoughts or memories to a peaceful environment and activity.

Environmental Factors

There are other factors involved in fly fishing, including environmental and timing components, that anglers must consider. The time of day that fish feed is important and observing the "hatching" of insects along with the temperature of the water requires attention. Additionally, an angler must understand the water, i.e., ripples, runs, slicks and pools.

The Fishing Experience

Spending time near a stream or river away from crowded city streets is often very calming and soothing. It is in trout streams and rivers where Veterans suffering from Post Traumatic Stress Disorder (PTSD), Traumatic Brain Injuries (TBI) and other injuries may experience less stress and are not under pressure to perform. Furthermore, there is a healing aspect to fly fishing that other, more clinical settings may not provide. At fly fishing outings, Veterans feel the common bond with fellow Veterans. They empathize with one another and speak of shared histories and experiences. They tell stories about the thrill of catching a beautiful rainbow trout on a "woolly bugger" fly and later, during the quiet evening hours, they may speak about a painful memory that has disturbed them. Fly fishing creates an environment to develop trust and friendships. It is a shared experience that often becomes a fulfilling hobby for Veterans with disabilities that can be practiced for a lifetime.

References

American Veterinary Medical Association (1975). *Journal of the American Veterinary Medical Association*, 212(11), 1–5.

Bowlby, J. (1969). *Attachment and Loss: Attachment* (Vol. I). New York: Basic Books.

Burnam, M.A., Meredith, T.T., & Jaycox, L.H. (2009). Mental health care for Iraq and Afghanistan war Veterans. *Health Affairs*, 28(3), 771–782.

Digges, J. (2009). Human–companion animal social relationships. *Reflections*, Winter, 35–41.

Friedman, E., Son, Heesok, & Tsai, CC (2010). The animal/human bond: Health and wellness. In Aubrey Fine (Ed.), *Handbook of Animal-Assisted Therapy* (pp. 85–106). Amsterdam: Elsevier.

Headey, B., Grabka, M., & Kelley, J. (2002). Pet ownership is good for your health and saves public expenditure too. *Australian Social Monitor*, 4, 93–99.

Lutwack-Bloom, P., Wijewickrama, R., & Smith, B. (2005). Effects of pets versus people visits with nursing home residents. *Journal of Gerontological Social Work*, 44(3/4), 137–159.

NARHA Retrieved April 20, 2011 from: http://www.narha.org/resources-education/resources/eaat/203-precautions-and-contraindications

Orlandi, M., Trangeled, K., Mambrini, A., Tagliani, M., Ferrarini, A. et al. (2007). Pet therapy effects on oncological day hospital patients undergoing chemotherapy treatment. *Anticancer Research*, 27, 4201–4303.

Rabschutz, L. (2009). The meaning of companionship between a person with a disability and an assistance dog. *Reflections*, Winter, 59–62.

Tedeschi, P., Fine, A., & Helgeson, J. (2010). Assistance animals: Their evolving role in psychiatric service applications. In Aubrey Fine (Ed.), *Handbook of Animal-Assisted Therapy* (pp. 421–438). Amsterdam: Elsevier.

16

VA INTEGRATED POST-COMBAT CARE

A Systemic Approach to Caring for Returning Combat Veterans

Deborah Amdur, Alfonso Batres, Janet Belisle, John H. Brown, Jr., Micaela Cornis-Pop, Marianne Mathewson-Chapman, Greg Harms, Stephen C. Hunt, Peggy Kennedy, Heather Mahoney-Gleason, Jennifer Perez, Carol Sheets, and Terry Washam

Introduction

Since 2001 over two million U.S. military personnel have been deployed to the conflicts in Iraq and Afghanistan. Of these individuals, over one million have separated from the military and are eligible for health care and other services through the Department of Veterans Affairs (VA) system of care. Approximately 50 percent of these eligible Operation Enduring Freedom/Operation Iraqi Freedom/Operation New Dawn (OEF/OIF/OND/) combat Veterans have used VA services since 2001 based on Global War on Terrorism (GWOT) data. (NB: A Veteran is defined as a person who served in active military service and who was discharged or released under conditions other than dishonorable. A Service Member is defined as a member of the active duty military service or a member of the National Guard or Reserve Forces. A member of the National Guard and Reserve Forces could also be a Veteran.)

The conflicts in Iraq and Afghanistan have exposed these individuals to a matrix of risks that may result in a wide variety of post-deployment health problems and general life concerns. These risks include physical injury including traumatic brain injury from blast wave exposure (Martin, Lu, Helmick, et al., 2008), psychological trauma (Hoge, Castro, Messer, et al., 2004), environmental agent exposure (Helmer, Rossignol, Blatt, et al., 2007) as well as numerous stressors impacting personal life. Complex constellations of medical concerns, mental health conditions and psychosocial difficulties are common among these Veterans (Seal, Metzler, Gimak, et al., 2009). Clinical presentations tend to involve combinations of symptoms and concerns that vary widely from Veteran to Veteran. These concerns run from major medical complications, mental health conditions (Hoge et al., 2004) and elevated suicide risk (Kang & Bullman, 2008) to relatively commonplace but potentially problematic impacts on marriages, family life and occupational financial concerns (Sayers, Farrow, Ross, & Oslin, 2009; McFarlane, 2009). Combinations of these concerns are the norm for these Veterans (Uomoto & Williams, 2009; Gironda, Clark, Ruff, et al., 2009; Lew, Otis, Tun, et al., 2009). Comprehensively assessing and prioritizing these concerns, sequencing services, coordinating ongoing care and insuring appropriate and effective long-term support and management of these health concerns is exceedingly challenging. In the face of this challenge, VA has developed and implemented a systematic approach to transition assistance and post-combat care. The purpose of this chapter is to describe VA's system of Veteran centered, post-combat care programs which rely on a significant involvement of social workers to support Service members, Veterans and their families through recovery, rehabilitation, and re-integration into their home communities.

Post Deployment System of Care

The VA has established a variety of programs which partner social work with primary care, mental health and rehabilitation services to address the full spectrum of risk exposure and complex health implications experienced by combat Veterans returning from Iraq and Afghanistan. The core features of this care include expression of appreciation for the Veteran's service and sacrifice, keeping the care Veteran centric (including comprehensive team-based initial assessments, treatment planning and ongoing care), insuring evidence-based treatments for all conditions, and organizing, sequencing and monitoring the post-combat services and the Veteran's progress by using care management strategies.

The system of care is built upon social work principles (connecting the Veteran with the right service and resource at the right time) utilizing a rehabilitative and health recovery orientation. Mental health services are integrated to reduce stigma and obstacles to Veterans receiving appropriate treatment for mental health conditions. Specialized programs have been developed and implemented for suicide risk reduction, polytrauma care for the assessment and treatment for individuals with multiple, more serious injuries, and specialized mental health treatment.

The social work assets involved in these programs are the foundation of the model. Social workers often lead the OEF/OIF/OND Care Management team and provide critical coordination of care for returning combat Veterans. In total there are 9,000 master's prepared social workers among the 235,000 individuals employed by the VA.

VHA Social Work Case Management

Social work case managers are skilled professionals who use their clinical training and skills to help Veterans create better lives for themselves and their families. They are a safety net, providing vital resources and support to those who need it most and work across a range of practice areas to make the greatest impact on the Veterans and families they serve.

Since the beginning of the OEF/OIF/OND wars following September 11, 2001, social workers have found the OEF/OIF/OND Veterans in need of a well coordinated care management system of health care delivery. Case management by social workers for these Veterans is now the core component in the provision of care and services to help them restore or maintain their functioning within the context of their family relationships and community reintegration post deployment.

Case management for patients with complex, multiple injuries including traumatic brain injury, amputation and psychological trauma require specialized knowledge and skills. Patients and families need long-term case management services to ensure coordination of services, evaluation of ongoing rehabilitation needs, and supportive services to assist with successful community reintegration. As patients move through the various levels of polytrauma care, coordinated services via case management ensure a warm "hand-off" to the next level of care. The outcome of this model of social work case management improves support and seamless services to patients and families for long-term care.

Social work case management is mission critical in ensuring ongoing coordination of services. Social work case managers use proactive case management, maintaining regular contacts with Veterans and their families to coordinate services and address emerging needs. Services are provided across a continuum of care that may include inpatient and outpatient rehabilitation, long-term care, transitional living, community re-integration programs, and vocational rehabilitation and employment services. Social work case managers support and guide Veterans to appropriate resources. Case management services are provided in a variety of settings including polytrauma and specialty programs, post-deployment integrated care clinics, and as part of the OEF/OIF/OND Care Management team.

VA Liaisons for Healthcare

VA has a robust system in place to transition severely ill and injured Service members from DoD to the VA system of care. Typically, a severely injured Service member returns from theater and is sent to a military treatment facility (MTF) where he/she is medically stabilized. A key component of transitioning these injured and ill Service members and Veterans are the VA Liaisons for Healthcare, either social workers or nurses strategically placed in MTFs with concentrations of recovering Service members returning from Iraq and Afghanistan. Having started with one VA Liaison at two MTFs, the VA now has 33 VA Liaisons for Healthcare stationed at 18 MTFs to transition ill and injured Service members from DoD to the VA system of care. The VA Liaisons facilitate the transfer of Service members and Veterans from the MTF to a VA health care facility closest to their home or most appropriate for the specialized services their medical condition requires.

VA Liaisons are co-located with DoD Case Managers at MTFs and provide onsite consultation and collaboration regarding VA resources and treatment options. VA Liaisons educate Service members and their families about the VA system of care, coordinate the Service member's initial registration with the VA, and secure outpatient appointments or inpatient transfer to a VA health care facility as appropriate. VA Liaisons make early connections with Service members and families to begin building a positive relationship with the VA. VA Liaisons coordinated 7,150 referrals for health care and provided over 26,825 professional consultations in fiscal year 2010.

Polytrauma System of Care

Traumatic Brain Injury (TBI) and polytrauma are significant health risks for Veterans returning from current combat operations in Iraq and Afghanistan. Trauma consequences may include physical, cognitive, behavioral, and emotional disabilities. The VA has developed comprehensive medical, psychological, rehabilitation, and prosthetic care for Veterans with TBI and polytrauma.

Beginning in 2005, VA developed an integrated nationwide Polytrauma/TBI System of Care (PSC) with over 100 facilities that provide specialized rehabilitation services. PSC facilities are distributed across the nation and include four components of care organized in a hub and spokes model:

1   four TBI/Polytrauma Rehabilitation Centers serve as hubs for acute medical and rehabilitation care, research, and education;
2   twenty-two TBI/Polytrauma Network Sites manage the post-acute symptoms of TBI/Polytrauma and coordinate rehabilitation services within their network;
3   eighty-two TBI/Polytrauma Support Clinic Teams provide specialized rehabilitation services for patients within their catchment area and address community re-integration needs;
4   forty-eight remaining VA facilities have identified TBI/Polytrauma Points of Contact responsible for managing consultations and referrals into the PSC as appropriate for the Veterans' needs.

Important benefits of the VA's Polytrauma System of Care (PSC) include coordinated, interdisciplinary care by teams of rehabilitation specialists; specialty care management; patient and family education and training; psychosocial support;

advanced rehabilitation technologies; and environment of care that meets the needs and expectations of the new generation of Veterans. An individualized rehabilitation and reintegration plan of care is developed for every Veteran and Service member who receives inpatient or outpatient rehabilitation services at one of the PSC facilities. The VA developed a standardized national template to document the plan of care in the computerized record of each patient. Elements of the plan address goals and resources to assist Veterans, Service members and families through recovery, rehabilitation, and reintegration into the community. A care manager is designated to oversee the implementation of the plan and to coordinate the necessary follow-up services.

Care management is the lynchpin of care coordination in PSC. Every Veteran and Service member recovering from polytrauma and TBI is assigned a case manager who assesses the psychosocial needs of the patient and family, provides the necessary services and support to address those needs, and coordinates services, including community resources. An extensive support system exists across PSC to ensure that patients and their families receive all necessary services, to enhance the rehabilitation process, and to minimize the inherent stress of recovery from severe injury.

Providing life-long care for TBI patients in an appropriate setting is a challenge. To address this challenge, VA, in collaboration with the Defense and Veterans Brain Injury Center, is implementing a five year pilot program to assess the effectiveness of providing assisted living services to eligible Veterans with moderate to severe functional deficits due to TBI. The pilot is being implemented through contracts with brain injury residential living programs that provide individualized treatment models of care to accommodate the specialized needs of patients with TBI.

Federal Recovery Coordination Program

To ensure continuity for the most seriously ill and injured of our returning OEF/OIF/OND Services members, VA, DoD, and Health and Human Services developed the Federal Recovery Coordination Program. Those individuals whose recovery is likely to require a complex array of specialists, transfers to multiple facilities, and long periods of rehabilitation are referred to a Federal Recovery Coordinator (FRC). The FRC will coordinate the care of the seriously ill or injured Service member or Veteran from MTF, to VA, even private sector, and then home. When a referral is made, a FRC conducts an evaluation that serves as the basis for problem identification and determination of the appropriate level of service. In conjunction with the Service member or Veteran, their family or caregiver, and members of the multidisciplinary health care team, a Federal individual recovery plan is developed. The FRCs works closely with Polytrauma and OEF/OIF/OND case managers to assist recovering Service members and their families with access to care, services, and benefits provided through the various programs in DoD, VA, other federal agencies, states and the private sector. The FRCs continue to coordinate care regardless of the location of the Service member or Veteran and for as long as is needed.

Care Management of OEF/OIF/OND Veterans

All 152 VA medical centers have a Care Management team consisting of both a clinical component (registered nurses and social workers) that includes the OEF/OIF/OND Program Manager and OEF/OIF/OND case managers and a non-clinical component led by Transition Patient Advocates (many of whom are OEF/OIF/OND Veterans). The Program Manager coordinates clinical care and oversees the transition and care for this population. OEF/OIF/OND case managers coordinate patient care activities and ensure that all clinicians providing care to the patient are doing so in a cohesive and integrated manner. Transition Patient Advocates help Veterans navigate the VA system, and Veterans Benefits Administration (VBA) team members assist Veterans with the benefit application process and provide education about VA benefits.

All severely ill and injured OEF/OIF/OND Service members and Veterans receiving care at VA are provided with a case manager. All others are screened for case management needs and, based upon the assessment, a case manager is assigned as indicated. The patient and family serve as integral partners in the assessment and treatment care plan. Since many of the returning OEF/OIF/OND Veterans connect to more than one specialty care system, the VA introduced a new concept of a "lead" case manager. The "lead" case manager now serves as a central communication point for the patient and his or her family. Our case managers maintain regular contact with Veterans and their families to provide support and assistance to address any health care and psychosocial needs that may arise. As of December 31, 2010, 6,244 OEF/OIF/OND severely ill and injured Service members and Veterans, as well as over 45,000 who are less seriously injured, were receiving on-going case management services. Case Managers collaborate with VA, DoD, and other Federal, state and community resources to address the needs of OEF/OIF/OND Veterans.

Now that VA has a robust system in place to identify severely ill and injured Veterans who require case management, VA's challenge is to identify those less severely ill and injured Veterans who would also benefit from case management. VA often refers to these Veterans as the "walking wounded." VA recently implemented a standardized screening tool to evaluate all returning combat Veterans for case management needs. The key will be to ensure that it is used in all settings where OEF/OIF/OND Veterans receive care.

Caregiver Support

Veterans are best served when they can live their lives as independently as possible in their home in the community surrounded by family and friends.

Caregivers are a valuable resource providing physical, emotional and other support to seriously ill and injured Veterans, making it possible for them to remain in their homes rather than requiring institutional care. Caregivers with the heaviest responsibilities are vulnerable to risk such as burnout, decline in health, emotional stress, and economic hardship. Recognizing the importance of providing support and services to the caregivers of severely ill and injured OEF/OIF/OND Veterans, VA offers a range of benefits and services that support Veterans and their family caregivers. These include such things as in-home care, specialized education and training, respite care, equipment and home and automobile modification, and financial assistance. The new Caregivers and Veterans Omnibus Health Services Act of 2010, signed into law by President Obama on May 5, 2010, enhances existing services for all caregivers of Veterans who are currently enrolled in VA care and provides unprecedented new benefits and services to those who care for Veterans who have a serious injury that was incurred or aggravated in the line of duty after September 1, 2001. VA is enhancing its current services and developing a comprehensive National Caregiver Support Program with a prevention and wellness focus that includes the use of evidence-based training and support services for caregivers. VA has designated Caregiver Support Points of Contact at each VA medical center who serve as the clinical experts on caregiver issues and are most knowledgeable of the VA and non-VA support resources that are available. VA has a Caregiver Support website (www.caregiver.va.gov) which provides a wealth of information and resources for Veterans, families and the general public. Providing ongoing support for caregivers of critically injured Veterans will be a challenge in the coming years. Many of these caregivers are parents and are themselves aging; many quit jobs to provide care and no longer have health insurance; young wives are raising children in addition to caring for an injured husband. There are many issues to consider in developing support programs to meet caregiver needs.

Vet Centers

Given that only half of eligible returning combat Veterans are seen in the VA, it is essential that we reach Veterans in the communities where they live. The Vet Center Program originated in 1979 to address the psycho-social sequela of combat Vietnam Veterans and their families. Vet Centers are located in the community at 282 sites across the United States to include Puerto Rico, St. Thomas, American Virgin Islands, Guam, and American Samoa. There will be 300 Vet Centers by the end of 2011, and approximately 80 percent of all staff are Veterans and 33 percent are combat Veterans having served in OEF, OIF, or OND. The program remains the gold standard in community based readjustment counseling in a safe and confidential setting, and over 97 percent of all Veteran clients would recommend the Vet Center to a fellow Veteran. Services include individual and group counseling for Veterans and their families, family counseling for military related issues, bereavement counseling for families who experience an active duty death, military sexual trauma counseling and referral, homeless Veteran services, outreach and education including Post Deployment Health Reassessment (PDHRA), community events, etc., substance abuse assessment and referral, employment assessment and referral, screening and referral for medical issues including TBI, depression, etc., and VBA benefits screening and referral.

To date the Vet Center program has touched approximately 40 percent of all discharged OEF/OIF/OND Veterans either by services at a Vet Center or on outreach. From November 2004 through August 2010, Vet Centers have participated in 1,789 distinct PDHRA events and facilitated 32,545 Vet Center referrals.

An additional tool that was rolled out in 2009 was the Mobile Vet Center (MVC) project. The mobile center, literally a mobile vehicle, provides counseling services to Veterans and their families in rural areas, and has satellite communication to VA medical records. The mobile vet center can also be used in medical emergencies as a triage clinic, and can also be turned into a disaster relief center and serve as a command, control and communication center. Currently, there are 50 MVCs spread throughout the United States, and it gives VA the ability to reach rural areas that are not accessible to other VA facilities; and there will be an additional 20 vehicles deployed in 2011. In addition to rural area outreach, MVC attends PDHRA, yellow ribbon ceremonies, pre- and post-deployment ceremonies, and provides a place for returning Veterans to discuss their issues in privacy as well as to assist them with referrals. During the Fort Hood incident, Vet Centers mobilized four MVCs and provided counseling to over 8,200 Veterans and family members.

The Vet Center Program also runs the Vet Center Combat Veterans Call Center. This is a 24/7 national service where combat Veterans and/or family members can call at anytime to talk to another combat Veteran regarding any readjustment issues related to military service. The Veteran on the receiving end of the call understands military culture and values military experience in a combat theater, is a trained counselor, and has knowledge of other VA services and benefits that may be needed by the Veteran or family member. The call-in number is 1-877-WAR-VETS (927-8387).

Seven Touches of Outreach: A Personal Approach

Only 50 percent of separated OEF/OIF/OND Veterans have accessed VA health care; therefore coordinated outreach initiatives are critical to the education of OEF/OIF/OND Service members and their family members about VA benefits and services. More importantly, it is a part of VA's Veteran centric strategy to assist

Veterans in accessing needed services during the post-deployment period. The VA has embraced a new paradigm in reaching out to returning Service members throughout the deployment cycle, within the first six months of returning home, and with a special focus on Reserve and National Guard Forces. This new paradigm is called the *Seven Touches of Outreach: A Personal Approach.*

The following seven initiatives comprise the *Seven Touches of Outreach*, and demonstrate the personal approach and collaborative efforts required under this new paradigm:

1   *Demobilization Initiative* in which VA staff conduct briefings to returning Reserve and National Guard Service members at 61 demobilization sites;
2   *Reserve and National Guard Yellow Ribbon Reintegration Program Support Initiative* that involves VA staff conducting benefit briefings, enrolling Veterans in VA health care and providing assistance and referral service to Veterans;
3   *VA's Partnership with the National Guard Bureau's Transition Assistance Advisors (TAAs) Initiative* in which 62 nationally placed TAAs assist Veterans and their families in accessing needed VA and community services;
4   *Combat Veteran Call Center Initiative* designed to contact all returning OEF/OIF/OND Veterans not currently enrolled in VA health care by telephone to inform them of benefits and link them to needed local VA services;
5   *Reserve and National Guard Post-Deployment Health Reassessment Support Initiative* in which DoD contract health care providers conduct health care screenings on Service members within 90–180 days post-deployment; VA staff provide health care enrollment, benefit information and assistance in arranging follow-up health care appointments for referred Veterans;
6   *Individual Ready Reserve (IRR) Muster Initiative* designed to reach out to Service members who may not have attended VA Transition Assistance Program (TAP) briefings prior to separation from active duty and to Reserve and National Guard Service members not assigned to local Units;
7   *Internet Webpage for OEF/OIF/OND Veterans* (www.OEF/OIF/OND.VA.Gov) a one-stop site for returning combat Veterans to obtain information on VA benefits and services and to participate in VA's new forms of social media such as blogs, Twitter and Facebook.

In addition to the above National outreach initiatives, VA staff conduct local outreach activities that extend well beyond these initiatives. They include outreach to active duty bases, military family support groups, homeless stand downs, job and employment fairs, college and universities, along with other community-sponsored events. In summary, outreach is a major part of VA's continuum of care and social workers play critical leadership and clinical roles in these efforts.

Conclusion

The experience of war and participation in combat often leaves a Veteran feeling disconnected from pre-deployment relationships, contexts and life trajectories. Veterans often report, "I thought everything would get better after I got home, but since getting back I almost feel like a stranger, even in my own home, even with my spouse and my kids and my old friends." They often describe feeling as if their lives have "fallen apart." Given this existential reality for some Veterans, we can see that successfully reintegrating into family and community life upon returning home from war involves a process of re-establishing connections and "putting the pieces together." Connection and integration are two core functions which are integral to social work practice. In the case of returning combat Veterans, it is the social worker who most directly supports the Veteran in the process of re-connection to loved ones, to resources, to opportunities and ultimately to that path leading to a healthy and functional life. It is the social worker who most directly supports the Veteran in the process of reintegration: putting the services, the opportunities, the disparate pieces of a life in transition back together in a way that results in a whole, healthy, functional Veteran and family.

In order to accomplish this mission we must create systems that model connection and integration, both within the VA in terms of interdisciplinary collaboration and teamwork, as well as between the VA and other agencies and providers (Huebner, et. al., 2009). Combat Veterans are fully aware of the importance of a well-trained, well-integrated team when one is faced with a challenging mission. What better way to express our appreciation for the service and sacrifice of these Veterans and their families than to offer them such a team, an integrated community of care both within the VA and throughout the community, to support them effectively in every way possible on this challenging and complex journey home from war.

The Department of Veterans Affairs is prepared to serve the Nation's newest generation of Veterans and invites readers to learn more about our comprehensive programs and services by visiting our websites at www.va.gov and www.oefoif. va.gov. Readers are also encouraged to follow us on Facebook (www.facebook. com/VeteransHealth) and Twitter (www.twitter.com/DeptVetAffairs).

References

Gironda, R.J., Clark, M.E., Ruff, R.L., Chait, S., Craine, M., Walker, R., et al. (2009). Traumatic brain injury, polytrauma, and pain: challenges and treatment strategies for the polytrauma rehabilitation. *Rehabilitation Psychology*, 54(3), 247–258.

Helmer, D., Rossigbnol, M., Blatt, M., Agarwal, R., & Lange, R. (2007). Health and exposure concerns for Veterans deployed to Iraq and Afghanistan. *Journal of Occupational and Environmental Medicine*, 49(5), 475–480.

Hoge, C.W., Castro, C.A., Messer, S.C., McGurk, D., Cotting, D.I., & Koffman, R.L. (2004). Combat duty in Iraq and Afghanistan, mental health problems, and barriers to care. *New England Journal of Medicine*, 351(1), 13–22.

Kang, H.K. & Bullman, T.A. (2008). Risk of suicide among U.S. Veterans after returning from the Iraq or Afghanistan war zones. *Journal of the American Medical Association*, 300(6), 652–653.

Lew, H.L., Otis, J.D., Tun, C., Kerns, R.D., Clark, M.E., & Cifu, D.X. (2009). Prevalence of chronic pain, posttraumatic stress disorder, and persistent postconcussive symptoms in OIF/OEF Veterans: polytrauma clinical trial. *Journal of Rehabilitational Research and Development*, 46(6), 697–702.

Martin, E.M., Lu, W.C., Helmick, K., French, L., & Warden, D.L. (2008). Traumatic brain injuries sustained in the Afghanistan and Iraq wars. *American Journal of Nursing*, 108(4), 40–47; quiz 47–48.

McFarlane, A.C. (2009). Military deployment: The impact on children and family adjustment and the need for care. *Current Opinion in Psychiatry*, 22(4), 369–373.

Sayers, S.L., Farrow, V.A., Ross, J., & Oslin, D.W. (2009). Family problems among recently returned military Veterans referred for a mental health evaluation. *Journal of Clinical Psychiatry*, 70(2), 163–170.

Seal, K.H., Metzler, T.J., Gima, K.S., Bertenthal, D., Maguen, S., & Marmar, C.R. (2009). Trends and risk factors for mental health diagnoses among Iraq and Afghanistan Veterans using Department of Veterans Affairs health care, 2002–2008. *American Journal of Public Health*, 99(9), 1651–1658.

Uomoto, J. & Williams, R. (2009). Post-acute polytrauma rehabilitation and integrated care of returning Veterans: Toward a holistic approach. *Rehabilitation Psychology*, 54(3), 259–269.

PART V

Unique Concerns for Practitioners

17

ETHICAL CHALLENGES WHEN WORKING WITH THE MILITARY

Nancy Beckerman

The Context of Social Work With the Military

The ongoing war on terror in Iraq and Afghanistan has created an array of profound physical and psychological challenges for our returning U.S. and allied troops. Mental health counselors providing care to this population are confronted by particularly complicated clinical and ethical dilemmas. Soldiers have always been asked to put aside their own emotional needs for the welfare of their combat unit and their country (Menninger, 1948); and they have been expected to perpetrate acts of violence, bear witness to acts of violence, and live under the specter of their own death at any moment of any day—this is within the nature of military service and combat.

However, the lengthy duration and unique combat challenges of military operations in Iraq and Afghanistan have resulted in differences such as: troop shortages; numerous repeated tours of duty; more reservists seeing active duty; and more traumatic brain injuries and loss of limbs due to improvised explosive devices (Nash, 2007; Solomon, Shklar, & Mikulincer, 2005). A remarkable percentage of wounded soldiers in these wars are surviving their injuries (90%), which is thanks to advances in infection control, body armor and quick evacuation to the United States for care (Hyer, 2006). As such, significantly more troops are returning home with complex physical and mental health challenges than in previous wars (Nash, 2007). Among the returning troops, there is a prevalence of depression, PTSD symptoms, subjective poor health, and alcohol abuse (Daley, 2003; Nash, 2007; Van Staden, Hacker, Hughes, et al., 2009). These situations present a palpable range of ethical concerns and dilemmas for the practitioner who works with the military population, both in the Veterans Administration (VA) or Department of Defense (DoD) system of care and in the civilian sector. This chapter will explore some of the ethical dilemmas faced by those who serve the military and will attempt to offer a perspective on how these dilemmas can be addressed.

Social workers in the military (those employed by the VA or DoD systems) have been prepared to work with issues of a soldier's readiness to enter and re-enter combat, substance abuse, psychological sequelae of wartime combat, pre-existing mental health vulnerabilities and a soldiers' full array of difficulties back home (Daley, 1999, 2003; Simmons & Rycraft, 2010; Solomon, Shklar, & Mikulincer, 2005). Both the Uniformed Code of Military Justice and the NASW Code of Ethics (1996) guide military social workers. The Uniformed Code of Military Justice states that the needs of the military missions prevail; the underlying principle is drawn from a utilitarian model which espouses that soldiers have the ethical obligation to sacrifice their individual freedoms for the greater good of society (Powers, 2006). The military experience and culture is one that emphasizes the group mentality over the individual, the mission over the needs of one, and values the mission over the individual introspection (Daley, 2003; Jones, Sparacino, Wilcox, et al., 1995; Nash, 2007). Therefore the primary ethical challenge for the military social worker is this underlying tension between the value system of the military versus that of social work (with a cornerstone value of client self-determination) (London, Rubenstein, Baldwin-Ragaven, & Van Es, 2006). The military social worker will be asked, and expected, to care for each individual soldier and simultaneously care for a unit and its mission. However, the underlying principles of the NASW Code of Ethics (1996) value individual freedoms such as autonomy, self-determination, privacy/confidentiality, and quality of life, drawing primarily from a framework of situational ethics (Congress, 2006; Reamer, 2006; Mattison, 2000). This can create a difficult situation for the worker who is bound by both codes.

Civilian Social Work and Ethical Dilemmas

How are civilian social workers prepared to cope with the unique ethical challenges of counseling a returning Veteran in their mental health agency or private practice? Given the breadth and depth of expected and unexpected psychosocial wounds of war over the past decade, civilian social workers have been faced with profound and complicated counseling and ethical challenges (Nash, 2007). Several studies have indicated that returning Veterans have manifested higher levels of PTSD, suicide attempts, alcohol abuse and incidents of domestic violence than in previous war efforts (Collier, 2010; Kapur, While, Blatchley, et al., 2009; Nash, 2007). This is a complicated endeavor as these areas of dysfunction can be attributed to numerous variables, e.g., pre-service vulnerabilities, repeated tours of duty and separations from families, the percentage of reservists who have been deployed as compared to active duty enlistees, the new and different forms of physical injuries from IEDs, etc. (Hyer, 2006; Kapur et al., 2009; Nash, 2007; Simmons & Rycraft, 2010).

Civilian social workers enter into a client's life at a most vulnerable and disorienting time. While he/she may have accessed care through the VA or DoD system, the service member may have opted to go beyond these venues of care for a variety of reasons including fear of reprisal and stigma, etc. The client is probably seeing the social worker/counselor because they or their family members are having difficulty coping with post-combat transition. The clinical challenges can of course range widely, but the typical set of issues includes depression, anxiety, PTSD, alcohol and substance abuse, and the potential for domestic violence (Kapur et al., 2007; Solomon et al., 2005).

Ethical Dilemma Cases

As we look at the following ethical dilemmas in civilian social work practice, the social worker/mental health counselor has to remember that there is always an ethical dimension to our work, and that the nature of an ethical dilemma is that the two or more choices appear equally bad or good and without an obvious satisfactory plan of action. That's what makes it a dilemma.

Personal vs. Professional

Joe B., a 23 year old Italian–American Marine, sits across from the social worker in an out-patient mental health setting. He has served three tours in Afghanistan; he has not suffered a physical injury of war, but a psychological one. He is uneasy in his civilian life, agitated, vigilant and easily impatient. He is seen in the context of difficulties with his son who has manifested behavioral problems in school and his wife who appears depressed. While Joe is rightfully concerned about his son and wife, he does not seem to understand that the difficulties they are experiencing may be in reaction to his shift in recent behavior. In assessment, it is clear that this was not Joe's "personality" before his service, but that he is not at risk of hurting himself or others. The client wishes and expects to return to active duty to fulfill his obligation to the military.

The worker, who is personally against the war, may have difficulty being objective. A civilian social worker will be confronted by the impact of wars they may feel personally conflicted about or even personally strongly against. Civilian workers will be confronted and affected by the larger political context as well as their own personal values regarding war and these wars in particular (Banks, 2008). The political context of these military operations cannot be seen or understood in the same way as previous wars. The depth of feelings about 9/11 and the response in Iraq and Afghanistan are different than previous military actions, and it is important for the civilian social worker to reflect on their own personal values regarding these events. The political events over the past decade have shaped how the social worker may perceive the war itself and, to some extent, the social and political context of the social worker and the individual client. As Abramson (1996) has noted, the social worker has to have a "holistic" review of their ethics as well as the unique values and ethics of the client across from her. In essence this means the worker has be aware of her own value system and how they inform their practice as well as attention to what values the client may hold about the war; where these values may coincide and where they may conflict.

While the NASW Code of Ethics provides the principles of the profession, they are often at too abstract a level to provide specific guidance when there are two competing actions. Regarding Joe B., the NASW Code of Ethics standard 1.01 states that the primary responsibility is to promote the well-being of the client (NASW 1996), and yet the NASW Code also includes ethical standard 1.02 which encourages the social worker to support and promote a client's right to self-determination. In this instance, the worker may feel that to promote the client's self-determination will result in not protecting his well-being.

This social worker may have to support the individual soldier's wish to return to combat, while simultaneously feeling strongly that no U.S. troops should be involved in a military action that feels unjust. In this scenario, both Levy (1976) and Abramson (1996) underscore that self-awareness of one's one personal value system will be an essential component of decision-making, so that personal biases are not polluting the professional framework of ethical principles. As in the case of the social worker who has any other personal and professional values in conflict, the professional value system takes precedence. Whether the client is seeking a termination to a pregnancy (and the social worker is pro-life), for example, it is a worker's ethical obligation to support their client's self-determination. Consequently, unless Joe has demonstrated that he is unstable and will be an imminent harm to himself, his family or his fellow soldiers, the worker will be expected to support Joe's identified goal of returning to active combat. The worker's presenting issue will be the son's behavioral issues and, time-permitting, helping the family unit adjust to Joe's entries and exits. If Joe expresses the motivation to address his shift in mood, individual counseling can be initiated.

Most social workers will confront an internal ethical conflict such as this and can refer to the NASW Code of Ethics which will ensure the primacy of our ethical obligation to our clients. Additional support can be found in understanding what Levy coined as the "personal vs. professional" dilemma. This is when the worker's personal value system is in opposition to the values espoused by the profession. Working with those involved in military combat, there will be instances when impartiality to the context of war is a daunting challenge. These moments with clients are informed by, and can be clouded by, all the complexities of religion, culture and politics that lie within the worker, within the client and, of course, between the worker and the client. In the final analysis in the above scenario, our worker has to be self-aware and then endeavor to contain their personal values and political viewpoints so that they do not enter into the client–worker relationship. The worker who is in personal opposition to these wars will need to reflect over and over to identify their own personal values, leave them outside of the client–worker relationship, and do their best to serve each client with their best clinical and ethical professionalism (Levy, 1976; NASW, 1996).

Confidentiality of Diagnosis

R., the social worker, in consultation with Sara, learns that Sara's husband "has not been the same" since his return from his last tour of duty in Iraq. In assessing the client's concern, the worker can surmise that this returning Veteran has been unable to transition adaptively to civilian life. When asked for specific details, the client explains that since he's back, "my husband doesn't get out of the bed, doesn't shower, sleeps all the time and has bouts of crying and drinking." With encouragement, Ms. R. is able to bring her husband into the next session.

In assessment with Sara's husband, Roger, it is apparent that he is experiencing a Major Depressive episode with bouts of suicidal ideation. The worker believes the client should be seen by a psychiatrist for a consultation as soon as possible. If he is referred for a psychiatric consultant, he may very well be diagnosed with a Major Depression. There are numerous dimensions to this ethical dilemma. When a soldier is diagnosed with a mental health condition, there are profound effects on the individual client and his future. On the one hand, the client may feel reassured and this consultation and diagnosis can open up treatment options to relieve his suffering. However, on the other hand, it can confound his sense of identity, purpose and career path. A diagnosis can result in stigma, and some have reported that carrying any mental health diagnosis can be seen as weakness and cowardice and be met with the loss of trust of their peers.

If the worker counsels the client to pursue a psychiatric consultation and Roger agrees, then the worker can support that action under Ethical Standard 1.07 (c) and (d), because the worker is breaching confidentiality to prevent serious, foreseeable harm to the client (c), and is doing so with an informed client (d) (NASW, 1996). If Roger does not agree to pursue such a consultation, our worker is left with a client who is experiencing a Major Depression, is in emotional pain, risk of suicidal behavior, and is unable to function in his domestic life. Here the dilemma intensifies. While the effect of a diagnosis might relieve the soldier from active duty, it might also provide a sense of relief and reassurance for him and his young family, and could result in the appropriate follow-up mental health care. Intrinsic in this scenario is the impact of the diagnosis on the soldier's career and aspirations within the military, as well as the limits of confidentiality. Once a client is labeled with a mental health diagnosis or issue, their military career will likely be adversely affected (Garber & McNelis, 1995). There are those within the military who have argued that "people surrender certain personal rights" (such as confidentiality) when they join the military. In fact, once back in the military, "the collective trumps the rights of the individual" (Collier, 2010, p. 821). Indeed, for the military social worker (one employed by the government) carrying a dual role as an officer and a mental health counselor, there is very little room to weigh the relative importance of competing obligations as they are expected to accede to their superior officers (London et al., 2006). It is important to note that if individual soldiers fear that seeking counseling will harm their military careers, they may be reluctant to initiate mental health counseling within the VA or DoD and seek help in the civilian sector even when it is critically important to do so.

By not forcing the issue of the psychiatric consultation with Roger, the social worker may be complicit in allowing this soldier to return to duty while he is ill-equipped to work with his unit; hence putting himself and others in jeopardy. Loewenberg and Dolgoff (1996), as well as Mattison (2000, 2008), would encourage the social worker to identify these underlying principles and to weigh out how they translate into action plans.

Writing about ethical dilemmas in the military, Tallant and Ryberg (1999) provide a straightforward way to measure one's alternatives in such a scenario. They allot the weight of each ethical principle to provide the further assistance necessary for identifying ethical principles that are in conflict with one another. While all ethical principles are important, the following ranking order can be utilized to promote prioritization in ethical decision-making.

1 Principle of the protection of life;
2 Quality and inequality;
3 Autonomy and freedom;
4 Least harm;
5 Quality of life;
6 Privacy and confidentiality;
7 Truthfulness and full disclosure.

Following their weighted principles, the protection of life (#1) supersedes privacy and confidentiality (#6) with definitive resolution. Also, Mattison (2000) would support this prioritizing and suggest that the worker should be actively engaged with identifying the possible actions, weighing the benefits and costs and projected outcomes, and then be able to justify the choice of action (Mattison, 2000). In this process, the potential courses of action are (a) allow the client to leave untreated, or (b) making every effort to ensure that Roger be seen by a psychiatrist (even if it breaches client confidentiality). Weighing the benefits and costs of allowing a disturbed client to go untreated (which could result in suicide and devastation of his family unit), or being diagnosed and treated (and perhaps unable to return to military action), the civilian social worker will arrive at the prioritization of protection of life over confidentiality breach or client-self-determination. While Tallent and Ryberg (1999) and Mattison's (2000) model can be utilized successfully in this scenario, each case will present their own unique and complex ethical challenges.

Self-determination vs. Beneficence

Reservist Sue C. is scheduled for re-deployment and she wants/needs to go back into active duty. She explains in a first counseling appointment that she comes from a family of soldiers and did not want to talk to a military social worker for fear of stigma and, therefore, sought counsel with a civilian social worker. She explains that she would be too ashamed to be discharged, but presents as highly erratic and requesting anti-anxiety medication. She hasn't told anyone that she has been incapacitated by panic attacks since the last few weeks of service and over these seven months since she has been home. She has been smoking marijuana and drinking to self-medicate, and has started to rely on over the counter sleep medications. She says she is determined to be a soldier and does not want anything to interfere with returning to the service; nor she does want her husband or her kids to know of her condition.

Of course there is the clinical social work assessment that would include pre-morbid functioning, psychiatric history, history of substance abuse, and the recent onset, acuity and frequency of the panic attacks. All of these variables will be looked at in terms of how they may be part of a larger diagnostic assessment and treatment plan. However, there is also an ethical dilemma present in this scenario. This social worker will need to weigh the underlying ethical principle of fostering client self-determination (Ethical Standard 1.02 of NASW Code of Ethics), against the client's best interest (beneficence), and the need for limitation of client self-determination, i.e., when a client's actions or potential actions pose imminent risk to themselves or others (also code 1.02) (Veatch, 1989). The other nuances in this scenario are: who is the client (Sue or Sue and her family), who decides, (civilian or military personnel), what if the social worker's assessment of beneficence is in direct opposition with the client's? As always in a case such as this, there will also be the question of confidentiality as well.

Loewenberg and Dolgoff (1996) provide an ethical decision–making model that can be utilized. The process of an ethical assessment can be developed by referring to the ethical steps listed below:

1   Identify the problem and the factors that contribute to its maintenance.
2   Identify the persons and institutions involved in this problem, such as clients, victim support systems, other professionals, and others.
3   Identify the values relevant to this problem held by several participants, including social work values, professional values, and client's and worker's personal values.
4   Identify the goals and objectives whose attainment may resolve (or at least reduce) the problem.
5   Identify alternative intervention strategies and targets.
6   Assess the effectiveness and efficiency of each alternative in terms of two identified goals.

7   Determine who should be involved in decision making.
8   Select the most appropriate strategy.
9   Implement the strategy selected.
10   Monitor the implementation, paying particular attention to unanticipated consequences.
11   Evaluate the results and identify additional problems.

(Loewenberg & Dolgoff, 1996)

Using Loewenberg and Dolgoff's Ethical Rules System (ERS), we can identify that Sue C. wishes to return to active military combat (her self-determination), while the professional assessment sees her unstable mental state and her substance abuse as a serious harm to herself and others (beneficence). Sue C. values her role and identity as a military person and the social worker values the safety and wellbeing of her client (and her client's family and unit members). Sue C. wishes to keep this situation confidential and the social worker wants to be able to receive comprehensive care for this client which would include breaches to client confidentiality (steps 1–3).

In identifying goals, a shared goal would be to rehabilitate and treat in the short-term so that Sue might be able to return to combat if necessary. Another goal, with which Sue would not be in agreement, would be to ensure that Sue does not return to active duty (step 4). In reviewing strategies, one strategy could be a short-term plan to have the client enter into AA and any other substance program unbeknownst to the military or family, provide anxiety management techniques that do not include psychotropic medications, and set a date to assess the level of improvement. A more long-term and comprehensive approach would include informing and working with the family, the military, a psychiatric consultation and any other helping professional to attend to this soldier's needs (steps 5–6). Decision-making could initially be just the client and social worker, or expand to include a supervisor or psychiatrist as well as her husband (step 7). Our social worker could contract to meet with Sue C. and implement the short-term interventions (without referring to psychiatrist or family), and evaluate for improvement at an agreed-upon time in the near future, with the understanding that some or all of the longer, more comprehensive plans may need to be enacted (steps 8, 9 and 10). Finally, as Loewenberg and Dolgoff recommend, an evaluation will have to be thoughtfully reviewed to determine if Sue's management of her anxiety has significantly improved and if she has been able to maintain sobriety. In this scenario, what at first may have presented as ethically untenable may be partialized—broken up into discrete steps—much the same way crisis intervention workers triage. Are there some areas of ethical overlap in a case that can provide the entry point so that clinical work can ethically be carried out? In the case of Sue, Loewenberg and Dolgoff (1996) provided a rubric to begin that process.

Discussion

In trying to make an ethical assessment and arriving at the most ethical outcome for all parties involved, the social worker has several places to turn for guidance. The first is the professional Codes of Ethics. The NASW Code of Ethics is recognized and used by professional social workers in the United States for guidance in their own conduct towards clients, colleagues, practice settings, as professionals, the social work profession and the society.

This Code, as well as other professional codes, are generally used to identify principles and values so that the worker can clarify the nature of the conflict and try to reason out the primary ethical obligation(s). However, it does not prioritize which ethical obligation or which ethical principle take precedence over others. It is written at a level of abstraction that fosters ethical thinking and reflection, but does not and cannot be relied upon as a specific guideline to resolve the many different complex ethical dilemmas social workers face on a daily basis.

Ethicists within the social work profession such as Levy (1976), Loewenberg and Dolgoff (1996), Mattison (2000), and Reamer (2006) have addressed the range of ethical dilemmas in social work practice and have all concurred that Codes do not provide guidance for specific ethical dilemmas in practice. The profession's ethical decision-making frameworks attempt to provide a more fully developed conceptual standard that facilitates an ethical assessment and outlines options in relation to the underlying ethical principles in competition. At the abstract levels, principles such as self-determination and beneficence (in the client's best interest) may both be viable ethical principles that guide practice, but they can also present in opposition to one another in an ethical dilemma. If a client's self-determination puts them or others in harm's way, the social worker will have to weigh out whether they can simultaneously support both client self-determination and the client's best interest. In reasoning this dilemma through, a social work practitioner can benefit from weighing out the anticipated consequences of each planned action so that the final outcome will result in the least harm done to the most.

Social work with the military is in some ways no different from social work in any setting. Whether social workers are providing services in prisons, schools or VA hospitals, the profession has a history of being utilized as both an arm of social action (advocacy) and social control (easing client anxiety so they will be compliant with the goals of the host setting). In a medical hospital, school or the military, where the primary goal is not overall functioning of clients but one particular area such as educational, penal, and medical, social work is instrumental as a support (Simmons & Rycraft, 2010). It does, however, leave us vulnerable to myriad ethical dilemmas of which we have to be aware. When working with those in the military, the competing needs of combat and the individual are frequently at odds, and are expressed in numerous ways. While this chapter does not dictate a clear path through some of these situations, it does suggest a procedure for clarification of the issues and needs of both sides.

References

Abramson, M. (1996). Reflections on knowing oneself ethically: Towards a working framework for social work practice. *Families in Society*, 77(4) 195–202.

Banks, S. (2008). Critical commentary: Social work ethics. *British Journal of Social Work*, 38, 1238–1249.

Collier, R. (2010). Ethical dilemmas in military social work. *Canadian Medical Association. Journal*,182.18 (Dec 14): E821–2.

Congress, E. (2006). Social work ethics: Professional codes in Australia and the United States. *International Social Work*, 49, 151–164.

Daley, J. (1999). *Social Work Practice in the Military*. New York; Haworth.

Daley, J.G. (2003). Military social work: A multi-country comparison. *International Social Work*, 46, 437–448.

Garber, D.L., & McNelis, P.J. (1995). Military social work. In L. Beebe, A. Winchester, F. Pflieger, & S. Lowman (Eds.), *Encyclopedia of Social Work* (19th Ed., pp. 1726–1736). Washington, DC: NASW Press.

Hyer, R. (2006). *Iraq and Afghanistan Producing New Pattern of Extremity Injuries*. Conference proceedings from American Academy of Orthopaedic Surgeons 2006 Annual Meeting. Retrieved from: http://www.medscpe.com/viewarticl;e/528624

Jones, F.D., Sparacino, L.R., Wilcox, V.L., Rothenberg, J.M., & Stokes, J.W. (Eds.) (1995). *War Psychiatry*. Washington, DC: Office of the Surgeon General at TMM Publications.

Kapur, N., While, D., Blatchley, N., Bray, I., & Harrison, K. (2009). Suicide after leaving the UK armed forces: A cohort study, *Clinical Psychology Review*, 29(8): 695–706.

Levy, C. (1976). *Social Work Ethics.* New York: Human Sciences Press.

Loewenberg, F.M. & Dolgoff, R. (1996). *Ethical Decisions for Social Work Practice* (5th Ed.). Itasca, IL: F.E. Peacock.

London, L., Rubenstein, L.S., Baldwin-Ragaven, L., & Van Es, A. (2006). Dual loyalty among military health professionals: Human rights and ethicism times of armed conflict. *Cambridge Quarterly Healthcare* Ethics, 15, 381–391.

Mattison, M. (2000). Ethical decision-making: The person in the process. *Social Work*, 15(3), 201–212.

Mattison, M. (2008). Professional Ethics Codes. Application to common ethical dilemmas. In C. Franklin, M.B. Harris, and P. Allen-Meares (Eds.), *School Social Work and Mental Health Workers Training Resource Manual*. Oxford: Oxford University Press.

Menninger, W.C. (1948). *Psychiatry in a Troubled World: Yesterday's war and today's challenge*. New York: Macmillan.

Nash, W. (2007). Combat/Operational stress adaptation and injuries. In C. Figley & W. Nash, (Eds.), *Combat Stress Injury.* New York: Routledge.

NASW (National Association of Social Workers) (1996). *Code of Ethics.* Washington, DC: NASW.

Powers, R. (2006). *Military Ethics and Conflicts of Interest: Standards of ethics and conflict*. Retrieved April 15, 2011 from: http://usmilitary.about.com/cs/generalinfo/a/stanconduct.htm

Reamer, F. (2006). *Social Work and Values & Ethics* (3rd Ed.), New York: Columbia University Press.

Simmons, C. & Rycraft, J. (2010). Ethical challenges of military social workers serving in a combat zone. *Social Work*, 55(1), 91–8. (*Academic OneFile*. Web. 31 Mar. 2011.)

Solomon, Z., Shklar, R., & Mikulincer, M. (2005). Frontline treatment of combat stress reaction: A 20-year longitudinal evaluation study. *American Journal of Psychiatry*, 162, 2309–2314.

Tallant, S.H. & Ryberg, R.A. (1999). Common and unique ethical dilemmas encountered by military social workers. In J.G. Daley (Ed.), *Social Work Practice in the Military* (pp. 179–216). Binghamton, NY: Haworth Press.

Van Staden, Hacker, L., Hughes, J., Browne, J., et al. (2009). The prevalence of common mental disorders and PTSD in the UK military: Using data from clinical interview-based study. *BMC Psychiatry*, 9, 68–79.

Veatch R.M. (1989) *Death, Dying, and the Biological Revolution: Our last quest for responsibility*. New Haven, CT: Yale University Press.

18

THE COST OF CARING REQUIRES SELF CARE

Charles R. Figley and Joan Beder

Sgt. Sanchez (not her real name) was among those interviewed recently in a study (Figley, Cabrera, & Chapman, 2010) of combat medics between deployments. Combat medics are those who often experience primary trauma (war experiences), secondary trauma (the emotional and psychosocial consequences of providing medical services), and shared trauma (experience shared trauma with others in her unit).

"How do you do it?" I asked this slightly built but proven combat Veteran toward the end of the interview and after I had recited the various stressors she and other medics must cope with as a part of their position in a fighting unit.

Sgt. Sanchez: I had no other choice. I soldiered on; applied my training as a medic. I went through a checklist of tasks. I didn't beat up on myself and I didn't let it happen in the unit; ya know, due to stress. That helped a lot.

We are beginning to see a pattern among medics and others who serve the military that is especially evident and is the focus of this chapter: *the cost of caring and the need for self care.*

War changes people; for all who participate, it is a powerful experience and one that has the potential to enhance life while addressing a need to serve one's country and act nobly. For others, the experience has negative connotations and can be emotionally draining and depleting. For the injured in war, there is the additional challenge of returning home and making whatever adjustments are needed with family and self. As social workers, and other health care professionals, we are entrusted with the care of many of our returning service members; those who are having difficulty adjusting to home and/or are having memories of war experiences and are not able to manage their memories and emotions related to their participation overseas. Our "job" is to help and care for those who are in emotional pain; we extend our professionalism, our empathy and often our hearts to help. This chapter will alert social workers to the need to understand that caring has the potential to impact our ability to give fully in our work and may extract more from us than is emotionally healthy. Suggestions for ways to care for ourselves are offered.

Introduction

"There is a cost to caring. Professionals who listen to clients' stories of fear, pain, and suffering may feel similar fear, pain, and suffering because they care" (Figley, 1995, p. 1). Those professionals who work with the traumatized—those who may have been the victim of rape, domestic violence, disaster or war—are most prone to developing secondary traumatic stress (STS). STS is manifested as compassion fatigue (CF), which refers to how and why we as helpers, even though we are not directly traumatized, can become traumatized ourselves and possibly become secondary victims of the trauma we are listening to and absorbing (Fox, 2003). Compassion fatigue is a direct result of exposure to client suffering—rather than a pathological condition for the caring professional, it is a natural consequence of working with, and listening to, people who have related their experiences of extremely stressful events. Professionals who listen to those who have been traumatized may themselves come to need assistance to cope with the effects of listening to others' traumatic experiences (Gentry, 2002). The double bind for the empathic professional is the higher tendency to develop CF as the professional immerses him/herself in the life and drama of the traumatized. In contrast, compassion satisfaction is experienced as the pleasure derived from being a helper, from being able to do your work well. Those who experience compassion satisfaction feel positively about their colleagues and feel secure in their ability to contribute to the work and the work setting (Stamm, 2010)—it is an antidote to CF.

Effective work with those who have experienced trauma often involves assisting the client in working through their traumatic event(s) through discussion and description, and often in graphic detail. The process of recall and description helps to bring closure to the event for the client; in the process, however, the clinician is exposed to the traumatic event through vivid imagery and the act of listening (Bride, Radey, & Figley, 2007).

An additional factor in the development of CF may be the day-to-day bureaucratic struggles inherent in working in settings (agencies, hospitals, etc.) where counseling takes place. A combination of forces—content, empathic engagement, setting—creates the potential for the clinician to experience secondary trauma and the development of CF. The experience of CF tends to develop cumulatively over time (Newell & MacNeil, 2010), and some helpers are at greater risk from it. It is more common in those workers with a personal history of trauma or negative life events, and in those who have limited social supports (Adams, Boscarino, & Figley, 2006).

Secondary Traumatic Stress/Burnout/Compassion Fatigue

Secondary traumatic stress occurs when one is exposed to traumatic and extreme events by another; in the act of listening to the content of the traumatic event(s), and wanting to help or ease the suffering of the traumatized individual, stress is created for the helper. The helper may develop a range of responses, similar to those of post-traumatic stress disorder, which include numbing, startle response, intrusive thoughts nightmares, insomnia and anxiety, and avoidance of situations. Burnout is a set of symptoms associated with feelings of hopelessness and difficulties in dealing with work or doing one's job effectively (Stamm, 2100). Often, burnout reflects bureaucratic and environmental difficulties that might include too much paperwork, office space, long hours, low pay, and limited opportunities for advancement. Compassion fatigue is defined as a syndrome consisting of symptoms of STS and burnout (Adams, Boscarino, & Figley, 2006; Bride, Radney, & Figley, 2007). Similar to burnout, CF tends to develop over time and is cumulative. While it is realistic to expect that most helping professionals will at some point in their work life experience STS and feelings of burnout leading to CS, the likelihood of developing CF is significantly heightened for those who bear witness to the traumatized.

Figley (1995) sees the development of CF as normative rather than pathological and as an occupational hazard for those working with trauma survivors. As with any condition, the degree and intensity of the CF may be borne and easily relieved or may become chronic and become debilitating to the helper and have impact on the clinician's work.

Social workers and other helpers experiencing CF may be at higher risk to make poor professional judgments, create poor treatment plans and take out some of their anguish on clients who are not experiencing trauma (Stamm, 2010). In addition, these helpers may start missing work, may decide that they cannot accept any more clients, or may become "unreliable" in the work environment. Some who struggle with CF report feeling numb, cut-off; they question their effectiveness as helpers and their ability to make decisions that are in the best interest of the client. They may lose their sense of hopefulness and optimism (Hesse, 2002).

A way of representing the various critical factors accounting for CF is included in Figure 18.1; consider it a road map to CF. This model (Figley, 1995) suggests that the route to CF is by way of numerous distressing and "toxic" circumstances. Compassion fatigue among social workers emerges from particularly toxic situations that started with genuine concern and caring on the part of such workers. Empathic ability is the innate ability to empathize with another, be it a client or her/his family. With this ability, social workers are able to provide the necessary empathic response in their work, to feel and respond to the emotional needs and experiences of the client and her/his family. However, to provide the necessary empathic response—sensitivity, caring,

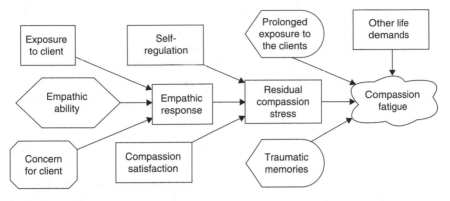

FIGURE 18.1 A model for predicting and preventing compassion fatigue

and professionalism—social workers must be concerned for, and exposed to, the client; thus, the risk of CF.

Social Workers Who Care for Returning Service Members

Social workers who are employed in the Department of Veterans Affairs, the Department of Defense hospital and out-patient systems, and those who work in the civilian sector, are charged with caring for those who have served in the Armed Forces. At present we are engaged in Operation Enduring Freedom (Afghanistan), Operation Iraqi Freedom, and Operation New Dawn (Modified Iraq force as of 9/2010). Since October, 2001, approximately 1.64 million U.S. troops have been deployed to Operation Enduring Freedom and Operation Iraqi Freedom. As of September, 2010, the total number of troops who have returned to the United States for medical care exceeds 247,000. This includes those who have Post-Traumatic Stress Disorder (PTSD), Traumatic Brain Injury (TBI), serious wounding and amputations (U.S. Military Casualty Statistics, 2010). Each of these service members is being treated in the Department of Defense and/or the VA medical system and by civilian social workers and mental health providers.

Rehabilitation of the injured service members is geared to restoring those who have served to their highest level of functionality. Social workers, as part of the multidisciplinary medical teams in the VA/DoD system and civilian providers as well, are involved in managing caseloads of patients with complex psychosocial, mental and physical needs. In the course of their work, social workers are encountering war casualties on a daily basis in most inpatient and outpatient units. Social work contact with service members is frequently focused on case management and counseling, with involvement of both the patient and her/his family. Social workers bear witness to the lives of their clients, their struggles and their anguish; they are involved in their progress and setbacks; and they hear their pain and accomplishments. Social workers entrusted with the care of the returning service members have high potential to develop CF.

In a recent study of Department of Defense social workers, Beder (2009) surveyed 161 social workers on levels of compassion satisfaction, burnout and CF using the Professional Quality of Life scale (ProQoL) developed by Stamm (2010). The developers of the scale suggest that there is an intersection between the three components of the scale; nevertheless, each component has validity and can be discussed alone or in combination. Each of the three components of the ProQoL has normed levels, above or below which have implications for the subject. Findings related to levels of CF were noted by the entire cohort of subjects, i.e., 59 percent of the subjects scored above the normed level of CF.

Those workers who were in the DoD system of care for up to five years had higher levels of CF compared to more senior workers. Social workers that worked at out-patient facilities (outside of a hospital setting) also had high levels of CF, compared to those who worked inside the hospital. These findings strongly support the assertion that social workers who work with returning service members may be especially impacted by their work with CF as a by-product since they tend to be younger and outside hospital settings.

Treatment and Prevention of Compassion Fatigue

Underlying any consideration of how to address CF is the need to reassure the worker that their symptoms are not an indication of some pathological weakness or disease or personal failing, but are instead a natural consequence of providing care for traumatized individuals. This urges an acceptance that allows the worker to share their concerns with colleagues, friends and other caregivers (Gentry, 2002). Acceptance of CF leads to acknowledgement and action to address the areas that are contributing to the feelings of CF.

The first step in preventing or treating STS/CF is to recognize the signs and symptoms of its emergence. As CF manifests at a symptoms level, workers need to be continually self-monitoring for the presence of numbing, startle response, intrusive thoughts, nightmares, insomnia and anxiety, and avoidance of situations. Many caregivers who experience symptoms of CF may attempt to ignore their distress until a threshold of discomfort is reached and their effectiveness in their work begins to suffer. Gentry (2002, p. 46) states that "… amelioration of compassion fatigue symptoms requires that the caregiver intentionally acknowledges and addresses, rather than avoids, these symptoms and their causes." Conscientious monitoring of both the worker's work environment and personal life needs to be implemented to address the build-up and continuation of CF (Bride & Figley, 2009).

The Work Environment

One factor that addresses compassion stress and accompanying CF is interactions with colleagues, clients, and personal supporters and the general workplace environment. Each of these groups of people can affect the overall emotional climate of the social work professional. In the context of work, factors that enable compassion are functions of the general morale and supportiveness of fellow workers, especially one's supervisor and the administration.

A positive work environment includes workers who care about each other and show it. They genuinely like one another, and they may joke around and/or pitch in when needed, and often without being asked to do so. They pick up on even the most subtle mood changes of fellow workers and ask about them in a caring and supportive manner. A negative work environment, on the other hand, can be emotionally toxic. In a supportive organizational culture, caregivers are able to validate their feelings through on-going supervision in a safe and supportive environment (Bride & Figley, 2009). This allows for ventilation and needed affirmation.

When relationships among workers, and especially with supervisory staff, are strained, staff morale tends to be negative. What is lacking in a toxic work environment is a sense of trust, optimism, and mutual support among and between staff members. As with other social psychological components, the vital resources of supportive colleagues, friends, and family enable the social worker to rebound from emotionally upsetting events, a key factor in the avoidance and minimization of CF.

The general workplace environment—with expectations for productivity, paperwork requirements, physical space and creature comforts—can contribute to burnout, which is a factor in CF. This is another area to be mindful of when making efforts to address CF. Caseload/workload management strategies to help avoid CF include balancing a clinical caseload with other professional activities, having traumatized clients as well as non-traumatized, engaging in advocacy activities on behalf of clients, and taking time off for respite.

On a Personal Level

In their personal lives, providers should strive to maintain a balance between their professional and personal lives. This balance includes stress management, meditation, and exercise, spending time with loved ones, and engaging in personal psychotherapy if needed.

Self-care is the ability to refill and refuel oneself in healthy ways. Healthy practices would include sharing with colleagues, exercise, meditation, nutrition, and spirituality. Conversely, many caregivers redouble their efforts, feeling that if they did more, they would reap more benefits from the work, i.e., they work harder to feel better. This is an unfortunate adaptation to the symptoms and feeling associated with CF, and potentially can worsen the condition rather than helping.

Another facet of self-care is that caregivers "... need to soften their critical and coercive self-talk and shift their motivational styles toward more self-accepting and affirming language and tone if they wish to resolve their compassion fatigue symptoms" (Gentry, 2002, p. 52).

Another factor that reduces CF is compassion satisfaction—a sense of fulfillment or gratification from the work. For social workers it is the joy of helping clients who are suffering and need support and care; it is inspiring and goes to the heart of social work practice. Sometimes social workers need to remember these very real satisfactions when feeling the weight of compassion stress and CF from the work. Caregivers must remember that they cannot fix everything and everyone, that there are situations that go beyond immediate repair, and that the best we can do for a traumatized client is to listen with them and acknowledge their pain and anguish. We must be content that allowing the verbalization of trauma gives the traumatized person a venue and permission to speak their worst fears and stories. We must be satisfied that this makes a significant contribution to the healing of the client; and this acknowledgement contributes to compassion satisfaction.

Other factors, over which we have some degree of control, contribute directly to CF. One is the prolonged exposure to suffering when social workers put in far too many hours without a sufficient break. Sometimes this is unavoidable, especially within the military environment with ever increasing caseloads and the constant influx of those returning from the wars continues to increase on a daily basis. Sometimes, however, prolonged exposure is self-imposed by the worker: skipping lunch, delaying vacations, working overtime, and other extensions of normal workloads.

The final factor that contributes to CF is the "other" category: other life demands. Often these demands have little to do with the job and everything to do with being stressful. Even positive activities such as getting a new car or falling in love demand time and attention and therefore restrict the resources needed to cope with work. More often, however, other life demands are negative, caused by personal issues, such as family obligations.

Collectively these factors, or roads, lead to CF. There are alternative roads leading to alternative destinations, however. They address ways of transforming CF into opportunities for change that enable social workers to be far more productive, useful, and happy at work and at home.

Ending Thoughts

Sgt. Sanchez provides a useful role model for someone who can say they has been exposed to some of the most horrific, dangerous, and stressful experiences. She, by virtue of this exposure, should have PTSD, a phobia, or some other type of anxiety disorder (mental illness). Her tests show that she is in good shape mentally, and far below the average among other soldiers regarding levels of anxiety. We are coming to believe that it is not so much the fact that we are overcome with emotion, cannot sleep, flashbacks, or some other disturbing consequence of using our hearts to heal others. It takes something out of us. What is given back, however, most often compensates for the cost of caring and that is compassion satisfaction (Stamm, 2005): the personal sense of satisfaction of doing the work. When Sgt. Sanchez said "*I had no other choice. I soldiered on,*" it represents her sense of purpose and duty. This sense is shared among other fields such as nursing, social work, first responders, physicians, and many others. Sgt. Sanchez also helps us to appreciate the "distraction" of paperwork, being busy with the "work of attending to your soldiers" that is so evident among combat medics. She is also suggesting that lowering the demand on one's self is good self care.

Trauma work can be extremely stressful and draining. Working with war Veterans is especially challenging because war often provokes behaviors that are extremely difficult to repeat and to hear. This is counterbalanced by the rewards of being trusted enough to witness the struggles of our service members to overcome war-related distress and its consequences. Feeling good about facilitating the traumatized to regain their strength and reintegrate into their lives by having been helped through our efforts is the essence of caring and the purpose of our work. The connections we make with those who have experienced trauma are often the strongest that people make, involving an intimacy and a trust that our service member clients may have lost as a result of their trauma (Hesse, 2002). We become the agents who help those traumatized in war to be able to regain trust in others and themselves. Because of our work, we risk CF. If we are vigilant about our self-care and can monitor our reactions, we will be able to continue to touch our clients and gain needed compassion satisfaction in the process and soldier on.

References

Adams, R.E., Boscarino, J., & Figley, C. (2006). Compassion fatigue and psychological distress among social workers. *American Journal of Orthopsychiatry*, 76, 103–118.

Beder, J. (2009). Social work in the Department of Defense Hospital: Impact, role and interventions. *Military Medicine*, 174(5), 486–490.

Bride, B.E., Radey, M., & Figley, C. (2007). Measuring compassion fatigue. *Clinical Social Work Journal*, 35, 155–163.

Bride, B. & Figley, C. (2009). Secondary trauma and military Veteran caregivers. *Smith College Studies in Social Work*, 79(3,4), 4314–4329.

Figley, C. (1995). *Compassion Fatigue: Coping with secondary traumatic stress disorder in those who treat the traumatized*. New York: Bruner/Mazel.

Figley, C.R., Cabrera, D., & Chapman, P. (2010). *Combat Medic Mettle Study*. Refereed presentation at the International Society for Traumatic Stress Studies, Montreal, Canada, November.

Fox, R. (2003). Traumaphobia: Confronting personal and professional anxiety. *Psychoanalytic Social Work*, 10(1), 43–55.

Gentry, J.E. (2002). Compassion fatigue: A crucible of transformation. *Journal of Trauma Practice*, 1(3/4), 37–61.

Hesse, A. (2002). Secondary trauma: How working with trauma survivors affects therapists. *Clinical Social Work Journal*, 30(3), 293–309.

Newell, J. & MacNeil, G. (2010). Professional burnout, vicarious trauma, secondary traumatic stress, and compassion fatigue: A review of theoretical terms, risk factors, and preventive methods for clinicians and researchers. *Best Practices in Mental Health*, 6(2), 57–68.

Stamm, B.H. (2005). *The ProQOL Manual. The professional quality of life scale: compassion satisfaction, burnout and compassion fatigue/secondary trauma scales.* Baltimore, MD: Sidran.

Stamm, B.H. (2010). *The Concise ProQoL Manual.* Pocatello, ID: ProQOL.org

U.S. Military Casualty Statistics (2010). *U.S. Military Casualty Statistics: Operation New Dawn, Operation Iraqi Freedom, and Operation Enduring Freedom.* Washington, DC: CRS Report for Congress.

INDEX